MAC OS X TIGER

IN A NUTSHELL

Other Macintosh resources from O'Reilly

Related titles

AppleScript: The Missing Manual
AppleScript: The Definitive Guide
iBook Fan Book
iPod Fan Book
Mac OS X Tiger Pocket Guide
Mac OS X: The Missing Manual, Tiger Edition

Mac OS X Power Hound
Mac OS X Hacks™
PowerBook Fan Book
Learning Unix for Mac OS X Tiger
Mac OS X Tiger for Unix Geeks

Macintosh Books Resource Center

mac.oreilly.com is a complete catalog of O'Reilly's books on the Apple Macintosh and related technologies, including sample chapters and code examples.

A popular watering hole for Macintosh developers and power users, the Mac DevCenter focuses on pure Mac OS X and its related technologies, including Cocoa, Java, AppleScript, and Apache, to name just a few. It's also keenly interested in all the spokes of the digital hub, with special attention paid to digital photography, digital video, MP3 music, and QuickTime.

Conferences

O'Reilly brings diverse innovators together to nurture the ideas that spark revolutionary industries. We specialize in documenting the latest tools and systems, translating the innovator's knowledge into useful skills for those in the trenches. Visit *conferences.oreilly.com* for our upcoming events.

Safari Bookshelf (*safari.oreilly.com*) is the premier online reference library for programmers and IT professionals. Conduct searches across more than 1,000 books. Subscribers can zero in on answers to time-critical questions in a matter of seconds. Read the books on your Bookshelf from cover to cover or simply flip to the page you need. Try it today for free.

MAC OS X TIGER

IN A NUTSHELL

*Andy Lester, Chris Stone, Chuck Toporek, and
Jason McIntosh*
with contributions from Leon Towns-von Stauber,
Brian Jepson, and Ernest E. Rothman

O'REILLY®

Beijing • Cambridge • Farnham • Köln • Paris • Sebastopol • Taipei • Tokyo

Mac OS X Tiger in a Nutshell

by Andy Lester, Chris Stone, Chuck Toporek, and Jason McIntosh

Copyright © 2006 O'Reilly Media, Inc. All rights reserved.
Printed in the United States of America.

Published by O'Reilly Media, Inc., 1005 Gravenstein Highway North, Sebastopol, CA 95472.

O'Reilly books may be purchased for educational, business, or sales promotional use. Online editions are also available for most titles (*safari.oreilly.com*). For more information, contact our corporate/institutional sales department: (800) 998-9938 or *corporate@oreilly.com*.

Editor:	Chuck Toporek
Production Editor:	Philip Dangler
Cover Designer:	Emma Colby
Interior Designer:	David Futato

Printing History:

January 2003:	First Edition, originally published as *Mac OS X in a Nutshell*.
June 2004:	Second Edition, published as *Mac OS X Panther in a Nutshell*.
November 2005:	Third Edition.

 This book uses RepKover™, a durable and flexible lay-flat binding.

ISBN: 0-596-00943-7

[M]

Table of Contents

v

Preface

Although Apple Computer ushered in the PC revolution in 1980 with the Apple II computer, the inventions that are most synonymous with the company are the Macintosh computer and its ground-breaking graphical operating system, both released in 1984. Let's think of this operating system as Mac OS 1, though Apple wouldn't coin the term "Mac OS" to describe its operating system until the 1990s. The early Mac made its mark in a world where all other popular computer interfaces were obscure.

In the years following the Mac's release, much has changed. Both bad and good things have happened, and some company in Washington called Microsoft started to take over the world. By 1996, Apple knew it needed to modernize the Mac OS (and make it more worthy competition to Windows) from the bottom up, but previous attempts and partnerships to bring this about had ended in failure. So, Apple made an unusual move and purchased NeXT. This company had made a nice Unix-based operating system called NeXTSTEP, in which Apple saw the seeds of its own salvation. As it happened, NeXT's leader was the ambitious Steve Jobs, one of Apple's founders, who left the company after a political rift in the 1980s. To make a long and interesting story short, Jobs quickly seized control of Apple Computer, stripped it down to its essentials, and put all its resources into reinventing the Mac. Five years later, the result was Mac OS X: a computing platform based around an entirely new operating system that merged the best parts of the old Mac OS, NeXTSTEP, and nearly two decades of user feedback on the Mac OS.

Mac OS X initially may seem a little alien to long-time Mac users; it is, quite literally, an entirely different operating system from Mac OS 9 and earlier versions (even though Mac OS X retains most of its predecessor's important interface idioms, such as the way the desktop and the user interface works). However, the Mac is now winning more converts than ever, not just from Windows, but from other Unix systems such as Linux, Solaris, and FreeBSD (from which Mac OS X's Unix core is derived).

Mac OS X brings all of the great things from earlier versions of the Mac OS and melds them with a BSD core, bringing Unix to the masses. Apple has created a rock-solid operating system to compete both on the user and enterprise level. In days gone by, the Mac was mostly looked at as a system for "fluffy-bunny designers." It's now becoming the must-have hardware and operating system of geeks and designers everywhere.

With Mac OS X, you can bring home the bacon and fry it up in a pan. Your Mac can be used not only for graphic design and creating web pages, but also as a web server. Not into flat graphics? Fine, Mac OS X sports Quartz Extreme and OpenGL. Want to learn how to program? Mac OS X is a developer's dream, packing in Perl, Python, Ruby, C, C++, Objective-C, compilers, and debuggers; if you're an X jockey, you can also run the X Window System on top of Mac OS X using Apple's X11 distribution or with other installations of XFree86. In addition to the standard programming languages, Mac OS X comes with a powerful set of frameworks for programming with Cocoa, Mac OS X's native language (adopted from NeXT).

Audience for This Book

This book should be of interest to Unix users and Unix programmers, as well as to anyone (such as a system administrator) who might offer direct support to users and programmers. The presentation is geared mainly toward people who are already familiar with the Unix system; that is, you know what you want to do, and you even have some idea how to do it. You just need a reminder about the details. For example, if you want to remove the third field from a database, you might think, "I know I can use the *cut* command, but what are the options?" In many cases, this book provides specific examples to show how a command is used.

This reference might also help people who are familiar with some aspects of Unix but not with others. Many chapters include an overview of the particular topic. While this isn't meant to be comprehensive, it's usually sufficient to get you started in unfamiliar territory.

Finally, if you're new to the Unix side of Mac OS X, and you're feeling bold, you might appreciate this book as a quick tour of what Unix has to offer. Chapter 1 can point you to the most useful commands, and you'll find brief examples of how to use them, but take note: this book should not be used in place of a good beginner's tutorial on Unix. For that, you might try O'Reilly's *Learning Unix for Mac OS X Tiger*. This reference should be a supplement, not a substitute. (There are references throughout the text to other relevant O'Reilly books that will help you learn the subject matter under discussion; in some cases, you may be better off detouring to those books first.)

How This Book Is Organized

There are three essential parts to this book, with the first part covering the shells and Unix commands found in Mac OS X Tiger. The two remaining parts cover text and text processing and include chapters on managing your Mac OS X system. The parts and chapters of this book are defined as follows:

Part I, Commands and Shells
> This part of the book introduces you to the basic concepts of networking and system administration, including coverage of Directory Services.

> Chapter 1, *Introduction*
>> This chapter provides you with a quick introduction to the Unix side of Mac OS X.

> Chapter 2, *Unix Command Reference*
>> This chapter lists descriptions and usage terms for over 300 of the Unix commands found in Mac OS X. The commands have been painstakingly run and verified against the manpages for accuracy; this is the most complete and accurate Mac-based Unix command reference in print.

> Chapter 3, *Using the Terminal*
>> With Mac OS X, you'll normally use one way to gain access to the Unix core: the Terminal application. This chapter introduces you to the Terminal application and shows you how to issue commands and tweak its settings.

> Chapter 4, *Shell Overview*
>> This chapter provides a quick overview of the differences between *bash*, Mac OS X Panther's default shell, and *tcsh*, the default shell for earlier versions of Mac OS X.

> Chapter 5, *bash: The Bourne-Again Shell*
>> This chapter provides a quick overview of the *bash* shell, along with a listing of its built-in commands for shell scripting.

Part II, Text and Text Processing
> The chapters in this part of the book provide insight to the tools you'll use to work with text files, the underlying structure of any Unix operating system, including Mac OS X Tiger.

> Chapter 6, *Pattern Matching*
>> A number of Unix text-processing utilities let you search for, and in some cases change, text patterns rather than fixed strings. These utilities include editing programs such as *vi* and Emacs, programming languages such as Perl and Python, and the commands *grep* and *egrep*. Text patterns (formally called *regular expressions*) contain normal characters mixed with special characters (called *metacharacters*).

Chapter 7, *The vi Editor*

vi is the classic screen-based text editing program for Unix. In Mac OS X Panther, *vim* is the default version of *vi* and runs when you invoke *vi* from the command line. This chapter covers some of *vi*'s most commonly used options and features.

Chapter 8, *The Emacs Editor*

The Emacs editor is found on many Unix systems, including Mac OS X, because it is a popular alternative to *vi*. For many Unix users, Emacs is more than "just an editor." While Emacs provides a fully integrated user environment, this chapter focuses on its editing capabilities.

Part III: Managing Mac OS X

This part of the book offers chapters on managing your Mac OS X Tiger system:

Chapter 9, *Filesystem Overview*

Like any Unix system, much of Mac OS X's functionality is based on its filesystem layout. This chapter tours the various folders found on a typical Mac OS X volume, including the Unix-centric directories that the Finder usually keeps out of sight.

Chapter 10, *Directory Services*

This chapter details the way Mac OS X stores and accesses its administrative information, ranging from the NetInfo system of network-linked databases to the "old-school" file-based system familiar to Unix administrators.

Chapter 11, *Running Network Services*

Mac OS X's suite of open source Unix software includes a full complement of network services programs (what the Unix wizards call *daemons*). This chapter details the major categories of services Unix supplies, including web servers, file sharing, and mail servers. This chapter also covers the control that Mac OS X gives you through either the Sharing preferences pane or the command line.

Chapter 12, *The X Window System*

This chapter highlights some of the key features of Apple's X11 distribution and explains how to install Apple's X11 and the X11 SDK. It also explains how to use X11 in both rootless and full-screen modes (using the GNOME and KDE desktops). You'll also learn how to connect to other X Window Systems using Virtual Network Computer (VNC), as well as how to remotely control the Mac OS X desktop from other X11 systems.

Chapter 13, *The Defaults System*

Like the old saying goes, there's more than one way to skin a cat. In this case, the cat we're skinning is Tiger. When you configure your system or an application to your liking, those preferences are stored in what's known as the *defaults database*. This chapter describes how to gain access to and hack these settings via the Terminal application and the *defaults* command.

Conventions Used in This Book

The following typographical conventions are used in this book:

Italic

> Used to indicate new terms, example URLs, filenames, file extensions, directories, commands and options, program names, and to highlight comments in examples. For example, a path in the filesystem appears as */Applications/Utilities*.

`Constant width`

> Used to show the contents of files or the output from commands. Also used to indicate code keywords, variables, values, parameters, and functions.

`Constant width bold`

> Used in examples and tables to show commands or other text that should be typed literally by the user.

`Constant width italic`

> Used in examples and tables to show text that should be replaced with user-supplied values.

Menus/navigation

> Menus and their options are referred to in the text as File → Open, Edit → Copy, etc. Arrows are also used to signify a navigation path when using window options. For example, "System Preferences → Desktop & Screen Saver → Screen Saver" means that you would launch System Preferences, click the icon for the "Desktop & Screen Saver" preference panel, and then select the "Screen Saver" pane within that panel.

Pathnames

> Pathnames are used to show the location of a file or application in the filesystem. Directories (or folders, for Mac and Windows users) are separated by a forward slash. For example, if you see something like, "...launch the Terminal application (*/Applications/Utilities*)" in the text, this means the Terminal application can be found in the Utilities subfolder of the Applications folder.
>
> The tilde character (~) refers to the current user's Home folder, so *~/Library* refers to the Library folder within your own Home folder.

↵

> A ↵ symbol at the end of a line of code denotes an unnatural line break; that is, you should not enter these as two lines of code, but as one continuous line. Multiple lines are used in these cases due to printing constraints.

$, #

> The dollar sign ($) is used in some examples to show the user prompt for the *bash* shell; the hash mark (#) is the prompt for the *root* user.

Menu symbols

> When looking at the menus for any application, you will see some symbols associated with keyboard shortcuts for a particular command. For example,

to open a document in Microsoft Word, you can go to the File menu and select Open (File→Open), or you can issue the keyboard shortcut, ⌘-O.

Figure P-1 shows the symbols used in the various menus to denote a keyboard shortcut.

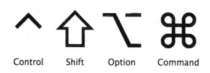

Control   Shift   Option   Command

Figure P-1. Keyboard modifiers for issuing commands

Rarely will you see the Control symbol used as a menu command option; it's more often used in association with mouse clicks or for working with the *bash* shell.

 Indicates a tip, suggestion, or general note.

 Indicates a warning or caution.

Comments and Questions

Please address comments and questions concerning this book to the publisher:

O'Reilly Media, Inc.
1005 Gravenstein Highway North
Sebastopol, CA 95472
(800) 998-9938 (in the U.S. or Canada)
(707) 829-0515 (international/local)
(707) 829-0104 (fax)

There is a web page for this book that lists errata, examples, or any additional information. You can access this page at:

http://www.oreilly.com/catalog/mactigerian

To comment or ask technical questions about this book, send email to:

bookquestions@oreilly.com

For more information about books, conferences, Resource Centers, and the O'Reilly Network, see the O'Reilly web site at:

http://www.oreilly.com

Acknowledgments

The authors would like to acknowledge the masses who helped make the book possible, and also would like to thank the authors of other O'Reilly books, from which some portions of this book were derived; including:

- *Linux in a Nutshell* (Ellen Siever, Stephen Spainhour, Stephen Figgins, and Jessica P. Hekman)
- *Mac OS X Tiger for Unix Geeks* (Brian Jepson and Ernest E. Rothman)
- *Unix in a Nutshell* (Arnold Robbins)

Acknowledgments for Andy Lester

My first thanks go to Chuck Toporek, my first and current editor at O'Reilly. It was Chuck who took me on the *Unix/Linux Power Tools, Third Edition* project years ago, and liked my work enough to bring me on the last two *Mac OS X in a Nutshell* projects. Thanks also to Kevin Bingham, for remembering me from my comments and corrections to *booktech@ora.com*, and passing my name to Chuck as someone who just might be worthy of working on an O'Reilly book.

Thanks to Leon Towns-von Stauber, who was invaluable in making sure I got the new stuff in and dropped the old. Thanks also to Brian Jepson and Ernie Rothman for *Mac OS X Tiger for Unix Geeks*. Besides having written a great book in its own right, their clear and complete explanations made it easy to summarize and encapsulate Tiger's new features for this book.

Thanks to my darling Quinn, who brought me countless pretend meals from her play kitchen. Daddy gets hungry when he's working, and plastic pizza, popcorn, and pickles really hit the spot.

Most of all, innumerable thanks to my wife, Amy, for being my best friend and the best mom to Quinn; for her (sometimes grudging) understanding on those weekends where I wasn't around much because I was holed up with a chapter; and for believing in and supporting me as I make my way down this new authorship trail. I love you as big as the sky.

Safari® Enabled

When you see a Safari® Enabled icon on the cover of your favorite technology book, that means the book is available online through the O'Reilly Network Safari Bookshelf.

Safari offers a solution that's better than e-Books: it's a virtual library that lets you easily search thousands of top tech books, cut and paste code samples, download chapters, and find quick answers when you need the most accurate, current information. Try it for free at *http://safari.oreilly.com*.

Commands and Shells

Part I presents a summary of Unix commands of interest to users and programmers. It also describes the three major Unix shells, including special syntax and built-in commands.

Chapters in this part of the book include:

- Chapter 1, Introduction
- Chapter 2, Unix Command Reference
- Chapter 3, Using the Terminal
- Chapter 4, Shell Overview
- Chapter 5, bash: The Bourne-Again Shell

Introduction

In 2001, Apple released Mac OS X (that's pronounced "mac oh ess ten"), building their next-generation operating system on the power of a Unix-like environment. Apple's famed "lickable" GUI is built on top of the open source Darwin, including the BSD source tree. Although many users may never realize it (and Apple's mainstream marketing has never made too much of it), when you're running Mac OS X, you're running a powerful Unix-like system.

The beauty of Mac OS X, besides its obvious visual beauty, is that it's turning out to be the way to get a real Unix system onto the desktops of the business world. IT departments around the world are finding that Mac OS X is an alternative to Microsoft Windows that can be used by anyone, not just Nick Burns, The Company Computer Guy. Mac OS X integrates effortlessly with Microsoft networks through the Samba package. Users familiar with Microsoft Office have a Mac version available to them. Most major software packages such as Adobe's Creative Suite (consisting of Photoshop, InDesign, Illustrator, etc.), QuarkXPress, and Maya have versions for Mac OS X. Internet packages, whether web browsers, email clients, or instant messaging clients are especially well represented on Mac OS X.

What You'll Find

It's for those who want to get at the Unix underpinnings of Mac OS X that this book is designed. Previous editions of *Mac OS X in a Nutshell* have been thick with chapters on System Preference panels, running Classic, and using the Finder and the Desktop. There are many more appropriate titles for this type of information, such as the Missing Manual series (O'Reilly/Pogue Press) or the *Mac OS X Tiger Pocket Guide* (O'Reilly). With *Mac OS X Tiger in a Nutshell*, we've come back to the Unix roots, more closely aligning with our ancestors, *Unix in a Nutshell* and *Linux in a Nutshell*.

The path to Unix on Mac OS X starts with the Terminal application. In Chapter 3, you'll find details on what for Unix fans is the most used application on their system. Even if you've been using Terminal for years, take a look to see what tidbits of configurability you might have missed.

Once in the Terminal, your login shell is your interface to your system. Chapter 4 gives a crash course in the basics of shell interaction and compares *bash*, the default shell for Mac OS X Tiger, with *tcsh*, the shell for the earliest versions of Mac OS X. Although both shells have much the same functionality, there can be big differences between how they approach different tasks. You should be familiar with these differences.

It's not surprising that *bash* is the default shell under Mac OS X. The *bash* shell has become a standard in the industry with its inclusion on almost every Linux distribution. It's also arguably the best shell available in terms of features, customization, and programming constructs. Chapter 5 provides a quick reference to *bash*'s inner powerful features. For a gentle introduction, and details on writing *bash*-specific shell scripts, see *Learning the bash Shell* (O'Reilly). For an introduction to shell scripting, see *Classic Shell Scripting* (O'Reilly).

If *bash* isn't to your liking, Tiger provides all the major shells, so you can choose what's best for you. In addition to *bash* and *tcsh*, you also get the Z shell, *zsh*, and the Korn shell, *ksh*. For details on *tcsh*, see *Using csh & tcsh* (O'Reilly), and for *ksh*, *Learning the Korn Shell* (O'Reilly). Details on *zsh* can be found at *http://www.zsh.org*.

When you're writing text, you're probably going to use *vi* or *Emacs*. Chapters 7 and 8 cover these two Unix stalwarts, including the latest information on versions that take advantage of Tiger's Aqua interface.

Section III of this book is about managing your Mac OS X system. For many, including this author, the jump to Mac OS X from a Unix background can be disorienting, with plenty of pondering "Where did the boys in Cupertino decide to put that?" The seasoned Unix user would do well to read Chapters 9 and 10 before installing new files or creating a user by editing */etc/passwd*.

The chapter you'll refer to most often is Chapter 2. In compiling this command reference, we've updated over 100 commands, added a dozen, and dropped outdated entries. If you're reading this book on paper, keep a highlighter handy whenever you turn here.

Tiger's biggest leap forward is the powerful Spotlight indexing service. Spotlight constantly indexes and monitors your system for documents, and adds them to a local document database. It's like Google for your hard drive, with extensible plug-ins that software vendors can provide. Even though it's most often seen in the upper-right corner of the screen, Tiger provides command-line programs to interface with Spotlight. See the *mdfind* command in Chapter 2.

Beginner's Guide

If you're just beginning to work on a Unix system, the abundance of commands might prove daunting. To help orient you, the following lists present a small sampling of commands on various topics.

Communication

Command	Use
ftp	File transfer protocol.
login	Sign on to Unix.
mailx	Read or send mail.
rlogin	Sign on to remote Unix.
talk	Write to other terminals.
telnet	Connect to another system.
vacation	Respond to mail automatically.

Comparisons

Command	Use
cmp	Compare two files, byte by byte.
comm	Compare items in two sorted files.
diff	Compare two files, line by line.
diff3	Compare three files.
sdiff	Compare two files, side by side.

File Management

Command	Use
cat	Concatenate files or display them.
cd	Change directory.
chmod	Change access modes on files.
cp	Copy files.
csplit	Break files at specific locations.
file	Determine a file's type.
head	Show the first few lines of a file.
ln	Create filename aliases.
ls	List files or directories.
mkdir	Create a directory.
more	Display files by screenful.
mv	Move or rename files or directories.
pwd	Print working directory.
rcp	Copy files to remote system.

Command	Use
rm	Remove files.
rmdir	Remove directories.
split	Split files evenly.
tail	Show the last few lines of a file.
wc	Count lines, words, and characters.

Printing

Command	Use
at_cho_prn	Allows you to choose an AppleTalk printer.
cancel	Cancel a printer request.
Enscript	Converts text files to PostScript.
lp	Send to the printer.
lpoptions	Display a list of printer options and defaults.
lprm	Cancel a print request.
lpstat	Get printer status.
pr	Format and paginate for printing.

Programming

Command	Use
cc	C compiler.
ctags	C function references (for *vi*).
ld	Loader.
lex	Lexical analyzer generator.
make	Execute commands in a specified order.
od	Dump input in various formats.
strip	Remove data from an object file.
yacc	Parser generator. Can be used with *lex*.

Searching

Command	Use
egrep	Extended version of *grep*.
fgrep	Search files for literal words.
find	Search the system for filenames.
grep	Search files for text patterns.
strings	Search binary files for text patterns.

Shell Programming

Command	Use
echo	Repeat command-line arguments on the output.
expr	Perform arithmetic and comparisons.
printf	Format and print command-line arguments.
sleep	Pause during processing.
test	Test a condition.

Storage

Command	Use
compress	Compress files to free up space.
cpio	Copy archives in or out.
gunzip	Expand compressed (*.gz* and *.Z*) files (preferred).
gzcat	Display contents of compressed files (may be linked to *zcat*).
gzip	Compress files to free up space (preferred).
tar	Tape archiver.
uncompress	Expand compressed (*.Z*) files.
zcat	Display contents of compressed files.

System Status

Command	Use
at	Execute commands later.
atq	Show jobs queued by *at*.
atrm	Remove job queued by *at*.
chgrp	Change file group.
chown	Change file owner.
crontab	Automate commands.
date	Display or set date.
df	Show free disk space.
du	Show disk usage.
env	Show environment variables.
finger	Display information about users.
kill	Terminate a running command.
printenv	Show environment variables.
ps	Show processes.
stty	Set or display terminal settings.
who	Show who is logged in.

Text Processing

Command	Use
col	Process control characters.
cut	Select columns for display.
emacs	Work environment with powerful text editing capabilities.
ex	Line editor underlying *vi*.
expand	Convert tabs to spaces.
fmt	Produce roughly uniform line lengths.
fold	Break lines.
groff	Format *troff* input.
join	Merge different columns into a database.
paste	Merge columns or switch order.
rev	Print lines in reverse.
sed	Noninteractive text editor.
sort	Sort or merge files.
tr	Translate (redefine) characters.
uniq	Find repeated or unique lines in a file.
vi	Visual text editor.
xargs	Process many arguments in manageable portions.

Miscellaneous

Command	Use
banner	Make posters from words.
bc	Arbitrary precision calculator.
cal	Display calendar.
clear	Clear the screen.
man	Get information on a command.
nice	Reduce a job's priority.
nohup	Preserve a running job after logging out.
passwd	Set your login password.
script	Produce a transcript of your login session.
su	Become a superuser.
tee	Simultaneously store output in file and send to screen.
which	Print pathname of a command.

2

Unix Command Reference

This chapter presents the Mac OS X user, programmer, and system administration commands available through the Terminal (see Chapter 3). Each entry is labeled with the command name on the outer edge of the page. The syntax line is followed by a brief description and a list of available options. Many commands come with examples at the end of the entry. If you need only a quick reminder or suggestion about a command, you can skip directly to the examples.

Typographic conventions for describing command syntax are in the Preface. For help in locating commands, see the Index at the back of this book.

We've tried to be as thorough as possible in listing the options. Basic command information and most options should be correct; however, new options are added, and sometimes older options may have been dropped. You may, therefore, find some differences between the options you find described here and the ones on your system. When there seems to be a discrepancy, check the manpage (by way of the *man* command). For most commands, you can also use the *--help* option to get a brief usage message. (Even when it isn't a valid option, it usually results in an "invalid option" error message, along with the usage message.)

Traditionally, commands take single-letter options preceded by a single hyphen, like *-d*. A more recent Unix convention allows long options preceded by two hyphens, like *--debug*. Often, a feature can be invoked through either the old style or the new style of options.

Some options can be invoked only by a user with root (superuser) privileges.

There are over 300 Unix commands listed in this chapter, many of which don't have manpages—or worse, inaccurate manpages—on the system. These commands give you the basics of what you need to know to get under the hood of your Mac OS X system...and more.

Alphabetical Summary of Commands

The sections that follow list the more commonly used Unix commands in alphabetical order. The page footer on righthand pages references the last command listed on that page.

---

ac

ac [*options*] [*users*]

Displays accumulative Aqua and shell login times for *users*, or for all users if none is specified. By default, *ac* reads from */var/log/wtmp* (see also *last*).

Options

-*d*   Show totals for each day.

-*p*   Show totals for each user.

-*w file*
        Read accounting data from *file* instead of */var/log/wtmp*.

---

appleping

appleping *host* [*packet-size* [*npackets*]]

Sends AppleTalk Echo Protocol (AEP) request packets to *host* and displays transmission statistics if successful. The AppleTalk *host* is specified in either of the following ways:

name:type[@zone]
        The host's *name* and *type*, as shown by the *atlookup* command. If *zone* isn't specified, the current zone is used.

network-node
        The host's network and node number in hexadecimal, as shown by the *atlookup* command.

Options

packet-size
        Send packets of *packet-size* bytes (a value between 14 and 599). The default value is 64.

npackets
        Send *npackets* number of packets before stopping. If *npackets* is not specified, *appleping* continues until you've sent an interrupt (using Control-C, for example).

---

appletalk

appletalk *options*

Displays or configures AppleTalk network interfaces. Any user may display settings, but only the superuser may change them. *appletalk* allows you to start and stop Apple-Talk on a single port (network interface), or configure AppleTalk routing or multihoming on multiple ports.

General options

-*d*   Deactivate AppleTalk.

-*n*   Show current AppleTalk interface, network number, node ID, and zone name.

-*p*   Show AppleTalk information stored in parameter RAM (PRAM).

-*s*   Show AppleTalk statistics.

-*C name*
   Set the computer name as seen on the network. Unprintable characters can be specified with hex characters between asterisks.

Single port options

-*h [zone]*
   Change the default AppleTalk zone to *zone*, or if *zone* isn't specified, display the current zone.

-*q*   Use with -*u* to start AppleTalk in quiet mode; doesn't prompt for zone selection.

-*u port*
   Start AppleTalk on the network interface *port* (*en0*, for example).

Multiple port options

-*c*   Verify the AppleTalk configuration file, */etc/appletalk.cfg*, without starting Apple-Talk. Use with -*r* or -*x*.

-*e*   Same as -*c*, but also display the AppleTalk configuration.

-*f file*
   Use *file* instead of the default */etc/appletalk.cfg* to start AppleTalk. Use with -*r* or -*x*.

-*j*   Display AppleTalk router status.

-*m n*
   Limit routing speed to a maximum *n* packets per second.

-*q*   Use with -*r* or -*x* to start AppleTalk in quiet mode; doesn't prompt for zone selection.

-*r*   Start AppleTalk in routing mode.

-*t*   Show the AppleTalk routing table.

-*v n*
   Set the maximum number of entries in the AppleTalk routing table to *n*. Use with -*r* or -*x*. Useful with large AppleTalk networks.

-*w n*
   Set the maximum number of entries in the Zone Information Protocol (ZIP) table to *n*. Use with -*r* or -*x*. Useful with large AppleTalk networks.

-x   Start AppleTalk in multihoming mode.

-z   List all AppleTalk zones.

Examples

Stop AppleTalk, using *sudo* to gain superuser privileges:

    `$ sudo appletalk -d`

Start AppleTalk on the *en1* interface:

    `$ sudo appletalk -u en1`

Start an AppleTalk router in quiet mode:

    `$ sudo appletalk -q -r`

appletviewer

appletviewer [*options*] *urls*

Connects to the specified *urls* and runs any Java applets they specify in their own windows, outside the context of a web browser.

Options

-debug
>   Run the applet viewer from within the Java debugger, *jdb*.

-encoding name
>   Specify the input HTML file encoding.

-J opt
>   Pass *opt* on to the *java* command. *opt* shouldn't contain spaces; use multiple *-J* options if necessary.

apply

apply [*options*] *command arguments*

Allows you to run a given command multiple times, each time with a different argument. By default, *apply* pairs and runs *command* followed by each argument listed in *arguments*. To place the argument elsewhere in *command*, mark that location in *command* with %*n*, where *n* is the *n*th unused item listed in *arguments* (see "Examples").

Options

-a character
>   Use *character* instead of %.

-number
>   Instead of pairing arguments one at a time with *command*, use them *number* at a time with *command*. If *number* is 0, none of the arguments will be used with *command*, but *command* will still run once for each item listed in *arguments*. If *command* contains %*n*, *number* is ignored.

Examples

Ping three different hosts, sending three packets to each:

```
$ apply 'ping -c3' host1.com host2.com host3.com
```

Ping three different hosts, sending a different number of packets to each:

```
$ apply -2 'ping -c' 3 host1.com 4 host2.com 5 host3.com
```

Ping three different hosts, and write output to file *pinglog*:

```
$ apply 'ping -c3 %1 >> pinglog' host1.com  host2.com ,⏎ host3.com
```

apropos

apropos *keywords*

Looks up one or more keywords in the online manpages. Same as *man -k*. See also *whatis*.

asr

asr -source *sourcepath* -target *targetpath* [*options*]
asr -imagescan *imagepath*

Copies the contents of a disk image or source volume onto a target volume. *asr* (Apple Software Restore) can also scan and prepare disk images when given the *-imagescan* option, allowing the images to be restored more efficiently. *asr* usually needs to run as root.

sourcepath can be the pathname of either a disk image or a volume, while *targetpath* can specify only a volume. Volumes can be specified by either their */dev* entries (e.g., */dev/disk0s10*) or mountpoints (e.g., */Volumes/Disk 2*).

For disk image creation, use either Disk Utility or the command-line utility *hdiutil*. Once a volume has been restored, it might be necessary to use the *bless* utility to make it bootable. (See *hdiutil* and *bless*).

For a complete description of the imaging and restoration process, as well as tips on optimizing restores using the buffer settings, see the *asr* manpage.

Options

-buffers n
> During block-copies, use *n* number of buffers instead of the default eight.

-blockonly
> When used with *-imagescan*, insert only information relevant to block-copies. This makes the scan much faster, but an image scanned with *-blockonly* can't be block-copied; an error will occur.

-buffersize n
> During block-copies, use buffers of size *n* bytes instead of the default 1000. *n* can also be specified in bytes, kilobytes, megabytes, or gigabytes by appending it with *b*, *k*, *m*, or *g*, respectively.

-csumbuffers n
> Use *n* number of buffers specifically for checksumming. By default, checksumming is performed with the same buffers used for copying.

-csumbuffersize n

Use checksum buffers of size *n* bytes. *n* can also be specified in bytes, kilobytes, megabytes, or gigabytes by appending it with *b*, *k*, *m*, or *g*, respectively.

-debug

Print additional information during operation to assist in troubleshooting.

-disableOwners

Don't enable the owners for the source and target. By default, *asr* ensures that all owners are enabled, allowing for more accurate file-by-file copying. If given, this option is ignored during block-copies.

 As of *asr* Version 14.4, this option doesn't function as described; if given, *-disableOwners* behaves as if the *-debug* option were given instead.

-erase

Erase the target volume before copying to it. If this option is not used, *asr* will instead restore in place, overwriting only those files that have the same name and location in both *sourcepath* and *targetpath* and copying from *sourcepath* anything not already in *targetpath*. Using the *-erase* option allows *asr* to perform a block-copy restore, which can be faster than the file-by-file copying procedure used when restoring in place.

-format [*format*]

Use *format* as the format of the target volume. Must be one of *HFS+*, *UFS*, or *HFSX*. Only valid with the *-erase* option.

-h Print a brief help message. This option can only be used by itself.

-imagescan imagepath

Scan disk image *imagepath* and generate checksums. Scanning optimizes images that *asr* will use as source images for restores. This option can only be used by itself.

-nocheck

Don't verify copied data. By default, *asr* uses checksums generated during the image scan for verification. This option will bypass that verification, allowing *asr* to restore from images that haven't first been scanned.

-noprompt

Don't prompt before erasing *targetpath* when the *-erase* option is used.

-nowrapper

Force an HFS wrapper to not be created on the target volume if the *-erase* option is used.

-rebuild

Rebuild the Classic system's desktop database on *targetpath*.

-v Print version information. This option can only be used by itself.

-verbose

Print verbose progress and error messages.

-wrapper

Create an HFS wrapper on the target volume if the *-erase* option is used.

Examples

Typically, `asr` requires root privileges, provided by the `sudo` command in these examples:

Clone one volume to another:

```
$ sudo asr -source "/Volumes/Mac HD" -target "/Volumes/Disk 2" -erase
```

Restore in place from a disk image:

```
$ sudo asr -source /Volumes/Images/image1.dmg  -target "/Volumes/Disk 2"
```

---

at

at [*options*] [*time*] [*date*] [+ *increment*]

Executes commands entered on standard input at a specified *time* and optional *date*. (See also *batch* and *crontab*.) End input with EOF. *time* can be formed either as a numeric hour (with optional minutes and modifiers) or as a keyword. *date* can be formed either as a month and date, a day of the week, or a special keyword. *increment* is a positive integer followed by a keyword. See the following lists for details.

at is disabled by default in Mac OS X. You must first enable *atrun* by uncommenting its line in */etc/crontab*.

Options

-*f file*
Execute commands listed in *file*.

-*m* Send mail to user after job is completed (if an MTA such as *sendmail* is configured to run).

-*q queuename*
Schedule the job in *queuename*. Values for *queuename* are the lowercase letters *a* through *l*. Queue *a* is the default queue for *at* jobs. Queue *b* is the queue for *batch* jobs. Queues with higher letters run with increased niceness (receive less priority).

Time

hh:mm [modifiers]
Hours can have one or two digits (a 24-hour clock is assumed by default); optional minutes can be given as one or two digits; the colon can be omitted if the format is *h*, *hh*, or *hhmm*; e.g., valid times are 5, 5:30, 0530, and 19:45. If modifier *am* or *pm* is added, *time* is based on a 12-hour clock.

midnight | noon | now | teatime
Use any one of these keywords in place of a numeric time. *now* must be followed by an *increment*. *teatime* is 4:00 P.M.

Date

month num [year] | MM/DD/YY | DD.MM.YY
month is one of the 12 months, abbreviated to its first three letters; *num* is the calendar day of the month; *year* is the four-digit year. If the given *month* occurs before the current month, *at* schedules that month next year.

today | tomorrow
Indicate the current day or the next day. If *date* is omitted, *at* schedules *today* when the specified *time* occurs later than the current time; otherwise, *at* schedules *tomorrow*.

Increment

Supply a numeric increment if you want to specify an execution time or day relative to the current time. The number should precede any of the keywords *minute*, *hour*, *day*, or *week* (or their plural forms).

Examples

Note that the first two commands are equivalent:

```
$ at 1945 Dec 9
$ at 7:45pm Dec 9
$ at now + 5 hours
$ at noon tomorrow
```

---

at_cho_prn

at_cho_prn [*type*[*@zone*]]

Specifies the default AppleTalk printer to use with *atprint*. With no arguments, *at_cho_prn* prompts you to choose from the list of zones, and then from the list of network-visible entities (NVEs) of type *LaserWriter* and *ImageWriter* in the chosen zone. Use *type* to specify a different type of NVE to list. Use *zone* to specify a zone to search, bypassing the zone selection prompt. *at_cho_prn* requires superuser privileges to run.

---

atlookup

atlookup [*options*] [*scope*]

Lists *network-visible entities* (NVEs) on the AppleTalk network. If *scope* isn't specified, *atlookup* lists all NVEs in the current zone.

Options

- -a Show only NVE names and types in the list; don't include network numbers.
- -C When used with -z, display zones in several columns instead of one.
- -d Print network numbers in decimal format instead of the default hexadecimal.
- -r *n* Retry unsuccessful lookups *n* times. The default is 8.
- -s *n* Retry unsuccessful lookups *n* seconds apart. The default is one second.
- -x Convert nonprintable characters in lists to their hexadecimal equivalents, prefaced with /.
- -z List all zones on the network. Used alone or with -C.

Scope

Specify the scope of the lookup by NVE *name*, *type*, and *zone* using this syntax:

[*name*[:*type*[*@zone*]]]

You can use the = wildcard anywhere in *name* or *type* to match zero or more characters, except with older AppleTalk Phase 1 nodes, which ignore such lookups. The = wildcard works with all AppleTalk nodes, however, when used by itself to match all names or types. Lookups are not case-sensitive.

Examples

Display all NVEs of type *darwin* in the current zone:

    `$ atlookup =:darwin`

Display all NVEs on printers named with *sales* in the current zone (not AppleTalk Phase 1 compliant):

    `$ atlookup sales=:=`

---

atprint

atprint [*printer*]

Sends data from standard input to AppleTalk printer *printer*, or the printer chosen with *at_cho_prn* if no printer is specified. Specify *printer* using the [*name*[:*type*[@*zone*]]] syntax as described for *atlookup*. If the printer is a PostScript device, you must first reformat non-PostScript data, such as plain text, to PostScript before printing with *atprint*. You can do this easily using *enscript*, as shown in the first example.

Examples

Print text file *addresslist* to the AppleTalk PostScript printer *sales*:

    `$ enscript -p- | atprint addresslist | sales`

Print *grep*'s manpage to the *at_cho_prn* chosen printer, using *man*'s -*t* option to format it for PostScript printing:

    `$ man -t grep| atprint`

---

atq

atq [*options*]

Lists jobs created by the *at* command that are still in the queue. Normally, jobs are sorted by the order in which they execute.

Options

-*q queuename*
    Show jobs pending in queue *queuename*.

-*v*   Show jobs that have completed but have not yet been deleted.

---

atrm

atrm *jobIDs*

Removes jobs queued with *at* that match the specified *jobIDs*.

atstatus

atstatus [*printer*]

Displays the status of AppleTalk printer *printer* or the printer chosen with *at_cho_prn* if no printer is specified. Specify *printer* using the [*name*[:*type*[@*zone*]]] syntax as described for *atlookup*.

automount

automount -help

automount -V

automount [-m *map_directory* map [-mnt *mount_directory*] [-1]]...
[-a *mount_directory*] [-d] [-D { mount | nsl | options | proc | select | all }]...
[-f] [-s] [-tcp] [-tl *timeout*] [-tm *timeout*]

Provides transparent, automated access to NFS and AFP shares. When running, any filesystem access to *map_directory* is intercepted by *automount*. Typically, *automount* will then set up a symbolic link from *map_directory* or one of its subdirectories to a mount point under *mount_directory*, automatically creating directories and mounting remote volumes as needed. It will also unmount remote volumes that have been idle for too long. Directories or mounts set up by *automount* are removed when *automount* exits.

automount makes use of *maps* to determine how to mount volumes. When using a file as a map, the format is similar to that used by NFS automounters on other Unix platforms. Each entry in the file consists of a single line, either a comment beginning with a hash mark (#) or a mount directive of the form:

    subdirectory server:/pathname

If this line were included in a file named */etc/mountmaps*, and *automount* were called like so:

    # automount -m /mount_directory /etc/mountmaps

upon accessing */mount_directory*, *automount* would mount the NFS-exported *server:/pathname* on */private/mount_directory/subdirectory* and create a symlink to that mount point from */mount_directory/subdirectory*.

It was once possible to use a map stored in a NetInfo database under */mountmaps/*, but that functionality has been deprecated in more recent versions of Mac OS X.

In addition to map files, there are several special maps available. Foremost among them are those used by default on Mac OS X systems, *-fstab*, *-static*, and *-nsl*. The following commands are run from the NFS startup item:

    automount -m /Network -nsl
    automount -m /automount/Servers -fstab -mnt /private/var/automount/ ⏎
    Network/Servers -m /automount/static -static -mnt /private/var/automount

Both *-fstab* and *-static* maps use similar configuration formats, stored in an Open Directory database under */mounts/*. The following configuration line triggers *automount* when using the *-fstab* map:

    server:/subdirectory /mount_point url

    net,url==afp://;AUTH=NO%20USER%20AUTHENT@server/share_name 0 0+

The AFP mount example is used for the remainder of this section, but an equivalent NFS configuration looks like this:

```
server:/subdirectory /mount_point nfs net 0 0
```

There are several options for getting this configuration into Open Directory; one is to use *niload fstab domain*, then enter the configuration line, followed by Control-D. It's stored in Open Directory like this (as displayed by *nidump -r /mounts domain*):

```
{
  "name" = ( "mounts" );
  CHILDREN = (
    {
      "dir" = ( "/mount_point" );
      "dump_freq" = ( "0" );
      "name" = ( "server:/subdirectory" );
      "opts" = ( "net", "url==afp://;
                              AUTH=NO%20USER%20AUTHENT@server/
share_name" );
      "passno" = ( "0" );
      "vfstype" = ( "url" );
    }
  )
}
```

The *net* option is the signal for this configuration line to be used by *automount* with the *-fstab* map. Without the *net* option, this configuration line is picked up by the *-static* map.

With this configuration, and *automount* called like so:

```
# automount -m /automount/Servers -fstab ↵
  -mnt /private/var/automount/Network/Servers
```

upon accessing */automount/Servers*, *automount* would mount *share_name* from *server* on */private/var/automount/Network/Servers/server/subdirectory*, and create a symlink from */automount/Servers/server*. (Alternatively, the mount may be accessed via */Network/Servers/server*, thanks to a symlink created by the NFS startup item.) The configured mount point (the value of the *dir* property) is ignored by the *-fstab* map.

Don't use a map_*directory* argument to *-m* that traverses a symlink, or any accesses to the mount will hang. For example, it's OK to do this:

```
# automount -m /private/tmp/map_dir -fstab
```

but not this:

```
# automount -m /tmp/map_dir -fstab
```

because */tmp* is a symlink to */private/tmp*.

While the *-static* map uses a configuration very much like that for *-fstab*, its mounting and linking behavior is significantly different. With a configuration like this (viewed as the output of *nidump fstab domain*):

```
server:/subdirectory /mount_point url
```

```
url==afp://;AUTH=NO%20USER%20AUTHENT@server/share_name 0 0
```

and *automount* called like so:

```
# automount -m /automount/static -static -mnt /private/var/automount
```

upon accessing */mount_point*, *automount* would mount *share_name* from *server* on */private/var/automount/mount_point*, create a symlink to this from */automount/ static/mount_point*, and then another from */mount_point* to */automount/static/mount_ point*. The configured *server:/subdirectory* (the value of the *name* property) is ignored by the *-static* map for AFP shares. (Incidentally, the term "static" is a misnomer. Mounts are made dynamically when they are accessed, just as with the *-fstab* map.)

AFP URLs

The format of the AFP URLs in the *automount* examples is described in the manpage for *mount_afp*, but there are constraints you should be aware of:

1. First, *server* must be a valid TCP/IP hostname or IP address, which may be different than the AFP name that shows up, for example, in a Connect to Server... dialog window.

2. Second, *share_name* is the AFP name for the share point, which is not necessarily the same as the full pathname to the share point on the server.

3. Finally, there are a few ways to handle authentication to the AFP server. If guest access to the share is allowed, you may use a URL like those in the examples:

   ```
   automount:afp://;AUTH=NO%20USER%20AUTHENT@server/share_name
   ```

If user authentication is required, you have two options. The first is to specify the necessary authentication information in the URL like so:

```
afp://username:password@server/share_name
```

However, this makes the authentication password available to anyone with access to the configuration stored in Open Directory. The other option is to leave out the authentication parameters:

```
afp://server/share_name
```

In this case, the user logged into the graphical console is presented with an authentication dialog to enable access to the share. Of course, if no one is logged into the GUI, this won't work, and the mount attempt will fail.

The *-nsl* map uses the Network Services Location service discovery API to automatically find available shares on the network (just as the Finder's Connect to Server... menu item does) and create mounts for them. With *automount* invoked like this:

```
# automount -m /Network -nsl
```

discovered shares are mounted on subdirectories of */private/var/automount/Network/ server*, with a symlink created from */Network/server*.

Before Version 10.3, the *-nsl* map didn't really work, and it generated I/O errors when access to a mount was attempted. The *automount* command, which uses the *-nsl* map in the NFS startup item, was added in Panther.

Another special map is the *-user* map. It doesn't actually cause any remote filesystems to be mounted on its own; it merely sets up symlinks to every user account's home directory from the *map_directory*, which may be useful if you want a single place to look in for everyone's home directory. But proceed cautiously if you have a very large number of user accounts.

The *-host* map is meant to automatically mount NFS exports from hosts listed in a NIS hosts map, when accessing a subdirectory of the *map_directory* with the same name as the host. For example, accessing */net/hostname/export* should mount *hostname:/export*, if */net* is the *map_directory*. This is similar to the *-hosts* map of other NFS automounters.

The *-null* map mounts...well, nothing. It will, however, intercept filesystem calls for the *map_directory*, thus effectively mounting an empty directory over whatever might have been there before. In the original *automount*, from which NeXT's and Apple's versions are descended, this was meant to nullify configuration entries included from a network-wide NIS map.

When running in daemon mode, *automount* stores its PID in */var/run/automount.pid* and responds to SIGHUP by reloading its configuration.

Options

-1   Create directories on the path to a *-fstab* mount point one at a time, as they're traversed, rather than creating the entire path to a mount point when the mount is accessed. However, using this option leads to I/O errors when trying to access the mount.

-a   Specify the directory in which mounts are made. Symbolic links from the directory specified in the *-m* option are used to access these mounts. The default is */private/var/automount*.

-d   Send debugging output to standard error and prevent daemonization.

-D   Output debugging messages of the specified type. If the *-d* option is used, output is to standard error; otherwise, it's via *syslog*. Multiple occurrences of this option may be used to specify multiple types.

-f   Used internally by *automount* to indicate that the process has already forked during daemonization. (You can see in the output of *ps -ax* that the *automount* daemon runs with the *-f* flag, even though it isn't invoked that way from the NFS startup item.)

-help
    Print a usage statement to standard output.

-m   Use the specified map to mount shares and create symlinks from the specified directory to the mount points. The map argument can be an absolute pathname to a file, a map in the */mountmaps/* directory of an Open Directory domain, or one of the special values *-fstab*, *-host*, *-nsl*, *-null*, *-static*, or *-user*. Multiple *-m* options enable the use of multiple maps. In the absence of a *-m* option, *automount* attempts to find maps in Open Directory.

-mnt
> Like *-a*, but specific to a single map.

-s   Supposedly create all mounts at startup and never unmount them. However, mounts are still only attempted upon access, at which point *automount* prints a bus error and dumps core when using this option.

-tcp
> Attempt to mount NFS volumes over TCP, instead of the default UDP.

-tl   Specify a time-to-live (TTL) for mount names, in seconds. After the timeout expires, mounts are rechecked. A timeout of 0 sets an infinite TTL. The default is 10000.

-tm Specify a timeout to retry failing mounts, in seconds. The timeout roughly doubles with each mount attempt, until giving up after a few tries. The default is 20.

-V   Print version number and host information to standard output.

---

banner

```
banner [-w width] message
```

Prints *message* as a poster on the standard output.

Options
-w width
> Specify the maximum width of the poster. Default is 132.

---

basename

```
basename pathname [suffix]
```

```
basename [-s suffix] pathname [...]
```

Given a *pathname*, strips the path prefix and leaves just the filename, which is printed on standard output. If specified, a filename *suffix* (e.g., *.c*) is removed also. The suffix may also be specified with the *-s* option, in which case multiple paths may be passed and stripped. *basename* is typically invoked via command substitution ('..') to generate a filename. See also *dirname*.

Option
-s suffix
> Removes *suffix* from the filename, if found.

Example
Given the following fragment from a Bourne shell script:

```
ofile=output_file
myname="`basename $0`"
echo "$myname: QUITTING: can't open $ofile" 1>&2
exit 1
```

If the script is called *do_it*, the following message is printed on standard error:

```
do_it: QUITTING: can't open output_file
```

batch

batch [*options*]

Executes commands entered on standard input. Ends with EOF. Unlike at, which executes commands at a specific time, *batch* executes commands one after another (waiting for each one to complete). This avoids the potentially high system load caused by running several background jobs at once. See also *at*.

batch is equivalent to issuing the command *at -q b now*.

Options

-f *file*
> Execute commands listed in *file*.

-m Send mail to user after job is completed (if an MTA such as *sendmail* is configured to run).

Example

```
$ batch
sort in > out
troff -ms bigfile > bigfile.ps
EOF
```

---

bc

bc [*options*] [*files*]

Interactively performs arbitrary-precision arithmetic or converts numbers from one base to another. Input can be taken from *files* or read from the standard input. To exit, type *quit* or *EOF*.

Options

-l   Make available functions from the math library.

-q   Quiet, don't print welcome message.

-s   Don't use extensions to POSIX *bc*.

-v   Print version number.

-w   Warn if extensions are used.

bc is a language (and compiler) whose syntax resembles that of C. *bc* consists of identifiers, keywords, and symbols, which are briefly described here. Examples follow at the end of this section.

Identifiers

An identifier is a single character, consisting of the lowercase letters a–z. Identifiers are used as names for variables, arrays, and functions. Within the same program, you may name a variable, an array, and a function using the same letter. The following identifiers would not conflict:

x   Variable *x*.

x[i]
> Element *i* of array *x*. *i* can range from 0 to 2047 and can also be an expression.

x(y,z)
>   Call function *x* with parameters *y* and *z*.

Input/output keywords

ibase, obase, and scale each store a value. Typing them on a line by themselves displays their current value. More commonly, you would change their values through assignment. Letters A-F are treated as digits whose values are 10-15.

ibase = *n*
>   Numbers that are input (e.g., typed) are read as base *n* (default is 10).

obase = *n*
>   Numbers displayed are in base *n* (default is 10). Note: once ibase has been changed from 10, use digit "A" to restore ibase or obase to decimal.

scale = *n*
>   Display computations using *n* decimal places (default is 0, meaning that results are truncated to integers). scale is normally used only for base-10 computations.

Statement keywords

A semicolon or a newline separates one statement from another. Curly braces are needed only when grouping multiple statements.

if (*rel-expr*) {*statements*}
>   Do one or more *statements* if relational expression *rel-expr* is true; for example:
>
>   if (x == y) i = i + 1

while (*rel-expr*) {*statements*}
>   Repeat one or more *statements* while *rel-expr* is true; for example:
>
>   while (i > 0) {p = p*n; q = a/b; i = i-1}

for (*expr1*; rel-expr; expr2) {statements}
>   Similar to while; for example, to print the first 10 multiples of 5, you can type:
>
>   for (i = 1; i <= 10; i++) i*5

break
>   Terminate a while or for statement.

quit
>   Exit *bc*.

Function keywords

define *j* (*k*) {
>   Begin the definition of function *j* having a single argument *k*. Additional arguments are allowed, separated by commas. Statements follow on successive lines. End with a }.

auto *x , y*
>   Set up *x* and *y* as variables local to a function definition, initialized to 0 and meaningless outside the function. Must appear first.

return(*expr*)
>   Pass the value of expression *expr* back to the program. Return 0 if (*expr*) is left off. Used in function definitions.

sqrt(*expr*)
>   Compute the square root of expression *expr*.

length(*expr*)
> Compute how many digits are in *expr*.

scale(*expr*)
> Same as previous, but count only digits to the right of the decimal point.

Math library functions

These are available when *bc* is invoked with -*l*. Library functions set *scale* to 20.

s(*angle*)
> Compute the sine of *angle*, a constant or expression in radians.

c(*angle*)
> Compute the cosine of *angle*, a constant or expression in radians.

a(*n*)
> Compute the arctangent of *n*, returning an angle in radians.

e(*expr*)
> Compute e to the power of *expr*.

l(*expr*)
> Compute the natural log of *expr*.

j(*n*, *x*)
> Compute Bessel function of integer order *n*.

Operators

These consist of operators and other symbols. Operators can be arithmetic, unary, assignment, or relational.

Table 2-1. Operators for use with the bc command

Type	Operator
Arithmetic	+, -, *, /, %, ^
Unary	-, ++, --
Assignment	=+, =-, =*, =/, =%, =^, =
Relational	<, <=, >, >=, = =, !=

Other symbols

/* */
> Enclose comments.

( ) Control the evaluation of expressions (change precedence). Can also be used around assignment statements to force the result to print.

{ } Used to group statements.

[ ] Array index.

"*text*"
> Use as a statement to print *text*.

Examples

Note that when you type some quantity (a number or expression), it is evaluated and printed, but assignment statements produce no display:

```
ibase = 8      Octal input
20             Evaluate this octal number
```

```
16                Terminal displays decimal value
obase = 2         Display output in base 2 instead of base 10
20                Octal input
10000             Terminal now displays binary value
ibase = A         Restore base-10 input
scale = 3         Truncate results to three places
8/7               Evaluate a division
1.001001000       Oops! Forgot to reset output base to 10
obase = 10        Input is decimal now, so "A" isn't needed
8/7
1.142             The Terminal displays result (truncated)
```

The following lines show the use of functions:

```
define p(r,n){    Function p uses two arguments
  auto v          v is a local variable
  v = r^n         r raised to the n power
  return(v)}      Value returned
scale = 5
x = p(2.5,2)      x = 2.5 ^ 2
x                 Print value of x
6.25
length(x)         Number of digits
3
scale(x)          Number of places to right of decimal point
2
```

---

biff

biff [y | n | b]

Turns mail notification on or off. With no arguments, *biff* indicates the current status.

When mail notification is turned on, each time you get incoming mail, the bell rings, and the first few lines of each message are displayed. *biff* needs the *comsat* daemon to be running. If the *b* option is specified, incoming mail rings the bell but doesn't print any lines of the message.

---

bless

bless [*folder options* | *device options* | *info options*]

Enables a device containing a Mac OS 9, Darwin, or Mac OS X system folder to be bootable and selects an enabled device or system folder to be the default boot system. *bless* can also report the current boot settings.

Folder options

Use *bless*'s folder options to enable and select system folders.

--bootinfo pathname

Enable a volume on New World Macintoshes to boot into Mac OS X by copying file *pathname* into the Mac OS X system folder (specified with *--folder*) to use as the BootX file. *pathname* is typically */usr/standalone/ppc/bootx.bootinfo*.

--bootBlocks

Enable a volume to boot into Mac OS 9 by setting the required boot blocks.

--bootBlockFile pathname

Enable a volume to boot into Mac OS 9 by setting the required boot blocks, which are extracted from the data fork of file *pathname*.

--folder pathname

Bless a Mac OS X system for booting, identified by its CoreServices directory *pathname*. (See example.)

--folder9 pathname

Bless a Mac OS 9 folder for booting or use by Classic, identified by its system folder *pathname*. (See example.)

--label name

Use *name* as the system volume label used by the OS Picker, which appears when the Option key is held during startup.

--labelfile file

Use *file* as an existing, pre-rendered label for the OS picker.

--mount pathname

Select to boot from volume *pathname* using its already blessed system folder, instead of selecting a specific folder. Specify a volume by its mount point pathname, such as */Volumes/Macintosh HD*.

--openfolder directory

Open *directory* when the volume is attached.

--save9

Retain the blessing of the blessed Mac OS 9 system folder when the *--folder* or *--mount* option is used but the *--folder9* option is not.

--saveX

Retain the blessing of the blessed Mac OS X system folder when the *--folder* or *--mount* option is used but the *--folder* option is not.

--setBoot

Set the specified partition as the boot partition.

--setOF

Set the computer to boot at next startup from the system specified by the *--folder* or *--folder9* option. *bless* writes to Open Firmware's boot-device variable.

--system pathname

Enable a volume to boot into Mac OS 9 by setting the required boot blocks, which are extracted from the system file *pathname*.

--systemfile pathname

Insert the data fork of system file *pathname* into the system file of the Mac OS 9 system folder specified by the *--folder9* option.

--use9

When both the *--folder* and *--folder9* options are given, use the Mac OS 9 system as the default system for that volume.

Device options

Use *bless*'s device options to set up new boot devices.

--bootBlockFile pathname

Enable the volume specified by *--device* to boot into Mac OS 9 by setting the required boot blocks, which are extracted from the data fork of file *pathname*.

--device pathname
> Select an unmounted device for setup by opening its block file *pathname*.

--format [fstype]
> Use filesystem type *fstype* to format the device specified by the *--device* option. If *fstype* isn't specified, *bless* format the device using HFS+ with an HFS wrapper.

--fsargs arguments
> Apply additional *arguments* when preparing the device specified by the *--device* option. *arguments* can be any options that exist for the *newfs* command.

--label name
> Use *name* as the label for the new filesystem specified by the *--device* option.

--mount pathname
> Use *pathname* as the temporary mount point for the HFS wrapper.

--setOF
> Set the computer to boot at next startup from the device specified by the *--device* option. *bless* sets this by writing to Open Firmware's boot-device variable.

--system pathname
> Use the file specifications from file *pathname* instead of from both the files specified by the *-bootBlockFile* and *--wrapper* options.

--wrapper pathname
> Mount the HFS wrapper on the mount point specified by *--mount* and insert the system file *pathname* into the wrapper, making it the default system file.

--xcoff pathname
> Enable a volume on Old World Macintoshes to boot into Mac OS X using file *pathname* as the HFS+ StartupFile. *pathname* is typically */usr/standalone/ppc/bootx. xcoff.*

Info options

--bootBlocks
> Display fields from the boot blocks of the volume specified by *--info*.

--info [pathname]
> Display the blessed system folder(s) on volume *pathname* or the default startup volume as set in Open Firmware if *pathname* isn't specified.

--plist
> Provide all information in *plist* format; used with *--info*.

General options

--quiet
> Operate in quiet mode; don't produce any output.

--verbose
> Be verbose; print extra output.

Examples

Bless a Mac OS X-only volume, and have it boot at next restart:

```
$ bless --folder "/Volumes/Mac OS X/System/ Library/ ⏎
CoreServices" -setOF
```

Set a current system volume that holds both a Mac OS X and a Mac OS 9 system to boot Mac OS 9 at next restart:

```
$ bless --folder9 "/Volumes/Mac  OS 9/System Folder" -saveX , ↵
--use9 --setOF
```

See the *bless* manpage for more examples.

cal

cal [*options*] [[*month*] *year*]

With no arguments, prints a calendar for the current month. Otherwise, prints either a 12-month calendar (beginning with January) for the given *year* or a one-month calendar of the given *month* and *year*. *month* ranges from 1 to 12; *year* ranges from 1 to 9999.

Options

-j   Print all days with Julian dates, which number from 1 (for January 1) to the last day of the year.

-y   Print the entire calendar for the current year.

Examples

```
$ cal -j 12 2003
$ cal 2003 > year_file
```

calendar

calendar [*option*]

Reads your *calendar* file and displays all lines that contain the current date. The *calendar* file is like a memo board. You create the file and add entries such as the following:

```
5/4     meeting with design group at 2 pm
may 6   pick up anniversary card on way home
```

When you run *calendar* on May 4, the first line is displayed. *calendar* can be automated by using *crontab* or *at*, or by including it in your startup files, *.profile* or *.login*.

Options

-A *num*
    Print the next *num* days in the future, including today.

-a
    Allow a privileged user to invoke *calendar* for all users, searching each user's login directory for a file named *calendar*. Entries that match are sent to a user via mail. This feature is intended for use via *cron*. It isn't recommended in networked environments with large user bases.

-B *num*
    Print the previous *num* days in the past, including today.

-d *MMDD* [[*YY*]*YY*]
    Display lines for the given date.

-F daynum
> Specify "virtual Friday," the last day before the weekend.

-f filename
> Display calendar items from file *filename* instead of the default *calendar* file in your home directory.

-l n Display calendar items up to *n* days ahead from the current date as well.

-W num
> Print the next *num* days in the future, including today, but not counting weekend days in the count.

-w n
> Force *calendar* to skip over weekends. Display calendar items up to *n* days ahead from the current date only when the current day is a Friday. The default for *n* is 2.

cancel

```
cancel [options] [printer]
```

Cancels print requests made with *lp*. The request can be specified by its ID, by the *printer* on which it is currently printing, or by the username associated with the request (only privileged users can cancel another user's print requests). Use *lpstat* to determine either the *id* or the *printer* to cancel.

Options

-a Cancel all queued requests to the specified *printer*.

-h [hostname]
> Specify the hostname of the print server. With no *hostname*, it uses the value of CUPS_SERVER or localhost.

-u username
> Cancel jobs for user *username*.

id Cancel print request *id*.

cat

```
cat [options] [files]
```

Reads one or more files and prints them on standard output. Reads standard input if no files are specified or if - is specified as one of the files; end input with EOF. Use the > shell operator to combine several files into a new file; >> appends files to an existing file.

Options

-b Like *-n*, but don't number blank lines.

-e Print a $ to mark the end of each line. Implies the *-v* option.

-n Number lines.

-s Squeeze out extra blank lines.

-t Print each tab as ^I. Implies the *-v* option.

-u   Print output as unbuffered (default is buffered in blocks or screen lines).

-v   Display control characters and other nonprinting characters.

Examples

Display a file:

```
$ cat ch1
```

Combine files:

```
$ cat ch1 ch2 ch3 > all
```

Append to a file:

```
$ cat note5 >> notes
```

Create file at terminal; end with EOF:

```
$ cat > temp1
```

Create file at terminal; end with STOP:

```
$ cat > temp2 << STOP
```

CCLEngine

CCLEngine -l *integer* -f *filename* -s { 0 | 1 } -e { 0 | 1 } -c { 0 | 1 } -p {

0 | 1 } -d { 0 | 1 } -m { 0 | 1 | 2 } [-v] [-E] -S *octal_integer* -I *string* -i

URL -C *string* -T *phone_num* -U *username* -P *password*

Parses a modem script and initiates a PPP dialout. When a PPP connection is attempted, *pppd* starts up, parses */Library/Preferences/SystemConfiguration/preferences. plist*, and calls *CCLEngine* with the appropriate arguments.

Options

-c   If set to 1, enable Van Jacobson TCP/IP header compression. This is the opposite of the *novj* option to *pppd*, and is obtained from the IPCPCompressionVJ parameter in */Library/Preferences/SystemConfiguration/preferences.plist*.

-C   If the modem script asks for input, this option provides the label for the alternate button (i.e., the one that's not labeled "OK") on the dialog that pops up. Normally this is set to "Cancel."

-d   If set to 1, start dialing the modem without waiting for a dial tone. This corresponds to the *modemdialmode* option to *pppd* and is obtained from the DialMode parameter in */Library/Preferences/SystemConfiguration/preferences.plist*.

-e   If set to 1, enable compression and error correction in the modem. This corresponds to the *modemcompress* and *modemreliable* options to *pppd*, and is obtained from the ErrorCorrection parameter in */Library/Preferences/ SystemConfiguration/preferences.plist*.

-E   Print output to standard error.

-f   Provide the name of a modem script, normally in */System/Library/Modem Scripts/*. This corresponds to the *modemscript* option to *pppd* and is obtained from the ConnectionScript parameter in */Library/Preferences/SystemConfiguration/ preferences.plist*.

-i   If the modem script asks for input, this option provides a URL for the icon on the dialog that pops up. Normally this is set to *file://localhost/System/Library/Extensions/PPPSerial.ppp/Contents/Resources/NetworkConnect.icns*.

-I   If the modem script asks for input, this option provides the title for the dialog that pops up. Normally this is set to "Internet Connect."

-l   Specify the service ID for the network configuration to use from */Library/Preferences/SystemConfiguration/preferences.plist*. This corresponds to the *serviceid* option to *pppd*.

-m   Determine whether the modem should try to connect (0), disconnect (1), or be set up to answer calls (2).

-p   If set to 1, the modem uses pulse dialing. This corresponds to the *modempulse* and *modemtone* options to *pppd*, and is obtained from the PulseDial parameter in */Library/Preferences/SystemConfiguration/preferences.plist*.

-P   Specify the password to use for PPP authentication.

-s   If set to 1, enable sound output from the modem through the computer speakers. This corresponds to the *modemsound* option to *pppd*, and is obtained from the Speaker parameter in */Library/Preferences/SystemConfiguration/preferences.plist*.

-S   Specify the *syslog* priority level and facility to use for logging errors. The argument is an octal integer that serves as the first argument to a *syslog* system call, as described in the *syslog* manpage and in */usr/include/sys/syslog.h*. The low-order digit specifies priority level from 0 (*emerg*) to 7 (*debug*), while the higher-order digits specify facility. The default is 150, which logs to the *remoteauth* facility at *emerg* level.

-T   Specify the telephone number to dial. This corresponds to the remoteaddress and altremoteaddress options to pppd, and is obtained from the CommRemoteAddress and CommAlternateRemoteAddress parameters in */Library/Preferences/SystemConfiguration/preferences.plist*.

-U   Specify the username to use for PPP authentication. This corresponds to the user option to pppd and is obtained from the AuthName parameter in */Library/Preferences/SystemConfiguration/preferences.plist*.

-v   If set to 1, enable verbose logging to */tmp/ppp.log*. Taken from the VerboseLogging parameter in */Library/Preferences/SystemConfiguration/preferences.plist*.

certtool

certtool { v | d | D } *filename* [h] [v] [d]

certtool y [h] [v] [k=*keychain* [c [p=*password*]]]

certtool c [h] [v] [a] [k=*keychain* [c [p=*password*]]]

certtool { r | I } *filename* [h] [v] [d] [a] [k=*keychain* [c [p=*password*]]]

certtool i *filename* [h] [v] [d] [a] [k=*keychain* [c [p=*password*]]] [r=*filename*]

[f={ 1 | 8 | f }]]

Manages X.509 SSL/TLS certificates. It uses the Common Data Security Architecture (CDSA) in much the same way that */System/Library/OpenSSL/misc/CA.pl* uses OpenSSL to ease the process of managing certificates.

As arguments, it takes a single-letter command, often followed by a filename, and possibly some options.

Options

a   When adding an item to a keychain, create a key pair including a private key with a more restrictive ACL than usual. (The default behavior creates a private key with no additional access restrictions, while specifying this option adds a confirmation requirement to access the private key that only *certtool* is allowed to bypass.)

c   As a command, walks you through a series of interactive prompts to create a certificate and a public/private key pair to sign and possibly encrypt it. The resulting certificate (in DER format) is stored in your default keychain.

 The first prompt, for a *key and certificate label*, is asking for two space-separated items. Common choices are an organization name for the key and a label designating the purpose of the certificate.

As an option, instructs *certtool* to create a new keychain by the name given in the *k* option.

d   As a command, displays the certificate contained in *filename*.

As an option, indicates that the format of the CSR or CRL contained in *filename* is DER (a binary format), instead of the default PEM (an ASCII format, which is essentially a DER certificate with Base64 encoding).

D   Display the *certificate revocation list* (CRL) contained in *filename*.

f   Specify the format of the private key in the file specified with the *r* option. The format is specified by a single character, either 1 (for OpenSSL's PKCS1, the default), 8 (PKCS8), or *f* (FIPS186, or BSAFE).

h   Print a usage statement to standard output, negating whichever command was given.

i   Import the certificate contained in *filename* into the default keychain.

I   Import the CRL contained in *filename* into the default keychain.

k   Specify the name of a keychain (in *~/Library/Keychains*) to use other than the default.

p   Specify the keychain password on the command line. To avoid password exposure, it's better to let *certtool* prompt for it.

r   As a command, walks you through a series of interactive prompts to create a certificate-signing request (CSR) and a public/private key pair to sign and possibly encrypt it. The resulting CSR is stored in *filename*.

As an option, specifies the file containing a private key for the certificate being imported. This is useful if you've used OpenSSL to generate a certificate, instead of *certtool*.

v   As a command, verifies the CSR contained in *filename*.

As an option, should enable verbose output, but it doesn't actually seem to make a difference.

y   As a command, displays the certificates and CRLs in the specified keychain.

chflags

chflags [*options*] *flags files*

Changes the file flags of one or more *files*. *flags* is a comma-separated list of file flags, described later. To unset a flag, use the same command but with *no* added to the front of the flag's name. To view a file's current flags, use the *ls -lo* command.

Options

-H   If any of the pathnames given in the command line are symbolic links, follow only those links during recursive operation. Works only with the -R option.

-L   Follow all symbolic links during recursive operation. Works only with the -R option.

-P   Follow no symbolic links during recursive operation. Works only with the -R option (the default).

-R   Recursively descend through the directory, including subdirectories and symbolic links, changing the specified file flags as it proceeds.

Flags

Table 2-2. Flags used with the chflags command

Flag name	Flag set	Who can change it
arch	Archived	Superuser only
opaque	Opaque	Owner or superuser only
nodump	Nodump	Owner or superuser only
sappnd	System append-only	Superuser only
schg	System immutable	Superuser only
uappnd	User append-only	Owner or superuser only
uchg	User immutable	Owner or superuser only

Though the system append-only (*sappend*) and system immutable (*schg*) flags can be set by the superuser in normal system mode, you can only *unset* them while in single-user mode.

Examples

Setting the user immutable (*uchg*) flag for a file prevents it from being deleted, changed, or moved. By locking a file in the Finder, you're actually setting its user immutable flag. Therefore, this command locks the file as well:

    $ chflags uchg importantfile.doc

Unset the user immutable flag and thus unlock the file:

    $ chflags nouchg importantfile.doc

chgrp

chgrp [*options*] newgroup *files*

Changes the ownership of one or more *files* to *newgroup*. *newgroup* is either a GID number or a group name known to directory services. You must own the file or be a privileged user to succeed with this command.

Options

-*f*   Force error messages to be suppressed.

-*h*   Change the permissions of the link, rather than the referent.

-*H*   If any of the pathnames given in the command line are symbolic links, follow only those links during recursive operation. Works only with the -*R* option.

-*L*   Follow all symbolic links during recursive operation. Works only with the -*R* option.

-*P*   Follow no symbolic links during recursive operation. Works only with the -*R* option (the default).

-*R*   Recursively descend through the directory, including subdirectories and symbolic links, setting the specified GID as it proceeds.

-*v*   Verbose output, showing files as they are changed.

chkpasswd

chkpasswd [-c] [-i *infosystem*] [-l *location*] [*username*]

Useful for scripts, this prompts for a password which is then compared against the appropriate directory service for the user specified. If the password is correct, *chkpasswd* returns 0; otherwise, it returns 1, and the string "Sorry" is printed to standard error.

Options

-*c*   Compare user input with the password hash directly, rather than running it through the *crypt* algorithm first.

-*i*   Specify the directory service to use, which may be *file*, *netinfo*, *nis*, or *opendirectory*.

-*l*   Depending on the directory service being used, it's either a file (defaults to */etc/master.passwd*), a NetInfo domain or server/tag combo, a NIS domain, or an Open Directory node (like */NetInfo/root*).

username
Designate whose password is checked. It defaults to that of the user running the command.

chmod

chmod [option] mode files

Changes the access *mode* or *access control lists* (ACLs) of one or more *files*. Only the owner of a file or a privileged user may change its mode. Create *mode* by concatenating the characters from *who*, *opcode*, and *permission*. *who* is optional (if omitted, default is *a*); choose only one *opcode*.

Options

+*a entry*
> Add ACL entry *entry* for the file.

+*apos entry*
> Add ACL entry *entry* for the file at position *pos*.

-*a entry*
> Remove ACL entry *entry* for the file.

=*apos entry*
> Rewrites the entry at position *pos* with *entry*.

-*f*   Suppress error message upon failure to change a file's mode.

-*h*   Change the permissions of the link, rather than the referent.

-*H*   If any of the pathnames given in the command line are symbolic links, follow only those links during recursive operation. Works only with the -*R* option.

-*L*   Follow all symbolic links during recursive operation. Works only with the -*R* option.

-*P*   Follow no symbolic links during recursive operation. Works only with the -*R* option (the default).

-*R*   Recursively descend directory arguments while setting modes.

-*v*   Verbose output, showing files as they are changed. If -*v* appears more than once, the old and new permissions are shown as well.

Who

u   User.

g   Group.

o   Other.

a   All (default).

Opcode

+   Add permission.

-   Remove permission.

=   Assign permission (and remove permission of the unspecified fields).

Permission

r   Read.

w   Write.

x   Execute (file) or search (directory).

X   Set the execute bit for all *who* values if any of the execute bits are already set in the specified file; meaningful only in conjunction with the *op* symbol +.

s   Set user (or group) ID.

t   Sticky bit; save text mode (file) or prevent removal of files by nonowners (directory).

u   User's present permission.

g   Group's present permission.

o   Other's present permission.

Alternatively, specify permissions by a three-digit sequence. The first digit designates owner permission; the second, group permission; and the third, others permission. Permissions are calculated by adding the following octal values:

4   Read.

2   Write.

1   Execute.

A fourth digit may precede this sequence. This digit assigns the following modes:

4   Set UID on execution.

2   Set GID on execution or set mandatory locking.

1   Sticky bit.

Examples

Add execute-by-user permission to *file*:

```
$ chmod u+x file
```

Either of the following assigns read-write-execute permission by owner (7), read-execute permission by group (5), and execute-only permission by others (1) to *file*:

```
$ chmod 751 file
$ chmod u=rwx,g=rx,o=x file
```

Any one of the following assigns read-only permission to *file* for everyone:

```
$ chmod =r file
$ chmod 444 file
$ chmod a-wx,a+r file
```

Set the UID, assign read-write-execute permission by owner, and assign read-execute permission by group and others:

```
$ chmod 4755 file
```

---

chown

```
chown [options] newowner[:newgroup] files
```

Changes the ownership of one or more *files* to *newowner*. *newowner* is either a UID number or a login name known to directory services. The optional *newgroup* is either a GID number or a group name known to directory services. When *newgroup* is supplied, the behavior is to change the ownership of one or more *files* to *newowner* and make it belong to *newgroup*.

Options

-f   Force error messages to be suppressed.

-h   Change the ownership of the link, rather than the referent.

-H   If any of the pathnames given in the command line are symbolic links, follow only those links during recursive operation. Works only with the -R option.

-L   Follow all symbolic links during recursive operation. Works only with the -R option.

-P   Follow no symbolic links during recursive operation. Works only with the -R option (the default).

-R   Recursively descend through the directory, including subdirectories, resetting the ownership ID.

-v   Verbose output, showing files as they are changed. If -v appears more than once, the old and new permissions will be shown as well.

cksum

cksum [*files*]

Calculates and prints a cyclic redundancy check (CRC) for each file. The CRC algorithm is based on the polynomial used for Ethernet packets. For each file, *cksum* prints a line of the form:

> sum *count* *filename*

Here, *sum* is the CRC, *count* is the number of bytes in the file, and *filename* is the file's name. The name is omitted if standard input is used.

clear

clear

Clears the Terminal display.

cmp

cmp [*options*] *file file2* [*skip1* [*skip2*]]

Compares *file1* with *file2*. Use standard input if *file1* or *file2* is -. To begin the comparison from byte offsets other than at the beginning of the files, use the optional arguments *skip1* and *skip2*, which specify the byte offsets from the beginning of each file. By default, the value is decimal. To use hexadecimal or octal values, precede them with a leading 0x or 0, respectively. See also *comm* and *diff*. The exit codes are as follows:

0   Files are identical.

1   Files are different.

2   Files are inaccessible.

Options

-c, --print-chars
> Print differing bytes as characters.

-i N, --ignore-initial= N
> Ignore differences in the first *N* bytes of input.

-n limit, --bytes=limit
> Compare at most `limit` bytes of input.

-l   For each difference, print the byte number in decimal and the differing bytes in octal.

-s   Work silently; print nothing, but return exit codes.

-v, --version
> Output version info.

Example

Print a message if two files are the same (exit code is 0):

```
$ cmp -s old new && echo 'no changes'
```

---

colcrt

```
colcrt [options] [files]
```

A postprocessing filter that handles reverse linefeeds and escape characters, allowing output from *tbl* or *nroff* to appear in reasonable form on a terminal. Puts half-line characters (e.g., subscripts or superscripts) and underlining (changed to dashes) on a new line between output lines.

Options

-    Don't underline.

-2   Double-space by printing all half lines.

---

colrm

```
colrm [start [stop]]
```

Removes specified columns from a file, where a column is a single character in a line. Reads from standard input, and writes to standard output. Columns are numbered starting with 1; begin deleting columns at (including) the *start* column, and stop at (including) the *stop* column. Entering a tab increments the column count to the next multiple of either the *start* or *stop* column; entering a backspace decrements it by 1.

Example

List all the contents of a directory and remove the permissions, UID and GID, file size, and the date/time information, leaving just the filenames:

```
$ ls -la | colrm 1 50
```

column

column [*options*] [*files*]

Formats input from one or more *files* into columns, filling rows first. Reads from standard input if no files are specified. Checks the COLUMNS environment variable for the current terminal width if necessary.

Options

-c num

   Format output into *num* columns.

-s char

   Delimit table columns with *char*. Meaningful only with *-t*.

-t   Format input into a table. Delimit with whitespace, unless an alternate delimiter has been provided with *-s*.

-x   Fill columns before filling rows.

comm

comm [*options*] *file1 file2*

Compares lines common to the sorted files *file1* and *file2*. Three-column output is produced: lines unique to *file1*, lines unique to *file2*, and lines common to both *files*. *comm* is similar to *diff* in that both commands compare two files. In addition, *comm* can be used like *uniq*; that is, *comm* selects duplicate or unique lines between two sorted files, whereas *uniq* selects duplicate or unique lines within the same sorted file. A filename of - means standard input, not an option.

Options

-1   Suppress printing of column 1.

-2   Suppress printing of column 2.

-3   Suppress printing of column 3.

-12 Print only lines in column 3 (lines common to *file1* and *file2*).

-13 Print only lines in column 2 (lines unique to *file2*).

-23 Print only lines in column 1 (lines unique to *file1*).

Example

Compare two lists of top 10 movies and display items that appear in both lists:

```
$ comm -12 shalit_top10 maltin_top10
```

compress

compress [*options*] [*files*]

Reduces the size of one or more *files* using adaptive Lempel-Ziv coding and move to *file.Z*. Restore with *uncompress* or *zcat*.

With a filename of -, or with no *files*, *compress* reads standard input.

Unisys claims a patent on the algorithm used by *compress*. Today, *gzip* is generally preferred for file compression.

compress doesn't preserve resource forks or HFS metadata when compressing files that contain them.

Options

-bn Limit the number of bits in coding to *n*; *n* is 9–16; 16 is the default. A lower *n* produces a larger, less densely compressed file.

-c Write to the standard output (don't change files).

-f Compress unconditionally; i.e., don't prompt before overwriting files. Also, compress files even if the resulting file would actually be larger.

-v Print the resulting percentage of reduction for *files*.

configd

configd [-b] [-B *bundle_ID*] [-d] [-t *pathname*] [-v] [-V *bundle_ID*]

The System Configuration Server monitors changes to network-related items such as link status, DHCP assignments, PPP connections, and IP configuration, and provides an API for applications to be notified of these changes. To monitor various items, it uses a set of plug-in configuration agents, including the Preferences Monitor, the Kernel Event Monitor, the PPP Controller Agent, the IP Configuration Agent, and the IP Monitor Agent. The agent plug-ins are located in */System/Library/SystemConfiguration/*. More information on the System Configuration framework can be found at *http://developer. apple.com/techpubs/macosx/Networking/SysConfigOverview926/*.

It's started as a bootstrap daemon, from */etc/mach_init.d/configd.plist* (processed by *register_mach_bootstrap_servers*). When running in daemon mode, *configd* stores its PID in */var/run/configd.pid*.

Options

-b Disable loading of all agents.

-B Disable loading of the specified agent.

-d Run the process in the foreground, preventing daemonization.

-t Load the agent specified by *pathname*.

-v Enable verbose logging.

-V Enable verbose logging for the specified agent.

cp

cp [*options*] *file1 file*

cp [*options*] *files directory*

Copies *file1* to *file2*, or copies one or more *files* to the same names under *directory*. If the destination is an existing file, the file is overwritten; if the destination is an existing directory, the file is copied into the directory (the directory is not over-written). If one of the inputs is a directory, uses the -R option.

cp doesn't preserve resource forks or HFS metadata when copying files that contain them. For such files, use *CpMac* or *ditto* instead.

Options

-*f* Remove the target file, if it exists, before creating the new copy. Also, don't prompt for confirmation of overwrites. Overrides previous -*i* or -*n* options.

-*H* If any of the pathnames given in the command line are symbolic links, follow only those links during recursive operation. Works only with the -*R* option.

-*i* Prompt for confirmation (y for yes) before overwriting an existing file.

-*L* Follow all symbolic links during recursive operation. Works only with the -*R* option.

-*n* Doesn't overwrite existing target file. Overrides previous -*f* or -*i* options.

-*p* Preserve the modification time and permission modes for the copied file. (Normally *cp* supplies the permissions of the invoking user.)

-*P* Follow no symbolic links during recursive operation. Works only with the -*R* option (the default).

-*R* Recursively copy a directory, its files, and its subdirectories to a destination *directory*, duplicating the tree structure. (This option is used with the second command-line format when at least one of the source *file* arguments is a directory.)

Example

Copy two files to their parent directory (keep the same names):

```
$ cp outline memo ..
```

---

cpio

cpio *control_options* [*options*]

Copies file archives in from or out to disk or to another location on the local machine. Note that until native drivers for tape drives exist for Mac OS X, *cpio* can't write to tape. Each of the three control options, -*i*, -*o*, or -*p*, accepts different options. (See also *ditto*, *pax*, and *tar*.)

cpio doesn't preserve resource forks or metadata when copying files that contain them. For such files, use *ditto* instead.

cpio -i [*options*] [*patterns*]
   Copy in (extract) files whose names match selected *patterns*. Each pattern can include filename metacharacters from the Bourne shell. (Patterns should be quoted or escaped so they are interpreted by *cpio*, not by the shell.) If no pattern is used, all files are copied in. During extraction, existing files aren't overwritten by older versions in the archive (unless -*u* is specified).

cpio -o [*options*]
   Copy out a list of files whose names are given on the standard input.

cpio -p [*options*] *directory*
   Copy files to another directory on the same system. Destination pathnames are interpreted relative to the named *directory*.

Comparison of valid options

Options available to the *-i*, *-o*, and *-p* options are shown respectively in the first, second, and third row below. (The - is omitted for clarity.)

```
i:    b B c C d E f F H I    m   r s S t u v 6
o: a A   B c C        F H      L  O          v
p: a          d               l L m         u v
```

Options

-a   Reset access times of input files.

-A   Append files to an archive (must use with -O).

-b   Swap bytes and half-words. Words are 4 bytes.

-B   Block input or output using 5120 bytes per record (default is 512 bytes per record).

-c   Read or write header information as ASCII characters; useful when source and destination machines are different types.

-C *n* Like -B, but block size can be any positive integer *n*.

-d   Create directories as needed.

-E *file*
      Extract filenames listed in *file* from the archive.

-f   Reverse the sense of copying; copy all files except those that match *patterns*.

-F *file*
      Synonym for -I in -i mode, or -O in -o mode. Uses *file* as the archive to operate on.

-H *format*
      Read or write header information according to *format*. Values for *format* are *ustar* (IEEE/P1003 Data Interchange Standard header) or *tar* (*tar* header).

-I *file*
      Read *file* as an input archive.

-l   Link files instead of copying. Can be used only with -p.

-L   Follow symbolic links.

-m   Retain previous file-modification time.

-O *file*
      Direct the output to *file*.

-r   Rename files interactively.

-s   Swap bytes.

-S   Swap half-words.

-t   Print a table of contents of the input (create no files). When used with the -v option, resembles output of *ls -l*.

-u   Unconditional copy; old files can overwrite new ones.

-v   Print a list of filenames.

-6   Process a PWB Unix 6th Edition archive format file. Useful only with the -i option, mutually exclusive with -c and -H.

Examples

Generate a list of old files using *find*; use list as input to *cpio*:

```
$ find . -name "*.old" -print | cpio -ocBvO ~/archive
```

Restore from a tape drive (if supported) all files whose name contains "save" (subdirectories are created if needed):

```
$ cpio -icdv "*save*" < /dev/rmt/0
```

To move a directory tree:

```
$ find . -depth -print | cpio -padml /mydir
```

CpMac

CpMac [-mac] [-p] [-r] *source_path* [*source_path*...] *dest_path*

Copies files, keeping multiple forks and HFS attributes intact.

Options

-mac

Arguments use legacy Mac OS pathname syntax (i.e., colons as path separators, paths as viewed from the Finder).

-p   Preserve file attributes.

-r   Recursively copy directory contents.

create_nidb

create_nidb [*tag* [*master_hostname* [*root_dir*]]]

A Perl program that creates and populates an Open Directory database from the contents of flat files in */etc/*. This may be especially useful if you have configuration information you wish to carry over from another Unix system. Currently, *create_nidb* uses the following files:

/etc/master.passwd
/etc/group
/etc/hosts
/etc/networks

create_nidb should be run with superuser privileges.

Options

master_hostname

The name of the host serving the master copy of the Open Directory database. The default is localhost if the tag is local; otherwise, it's the hostname of the system on which *create_nidb* is run.

root_dir

The directory in which *var/db/netinfo/tag.nidb* is created. The default is /.

tag

The tag of the Open Directory database. The default is local.

crontab

```
crontab [-u user] [file]
```

```
crontab [-u user] options
```

Runs *crontab* on your current crontab file, or specifies a crontab *file* to add to the crontab directory. A privileged user can run *crontab* for another user by supplying *-u user* before any of the other options.

A crontab file is a list of commands, one per line, that executes automatically at a given time. Numbers are supplied before each command to specify the execution time. The numbers appear in five fields, as follows:

```
Minute          0-59
Hour            0-23
Day of month    1-31
Month           1-12
Day of week     0-6, with 0 = Sunday
```

Use a comma between multiple values, a hyphen to indicate a range, and an asterisk to indicate all possible values. For example, assuming the following crontab entries below:

```
59 3 * * 5        find / -print | backup_program
0 0 1,15 * *      echo "Timesheets due" | mail user
```

The first command backs up the system files every Friday at 3:59 a.m., and the second command mails a reminder on the 1st and 15th of each month.

Options

-e   Edit the user's current crontab file (or create one).

-l   List the user's file in the crontab directory.

-r   Delete the user's file in the crontab directory.

curl

```
curl [options] [URL...]
```

Transfers files to and from servers using one or more URLs. *curl* supports several common protocols specified in *URL*: HTTP, HTTPS, FTP, GOPHER, DICT, TELNET, LDAP, and FILE. The following descriptions and examples cover *curl*'s basic operation; for a complete description, refer to *curl*'s manpage.

URL expressions

{a, b, c, ...}

Form multiple URLs, each using one of the alternate variables specified within the braces as part of its string. For example, this string expands into three different URLs: *http://www. somesite.com/~{jonny,andy,miho}*.

[n1-n2]

Form multiple URLs, each using one of the letters or numbers in the range specified within the brackets as part of its string. For example, this string expands into five different URLs: *http://www[1-5].somesite.com/*. Note that brackets need to be escaped from the shell (i.e., preceded with a backslash or surrounded in quotes).

Selected options

-B offset, --use-ascii
  Use ASCII mode for FTP and LDAP transfers.

-C offset, --continue-at offset
  Resume transfer after skipping the first *offset* bytes of the source file, for cases in which the previous transfer attempt was interrupted.

-D filename, --dump-header filename
  Save the HTTP headers or FTP server response lines in *filename*.

-M, --manual
  Display a detailed usage manual.

-o filename, --output filename
  Save downloaded data to *filename* instead of standard output. If you specify multiple URLs using braces or brackets and use *#n* within *filename*, it is replaced in each new filename by each of the multiple values inside the *n*th braces or brackets in the URL (see example).

-O, --remote-name
  Save downloaded data to a local file of the same name as the remote file, instead of standard output.

-T filename, --upload-file filename
  Upload local file *filename* to *URL*. If *URL* ends with a slash, *curl* uses the local file-name for the uploaded copy. Otherwise, the name at the end of *URL* is used.

-#, --progress-bar
  Display a progress bar instead of the default statistics during transfers.

Examples

Perform an anonymous FTP download into the working directory:

```
$ curl -O ftp://ftp.xyzsite.com/installer.sit
```

Download three sequentially named files from two different servers as user *jon*:

```
$ curl "ftp://jon@ftp.{abc,xyz}site.com/ installer[1-3].sit" ↵
-o "#1_installer#2.sit"
```

Upload a file to an iDisk's Public folder:

```
$ curl -T archive.tar http://idisk.mac.com/jon4738/Public/
```

---

cut

cut *options* [*files*]

Selects a list of columns or fields from one or more files. Either *-c* or *-f* must be specified. *list* is a sequence of integers. Use a comma between separate values and a hyphen to specify a range (e.g., *1-10,15,20* or *50-*). See also *paste* and *join*.

Options

-b list
  This *list* specifies byte positions, not character positions. This is important when multibyte characters are used. With this option, lines should be 1023 bytes or less in size.

-c list
> Cut the character positions identified in *list*.

-d c
> Use with *-f* to specify field delimiter as character *c* (default is tab); special characters (e.g., a space) must be quoted.

-f list
> Cut the fields identified in *list*.

-n Don't split characters. When used with *-b*, *cut* doesn't split multibyte characters.

-s Use with *-f* to suppress lines without delimiters.

Examples

Display only *ping* times while *ping*ing a host:

```
$ ping 192.168.10.58 | cut -sd= -f4
```

Find out who is logged on, but list only login names:

```
$ who | cut -d" " -f1
```

Cut characters in the fourth column of *file*, and paste them back as the first column in the same file. Send the results to standard output:

```
$ cut -c4 file | paste - file
```

---

date

```
date [option] [+format]
date [options] [string]
```

In the first form, prints the current date and time, specifying an optional display *format*. In the second form, a privileged user can set the current date by supplying a numeric *string*. *format* can consist of literal text strings (blanks must be quoted) as well as field descriptors, whose values will appear as described next (the listing shows some logical groupings).

Format

%n Insert a newline.

%t Insert a tab.

%m Month of year (01–12).

%d Day of month (01-31).

%y Last two digits of year (00–99).

%D Date in %m/%d/%y format.

%b Abbreviated month name.

%e Day of month (1–31); pad single digits with a space.

%Y Four-digit year (e.g., 2004).

%C "Century," or year/1000, as an integer.

%g Week-based year within century (00–99).

%G Week-based year, including the century (0000–9999).

%h Same as %b.

%B   Full-month name.

%H   Hour in 24-hour format (00–23).

%M   Minute (00–59).

%S   Second (00–61); 61 permits leap seconds and double-leap seconds.

%R   Time in %H:%M format.

%T   Time in %H:%M:%S format.

%k   Hour (24-hour clock; 0–23); single digits are preceded by a space.

%l   Hour (12-hour clock; 1–12); single digits are preceded by a space.

%I   Hour in 12-hour format (01–12).

%p   String to indicate a.m. or p.m. (default is AM or PM).

%r   Time in %I:%M:%S %p format.

%a   Abbreviated weekday.

%A   Full weekday.

%w   Day of week (Sunday = 0).

%u   Weekday as a decimal number (1–7, Sunday = 1).

%U   Week number in year (00–53); start week on Sunday.

%W   Week number in year (00–53); start week on Monday.

%V   The ISO-8601 week number (01–53). In ISO-8601, weeks begin on a Monday, and week 1 of the year is the one that includes both January 4th and the first Thursday of the year. If the first Monday of January is the 2nd, 3rd, or 4th, the preceding days are part of the last week of the previous year.

%j   Julian day of year (001–366).

%Z   Time-zone name.

%x   Country-specific date format.

%X   Country-specific time format.

%c   Country-specific date and time format (the default is %a %b %e %T %Z %Y; e.g., Mon Feb 23 14:30:59 PST 2004).

The actual formatting is done by the *strftime(3)* library routine.

Options

-r seconds
    Print the date and time that is *seconds* from the Epoch (00:00:00 UTC, January 1, 1970).

-u   Display or set the time using Greenwich Mean Time (UTC).

Strings for setting the date

A privileged user can set the date by supplying a numeric *string*. *string* consists of time, day, and year concatenated in one of three ways: *time* or [*day*]*time* or [*day*]*time*[*year*]. Note: don't type the brackets.

time
    A two-digit hour and two-digit minute (*HHMM*); *HH* uses 24-hour format.

day
    A two-digit month and two-digit day of month (*mmdd*); the default is current day and month.

year

The year specified as either the full four digits or just the last two digits; the default is current year.

Examples

Set the date to February 23 (0223), 4 A.M. (0400), 2005 (04):

```
$ date 0223040005
```

The following command:

```
$ date +"Greetings master, the current date and time is:%nDate: ⏎
%D%nTime: %T"
```

produces a formatted date as follows:

```
Greetings master, the current date and time is:
Date: 07/09/05
Time: 13:23:49
```

---

dc

dc [*file*]

An interactive desk calculator program that performs arbitrary-precision integer arithmetic (input may be taken from a *file*). Normally you don't run *dc* directly because it's invoked by *bc* (see *bc*). *dc* provides a variety of one-character commands and operators that perform arithmetic; *dc* works like a Reverse Polish calculator; therefore, operators and commands follow the numbers they affect. Operators include +, -, /, *, %, and ^ (as in C, although ^ signifies exponentiation); some simple commands include:

p Print current result.

q Quit *dc*.

c Clear all values on the stack.

v Take square root.

i Change input base; similar to *bc*'s *ibase*.

o Change output base; similar to *bc*'s *obase*.

k Set scale factor (number of digits after decimal); similar to *bc*'s *scale*.

! Remainder of line is a Unix command.

Examples

```
3 2 ^ p    Evaluate 3 squared, then print result
9

8 * p      Current value (9) times 8, then print result
72

47 - p     Subtract 47 from 72, then print result
25

v p        Square root of 25, then print result
5
```

2 o p   *Display current result in base 2*
101

Spaces aren't needed except between numbers.

---

dd

dd [*option = value*]

Makes a copy of an input file (*if=*) or standard input if there's no named input file, using the specified conditions, and sends the results to the output file (or standard output if *of* isn't specified). Any number of options can be supplied, although *if* and *of* are the most common and are usually specified first. Because *dd* can handle arbitrary block sizes, it is useful when converting between raw physical devices.

dd doesn't preserve resource forks or HFS metadata when copying files that contain them.

Options

bs=n

  Set input and output block size to *n* bytes; this option supersedes *ibs* and *obs*.

cbs=n

  Set the size of the conversion buffer (logical record length) to *n* bytes. Use only if the conversion *flag* is *ascii*, *asciib*, *ebcdic*, *ebcdicb*, *ibm*, *ibmb*, *block*, or *unblock*.

conv=flags

  Convert the input according to one or more (comma-separated) *flags* listed next. The first six *flags* are mutually exclusive. The next two are mutually exclusive with each other, as are the following two.

  ascii

    EBCDIC to ASCII.

  asciib

    EBCDIC to ASCII, using BSD-compatible conversions.

  ebcdic

    ASCII to EBCDIC.

  ebcdicb

    ASCII to EBCDIC, using BSD-compatible conversions.

  ibm

    ASCII to EBCDIC with IBM conventions.

  ibmb

    ASCII to EBCDIC with IBM conventions, using BSD-compatible conversions.

  block

    Variable-length records (i.e., those terminated by a newline) to fixed-length records.

  unblock

    Fixed-length records to variable length.

  lcase

    Uppercase to lowercase.

---

ucase
> Lowercase to uppercase.

noerror
> Continue processing when errors occur (up to five in a row).

notrunc
> Don't truncate the output file. This preserves blocks in the output file that this invocation of *dd* didn't write.

swab
> Swap all pairs of bytes.

sync
> Pad input blocks to *ibs*.

count=n
> Copy only *n* input blocks.

files=n
> Copy *n* input files (e.g., from magnetic tape), then quit.

ibs=n
> Set input block size to *n* bytes (default is 512).

if=file
> Read input from *file* (default is standard input).

obs=n
> Set output block size to *n* bytes (default is 512).

of=file
> Write output to *file* (default is standard output).

iseek=n
> Seek *n* blocks from start of input file (like *skip*, but more efficient for disk file input).

oseek=n
> Seek *n* blocks from start of output file.

seek=n
> Same as *oseek* (retained for compatibility).

skip=n
> Skip *n* input blocks; useful with magnetic tape.

You can multiply size values (*n*) by a factor of 1024, 512, or 2 by appending the letters *k*, *b*, or *w*, respectively. You can use the letter x as a multiplication operator between two numbers.

Examples

Convert an input file to all lowercase:

```
$ dd if=caps_file of=small_file conv=lcase
```

Retrieve variable-length data; write it as fixed-length to *out*:

```
$ data_retrieval_cmd | dd of=out conv=sync,block
```

defaults

defaults [-*currentHost* | -host *name*] *command*

Modifies the defaults system. When you customize your Mac using the System Preferences, all those changes and settings are stored in the defaults system. Everything that you've done to make your Mac your own is stored as XML data in the form of a property list (or *plist*). This property list is, in turn, stored in ~/*Library/Preferences*.

Every time you change one of those settings, that particular property list is updated. There are two other ways to alter the property lists: using the Property List Editor application (/*Developer/Applications*) or using the *defaults* command in the Terminal. Whether you use System Preferences, Property List Editor, or the *defaults* command, any changes you make affect the current user.

Options

-*currentHost*
> Perform operations on the local machine.

-*host name*
> Perform operations on the specified host.

Commands

read
> Print all your current settings.

read domain
> Print your settings for the specified domain, such as *com.apple.dock*.

read domain key
> Print the value of the specified key. For example, to see the current Dock orientation, use: *defaults read com.apple.dock orientation*

read-type domain key
> Print the datatype of the specified key. For example, *defaults read-type com.apple. dock orientation* tells you that the type of the orientation key is string.

write domain key value
> Write a value to the specified key.

rename domain old_key new_key
> Rename the specified key.

delete domain
> Delete the specified domain. So, if you issue the command *defaults delete com. apple.dock*, the Dock forgets everything. The next time you log in, the Dock's settings are set to the system default.

delete domain key
> Delete the specified key. So, if you issue the command *defaults delete com.apple. dock orientation*, the Dock forgets its orientation. The next time you log in, the Dock's settings are set to the system default.

domains
> List all the domains in your defaults.

find string
> Search all defaults for the specified string.

help
> Print a list of options.

Domains

By default, the domain is specified by the general form *com.companyname.appname*, as in *defaults read com.apple.Safari*. Other options available include:

-app appname
> Specify the name of the application instead of the domain, as in *defaults read -app Safari*.

filepath
> Specify the full path to the plist file, without the *.plist* extension, as in *defaults read ~/Library/Preferences/com.apple.Safari*.

-g, -globaldomain, NSGlobalDomain
> Specify the global domain.

Values

A value may take one of the following forms:

string
> Specify a string value. For example: *defaults write com.apple.dock orientation right*.

-type value
> Specify a value of the specified type. The type may be *string*, *float*, or *boolean*. For example, *defaults write com.apple.dock autohide -boolean true*.

-array [-add] value [value...]
> Create or add to a list of defaults. For example, you can create a list of your favorite colors with *defaults write personal.favorites colors -array red, blue*. Use *-add* to add values to an existing array.

-dict [-add] key value [key value...]
> Create or add to a dictionary list. For example, you can create a dictionary of preferred pet foods with *defaults write personal.pets food -dict cat salmon dog steak*.

 Using the *defaults* command is not for the foolhardy. If you manage to mangle your settings, the easiest way to correct the problem is to go back to that application's Preferences pane and reset your preferences. In some cases, you can use *defaults delete*, which will be reset to the same defaults when you next log in. Because the *defaults* command affects only the current user, you can also create a user just for testing random *defaults* tips you pick up.

Examples

View all the user defaults on your system:

```
$ defaults domains
```

This prints a listing of all the domains in the user's defaults system. The list you see is run together with spaces in between—not quite the prettiest way to view the information.

View the settings for your Terminal:

```
$ defaults read com.apple.Terminal
```

This command reads the settings from the *com.apple.Terminal.plist* file, found in *~/Library/Preferences*. This listing is rather long, so you might want to pipe the output to *less* or *more* to view the contents one screen at a time:

```
$ defaults read com.apple.Terminal | more
```

Change your Dock's default location to the top of the screen:

```
$ defaults write com.apple.Dock orientation top
```

This moves the Dock to the top of the screen underneath the menu bar. After changing that setting, you'll need to log out from the system and then log back in to see the Dock under the menu bar, or just issue the following command to kill and restart the Dock:

```
$ killall Dock
```

---

df

df [*options*] [*name*]

Reports the number of free disk blocks and inodes available on all mounted filesystems or on the given *name*. (Unmounted filesystems are checked with -F.) *name* can be a device name (e.g., */dev/disk0s9*), the directory name of a mount point (e.g., */Volumes/Drive2*), a directory name, or a remote filesystem name (e.g., an NFS filesystem). Besides the options listed, there are additional options specific to different filesystem types or *df* modules.

Options

-a   Show all mount points, even if mounted with MNT_IGNORE.

-b   Print sizes in 512-byte blocks.

-g   Print sizes in gigabytes.

-H   Print sizes in human-readable form. Sizes are reported in B,K,M,G,T,P for bytes, kilobytes, megabytes, gigabytes, terabytes, and petabytes, respectively. (If you have petabytes of storage for your Macintosh, we want to hear from you.) All sizes use powers of 10, so 1M = 1,000,000 bytes.

-h   Print sizes in human-readable form. Sizes are reported in B,K,M,G,T,P for bytes, kilobytes, megabytes, gigabytes, terabytes, and petabytes, respectively. All sizes use powers of 2, so 1M = 1,048,576 bytes.

-i   Report free, used, and percent-used inodes.

-k   Print sizes in kilobytes.

-l   Show local filesystems only.

-m   Print sizes in megabytes.

-n   Print already known, potentially stale statistics about the filesystems, without requesting or calculating new statistics. This should be used only when requesting statistics would cause a large delay.

-T *type1* [, *type2* , ...]
    Show only filesystem types specified. Types may be prefixed with "no" to exclude that filesystem type. Use the *lsvfs* command to see filesystems available. For example, to see only local drives and CD-ROMs, use *df -T hfs,cd9660*.

diff

`diff [options] [diroptions] file1 file2`

Compares two text files. *diff* reports lines that differ between *file1* and *file2*. Output consists of lines of context from each file, with `file1` text flagged by a < symbol, and `file2` text by a > symbol. Context lines are preceded by the *ed* command (*a*, *c*, or *d*) that converts `file1` to `file2`. If one of the files is -, standard input is read. If one of the files is a directory, *diff* locates the filename in that directory corresponding to the other argument (e.g., *diff dir junk* is the same as *diff dir/junk junk*). If both arguments are directories, *diff* reports lines that differ between all pairs of files having equivalent names (e.g., *olddir/program* and *newdir/program*); in addition, *diff* lists filenames unique to one directory, as well as subdirectories common to both. See also *cmp*.

Options

Options *-c*, *-C*, *-D*, *-e*, *-f*, *-h*, and *-n* can't be combined with one another (they are mutually exclusive).

-a, --text
> Treat all files as text files. Useful for checking to see if binary files are identical.

-b, --ignore-space-change
> Ignore repeating blanks and end-of-line blanks; treat successive blanks as one.

-B, --ignore-blank-lines
> Ignore blank lines in files.

-c, -C n, --context[=n]
> Context *diff*: print *n* lines surrounding each changed line. The default context is three lines.

--changed-group-format=format
> Use *format* to output a line group containing differing lines from both files in if-then-else format.

-d, --minimal
> Ignore segments of numerous changes and output a smaller set of changes. This may cause a significant slowdown in *diff*.

-D symbol, --ifdef=symbol
> When handling C files, create an output file that contains the contents of both input files, including `#ifdef` and `#ifndef` directives that reflect the directives in both files.

-e, --ed
> Produce a script of commands (*a*, *c*, *d*) to recreate `file2` from `file1` using the *ed* editor.

-E, --ignore-tab-expansion
> Ignore changes that are only due to expanded tabs.

-f
> Produce a script to recreate `file1` from `file2`; the script is in the opposite order, so it isn't useful to *ed*.

-F regexp, --show-function-line[=regexp]
> For context and unified *diff*, show the most recent line containing *regexp* before each block of changed lines.

--forward-ed

> Make output that looks vaguely like an *ed* script but has changes in the order they appear in the file.

--from-file=file

> Compare *file* to all operands. *file* can be a directory.

-H Speed output of large files by scanning for scattered small changes; long stretches with many changes may not show up.

-help

> Print brief usage message.

--horizon-lines=n

> In an attempt to find a more compact listing, keep *n* lines on both sides of the changed lines when performing the comparison.

-i, --ignore-case

> Ignore case in text comparison. Uppercase and lowercase are considered the same.

-I regex, --ignore-matching-lines=regex

> Ignore lines in files that match the regular expression *regex*.

--ifdef=name

> Make merged if-then-else format output, conditional on the preprocessor macro *name*.

--ignore-file-name-case, --no-ignore-filename-case

> Ignore case when comparing filenames. Maybe be prepended with *-no* to make case significant in filename comparisons.

-l, --paginate

> Paginate output by passing it to *pr*.

-L label, --label label, --label=label

> For context and unified *diffs*, print *label* in place of the filename being compared. The first such option applies to the first filename and the second option to the second filename.

--left-column

> For two-column output (*-y*), show only left column of common lines.

--line-format=format

> Use *format* to output all input lines in if-then-else format.

-n, -rcs

> Produce output in RCS *diff* format.

-N, --new-file

> Treat nonexistent files as empty.

--new-group-format=format

> Use *format* to output a group of lines taken from just the second file in if-then-else format.

--new-line-format=format

> Use *format* to output a line taken from just the second file in if-then-else format.

--old-group-format=format

> Use *format* to output a group of lines taken from just the first file in if-then-else format.

--old-line-format=format
> Use *format* to output a line taken from just the first file in if-then-else format.

-p, --show-c-function
> When handling files in C or C-like languages such as Java, show the function containing each block of changed lines. Assumes *-c*, but can also be used with a unified *diff*.

-P, --unidirectional-new-file
> If two directories are being compared, and the first lacks a file that is in the second, pretend that an empty file of that name exists in the first directory.

-q, --brief
> Output only whether files differ.

--sdiff-merge-assist
> Print extra information to help *sdiff*. *sdiff* uses this option when it runs *diff*.

--speed-large-files
> Assume large files and many scattered small changes.

--strip-trailing-cr
> Remove trailing input's carriage return.

--suppress-common-lines
> Don't print common lines in side-by-side format.

-t, --expand-tabs
> Produce output with tabs expanded to spaces.

-T, --initial-tab
> Insert initial tabs into output to line up tabs properly.

--to-file=file
> Compare all operands to *file*, which can be a directory.

-u, -U n, --unified[=n]
> Unified *diff*: print old and new versions of lines in a single block, with *n* lines surrounding each block of changed lines. The default context is three lines.

--unchanged-group-format=format
> Use *format* to output a group of common lines taken from both files in if-then-else format.

--unidirectional-new-file
> Treat absent first files as empty.

-v, --version
> Print version number of this version of *diff*.

-w, --ignore-all-space
> Ignore all whitespace in files for comparisons.

-W n, --width=n
> For two-column output (*-y*), produce columns with a maximum width of *n* characters. Default is 130.

-x regex, --exclude=regex
> Don't compare files in a directory whose names match *regex*.

-X filename, --exclude-from=filename
> Don't compare files in a directory whose names match patterns described in the file *filename*.

-y, --side-by-side
> Produce two-column output.

-n
> For context and unified *diff*, print *n* lines of context. Same as specifying a number with *-C* or *-U*.

Diroptions

The following *diroptions* are valid only when both file arguments are directories.

-r, --recursive
> Compare subdirectories recursively.

-s, --report-identical-files
> Indicate when files don't differ.

-S filename, --starting-file=filename
> For directory comparisons, begin with the file *filename*, skipping files that come earlier in the standard list order.

---

diff3

```
diff3 [options] file1 file2 file3
```

Compares three files and reports the differences. No more than one of the files may be given as - (indicating that it is to be read from standard input). The output is displayed with the following codes:

`====`
> All three files differ.

`====1`
> *file1* is different.

`====2`
> *file2* is different.

`====3`
> *file3* is different.

diff3 is also designed to merge changes in two differing files based on a common ancestor file (i.e., when two people have made their own sets of changes to the same file). *diff3* can find changes between the ancestor and one of the newer files and generate output that adds those differences to the other new file. Unmerged changes are places where both newer files differ from each other and at least one of them is from the ancestor. Changes from the ancestor that are the same in both of the newer files are called *merged changes*. If all three files differ in the same place, it is called an *overlapping change*.

This scheme is used on the command line with the ancestor being *file2*, the second filename. Comparison is made between *file2* and *file3*, with those differences then applied to *file1*.

Options

-3, --easy-only
> Create an *ed* script to incorporate into *file1* unmerged, non-overlapping differences between *file1* and *file3*.

-a, --text
> Treat files as text.

-A, --show-all
> Create an *ed* script to incorporate all changes, showing conflicts in bracketed format.

-e, --ed
> Create an *ed* script to incorporate into *file1* all unmerged differences between *file2* and *file3*.

-E, --show-overlap
> Create an *ed* script to incorporate unmerged changes, showing conflicts in bracketed format.

-i Append the *w* (save) and *q* (quit) commands to *ed* script output.

-L label, --label=label
> Use *label* to replace filename in output.

-m, --merge
> Create file with changes merged (not an *ed* script).

-T, --initial-tab
> Begin lines with a tab instead of two spaces in output to line tabs up properly.

-v, --version
> Print version information, and then exit.

-x, --overlap-only
> Create an *ed* script to incorporate into *file1* all differences in which all three files differ (overlapping changes).

-X Same as *-x*, but show only overlapping changes, in bracketed format.

---

dig

dig [@*server*] *host* [*querytype*] [*queryclass*] [*options*]

Queries Internet domain name servers. Like the *nslookup* command, *dig* displays information about *host* as returned by the default or a specified nameserver. With *dig*, you specify all aspects of the query on the command line; there's no interactive mode as with *nslookup*.

Specify the nameserver to query with @*server*, using either a domain name or an IP in *server*. The default is to query the nameservers in *resolv.conf*. Specify the type of query in *querytype*; the default is to look up address records. The supported types are:

A Host's Internet address.

ANY
> Any available information (default).

AXFR
> Request zone transfer.

HINFO
> Host CPU and operating system type.

MX Mail exchanger.

NS Nameserver for the named zone.

SOA
> Domain start-of-authority.

Use *queryclass* to specify query class of either IN (Internet) or ANY. Default is IN.

Options

The following descriptions cover *dig*'s basic operation; for a complete description, refer to *dig*'s manpage.

-x address
> Reverse map *address*, which allows you to locate a hostname when only an IP number is available. Implies *ANY* as the query type.

-p port
> Send queries to the specified port instead of port 53, the default.

+norec[urse]
> Turn off recursion (on by default).

+trace
> Iteratively trace queries from the root servers. Show the results of each subquery as it resolves from the root servers to the final destination.

+vc
> Send TCP-based queries (queries are UDP by default).

DirectoryService

```
DirectoryService [-h | -v]

DirectoryService [-appledebug | -appleframework | -applenodaemon | -appleoptions
| -appleperformance | -appleversion]
```

The server process for the Directory Service framework. It's started as a bootstrap daemon, from */etc/mach_init.d/DirectoryService.plist* (processed by *register_mach_bootstrap_servers*).

The manpage for *DirectoryService* on Tiger is very good, but this entry details the additional *-apple* options.

Options

-appledebug
> Run the service in debug mode, disabling daemonization and logging to */Library/Logs/DirectoryService/DirectoryService.debug.log*.

-appleoptions
> Print a usage statement for the second form of command invocation to standard output.

-appleperformance
> Run the service in the foreground and log extensively.

-appleversion
> Print software build version to standard output.

-h
> Print a usage statement for the first form of command invocation to standard output.

-v
> Print software release version to standard output.

dirname

dirname *pathname*

Prints *pathname*, excluding the last level. Useful for stripping the actual filename from a pathname. If there are no slashes (no directory levels) in *pathname*, *dirname* prints . to indicate the current directory. See also *basename*.

diskarbitrationd

diskarbitrationd [-d]

Manages communication between processes about the mounting and unmounting of disk volumes. On Tiger, this takes on part of the role formerly held by *autodiskmount* in Jaguar.

diskarbitrationd starts as a bootstrap daemon, from */etc/mach_init.d/diskarbitrationd. plist* (processed by *register_mach_bootstrap_servers*), and stores its PID in */var/run/ diskarbitrationd.pid*.

Option

-d   Run in debug mode, preventing daemonization.

diskutil

diskutil list [*device*]

diskutil mount[Disk] *device*

diskutil { info[rmation] | unmount[Disk] | eject | reformat | verifyDisk | repairDisk |

enableJournal | disableJournal | verifyPermissions | repairPermissions | eraseOptical [quick] | secureErase | zeroDisk | randomDisk [*integer*] } { *mount_ point* | *device* } diskutil repairOS9Permissions

diskutil rename { *mount_point* | *device* } *vol_name*

diskutil eraseVolume *format vol_name* { *mount_point* | *device* }

diskutil eraseDisk *format vol_name* [OS9Drivers] { *mount_point* | *device* }

diskutil secureErase [freespace] [*format*] { *mount_point* | *device* }

diskutil partitionDisk *device num_partitions* [OS9Drivers | MBRFormat] *part1_ format part1_name part1_size* [*part2_format part2_name part2_size ...*]

diskutil checkRAID

diskutil createRAID { mirror | stripe } *set_name format device1 device2* [*device3...*]

diskutil enableRAID mirror *device*

diskutil destroyRAID { *set_UUID* | *device* }

diskutil addToRAID { member | spare } *set_name device1*

```
diskutil removeFromRAID set_name device1

diskutil updateRAID key value device1

diskutil repairMirror { set_UUID | device } partition_num from_device to_device
```
Controls disk volumes, including mounting, unmounting, ejecting, erasing, journaling, partitioning, fixing permissions, and setting up RAIDs. This is a command-line analog of the Disk Utility application and contains functionality beyond the somewhat less user-friendly *disktool*.

Volumes are specified by mount point (directory on which the volume is mounted) or device name (e.g., *disk0s1*). Filesystem types specified by *format* arguments may be *HFS+*, *JournaledHFS+*, *HFS*, *UFS*, or *MS-DOS*.

Options

AddToRAID
> Add a slice or spare to an existing RAID set. Requires privileged access.

checkRAID
> Check the status of RAID sets. Requires privileged access.

createRAID
> Create a mirror (RAID 1) or a stripe (RAID 0) on a set of devices. Requires privileged access.

destroyRAID
> Destroy an existing mirrored or striped RAID set. Requires privileged access.

disableJournal
> Disable journaling on an HFS+ volume. Requires privileged access.

eject
> If a disk is ejectable, unmount and eject the disk. Requires privileged access, unless the user running *diskutil* is logged into the graphical console.

enableJournal
> Enable journaling on an HFS+ volume. The journal keeps a record of all filesystem operations, which allows the system to roll back to a consistent filesystem state in the event of a crash. This eliminates the need for disk verification after a crash. Requires privileged access.

enableRAID
> Convert a single disk into an unpaired member of a mirrored RAID set. Requires privileged access.

eraseDisk
> Unmount and reformat an entire disk. Requires privileged access.

eraseOptical
> Unmount and erase a read/write optical disk. Requires privileged access.

eraseVolume
> Unmount and reformat a disk partition. Requires privileged access.

info, information
> Prints data about the device to standard output, including device name, volume name and mount point, filesystem format, disk hardware access protocol, total and free disk space, and whether the device is read-only or ejectable.

list

List partitions on the system or just on the specified disk device, including device names, volume names, and sizes.

mount

Mount the specified partition. Requires privileged access, unless the user running *diskutil* is logged into the graphical console.

mountDisk

Mount all partitions on the specified disk. Requires privileged access, unless the user running *diskutil* is logged into the graphical console.

partitionDisk

Repartition the specified disk. The *MBRFormat* flag causes the partition map to be DOS-compatible, with a Master Boot Record (MBR). The number of partitions (*num_partitions*) is limited to 8. Partition sizes are given as a number concatenated with a letter, where the letter is *B* (for bytes), *K* (for kilobytes), *M* (for megabytes), *G* (for gigabytes), or *T* (for terabytes). The current boot disk can't be repartitioned. Requires privileged access.

randomDisk

Erase a disk while overwriting its contents with random data (optionally, more than once, as specified by an additional argument). Requires privileged access.

reformat

Reformat *device* with the same name and format. Requires privileged access.

rename

Give the device a new volume name. For HFS, HFS+, and UFS partitions only.

repairDisk

Unmount the device, attempt to repair any filesystem inconsistencies it finds, and remount the device. Requires privileged access.

repairMirror

Repair a mirrored RAID set. If *checkRAID* reports a problem with a mirrored partition, this lets you sync the data for that partition from the good copy to the bad copy. Requires privileged access.

repairOS9Permissions

Reset file permissions on the System and Applications folders associated with a user's Classic environment.

repairPermissions

Scan the *Archive.bom* files in */Library/Receipts* for installed software packages and reset file permissions according to what they should have been upon installation. Requires privileged access.

secureErase

Erases a disk, or just the free space on it, using a secure algorithm. Requires privileged access to the disk.

If specified, *level* should be one of the following: 1 for a single pass random erase, 2 for US DoD 7-pass secure erase, or 3 for a Gutmann 35-pass secure erase.

unmount

Unmount the specified partition. Requires privileged access, unless the user running *diskutil* is logged into the graphical console.

unmountDisk

Unmount all partitions on the specified disk. Requires privileged access, unless the user running *diskutil* is logged into the graphical console.

verifyDisk

Unmount the device, scan it for filesystem inconsistencies, and remount the device. Requires privileged access.

verifyPermissions

Scan the *Archive.bom* files in */Library/Receipts* for installed software packages and verify whether file permissions are set according to what they should have been upon installation. Requires privileged access.

zeroDisk

Erase a disk while overwriting its contents with zeros. Requires privileged access.

ditto

```
ditto [options] files directory
```

```
ditto [options] directory1 directory2
```

Copies files and directories while preserving most file information, including resource fork and HFS metadata information when desired. *ditto* preserves the permissions, ownership, and timestamp of the source files in the copies. *ditto* overwrites identically named files in the target directory without prompting for confirmation.

ditto works like *cp* in the first synopsis form. However, the second form differs in that *cp -r* copies the entire *directory1* into an existing *directory2*, while *ditto* copies the contents of *directory1* into *directory2*, creating *directory2* if it doesn't already exist.

Options

-arch arch

When copying fat binary files, copy only the code for chip type *arch*. Fat binary files contain different code for different chip architectures. The *-arch* flag allows you to "thin" the binary by copying only the code for the specified chip. Possible values for *arch* include *ppc*, *m68k*, *i386*, *hppa*, and *sparc*.

-bom pathname

When copying a directory, include in the copy only those items listed in *BOM* file *pathname*. See also *mkbom* for information on making a *BOM* file.

-c   Create a CPIO archive at *directory2*.

--extattr

Preserve POSIX extended attributes. This is on by default.

-k   Specify that archives are in PKZip format.

--keepParent

Embed *directory1*'s parent directory in *directory2*.

--nocache

Do not use Mac OS X Unified Buffer Cache for copying.

--noextattr

Do not preserve POSIX extended attributes.

--norsrc

When copying files, include any resource fork and HFS metadata information.

-rsrcFork, -rsrc
> When copying files, include any resource fork and HFS metadata information.

--sequesterRsrc
> Put resource forks and HFS data in directory *__MACOSX*.

-v   Be verbose; report each directory copied.

-V   Be very verbose; report each file, symlink, and device copied.

-x   Unpack the CPIO archives at *directory1*.

-X   Don't descend into directories on another device.

-z   Specify compressed CPIO archives.

Example

Duplicate an entire home directory, copying the contents of directory */Users/chris* into the directory */Volumes/Drive 2/Users/chris* and preserving resource forks and HFS metadata:

```
$ ditto -rsrc /Users/chris "/Volumes/Drive 2/Users/chris"
```

dmesg

```
dmesg [options]
```

Displays the system control messages from the kernel ring buffer. This buffer stores all messages since the last system boot or the most recent ones, if the buffer has been filled.

Options

-M core
> Use the specified *core* file from which to extract messages instead of */dev/kmem*.

-N system
> Use the specified *system* instead of the default */mach_kernel*.

dns-sd

```
dns-sd [-E | -F | -A | -I | -M | -N | -T | -U]
```

```
dns-sd -B _app_protocol._transport_protocol domain
```

```
dns-sd -L service_name _app_protocol._transport_protocol domain
```

```
dns-sd -R service_name _app_protocol._transport_protocol domain port [key=value]…
```

```
dns-sd -P service_name _app_protocol._transport_protocol domain port hostname ip_
addr [key=value]…
```

```
dns-sd -Q fqdn rr_type [rr_class]
```

This command is the same as *mDNS* (see the entry later in this section), with the addition of the -*P* and -*Q* options.

Options

-P   As -R, but registers a service provided by a different host than
the one on which *dns-sd* is run. It also creates a multicast DNS address record for
that host.

-Q   Queries for arbitrary DNS resource records. The arguments are the fully qualified
domain name of what you want to learn about, an RR type (such as *A*, *PTR*, *TXT*,
SRV, etc.), and optionally an RR class (which defaults to 0, the IN class).

---

drutil

drutil help [*subcommand*]

drutil { version | list | poll }

drutil { info | discinfo | trackinfo | status | cdtext | subchannel | eject } [-drive *drive_spec*]

drutil { erase | bulkerase } { full | quick } [-drive *drive_spec*]

drutil tray { eject | open | close } [-drive *drive_spec*]

drutil getconfig { current | supported } [-drive *drive_spec*]

drutil filename *filename*

drutil dumpiso *device block_num* [*format*]

drutil burn [-test] [-appendable] [-erase] [-mount] [-noverify] [-nohfsplus] [-noiso9660] [-nojoliet] [-noudf] [-nofs] [-disctitle *title*] [-audio] [-pregap] *path*

Manages disk drives that can write to optical media, using the Disc Recording framework.

Options

atip
> Prints the Absolute Time in Pre-Groove (ATIP).

bulkerase
> Erase an optical disk as the *erase* subcommand, and then prompt for another disk to erase. This repeats until the process is killed.

burn
> Burn a file or directory to disc. For burning a disk image, use the *burn* verb in *hdiutil*.

cdtext
> Display CD-Text data contained on an audio CD.

discinfo
> Print information about the optical disk in the drive to standard output.

dumpiso
> Dump ISO-9660 and Joliet formatting data from an optical disk. The *device* argument is a disk device filename, such as */dev/disk1*. The *block_num* argument specifies the block to dump. The *format* argument is one of *None*, *Boot*, *Dir*, *HFSPlusVH*, *LPath*, *MPath*, *PVD*, *SVD*, *VDST*, or *VPD*.

eject

Unmount and eject an optical disk. Same as *drutil tray eject*.

erase

Erase a rewritable optical disk and eject it. A *quick* erasure removes only formatting information so that the disk appears to be blank; a *full* erasure overwrites the entire disk but takes considerably longer.

filename

Show how the given filename is converted when burning to an optical disk, given the support available with different formats, including ISO-9660 levels 1 and 2, ISO-9660 with Joliet extensions, and HFS+.

getconfig

Print the features supported by an optical disk drive to standard output. Using *current* lists enabled features, while *supported* lists all possible features. Features include audio CD support, DVD support, power management, and real-time streaming.

help

Print a usage statement to standard output, either for the specified subcommand or for *drutil* as a whole.

info

Print information about drives to standard output, such as vendor, hardware interface, cache size, and write capabilities.

list

Print a list of all disk drives attached to the system that can burn optical disks.

poll

Repeatedly poll an optical drive for information until terminated.

status

Print status information about an optical disk to standard output, such as disk type, number of sessions and tracks, and remaining disk space.

subchannel

Unmount a CD and print subchannel information to standard output, including the CD's media catalog number (MCN) and each track's International Standard Recording Code (ISRC).

toc   Print the table of contents.

trackinfo

Print information about tracks on an optical disk to standard output.

tray

Manipulate drives with motorized trays. Some optical disk drives have trays that can be automatically opened and closed; some can only be opened (and must be closed) manually; some have nonmotorized trays; and slot-loading drives have no trays. The *eject* argument unmounts a disk and opens the tray; the *open* argument opens a tray only if the drive is empty; and the *close* argument closes the tray.

version

Print the operating system and version, and version identifiers for the Disc Recording framework and I/O Kit to standard output.

-drive

Some systems have multiple writable optical drives. The *-drive* option lets you manipulate a drive other than the one chosen automatically by system. The *drive_spec* argument may be one of the following: an integer used to select a particular drive (according the numbering produced by *drutil list*), a string used to match a drive's vendor or product name, or a keyword used to restrict the list of drives that may be manipulated. The keyword is one of *internal*, *external*, *atapi*, *firewire*, *scsi*, or *usb*.

dscl

dscl [*options*] [*datasource* [*command*]]

Allows operations on Directory Service nodes, as a replacement to the older *niutil*.

Options

-p   Prompt for password.

-P password

Use *password* as the password. Use *-p* to be prompted for a password.

-q   Quiet mode.

-raw

Doesn't strip the dsAttrType prefixes from DirectoryService API constants.

-u user

Run as user *user*.

-url Print record attribute values in URL-style encoding. This can help if your values have spaces or colons in them.

Commands

-read path [*key(s)*]

Reads and displays the contents of the directory at path, one key/value pair per line. If any *key(s)* are specified, only those keys are listed.

-list path [*key*]

Displays the subdirectories in *path*. If *key* is specified, only those keys are listed.

-search path key val

Searches *path* for the matching *key/val* pair. For example, to find a specific user by real name, use *dscl . -search /Users RealName "Andy Lester"*.

-create path [*key* [*val(s)*]]

Creates a directory at *path*, including the optional property *key* and optional values *val(s)*. Note that if the property *key* already exists, it will be overwritten with the new key and values.

-append path key val(s)

Appends values to the property *key* at *path*. If *key* does not exist, it will be created.

-merge path key val(s)

Appends values to the property *key* at *path*. Any values in *val(s)* that already exist will be ignored. If *key* does not exist, it will be created.

-delete path [key [val(s)]]
> Deletes directories, keys, or values. If only *path* is specified, that entire directory is deleted. If *key* is specified, that property is deleted. If any *val(s)* are specified, only those values are deleted.

-change record_path key old_val new_val
> Changes any values *old_val* to *new_val* in the property *key* at *path*.

-changei record_path key val_index new_val
> Changes the value at index *val_index* in the property *key* at *path* to *new_val*. The index is based on 1, so 1 is the first value.

-passwd user_path [new_pw | old_pw new_pw]
> Changes a user's password, specified by the full path, not just the username. If only *new_pw* is specified, you will be prompted for the old password. If no passwords are specified, you will be prompted for both.

UnixCommand
Reference

du

du [options] [directories]

Prints disk usage (as the number of 512-byte blocks used by each named directory and its subdirectories; default is current directory).

Options

-a Print usage for all files, not just subdirectories.

-c In addition to normal output, print grand total of all arguments.

-d depth
> Summarize usage for each directory at most *depth* directories down.

-H Follow symbolic links, but only if they are command-line arguments.

-h Human-readable output, with units spelled out: bytes, kilobytes, etc.

-I mask
> Ignore entries matching *mask*.

-k Print sizes in kilobytes.

-L Follow symbolic links.

-P Don't follow any symbolic links.

-s Print a total for each file specified.

-x, --one-file-system
> Display usage of files in current filesystem only.

dynamic_pager

dynamic_pager [-E] [-F *filename*] [-H *hire_point*] [-L *layoff_ point*] [-P *priority*]

[-S *file_size*]

Manages virtual memory swap files. This tool is started from */etc/rc* during the boot process.

Starting with Panther, when *dynamic_pager* is invoked without -H, -L, or -S options, it creates swap files that are sized dynamically according to paging needs and available disk space.

Options

-E   Encrypt the swap file.

-F   Specify the base absolute pathname for swap files. Swap filenames consist of this base and a whole number suffix, starting at 0. The default is */private/var/vm/ swapfile*.

-H   Create an additional swap file when free swap space drops below the *hire_point* in bytes. The default is 0, which disables the use of this swap space.

-L   Attempt to consolidate memory and remove a swap file when free swap space rises above the *layoff_point* in bytes. The *layoff_point* must be set higher than the sum of the swap file size and the *hire_point*, unless it is set to 0 (the default), which disables layoffs.

-P   Determine the priority of this swap space. The default is 0.

-S   Determine the size of swap files created, in bytes. The default is 20000000.

---

echo

echo [-n] [*string*]

Echoes arguments to standard output. Often used for producing prompts from shell scripts.

Option

-n   Suppress printing of newline after text.

Example

```
$ echo "testing printer" | lp
```

---

egrep

egrep [*options*] [*regexp*] [*files*]

Searches one or more *files* for lines that match an extended regular expression *regexp*. egrep doesn't support the regular expressions \ (, \), \n, \<, \>, \{, or \}, but does support the other expressions, as well as the extended set +, ?, |, and ( ). Remember to enclose these characters in quotes. Regular expressions are described in Chapter 6. Exit status is 0 if any lines match, 1 if none match, and 2 for errors.

See *grep* for the list of available options. Also see *fgrep*. egrep typically runs faster than those commands.

Examples

Search for occurrences of *Victor* or *Victoria* in *file*:

```
$ egrep 'Victor(ia)*' file
$ egrep '(Victor|Victoria)' file
```

Find and print strings such as *old.doc1* or *new.doc2* in *files*, and include their line numbers:

```
$ egrep -n '(old|new)\.doc?' files
```

enscript

enscript [*options*] [*files*]

Converts text files to PostScript for output to a printer or file. This conversion is necessary when printing text files from the command line to most laser printers, for example, because most laser printers are PostScript devices. *enscript* is a feature-rich application that allows you to modify the printed output in many ways. The following descriptions and examples cover *enscript*'s basic operation; for a complete description, refer to *enscript*'s manpage.

Used with no arguments, *enscript* receives text from standard input and sends it to the default printer. Otherwise, *enscript* converts the text files specified in *files*, and directs output to a named printer, file, or standard output as specified by *options* (or the default printer, if no options are specified).

Common options

-# n, -n n, --copies=n
   Print *n* copies of every page.

-a pages, --pages=pages
   Print selected *pages*, as specified in the following format:

begin-end
   Print from page number *begin* to page number *end*.

-end
   Print until page number *end*.

begin-
   Print from page number *begin* to the last page.

page
   Print only *page* number page.

odd
   Print only the odd numbered pages.

even
   Print only the even numbered pages.

-B, --no-header
   Don't print page headers.

-b header, --header=header
   Print *header* at the top of each page. This *header* can contain formatting directives. See the manpage for details.

-c, --truncate-lines
   Cut off long lines instead of wrapping.

-d printer, -P printer, --printer=printer
   Send output to *printer*.

-h, --no-job-header
   Don't print job header page.

-j, --borders
   Print borders around columns in N-up output.

--list-options
   List the current *enscript* option settings.

-m, --mail
> Send notification to user when job has finished.

-r, --landscape
> Print the page in landscape mode, rotated 90 degrees.

-R, --portrait
> Print the page in portrait mode, the default.

-U n, --nup=n
> Print *n*-up; place *n* pages on each sheet of output.

--margins=left:right:top:bottom
> Print with margins of *left*, *right*, *top* and *bottom*, each specified in PostScript points. To use the default value for a margin, omit that argument.

Examples

Print pages 5 through 10, 2-up, of text document *notes.txt*:

```
$ enscript -a 5-10 -U 2 notes.txt
```

Print page 1 of text document *notes.txt*, setting a top margin of 50 points and a bottom margin of 25 points:

```
$ enscript -a 1 --margins=::50:25 notes.txt
```

env

```
env [-i] [variable=value...] [command]
```

Displays the current environment or, if environment *variables* are specified, sets them to a new *value* and displays the modified environment. If *command* is specified, executes it under the modified environment.

Option

-i   Ignore current environment entirely.

expand

```
expand [options] [files]
```

Expands tab characters into appropriate number of spaces. *expand* reads the named files or standard input if no files are provided. See also *unexpand*.

Option

-t tab1,tab2,...,tabn
> Set tab stops at *tab1*, *tab2*, etc. If only *tab1* is specified, sets tab stops every *tab1* spaces.

Example

Cut columns 10 through 12 of the input data, even when tabs are used:

```
$ expand data | cut -c 10-12 > data.col2
```

expr

`expr arg1 operator arg2 [operator arg3...]`

Evaluates arguments as expressions and prints the result. Strings can be compared and searched. Arguments and operators must be separated by spaces. In most cases, an argument is an integer, typed literally or represented by a shell variable. There are three types of operators: arithmetic, relational, and logical. Exit status for *expr* is 0 (expression is nonzero and nonnull), 1 (expression is 0 or null), or 2 (expression is invalid).

expr is typically used in shell scripts to perform simple mathematics, such as addition or subtraction. It is made obsolete in the Korn shell by that program's built-in arithmetic capabilities.

Arithmetic operators

Use the following operators to produce mathematical expressions whose results are printed:

+   Add *arg2* to *arg1*.

-   Subtract *arg2* from *arg1*.

*   Multiply the arguments.

/   Divide *arg1* by *arg2*.

%   Take the remainder when *arg1* is divided by *arg2*.

Addition and subtraction are evaluated last, unless they are grouped inside parentheses. The symbols *, (, and) have meaning to the shell, so they must be escaped (preceded by a backslash or enclosed in single or double quotes).

Relational operators

Use relational operators to compare two arguments. Arguments can also be words, in which case comparisons assume a < z and A < Z. If the comparison statement is true, the result is 1; if false, the result is 0. Symbols < and > must be escaped.

=   Are the arguments equal?

!=   Are the arguments different?

>   Is *arg1* greater than *arg2*?

>=   Is *arg1* greater than or equal to *arg2*?

<   Is *arg1* less than *arg2*?

<=   Is *arg1* less than or equal to *arg2*?

Logical operators

Use logical operators to compare two arguments. Depending on the values, the result can be *arg1* (or some portion of it), *arg2*, or 0. Symbols | and & must be escaped.

| Logical OR; if *arg1* has a nonzero (and nonnull) value, the result is *arg1*; otherwise, the result is *arg2*.

&   Logical AND; if both *arg1* and *arg2* have nonzero (and nonnull) values, the result is *arg1*; otherwise, the result is 0.

: Similar to *grep*; *arg2* is a pattern to search for in *arg1*. *arg2* must be a regular expression in this case. If the *arg2* pattern is enclosed in \(\), the result is the portion of *arg1* that matches; otherwise, the result is simply the number of characters that match. By default, a pattern match always applies to the beginning of the first argument (the search string implicitly begins with a ^). To match other parts of the string, start the search string with .*.

Examples

Division happens first; result is 10:

```
$ expr 5 + 10 / 2
```

Addition happens first; result is 7 (truncated from 7.5):

```
$ expr \( 5 + 10 \) / 2
```

Add 1 to variable i; this is how variables are incremented in shell scripts:

```
$ i=`expr $i + 1`
```

Print 1 (true) if variable a is the string "hello":

```
$ expr $a = hello
```

Print 1 (true) if variable b plus 5 equals 10 or more:

```
$ expr $b + 5 \>= 10
```

In the following examples, variable p is the string "version.100". This command prints the number of characters in p:

```
$ expr $p : '.*'          Result is 11
```

Match all characters and print them:

```
$ expr $p : '\(.*\)'      Result is "version.100"
```

Print the number of lowercase letters at the beginning of p:

```
$ expr $p : '[a-z]*'      Result is 7
```

Match the lowercase letters at the beginning of p:

```
$ expr $p : '\([a-z]*\)'  Result is "version"
```

Truncate $x if it contains five or more characters; if not, just print $x. (Logical OR uses the second argument when the first one is 0 or null; i.e., when the match fails.) Double- quoting is a good idea, in case $x contains whitespace characters.

```
$ expr "$x" : '\(.....\)' \| "$x"
```

In a shell script, rename files to their first five letters:

```
$ mv "$x" `expr "$x" : '\(.....\)' \| "$x"`
```

(To avoid overwriting files with similar names, use *mv -i*.)

---

false

```
false
```

A null command that returns an unsuccessful (nonzero) exit status. Normally used in *bash* scripts. See also *true*.

fdisk

fdisk [-t | -d | -e | -u | -S integer | -c integer -h integer -s integer]
[device]

fdisk -i [-a { boothfs | bootufs | hfs | ufs | dos | raid } | -f filename | -r]
[-y] device

Description
Provides control over DOS partition tables on disk devices in Darwin x86 systems. If invoked without arguments, *fdisk* prints a usage statement to standard error. If invoked with only a device name as an argument, it displays the device's partition table.

Options

-a   Partitions the disk according to the specified automatic style. The *boothfs* and *bootufs* styles each include an 8 MB boot partition, with the remainder formatted as the specified type. The *hfs*, *ufs*, *dos*, and *raid* styles each create a single partition of the specified type, which spans the entire disk. The default is *boothfs*.

-c   Forces an assumption of a disk geometry with the specified number of cylinders.

-d   Displays the disk's partition table, in a format usable with -*r*.

-e   Enters an interactive edit mode. Commands available in this mode are listed in the "Commands" section.

-f   Specifies a template file to use in creating the partition table.

-h   Forces an assumption of a disk geometry with the specified number of heads.

-i   Initializes the Master Boot Record (MBR) on the disk, which contains the partition table.

-r   Reads in a new set of partition entries from standard input.

-s   Forces an assumption of a disk geometry with the specified number of sectors per track.

-S   Specifies the disk's size, in blocks.

-t   Tests whether the disk has a DOS partition table on it.

-u   Updates the MBR code, leaving the existing partition table intact.

-y   Skips requests for confirmation.

device
    The raw disk device filename, e.g., */dev/rdisk0*.

Commands

abort
    Exits interactive mode without making changes.

auto
    Partitions the disk according to the specified automatic style.

disk
    Displays the disk's partition table.

edit
    Edits a partition table entry.

erase
> Erases the MBR.

exit
> Exits from edit mode without making changes.

flag
> Marks the specified partition as the boot partition.

help
> Displays a command summary.

manual
> Displays the *fdisk* manpage.

print
> Displays the partition table being edited as it currently exists in memory.

quit Exits from edit mode, saving changes.

reinit
> Reinitializes the copy of the partition table held in memory.

select
> Selects the specified extended partition table entry.

setpid
> Sets the partition identifier of the specified partition.

update
> Updates the MBR code, leaving the existing partition table intact.

write
> Writes the in-memory partition table to disk, thus making changes to the partition table take effect.

---

fetchmail

fetchmail [*options*] [*servers*...]

Retrieves mail from mail servers and forwards it to the local mail delivery system. *fetchmail* retrieves mail from servers that support the common mail protocols POP2, POP3, IMAP2bis, and IMAP4. Messages are delivered via SMTP through port 25 on the local host and through your system's mail delivery agent (such as *sendmail*), where they can be read through the user's mail client. *fetchmail* settings are stored in the ~/.fetchmailrc file. Parameters and servers can also be set on the command line, which will override settings in the .*fetchmailrc* file. For a complete list of options, refer to the *fetchmail* manpage.

Common options
-a, --all
> Retrieve all messages from server, even those that have already been seen but left on the server. The default is to retrieve only new messages.

-A type, --auth type
> Specify the type of authentication. *type* may be *password*, *kerberos_v5*, or *kerberos*. Authentication type is usually established by *fetchmail* by default, so this option isn't very useful.

-B n, --fetchlimit n

Set the maximum number of messages (*n*) accepted from a server per query.

-b n, --batchlimit n

Set the maximum number of messages sent to an SMTP listener per connection. When this limit is reached, the connection is broken and reestablished. The default of 0 means no limit.

-c, --check

Check for mail on a single server without retrieving or deleting messages. Works with IMAP, but does not work well with other protocols, if at all.

-D [domain], --smtpaddress [domain]

Specify the *domain* name placed in RCPT TO lines sent to SMTP. The default is the local host.

-E header, --envelope header

Change the header assumed to contain the mail's envelope address (usually "X-Envelope-to:") to *header*.

-e n, --expunge n

Tell an IMAP server to *expunge* (i.e., purge messages marked for deletion) after *n* deletes. A setting of 0 indicates expunging only at the end of the session. Normally, an *expunge* occurs after each delete.

-F, --flush

For POP3 and IMAP servers, remove previously retrieved messages from the server before retrieving new ones.

-f file, --fetchmailrc file

Specify a nondefault name for the *fetchmail* configuration file.

-I specification, --interface specification

Require that the mail server machine is up and running at a specified IP address (or range) before polling. The *specification* is given as *interface/ipaddress/mask*. The first part indicates the type of TCP connection expected (sl0, ppp0, etc.), the second is the IP address, and the third is the bit mask for the IP, assumed to be 255.255.255.255.

-K, --nokeep

Delete all retrieved messages from the mail server.

-k, --keep

Keep copies of all retrieved messages on the mail server.

-l size, --limit size

Set the maximum message size that will be retrieved from a server. Messages larger than *size* bytes are left on the server and marked unread.

-M interface, --monitor interface

In daemon mode, monitor the specified TCP/IP *interface* for any activity beside itself, and skip the poll if there is no other activity. Useful for PPP connections that automatically time out with no activity.

-m command, --mda command

Pass mail directly to mail delivery agent, rather than send to port 25. The *command* is the path and options for the mailer, such as */usr/lib/sendmail -oem*. A %T in the command is replaced with the local delivery address, and an %F is replaced with the message's From address.

-n, --norewrite
>   Don't expand local mail IDs to full addresses. This option disables expected
>   addressing and should only be used to find problems.

-P n, --port n
>   Specify a port to connect to on the mail server. The default port numbers for
>   supported protocols are usually sufficient.

-p proto, --protocol proto
>   Specify the protocol to use when polling a mail server. *proto* can be:

>   *POP2*
>>   Post Office Protocol 2.

>   *POP3*
>>   Post Office Protocol 3.

>   *APOP*
>>   POP3 with MD5 authentication.

>   *RPOP*
>>   POP3 with RPOP authentication.

>   *KPOP*
>>   POP3 with Kerberos v4 authentication on port 1109.

>   *IMAP*
>>   IMAP2bis, IMAP4, or IMAP4rev1. *fetchmail* autodetects their capabilities.

>   *IMAP-K4*
>>   IMAP4 or IMAP4rev1 with Kerberos v4 authentication.

>   *IMAP-GSS*
>>   IMAP4 or IMAP4rev1 with GSSAPI authentication.

>   *ETRN*
>>   ESMTP.

-Q string, --qvirtual string
>   Remove the prefix *string*, which is the local user's host ID, from the address in
>   the envelope header (such as "Delivered-To:").

-r folder, --folder folder
>   Retrieve the specified mail *folder* from the mail server.

-s, --silent
>   Suppress status messages during a *fetch*.

-t seconds, --timeout seconds
>   Stop waiting for a connection after *seconds* seconds.

-U, --uidl
>   For POP3, track the age of kept messages via unique ID listing.

-u name, --username name
>   Specify the user *name* to use when logging into the mail server.

-V, --version
>   Print the version information for *fetchmail* and display the options set for each
>   mail server. Performs no *fetch*.

-v, --verbose
> Display all status messages during a *fetch*.

-Z nnn, --antispam nnn
> Specify the SMTP error *nnn* to signal a spam block from the client. If *nnn* is -1, this option is disabled.

fgrep

fgrep [options] pattern [files]

Search one or more *files* for lines that match a literal text string *pattern*. Exit status is 0 if any lines match, 1 if not, and 2 for errors.

See *grep* for the list of available options. Also see *egrep*.

Examples

Print lines in *file* that don't contain any spaces:

```
$ fgrep -v '' file
```

Print lines in *file* that contain the words in *spell_list*:

```
$ fgrep -f spell_list file
```

file

file [options] files

Classify the named *files* according to the type of data they contain. *file* checks the magic file (*/etc/magic*) to identify some file types.

Options

-b, --brief
> Brief mode: don't print filenames.

-c, --checking-printout
> Check the format of the magic file (*files* argument is invalid with -c). Usually used with -m.

-F separator, --separator separator
> Print *separator* between file and type, instead of a colon.

-f file, --files-from file
> Read the names of files to be checked from *file*.

-i, --mime
> Print the MIME type of the file instead of a human-readable description.

-k, --keep-going
> Don't stop after the first match.

-L, --dereference
> Follow symbolic links. By default, symbolic links are not followed.

-m file, --magic-file file
> Search for file types in *file* instead of */etc/magic*.

-N, --no-pad
> Don't pad filenames for alignment.

-v, --version
> Print the version.

-z, --uncompress
> Attempt checking of compressed files.

Many file types are understood. Output lists each filename, followed by a brief classification such as:

```
Apple QuickTime movie file (moov)
ASCII text
data
directory
gzip compressed data
empty
PDF document, version 1.4
Mach-O executable ppc
sticky symbolic link to private/tmp
```

Example
List all PDF Version 1.1 files:

```
$ file * | grep "PDF document, version 1.1"
```

---

find

```
find [options] [pathnames] [conditions]
```

An extremely useful command for finding particular groups of files (numerous examples follow this description). *find* descends the directory tree beginning at each *pathname* and locates files that meet the specified *conditions*. The default pathname is the current directory. The most useful conditions include *-print* (which is the default if no other expression is given), *-name* and *-type* (for general use), *-exec* and *-size* (for advanced users), and *-mtime* and *-user* (for administrators).

Conditions may be grouped by enclosing them in \(\) (escaped parentheses), negated with ! (use \! in the C shell), given as alternatives by separating them with *-o*, or repeated (adding restrictions to the match; usually only for *-name*, *-type*, *-perm*). Modification refers to editing of a file's contents. Change refers to modification, permission or ownership changes, and so on; therefore, for example, *-ctime* is more inclusive than *-atime* or *-mtime*.

Options

-d   Descend the directory tree, skipping directories and working on actual files first (and then the parent directories). Useful when files reside in unwritable directories (e.g., when using *find* with *cpio*).

-E   When used with the *-regex* or *-iregex* conditions, interpret the regular expression as extended instead of basic. For more information on regular expressions, see Chapter 6.

-H   If any of the pathnames given in the command line are symbolic links, consider the file information of the referenced files and not the links themselves. However, if the referenced file no longer exists, consider the link itself.

-L   If any of the files encountered during the search are symbolic links, consider the file information of the referenced files and not the links themselves. However, if the referenced file no longer exists, consider the link itself.

-P   If any of the files encountered during the search are symbolic links, consider the file information of the links themselves (the default behavior).

-s   Move through directory contents in alphabetical order.

-x   Don't scan filesystems (mounted volumes) other than the one that the command begins with.

-X   When used with the -xargs action, identify and skip any files whose names contain characters used by -xargs as delimiters (', ", \, space, tab, and newline characters).

Conditions and actions

-amin +n | -n | n
>   Find files last accessed more than *n* (+*n*), less than *n* (-*n*), or exactly *n* minutes ago. Note that *find* changes the access time of directories supplied as *pathnames*.

-anewer file
>   Find files that were accessed after *file* was last modified.

-atime +n | -n | n
>   Find files that were last accessed more than *n* (+*n*), less than *n* (-*n*), or exactly *n* days ago.

-cmin +n | -n | n
>   Find files last changed more than *n* (+*n*), less than *n* (-*n*), or exactly *n* minutes ago. A change is anything that changes the directory entry for the file, such as a *chmod*.

-cnewer file
>   Find files that were changed after they were last modified.

-ctime +n | -n | n
>   Find files that were changed more than *n* (+*n*), less than *n* (-*n*), or exactly *n* days ago.

-delete +n | -n | n
>   Delete found files and directories, operating as if the -*d* flag were being used as well (files first).

-empty
>   Continue if file is empty. Applies to regular files and directories.

-exec command { } \;
>   Run the Unix *command* from the starting directory on each file matched by *find* (provided command executes successfully on that file; i.e., returns a 0 exit status). When command runs, the argument { } substitutes the current file. Follow the entire sequence with an escaped semicolon (\;).

-execdir command { } \;
>   Same as -*exec*, but run the Unix *command* from the directory holding the file matched by *find*.

-flags [+ | -] flags, notflags
>   Find files by their file flag settings (see *chflags*). To specify flags that are set, list them in *flags*. To specify flags that are not set, list those flags (with their "no" prefixes) in *notflags*. To match files with at least all of the settings specified by

both *flags* and *notflags*, use the - before *flags*. To match files with any of the flags specified in *flags* or *notflags*, use the + before *flags*. Without the - or the +, *find* finds only files with flag settings matching exactly with those in *flags* and *notflags*.

-*fstype fstype*
> Match files only on *type* filesystems. (Run *sysctl vfs* to view currently mounted filesystem types). You can also specify two pseudotypes, *local* and *rdonly*, which allows you to match files only on physically mounted volumes and read-only volumes, respectively.

-*group gname*
> Find files belonging to group *gname*. *gname* can be a group name or a GID number.

-*iname pattern*
> A case-insensitive version of -*name*.

-*inum n*
> Find files whose inode number is *n*.

-*ipath pattern*
> A case-insensitive version of -*path*.

-*iregex pattern*
> A case-insensitive version of -*regex*.

-*links n*
> Find files having *n* links.

-*ls* Write the list of found files to standard output as if provided by the *ls -dgils* command. Return true.

-*maxdepth num*
> Don't descend more than *num* levels of directories.

-*mindepth num*
> Begin applying tests and actions only at levels deeper than *num* levels.

-*mmin +n | -n | n*
> Find files last modified more than *n* (+*n*), less than *n* (-*n*), or exactly *n*.

-*mtime +n | -n | n*
> Find files that were last modified more than *n* (+*n*), less than *n* (-*n*), or exactly *n* days ago.

-*name pattern*
> Find files whose names match *pattern*. Filename metacharacters may be used but should be escaped or quoted.

-*newer file*
> Find files that have been modified more recently than *file*; similar to -*mtime*.

-*nogroup*
> The file's GID doesn't correspond to any group.

-*nouser*
> The file's UID doesn't correspond to any user.

-*ok command { }\;*
> Same as -*exec*, but prompt user to respond with y before *command* is executed.

-*okdir command { } \;*
> Same as -*ok*, but run the Unix *command*, from the directory holding the file matched by *find*.

-path pattern

    Find files whose names match *pattern*. Expect full pathnames relative to the starting pathname (i.e., don't treat / or . specially).

-perm nnn

    Find files whose permission flags (e.g., *rwx*) match octal number *nnn* exactly (e.g., 664 matches -rw-rw-r--). Use a minus sign before *nnn* to make a wildcard match of any unspecified octal digit (for example, *-perm -600* matches -rw-******, where * can be any mode).

-print

    Print the matching files and directories, using their full pathnames. Return true.

-print0

    Print the matching files and directories, using their full pathnames and separating each with the ASCII NUL character. This allows *find* to properly work with the *xargs* utility and pathnames containing spaces, for example. Return true.

-prune

    Prevent *find* from descending into the directory found by the previous condition in the command line. Useful when used with an alternative condition (*-o*) that specifies which directories must be traversed. Return true.

-regex pattern

    Like *-path* but use *grep*-style regular expressions instead of the shell-like globbing used in *-name* and *-path*.

-size n[c]

    Find files containing *n* blocks, or if *c* is specified, *n* characters long.

-type c

    Find files whose type is *c*. *c* can be *b* (block special file), *c* (character special file), *d* (directory), *p* (FIFO or named pipe), *l* (symbolic link), *s* (socket), or *f* (plain file).

-user user

    Find files belonging to *user* (name or ID).

-xdev

    Search for files that reside only on the same filesystem as pathname.

Examples

List all files (and subdirectories) in your home directory:

```
$ find ~ -print
```

List all files named *chapter1* in the *~/Documents* directory:

```
$ find /Documents -name chapter1 -print
```

List all files beginning with *memo* owned by *ann*:

```
$ find /Documents -name 'memo*' -user ann -print
```

Search the filesystem (begin at root) for manpage directories:

```
$ find / -type d -name 'man*' -print
```

Search the current directory, look for filenames that don't begin with a capital letter, and send them to the printer:

```
$ find . \! -name '[A-Z]*' -exec lpr { }\;
```

Find and compress files whose names don't end with *.gz*:

```
$ gzip `find . \! -name '*.gz' -print`
```

Remove all empty files on the system (prompting first):

```
$ find / -size 0 -ok rm {} \;
```

Search the system for files that were modified within the last two days (good candidates for backing up):

```
$ find / -mtime -2 -print
```

Recursively *grep* for a pattern down a directory tree:

```
$ find ~/Documents -print0 | xargs -0 grep '[Nn]utshell'
```

Search the system excluding all but the system volume:

```
$ find / -path '/Volumes/*' -prune -o -name "*. doc" -print
```

FixupResourceForks

```
FixupResourceForks [-nodelete] [-nosetinfo] [-q[uiet]] pathname...
```

Recombines the resource fork and HFS metadata split out into a separate file (named .
filename) with the file's data fork (in a file named *filename*), resulting in a single multiforked file (named *filename*) with HFS attributes. As such, this works only on HFS and HFS+ volumes. It reverses the effect of running *SplitForks*.

FixupResourceForks does a recursive descent into the directory specified by *pathname*, working on every file within it.

Options

-nodelete

Prevent deletion of ._filename_ after recombination with *filename*.

-nosetinfo

Disable setting of HFS attributes on the recombined files.

-quiet

Suppress printing the name of each recombined file to standard output.

fmt

```
fmt [goal [maximum]] [files]
```

Converts text to specified width by filling lines and removing newlines. Width is specified as being close to *goal* characters, but not over *maximum* characters wide (65 and 75 characters by default). Concatenate files on the command line, or read text from standard input if no file is specified. By default, preserve blank lines, spacing, and indentation. *fmt* attempts to break lines at the end of sentences and to avoid breaking lines after a sentence's first word or before its last.

Options

-c   Center each line.

-d chars

Define *chars* as the characters that end a sentence. By default, these are period, exclamation point, and question mark.

-l width

> Replaces each *width* spaces at the beginning of a line with a tab character. Default is 8. Specify *width* of 0 to turn off this tab unexpansion.

-m Try to format mail headers correctly.

-n Format each line, even if it starts with a dot.

-p Handle indented paragraphs. Without this flag, changes in the amount of whitespace at the beginning of a line indicates a new paragraph.

-s Compress multiple whitespace characters into a single space.

-t width

> Assume *width* spaces per tab in the input files.

fold

fold [*option*] [*files*]

Breaks the lines of the named *files* so they are no wider than the specified width (default is 80). *fold* breaks lines exactly at the specified width, even in the middle of a word. Reads from standard input when given - as a file.

Options

-b Count bytes, not columns (i.e., consider tabs, backspaces, and carriage returns to be one column).

-s Break at spaces only, if possible.

-w width

> Set the maximum line width to *width*. Default is 80.

fs_usage

fs_usage [*options*] [*processes*]

Shows a continuous display of filesystem-related system calls and page faults. You must run *fs_usage* as root. By default, it ignores anything originating from *fs_usage*, *Terminal*, *telnetd*, *sshd*, *rlogind*, *tcsh*, *csh*, or *sh*, but shows all other system processes. To have *fs_usage* track only specific processes, specify those process names or IDs in *processes*.

Options

-e [processes]

> Exclude from tracking those processes specified in *processes*. If no processes are given, exclude only the current *fs_usage* process.

-f mode

> Filter output according to the *mode*, which must be *network*, *filesys*, or *cachehit*.

-w Display in a more detailed, wider format. Lines longer than the window width will be wrapped.

fsaclctl

fsaclctl [-v]

fsaclctl { -a | -p *pathname* } [-e | -d]

Enables or disables the use of file access control lists (ACLs) on specified filesystems. (They're disabled by default.) When invoked with no arguments, it prints a usage statement to standard output.

Options

-a   Enables or disables ACLs on all local HFS+ filesystems. If neither -e nor -d are specified, prints the status of ACLs on these filesystems.

-d   Disables ACLs on the specified filesystems.

-e   Enables ACLs on the specified filesystems.

-p   Enables or disables ACLs on the filesystem containing the specified *pathname*. If neither -e nor -d are specified, prints the status of ACLs on the filesystem.

-v   Prints software version to standard output.

fsck

fsck [-l *num_procs*] [-b *block_num*] [-m *mode*] [-c { 0 | 1 | 2 | 3 }]
[-p | -n | -y] *device*...

Performs consistency checks of UFS volumes, and attempts to fix any inconsistencies found.

Options

-b   Specify an alternate super block for the filesystem.

-c   Convert the filesystem to the specified version level. See the *fsck* manpage for details.

-f   Force a check, even if the filesystem is clean.

-l   Limit the number of parallel *fsck* processes. Defaults to the number of disks.

-m   Specify the permissions of the *lost+found* directory, where files that have become detached from their place in the directory hierarchy due to filesystem corruption can be located. The argument is an octal mode, as described in the *chmod* manpage. The default is 1777.

-n   Automatically answer "no" whenever *fsck* asks to resolve an inconsistency.

-p   Run in preening mode, in which only purely innocuous inconsistencies are resolved.

-q   Quick check to see if filesystem was unmounted properly.

-y   Automatically answer "yes" whenever *fsck* asks to resolve an inconsistency.

device
     The volume's device filename, e.g., */dev/disk1s2*.

fsck_hfs

```
fsck_hfs -u
```

```
fsck_hfs [-d] [-f] [-r] { -q | -p | [-n | -y] } device...
```

Performs consistency checks of HFS and HFS+ volumes, and attempts to fix any inconsistencies found.

Options

-d   Enable debugging output.

-f   Force check even if the volume is marked as clean.

-l   Lock and check the volume without writing. This allows checks on mounted volumes.

-m   Specify the permissions of the *lost+found* directory, where files that have become detached from their place in the directory hierarchy due to filesystem corruption can be located. The argument is an octal mode, as described in the *chmod* manpage. The default is 1777.

-n   Automatically answer "no" whenever *fsck_hfs* asks to resolve an inconsistency.

-p   Run in preening mode, in which only purely innocuous inconsistencies are resolved.

-q   Check the filesystem but don't resolve any inconsistencies. Return filesystem status of clean, dirty, or failure to standard error.

-r   Cause a rebuild of the volume's catalog *btree* to occur.

-u   Print a usage statement to standard output.

-y   Automatically answer "yes" whenever *fsck_hfs* asks to resolve an inconsistency.

device
> The volume's device filename, e.g., */dev/disk1s2*.

fsck_msdos

```
fsck_msdos { -q | -p | [-n | -y] } device...
```

Performs consistency checks of FAT volumes and attempts to fix any inconsistencies found.

Options

-n   Automatically answer "no" whenever *fsck_msdos* asks to resolve an inconsistency.

-p   Run in preening mode, in which only purely innocuous inconsistencies are resolved.

-q   Check the filesystem but don't resolve any inconsistencies. Print filesystem status to standard output.

-y   Automatically answer "yes" whenever *fsck_msdos* asks to resolve an inconsistency.

device
> The volume's device filename, e.g., */dev/disk1s2*.

ftp

ftp [*options*] [*hostname*]

Transfers files to and from remote network site *hostname*. *ftp* prompts the user for a command. Type *help* to see a list of known commands, and use the *help* command to view help on a specific command.

The *ftp* client included with Mac OS X supports auto-fetch, which allows you to perform a download with a single command line. To auto-fetch a file, supply its location as an argument to *ftp* in one of several formats:

- *ftp* [*user@*]*host*:[*path*][/]
- *ftp* [ftp://[*user*[:*password*]@]*host*[:*port*]/*path*[/]]
- *ftp* [http://[*user*[:*password*]@]*host*[:*port*]/*path*]

Options

-4   Only use IPv4 addresses.

-6   Only use IPv6 addresses.

-A   Force active mode for use with older servers.

-a   Perform anonymous login automatically.

-d   Enable debugging.

-e   Disable command-line editing.

-f   Perform a forced reload of the cache. Useful when transferring through proxies.

-g   Disable filename globbing.

-i   Turn off interactive prompting.

-n   No autologin upon initial connection.

-N *filename*
    Use *filename* instead of ~/.netrc.

-o *pathname*
    Save file as *pathname* when auto-fetching.

-p   Enable passive mode (the default).

-P *port*
    Specify alternate *port* number.

-r *wait*
    Attempt to connect again after *wait* seconds if initial attempt fails.

-R   When auto-fetching, resume incomplete transfers (if not transferring through a proxy).

-t   Enable packet tracing.

-T *direction, maximum [,increment]*
    Throttle transfer rates by specifying *direction* of transfer, *maximum* transfer speed in bytes/second, and an *increment* value that allows changing *maximum* on the fly. Direction can be *get* for incoming transfers, *put* for outgoing transfers, and *all* for both.

-u *url file [...]*
    Upload *file* to *url* from the command line.

-*v*   Verbose. Show all responses from remote server.

-*V*   Disable verbose.

gcc_select

gcc_select [-v | --version] [-h | --help] [-l | --list]

gcc_select [-v | --version] [-n] [-force] [-root] { 2 | 3 | 3.*x* | 4.*x* }

A shell script that sets the default version of GCC—either 2.95.2 (specified as 2), 3.1 (3), 4.0 (4), or some other version (specified as 3.x)—by creating various symlinks for compiler tools, libraries, and headers. With no arguments (or with just -*v*), the current default version is printed to standard output.

Options

-force
> Recreate symlinks for the specified version, even if it is already the current default version.

-h, --help
> Print a usage statement to standard output.

-l, --list
> List available GCC versions.

-*n*   Print the list of commands that would be executed to standard output, but don't actually execute them.

-root
> Disable the initial check for *root* access before executing commands.

-v, --version
> Print the version of *gcc_select* to standard output.

GetFileInfo

GetFileInfo [*options*] *pathname*

Displays HFS+ file attributes (metadata) of file *pathname*. If you specify no options, *GetFileInfo* shows all the file's attributes. *GetFileInfo* is installed with the Xcode Tools (*/Developer/Tools*). Because this directory isn't in the shell's search path by default, you might to need to specify *GetFileInfo*'s pathname to invoke it. See also *SetFile*.

Options

-a[attribute]
> Display the settings for those attributes that toggle on or off (sometimes called "Finder flags"). If *attribute* is empty, the settings of all attributes are displayed as a series of letters. If the letter is shown in uppercase, that attribute is on (its bit is set). If the letter is shown in lowercase, that attribute is off. To view the setting for a single attribute (either 1 for on or 0 for off), specify that attribute by its letter in *attribute*. Refer to the following table for the specific attributes.

Table 2-3. Attributes for GetFileInfo's -a option

Attribute	Set | unset	Meaning
Alias	A | a	File is/isn't an alias.
Bundle	B | b	File has/hasn't bundle resource.
Custom Icon	C | c	File has/hasn't a custom icon.
Desktop Item	D | d	File is/isn't on the desktop.
Extension	E | e	Filename extension is/isn't hidden.
Inited	I | i	File is/isn't inited.
Locked	L | l	File is/isn't locked.
Shared	M | m	Multiple users can/can't run a file at once (applies to application files).
INIT	N | n	File has/hasn't INIT resource.
System	S | s	File is/isn't a system file (locks name).
Stationary	T | t	File is/isn't a stationary file.
Invisible	V | v	File is/isn't invisible to Finder.

-c   Display the file's four-character creator code.

-d   Display the file's creation date.

-m   Display the file's modification date.

-t   Display the file's four-character type code.

Examples

Display all toggled attributes:

```
$ /Developer/Tools/GetFileInfo -a Quinn.jpg
```

Display only the locked setting:

```
$ /Developer/Tools/GetFileInfo -aL Quinn.jpg
```

---

gnutar

gnutar [*options*] [*tarfile*] [*other-files*]

Copies *files* to or restores *files* from an archive medium. An enhanced version of *tar*, *gnutar* is usually the preferred utility because *gnutar* can handle much longer path-names than *tar*, and *gnutar*'s default omission of the leading slash in pathnames allows archives to be more easily opened on other systems. Note that until native drivers for tape drives exist for Mac OS X, *gnutar* can't write to tape. Note also that *gnutar* doesn't preserve resource forks or HFS metadata when copying files that contain them.

gnutar is installed on Mac OS X as part of Apple's Xcode Tools.

Function options

You must use exactly one of these, and it must come before any other options:

-A, --catenate, --concatenate
    Concatenate a second tar file onto the end of the first.

-c, --create
    Create a new archive.

-d, --diff, --compare
> Compare the files stored in *tarfile* with *other-files*. Report any differences, such as missing files, different sizes, different file attributes (such as permissions or modification time).

--delete
> Delete *other-files* from the archive.

-r, --append
> Append *other-files* to the end of an existing archive.

-t, --list
> Print the names of *other-files* if they are stored on the archive (if *other-files* aren't specified, print names of all files).

-u, --update
> Add files if not in the archive or if modified.

-x, --extract, --get
> Extract *other-files* from an archive (if *other-files* aren't specified, extract all files).

--help
> Display help information.

Options

--atime-preserve
> Preserve original access time on extracted files.

-b, --block-size=n
> Set block size to *n* 512 bytes.

-B, --read-full-blocks
> Form full blocks from short reads.

--backup
> If *tarfile* already exists, make a backup copy before overwriting.

-C, --directory=directory
> *cd* to *directory* before beginning *tar* operation.

--checkpoint
> List directory names encountered.

--exclude=file
> Remove *file* from any list of files.

-f arch, --file=filename
> Store files in or extract files from archive *arch*. Note that *filename* may take the form *hostname:filename*. Also, because Mac OS X has no native tape drive support, *gnutar* produces an error unless the *-f* option is used.

-F filename, --info-script=filename, --new-volume-script=filename
> Run the script found in *filename* when *tar* reaches the end of a volume. This can be used to automatically swap volumes with a media changer. This option implies *-M*.

--force-local
> Interpret filenames in the form *hostname:filename* as local files.

-g, --listed-incremental
> Create new-style incremental backup.

-G, --incremental
> Create old-style incremental backup.

-h, --dereference
> Dereference symbolic links.

-i, --ignore-zeros
> Ignore zero-sized blocks (i.e., EOFs).

--ignore-failed-read
> Ignore unreadable files to be archived. Default behavior is to exit when encountering these.

-k, --keep-old-files
> When extracting files, don't overwrite files with similar names. Instead, print an error message.

-K, --starting-file=file
> Start at *file* in the archive.

-l, --one-file-system
> Don't archive files from other filesystems.

-L, --tape-length=length
> Write a maximum of *length* 1024 bytes to each tape.

-m, --modification-time
> Don't restore file modification times; update them to the time of extraction.

-M, --multivolume
> Expect archive to multivolume. With *-c*, create such an archive.

--mode=filemode
> Set symbolic file mode (permissions) of added files to *filemode*.

-N date, --newer=date, --after-date=date
> Ignore files older than *date*.

--newer-mtime=date
> Ignore files whose modification times are older than *date*.

--no-recursion
> Don't descend into directories.

--no-same-owner
> Set the owner of the extracted files to be the current user, not the owner as defined in the archive.

--no-same-permissions
> Set the permissions of the extracted files to the default permissions for the current user, not as defined in the archive.

--null
> Allow filenames to be null-terminated with *-T*. Override *-C*.

--numeric-owner
> Use the ID numbers instead of names for file owners and groups.

-o, --old, old-archive, --portability
> Don't create archives with directory information that V7 *tar* can't decode.

-O, --to-stdout
> Print extracted files on standard out.

--overwrite
> Overwrite existing files when extracting.

--overwrite-dir
> Overwrite existing directory data when extracting.

--owner=name
> Set owner of added files to *name*.

-p, --preserver-permissions
> Keep ownership of extracted files same as that of original permissions.

-P, --absolute-paths
> Don't remove initial slashes (/) from input filenames.

--preserve
> Equivalent to invoking both the *-p* and *-s* options.

--posix
> Create archives that conform to POSIX standards. Such files aren't readable by older versions of *gnutar*.

-R, --block-number
> Display record number with each file in the archive.

--record-size=size
> Set size of records to *size* bytes, with *size* a multiple of 512.

--recursive-unlink
> Remove directories and files prior to extracting over them.

--remove-files
> Remove originals after inclusion in archive.

--rsh-command=command
> Don't connect to remote host with *rsh*; instead, use *command*.

-s, --same-order, --preserve-order
> When extracting, sort filenames to correspond to the order in the archive.

-S, --sparse
> Treat short files specially and more efficiently.

--same-owner
> Try to set ownership of extracted files as defined in the archive.

--show-omitted-dirs
> Show directories that were omitted during processing.

--suffix=c
> If *tarfile* already exists, make a backup copy before overwriting. Name the backup file by appending the character *c* to *tarfile* instead of the default "~".

-T filename, --files-from filename
> Consult *filename* for files to extract or create.

--totals
> Print byte totals.

-U, --unlink-first
> Remove files prior to extracting them.

--recursive-unlink
> Empty hierarchies before extracting directories.

--use-compress-program=program
> Compress archived files with *program* or uncompress extracted files with *program*.

-v, --verbose
> Verbose. Print filenames as they are added or extracted, or show permissions when files are listed.

-V name, --label=name
> Name this volume *name*.

--version
> Show version of *gnutar*.

--volno-file=n
> Force decimal number *n* to be used in *gnutar*'s prompt to change tapes.

-w, --interactive, --confirmation
> Wait for user confirmation (y) before taking any actions.

-W, --verify
> Check archive for corruption after creation.

-z
> Compress files with *gzip* before archiving them or uncompress them with *gunzip* before extracting them.

-X file, --exclude-from file
> Consult *file* for list of files to exclude.

--[no-]anchored
> Exclusion patterns match filename start (default: on).

--[no-]ignore-case
> Exclusion patterns ignore case (default: off, case-sensitive).

--[no-]wildcards
> Exclusion patterns use wildcards (default: on).

--[no-]wildcards-match-slash
> Exclusion pattern wildcards match "/" (default: on).

-z, --gzip, --ungzip
> Compress files with *gzip* before archiving them or uncompress them with *gunzip* before extracting them.

-Z, --compress, --uncompress
> Compress files with *compress* before archiving them or uncompress them with *uncompress* before extracting them.

[drive][density]
> Set drive (0-7) and storage density (*l*, *m*, or *h*, corresponding to low, medium, or high).

Examples

Create an archive of *~/Documents* and *~/Music* (*c*), show the command working (*v*), and write to an external volume, */Volumes/Backups/archive.tar*, saving the previous backup file as *archive.tar~* (*-backup*):

```
$ gnutar cvf /Volumes/Backups/archive.tar -backup ↵
~/Documents ~/Music
```

Extract only *~/Music* directory from *archive.tar* to the current directory:

```
$ gnutar xvf  ~/archive.tar Music
```

Compare extracted files with those in the archive (*d*):

```
$ gnutar dvf ~/archive.tar Music
```

---

grep

grep [*options*] *pattern* [*files*]

Searches one or more *files* for lines that match a regular expression *pattern*. Regular expressions are described in Chapter 6. Exit status is 0 if any lines match, 1 if none match, and 2 for errors. See also *egrep* and *fgrep*.

Options

-a, --text
> Don't suppress output lines with binary data; treat as text.

-A num, --after-context=num
> Print *num* lines of text that occur after the matching line.

-b, --byte-offset
> Print the byte offset within the input file before each line of output.

-B num, --before-context=num
> Print *num* lines of text that occur before the matching line.

--binary-files=type
> Treat binary files as specified. By default, *grep* treats binary files as such (*type* is *binary*). If a matching string is found within a binary file, *grep* reports only that the file matches; nothing is printed for nonmatching binary files. If *type* is *without-match*, *grep* assumes binary files don't match and skips them altogether. Same as *-I*. Using a *type* of *text* causes *grep* to treat binary files as text and print all matched lines. Same as *-a*.

-c, --count
> Print only a count of matched lines. With the *-v* or *--invert-match* option, count nonmatching lines.

-C[num], --context[=num], -num
> Print *num* lines of leading and trailing context. Default context is 2 lines.

-color[=when], --colour[=when]
> Marks matched text in red, or the contents of GREP_COLOR environment variable. Optional *when* can be *auto*, *always*, or *never*.

-d action, --directories=action
> Define an *action* for processing directories. Possible actions are:
>
> *read*
> > Read directories like ordinary files (default).
>
> *skip*
> > Skip directories.
>
> *recurse*
> > Recursively read all files under each directory. Same as *-r*.

-e pattern, --regexp=pattern
> Search for *pattern*. Same as specifying a pattern as an argument, but useful in protecting patterns beginning with -.

-E, --extended-regexp
> Treat *pattern* as an extended regular expression. Same as using the *egrep* command.

-f file, --file=file
> Take a list of patterns from *file*, one per line.

-F file, --fixed-strings
> Treat *pattern* as a list of fixed strings. Same as using the *egrep* command.

-G file, --basic-regexp
> Treat *pattern* as a basic regular expression, the default behavior.

-h, --no-filename
> Print matched lines but not filenames (inverse of *-l*).

-H, --with-filename
> Print matched lines with filenames, the default behavior.

--help
> Display a help message.

-i, --ignore-case
> Ignore uppercase and lowercase distinctions.

-I   Skip binary files. Same as *--binary-files=without-match*.

-l, --files-with-matches
> List the names of files with matches but not individual matched lines; scanning per file stops on the first match.

-L, --files-without-match
> List files that contain no matching lines.

--label=name
> Lines that come from standard input are shown as coming from file *name*.

--mmap
> For possibly better performance, read input using the *mmap* system call, instead of *read*, the default. Can cause unexpected system behavior.

-m num, --max-count= num
> Stops printing after *num* matching lines. If *-v* (non-matching lines) is in effect, then *num* nonmatching lines are printed

-n, --line-number
> Print lines and their line numbers.

-q, --quiet, --silent
> Suppress normal output in favor of quiet mode; the scanning stops on the first match.

-r, --recursive
> Recursively read all files under each directory. Same as *-d recurse*.

> *--include=pattern*
>> Only read files matching *pattern*.

> *--exclude=pattern*
>> Skip files matching *pattern*.

-s, --no-messages
> Suppress error messages about nonexistent or unreadable files.

-v, --invert-match
> Print all lines that don't match pattern.

-V, --version
> Print the version number and then exit.

-w, --word-regexp
> Match on whole words only. Words are divided by characters that aren't letters, digits, or underscores.

-x, --line-regexp
> Print lines only if pattern matches the entire line.

-Z, --null
> Print the matching files using their full pathnames and separating each with the ASCII NULL character instead of the newline character. This allows *grep* to properly work with the *xargs* utility and pathnames that contain spaces, for example.

Examples

List the number of email messages from a specific domain:

```
$ grep -c '^From .*@mac\.com' mbox
```

List files that have at least one URL:

```
$ grep -Eil '*p:\/\/*' *
```

List files that don't contain *pattern*:

```
$ grep -c pattern files | grep :0
```

---

gunzip

gunzip [gzip *options*] [*files*]

Identical to *gzip -d*. Provided as a hard link to *gzip*. The *-1 ... -9* and corresponding long-form options are not available with *gunzip*; all other *gzip* options are accepted. See *gzip* for more information.

---

gzcat

gzcat [gzip *options*] [*files*]

A link to *gzip* instead of using the name *zcat*, which preserves *zcat*'s original link to *compress*. Its action is identical to *gunzip -c*. Also installed as *zcat*. See *gzip* for more information.

---

gzip

gzip [*options*] [*files*]

gunzip [*options*] [*files*]

zcat [*options*] [*files*]

Compresses specified files (or read from standard input) with Lempel-Ziv coding (LZ77). Renames compressed file to *filename.gz*; keeps ownership modes and access/modification times. Ignores symbolic links. Uncompresses with *gunzip*, which takes all of *gzip*'s options, except those specified. *zcat* is identical to *gunzip -c* and takes the options *-fhLV*, described here. Files compressed with the *compress* command can be decompressed using these commands.

gzip doesn't preserve resource forks or HFS metadata when compressing files that contain them.

Options

-1 .. -9, --fast, --best
> Regulate the speed of compression using the specified digit *n*, where *-1* or *--fast* indicates the fastest compression method (less compression) and *-9* or *--best* indicates the slowest compression method (most compression). The default compression level is *-6*.

-c, --stdout, --to-stdout
> Print output to standard output, and don't change input files.

-d, --decompress, --uncompress
> Same as *gunzip*.

-f, --force
> Force compression. *gzip* normally prompts for permission to continue when the file has multiple links, its *.gz* version already exists, or it is reading compressed data to or from a terminal.

-h, --help
> Display a help screen and then exit.

-l, --list
> Expects to be given compressed files as arguments. Files may be compressed by any of the following methods: *gzip*, *deflate*, *compress*, *lzh*, and *pack*. For each file, list uncompressed and compressed sizes (the latter being always *-1* for files compressed by programs other than *gzip*), compression ratio, and uncompressed name. With *-v*, also print compression method, the 32-bit CRC of the uncompressed data, and the timestamp. With *-N*, look inside the file for the uncompressed name and timestamp.

-L, --license
> Display the *gzip* license and quit.

-n, --no-name
> When compressing, don't save the original filename and timestamp by default. When decompressing, don't restore the original filename if present, and don't restore the original timestamp if present. This option is the default when decompressing.

-N, --name
> Default. Save original name and timestamp. When decompressing, restore original name and timestamp.

-q, --quiet
> Print no warnings.

-r, --recursive
> When given a directory as an argument, recursively compress or decompress files within it.

-S suffix, --suffix suffix
> Append *.suffix*. Default is *.gz*. A null suffix while decompressing causes *gunzip* to attempt to decompress all specified files, regardless of suffix.

-t, --test
> Test compressed file integrity.

-v, --verbose
> Print name and percent size reduction for each file.

-V, --version
> Display the version number and compilation options.

halt

```
halt [options]
```

Prepares the system and then terminates all processes, usually ending with a hardware power-off. During preparation, all filesystem caches are flushed, and running processes are sent SIGTERM followed by SIGTERM.

Options

-l   Don't log the halt via *syslog* (i.e., *mach_kernel: syncing disks...*).

-n   Don't flush filesystem caches. Should not be used indiscriminately.

-q   The filesystem caches are flushed, but the system is otherwise halted ungracefully. Should not be used indiscriminately.

hdid

```
hdid -help
```

```
hdid image_file [options]
```

Loads disk images, attaches them to device nodes (files in */dev*), and signals Disk Arbitration to mount them into the directory hierarchy.

hdid is a synonym for *hdiutil -attach* and takes the same set of options and arguments. See the *hdid* manpage for more details.

hdiutil

```
hdiutil command [cmd-specific_args_and_opts] [-quiet | -verbose | -debug]
```

```
[-plist]
```

Manages disk images, performing some of the same functions as the Disk Utility application. The "Options" section highlights some common uses, but the full set of commands (and associated arguments and options) is extensive and isn't detailed here. See the *hdiutil* manpage or run *hdiutil help* for more assistance.

Options

attach

Attach a disk image to a device node and mount it. As arguments, it takes the file-name of a disk image and a possible list of options, some of which are:

-autoopenrw

Automatically open read/write volumes in the Finder after they're mounted.

-help

Print a usage summary to standard output.

-mountpoint

If there's only one volume in the disk image, mount it at mount point specified as an argument, instead of under */Volumes/*.

-mountroot

Mount volumes under a directory specified as an argument instead of under */Volumes/*.

-noautoopenro

Disable automatic opening of read-only volumes in the Finder after they're mounted.

-nomount

Create device nodes in */dev* and attach the image or its partitions to them, but don't mount them.

-noverify

Disable verification of disk images containing checksums.

-readonly

Disable write access to the mounted image.

-shadow

Pass modifications to the disk image through to a shadow image. Subsequent access to the modified data will be from the shadow, which allows effective read/write access to data on a disk image that shouldn't or can't be modified. This option takes the filename of a shadow disk image as an argument but defaults to the name of the attached image with a *.shadow* extension. The shadow image is created if it doesn't already exist.

burn

Burns a disk image to an optical disk (a writable CD or DVD). As arguments, it takes the filename of a disk image and a possible list of options, some of which are:

-erase

Erase an optical disk if the drive and media support erasure.

-forceclose

Close the optical disk after burning the image, preventing any future burns to the disk.

-fullerase

Perform a sector-by-sector erasure of an optical disk if the drive and media support it.

-noeject

Disable ejection of the disk after burning.

-optimizeimage

Optimize the size of the image for burning, reducing the size of HFS and HFS+ volumes to the size of the data on them.

create
>Create a blank disk image. It takes the filename for the disk image as an argument. One of these options is required to specify the size of the image:

>*-megabytes*
>>Specify the size of the image in megabytes. Takes an integer argument.

>*-sectors*
>>Specify the size of the image in 512-byte sectors. Takes an integer argument.

>*-size*
>>Specify the size of the image with a choice of unit. Takes an argument consisting of an integer concatenated with a letter, where the letter is *b* (for bytes), *k* (for kilobytes), *m* (for megabytes), *g* (for gigabytes), *t* (for terabytes), *p* (for petabytes), or *e* (for exabytes).

>*-srcfolder*
>>Create an image large enough to hold the contents of a directory specified as an argument.

>Finally, *create* can take a list of discretionary options, some of which are:

>*-fs*
>>Format the disk image with a filesystem, the format being given as an argument to this option. Possible formats are HFS+, HFS, UFS, and MS-DOS. After the image is created, it's attached, formatted, and detached.

>*-stretch*
>>If creating an HFS+ filesystem, initialize it so that it can later be stretched with *hdiutil resize*. Takes an argument with the same format as the *-size* option, which determines the maximum size to which the filesystem can be stretched.

>*-volname*
>>Specify the volume name for the image. Takes a string argument; the default volume name is *untitled*.

detach
>Unmount an image or its partitions and detach them from their device nodes. Takes a device name (e.g., *disk1*) as an argument.

eject
>Same as *detach*.

header
>Print the disk image header to standard output. Takes the filename of a disk image as an argument.

help
>Print an extensive usage summary to standard output.

imageinfo
>Print information about a disk image or device to standard output, including properties (such as whether the image is compressed, encrypted, or partitioned), format, size, and checksum. As arguments, it takes a device name (e.g., */dev/disk1*) or the filename of a disk image, and a possible list of options, some of which are:

>*-checksum*
>>Display only the checksum.

>*-format*
>>Display only the image format.

info

> Print the version of the DiskImages framework to standard output, as well as information about mounted images (such as image filename, format, associated device node, mount point, and mounting user's identity).

internet-enable

> After being applied to a disk image and when the image is mounted, its contents are automatically copied to the directory containing the image file, and then the image is unmounted and moved to the user's Trash. The effect is to replace the disk image by its contents, in place. It takes an argument of either *-yes*, *-no*, or *-query*, as well as a disk image filename.

makehybrid

> Create a hybrid HFS+/ISO-9660 disk image suitable for use on other operating systems. As an argument, it takes *-o* followed by an image source, which can be either another disk image or a directory. It also takes a list of discretionary options, some of which are:

> *-hfs*
>
> > Include HFS+ filesystem information in the image. This happens by default, unless the *-iso* or *-joliet* options are specified without *-hfs*.

> *-hfs-blessed-directory*
>
> > Specify the directory on an HFS+ volume containing a valid *BootX* file, which may created by the *bless* command.

> *-hfs-openfolder*
>
> > Specify the directory on an HFS+ volume that should be automatically opened in the Finder after mounting.

> *-iso*
>
> > Include ISO-9660 filesystem information in the image. This happens by default, unless the *-hfs* option is specified without *-iso*.

> *-joliet*
>
> > Include ISO-9660 filesystem information with Joliet extensions in the image. This happens by default, unless the *-hfs* or *-iso* options are specified without *-joliet*.

mount

> Same as *attach*.

mountvol

> Mount a device into the filesystem hierarchy using Disk Arbitration (similar to *diskutil mount*). Takes a device name (e.g., *disk1*) as an argument. This can be used to complete the process of mounting a disk image after using *hdiutil attach -nomount*.

plugins

> Print information about plug-ins for the DiskImages framework to standard output.

pmap

> Print the partition map of a disk image or device to standard output. As arguments, it takes a device name (e.g., */dev/disk1*) or the filename of a disk image, and a possible list of options.

testfilter

> Test whether a file is a valid disk image and return YES or NO to standard error.

unmount

 Unmount an image or its partitions without detaching them from their device nodes. Takes a device name (e.g., *disk1*) or a mount point as an argument.

-debug

 Enable debugging output to standard error.

-plist

 Display output in XML property list format, if the command can do it.

-quiet

 Minimize output.

-verbose

 Enable verbose output.

head

head [*options*] [*files*]

Prints the first few lines of one or more *files* (default is 10).

Options

-*n* Print the first *n* lines of the file.

-*n n* Print the first *n* lines of the file.

Example

Display the first 20 lines of *phone_list*:

 $ **head -20 phone_list**

host

host [*options*] *host* [*server*]

host [*options*] *domain* [*server*]

Prints information about specified hosts or zones in DNS. Hosts may be IP addresses or hostnames; *host* converts IP addresses to hostnames by default and appends the local domain to hosts without a trailing dot. Default servers are determined in */etc/resolv.conf*. For more information about hosts and zones, refer to Chapters 1 and 2 of *DNS and BIND* (O'Reilly).

Options

-*a* All, same as -*t* ANY.

-*c class*

 Search for specified resource record class (*in*[ternet], *cs*[net], *ch*[aos], *hs/hesiod*, or *any*). Default is *in*. The *chaos* and *csnet* classes, although defined in RFC1035, are rejected as invalid classes by the *host* command.

-*C* Print the SOA (start of authority) records for the host.

-*d* Verbose. Same as -*v*.

-*l domain*

 List all machines in *domain*.

-r   No recursion. Don't ask contacted server to query other servers, but require only the information that it has cached.

-s   Chase signatures back to parent key (DNSSEC).

-t type
    Look for *type* entries in the resource record. Acceptable values for *type* are: *a*, *ns*, *md*, *mf*, *cnames*, *soa*, *mb*, *mg*, *mr*, *null*, *wks*, *ptr*, *hinfo*, *minfo*, *mx*, *any*, and *** (careful, the shell loves those asterisks; be sure to escape them).

-v   Verbose. Include all fields from the resource record, even time-to-live and class, as well as "additional information" and "authoritative nameservers" (provided by the remote nameserver).

-w   Wait forever for a response from a queried server.

hostinfo

hostinfo

Prints basic information about the system to standard output, including Darwin version number, number and types of processors, amount of physical memory, current number of Mach tasks and threads running in the kernel, and CPU load.

Example

```
$ hostinfo
Mach kernel version:
         Darwin Kernel Version 8.2.0: Fri Jun 24 17:46:54 PDT 2005;
root:xnu-792.2.4.obj~3/RELEASE_PPC
Kernel configured for a single processor only.
1 processor is physically available.
Processor type: ppc7450 (PowerPC 7450)
Processor active: 0
Primary memory available: 768.00 megabytes
Default processor set: 57 tasks, 197 threads, 1 processors
Load average: 0.57, Mach factor: 0.69
```

hostname

hostname [*option*] [*nameofhost*]

Sets or prints name of current host system. A privileged user can temporarily set the hostname with the *nameofhost* argument. Edit */etc/hostconfig* to make a permanent change.

Option

-s   Trim domain information from the printed name.

hwprefs

hwprefs [-h]

hwprefs [-v] *parameter*[*=value*] [*parameter*[*=value*]]...

Prints some information about the system to standard output. This is installed as part of the Computer Hardware Understanding Development (CHUD) set of developer tools.

Options

-h   Print a usage statement to standard error.

-v   Print information verbosely.

parameter
> One of the following: *cpus* reports the number of CPUs (either 1 or 2), *cpunap* reports whether the CPU may slow down to conserve energy (either 0 or 1), *hwprefetch* reports the number of prefetch engines used by a G5 CPU (either 4 or 8), and *ostype* reports the code name for the system's OS (either *Cheetah*, Mac OS X 10.0; *Puma*, 10.1; *Jaguar*, 10.2; *Smeagol*, 10.2.7; *Panther*, 10.3; or *Tiger*, 10.4).

id

id [*options*] [*username*]

Displays information about yourself or another user: UID, GID, effective UID and GID if relevant, and additional GIDs.

Options

-g   Print GID.

-G   Print supplementary GIDs.

-n   With *-u*, *-g*, or *-G*, print user or group name, not number.

-p   Print the output in a more easily read format. Not used with other options.

-P   Print in the format used by the system password file, */etc/passwd*.

-r   With *-u*, *-g*, or *-G*, print real, not effective, UID or GID.

-u   Print UID only.

ifconfig

ifconfig [*options*] [*interface address_family address parameters*]

Assigns an address to a network interface and/or configures network interface parameters. *ifconfig* is typically used at boot time to define the network address of each interface on a machine. It may be used at a later time to redefine an interface's address or other parameters. Without arguments, *ifconfig* displays the current configuration for a network interface. Used with a single *interface* argument, *ifconfig* displays that particular interface's current configuration.

Display options

-*a*   Display information about all configured interfaces. This is the default when no options and arguments are specified.

-*d*   Display information about interfaces that are down.

-*L*   Display address lifetime for IPv6 addresses.

-*l*   Display all configured interfaces, names only.

-*m*   Display all supported media for specified interface.

-*u*   Display information about interfaces that are up.

Arguments

interface
> String of the form *name unit*—for example, en0.

address
> Hostname or address in "dotted-octet" notation; for example, 172.24.30.12.

address_family
> Because an interface may receive transmissions in differing protocols, each of which may require separate naming schemes, you can specify the *address_family* to change the interpretation of the remaining parameters. You may specify *inet* (the default; for TCP/IP) or *inet6*.

dest_address
> Specify the address of the correspondent on the other end of a point-to-point link.

The following parameters may be set with *ifconfig*:

add/delete

[-]alias
> Create/delete an additional/existing network address for this interface.

anycast
> Specify address as an anycast address (*inet6* only).

[-]arp
> Enable/disable use of the Address Resolution Protocol in mapping between network-level addresses and link-level addresses.

broadcast
> Specify address to use to represent broadcasts to the network (*inet* only). The default is the address with a host part of all 1s (i.e., x.y.z.255 for a class C network).

create/plumb *and* destroy/unplumb
> These commands perform operations related to interface cloning. However, Mac OS X itself doesn't support interface cloning. Therefore, the manpage descriptions of these parameters are of historical significance only.

[-]debug
> Enable/disable driver-dependent debugging code.

down
> Mark an interface "down" (unresponsive).

ether
> Same as lladdr.

[-]link[0-2]
> Enable/disable special link-level processing modes. Refer to driver's manpage for more information.

lladdr *addr*
> Set the link-level *addr*ess on an interface as a set of colon-separated hex digits; for example, 00:03:93:67:7a:4a.

media *type*
> Set the interface media type to *type*; for example, 10base5/AUI.

[-]mediaopt *opts*
> Comma-separated list of media options for a supported media selection system.

metric *n*
> Set routing metric of the interface to *n*. Default is 0.

mtu *num*
> Set the interface's Maximum Transfer Unit (MTU) to *mtu*.

netmask *mask*
> Specify how much of the address to reserve for subdividing networks into subnetworks (*inet* only). *mask* can be specified as a single hexadecimal number with a leading 0x, with a dot notation Internet address, or with a pseudonetwork name listed in the network table */etc/networks*.

up   Mark an interface "up" (ready to send and receive).

---

info

info [*options*] [*topics*]

Info files are arranged in a hierarchy and can contain menus for subtopics. When entered without options, the command displays the top-level information file (usually */usr/local/info/dir*). When *topics* are specified, find a subtopic by choosing the first *topic* from the menu in the top-level information file, the next *topic* from the new menu specified by the first *topic*, and so on. The initial display can also be controlled by the *-f* and *-n* options.

Options

--apropos string
> Looks up *string* in all manual indexes.

-d directories, --directory directories
> Search *directories*, a colon-separated list, for information files. If this option isn't specified, use the INFOPATH environment variable or the default directory (usually */usr/local/info*).

--dribble file
> Store each keystroke in *file*, which can be used in a future session with the *--restore* option to return to this place in *info*.

-f file, --file file
> Display specified info *file*.

-h, --help
> Display brief help.

--index-search=string
> Go to node pointed to by index entry *string*.

-n node, --node node
> Display specified *node* in the information file.

-O, --show-options, --usage
> Don't remove ANSI escapes from manpages.

-o file, --output file
> Copy output to *file* instead of displaying it at the screen.

-R, --raw-escapes
> Don't remove ANSI escapes from manpages.

--restore=file
> When starting, execute keystrokes in *file*.

--subnodes
> Display subtopics recursively.

--version
> Display version.

--vi-keys
> Use *vi*-like key bindings.

install

```
install [options] file1 file2
```

```
install [options] files directory
```

```
install -d [options] [file] directory
```

Used primarily in Makefiles to update files. *install* copies files into user-specified directories. Similar to *cp*, with additional functionality regarding inode-based information like UID, GID, mode, flags, etc.

Options

-b Create backup copies of existing target files by renaming existing *file* as *file.old*. See -B for specifying extension name (i.e., default is *.old*).

-B suffix
> Use *suffix* as a filename extension when -b is in effect.

-c Copy the specified file(s). This is the default behavior of the *install* command.

-C Copy the file. Don't change the modification timestamp if the target exists and is the same as the source.

-d Create any missing directories.

-f flags
> Set the file flags of the target file(s). Flags are a comma-separated list of keywords. See the *chflags(1)* manpage for further details.

-g gid or groupname
> Set GID of target file to *group* (privileged users only or user is member of specified group).

-m mode
> Set the mode of the target files to *mode*. The default is 0755, or *rwxr-xr-x*.

-M Don't use *mmap(2)*.

-o uid or username
> Set ownership to *uid* or *username* or, if unspecified, to root (privileged users only).

-p Preserve modification times.

-s Strip binaries to enhance portability.

-S Safe copy. The source file is copied to a temporary file and then renamed. The default behavior is to first unlink the existing target before the source is copied.

-v Verbose. *install* prints symbolic representations for each copy action.

installer

`installer` *options* `-pkg` *pkgpath* `-target` *volpath*

Installs standard Mac OS X package files from the command line. *install* is an alternative to the *Installer.app* GUI application.

Options
-allow
> Install over an existing version of the software, even when the version being installed is older. The package must have special support for this option.

-config
> Send the list of command-line arguments, formatted in *plist* XML, to standard output without performing the installation. If you direct the output to a file, you can use that file with the *-file* option to perform multiple identical installations.

-dumplog
> Log installer's messages to standard output.

-file pathname
> Read arguments from file *pathname*. The file needs to be a product of the *-config* option or a file of the same format.

-help
> Display a help screen, and then exit.

-lang language
> Identify *language* (specified in ISO format) as the default language of the target system. Used only with OS installations.

-listiso
> Display the languages *installer* recognizes, in ISO format.

-pkginfo
> List the packages to be installed without performing the installation. Metapackages contain multiple subpackages; this option lists those subpackages as well.

-plist
> When used with *-pkginfo* and *-volinfo*, format the output into *plist* XML.

-verbose
> Print more package and volume information. Used with *-pkginfo* and *-volinfo*.

-verboseR

    Print more package and volume information, formatted for parsing. Used with *-pkginfo* and *-volinfo*.

-vers

    Display the version of *installer*, and then exit.

-volinfo

    List the volumes mounted at the time the command is run without performing the installation.

Examples

List only available packages and target volumes:

```
$ installer -volinfo -pkginfo -pkg newpkg.pkg
```

Install *newpkg.pkg* on the current system volume:

```
$ installer -pkg newpkg.pkg -target /
```

Install *newpkg.pkg*, using arguments from *installfile*:

```
$ installer -pkg newpkg.pkg -file installfile
```

ipconfig

```
ipconfig getifaddr interface

ipconfig getoption { interface | "" } { option_name | option_code }

ipconfig getpacket interface

ipconfig ifcount

ipconfig set interface { BOOTP | DHCP }

ipconfig set interface { INFORM | MANUAL } IP_addr netmask

ipconfig waitall
```

Interacts with the IP Configuration Agent of *configd* to manage network configuration changes.

Options

getifaddr

    Print the specified network interface's IP address to standard output.

getoption

    Print the value of the specified DHCP option to standard output. If *interface* is specified, the option is interface specific. If empty quotes are used instead, the option is global. Option names and numeric codes are DHCP-standard (such as *host_name*, *domain_name*, *netinfo_server_address*, etc.).

getpacket

    Print DHCP transaction packets to standard output.

ifcount

    Print the number of network interfaces to standard output.

set   Set the method by which the specified network interface is assigned an IP address. Using *BOOTP* or *DHCP* causes the system to attempt to contact a server of the appropriate type to obtain IP configuration information. Using *INFORM* sets the IP address locally, but initiates a DHCP request to obtain additional IP configuration information (DNS servers, default gateway, etc.). Using *MANUAL* indicates that all IP configuration information is set locally.

setverbose *level*
> Turns on logging if *level* is 1, or turns off logging if *level* is 0.

waitall
> Set the configurations of all network interfaces according to the specifications in */etc/iftab*.

join

join [*options*] *file1* *file2*

Joins the common lines of sorted *file1* and sorted *file2*. Reads standard input if *file1* is -. The output contains the common field and the remainder of each line from *file1* and *file2*. In the following options, *n* can be 1 or 2, referring to *file1* or *file2*.

Options

-a[*n*]
> List unpairable lines in file *n* (or both if *n* is omitted).

-e *s*
> Replace any empty output field with the string *s*.

-j*n* *m*
> Join on the *m*th field of file *n* (or both files if *n* is omitted).

-o *n.m*
> Each output line contains fields specified by file number *n* and field number *m*. The common field is suppressed unless requested.

-t*c*   Use character *c* as a field separator for input and output.

-v *n*   Print only the unpairable lines in file *n*. With both -v 1 and -v 2, all unpairable lines are printed.

-1 *m*
> Join on field *m* of *file1*. Fields start with 1.

-2 *m*
> Join on field *m* of *file2*. Fields start with 1.

Examples

Assuming the following input files:

```
$ cat score
olga    81      91
rene    82      92
zack    83      93

$ cat grade
olga    B       A
rene    B       A
```

List scores followed by grades, including unmatched lines:

```
$ join -a1 score grade
olga 81 91 B A
rene 82 92 B A
zack 83 93
```

Pair each score with its grade:

```
$ join -o 1.1 1.2 2.2 1.3 2.3 score grade
olga 81 B 91 A
rene 82 B 92 A
```

jot

jot [*option*] [*repetitions* [begin [end [seed]]]]

Generates a list of random or sequential data *repetitions* lines long. Sequential lists start from the number given in the *begin* value and finish with the *end* value. Random data is generated using the seed value *seed*.

Options

-b word

Print *word* only.

-c   Print ASCII character equivalents instead of numbers.

-n   Don't print a trailing newline character at the end of the list.

-p precision

Print the data using the number of digits or characters specified by the number *precision*.

-r   Generate random data. *jot* generates sequential data by default.

-s string

Print the list separated by *string* instead of by newlines, the default.

-w word

Print *word* along with the other generated data.

Examples

Return a list of sequentially numbered names:

```
$ jot -w box- 20 1 20
```

Return the ASCII values of numbers 43 to 52:

```
$ jot -c 10 43 52
```

kdump

kdump [*option*]

Decode and display a kernel trace file produced by *ktrace*. By default, *kdump* processes any *ktrace.out* file found in the current working directory.

Options

-d   Show all numbers in decimal format.

-f tracefile
  Process the file *tracefile* instead of *ktrace.out*.

-l   Continue to read and display the trace file as new trace data is added.

-m maxdata
  When decoding I/O data, show no more than *maxdata* bytes.

-n   Don't decode completely; display some values, such as those from *ioctl* and *errno*, in their raw format.

-R   With each entry, show time since previous entry (relative timestamp).

-t tracepoints
  Show only the traces specified in *tracepoints* (see *kdump*'s -t option).

-T   With each entry, show seconds since the epoch (absolute timestamp).

---

kdumpd

kdumpd [-1] [-s *directory*] [-u *username*] [-c | -C]] [-n] [*directory*]

Provides a service meant to accept transfers of kernel core dumps from remote Mac OS X clients. Based on *tftpd*, it offers a simplistic file drop service. Setting it up involves:

- Adding a *kdump* entry to */etc/services*, recommended on UDP port 1069.
- Creating a *kdump* service file in */etc/xinetd.d/*, modeled after that for *tftp*.
- Executing *sudo service kdump start*.

Once that's done, you can invoke *tftp* on a client system, enter **connect server_name 1069**, and then **put** *filename* to transfer a file. The file is saved on the server in the directory specified in the arguments to *kdumpd*. There are restrictions: the filename can't include / or .., so the file is deposited into the target directory only; and the target file must not already exist.

This service is apparently not used by any current facility but may exist for future use by Apple.

Options

-c   Same as -C. Using this option should reject the connection if the path including the client IP address doesn't exist, but a bug prevents it from doing so.

-C   Add the client's IP address to the end of the *chroot* directory path. If this path doesn't already exist, it falls back to that specified for -s.

-l   Enable logging via *syslog* using the *ftp* facility. However, logging is enabled by default, so this option doesn't actually do anything.

-n   Suppress a negative acknowledgment if the client requests a relative pathname that doesn't exist.

-s   Perform a *chroot* to the specified directory.

-u   Change UID to the specified username. Defaults to *nobody*.

kill

kill [*option*] PID

This is the */bin/kill* command; there is also a shell command of the same name that works similarly. Send a signal to terminate one or more process IDs (PID). You must own the process or be a privileged user. If no signal is specified, TERM is sent. If the PID is -1, the signal is sent to all processes you own. If you are superuser, a PID of -1 sends the signal to all processes.

Options

-*l*   List the signal names. (Used by itself.)

-*s signal*
  Send signal *signal* to the given process or process group. *signal* can be the signal number (from */usr/include/sys/signal.h*) or name (from *kill -l*). With a signal number of 9, the kill is absolute.

-*signal*
  Send signal *signal* to the given process or process group.

killall

killall [*options*] procname...

Kills processes specified by command or pattern match. The default signal sent by *killall* is TERM but may be specified on the command line. *killall* assembles and executes a set of *kill* commands to accomplish its task.

Options

-*c procname*
  Use with the -*t* or -*u* options to limit processes that sent a signal to those matching *procname*.

-*d*   Print diagnostic information only about targeted processes; doesn't send signal.

-*h, -help, -?*
  Print usage and exit.

-*l*   List known signal names.

-*m*   Interpret the *procname* as a case-insensitive regular expression for selecting real process names to send a signal to.

-*s*   Show the *kill* command lines that send the signal but don't actually execute them.

-*SIGNAL*
  Send specified *signal* to process. *signal* may be a name (see -*l* option) or number.

-*t tty*
  Used to further select only those processes attached to the specified *tty* (procname tty), or to select all processes attached to the specified *tty* (i.e., no *procname* specified).

-u user

> Used to further select only those processes owned by the specified *user* (proc-name user), or to select all processes owned by the specified *user* (i.e., no *procname* specified).

-v Verbose output. Print the *kill* command lines that send the signal.

ktrace

ktrace [*options*] command

Trace kernel operations for process *command* and log data to file *ktrace.out* in the current working directory. The tracing continues until you either exit *command* or clear the trace points (with the *-c* or *-C* options). Use *kdump* to view the trace log.

Options

-a Append new data to the trace file instead of overwriting it.

-C Stop tracing all processes run by a user invoking *ktrace*. If this option is used with superuser privileges, the tracing of all processes is stopped.

-c Stop tracing process command.

-d Also trace any current child processes of the specified process.

-f file

> Log to *file* instead of *ktrace.out*, the default.

-g pgid

> Toggle tracing of all processes that are part of the process group *pgid*.

-i Also trace any future child processes of the specified process.

-p pid

> Toggle tracing of process *pid*.

-t tracepoints

> Trace only kernel operations specified in *tracepoints*. Use the appropriate letters from this list to indicate which type of operation(s) to trace:
>
> *c* System calls
>
> *i* I/O
>
> *n* Name translations
>
> *s* Signal processing
>
> *u* Userland operations
>
> *w* Context switches

Examples

Trace only system calls and I/O on process 489:

    $ ktrace -t ci -p 489

Run the *atlookup* command and trace all its kernel operations:

    $ ktrace atlookup

Turn off tracing for all user processes:

    $ ktrace -C

languagesetup

```
languagesetup -h
```

```
languagesetup -langspec language
```

```
languagesetup [-English | -Localized]
```

Changes the default language used by the system. If invoked with no arguments, or with the *-English* or *-Localized* flags, it enters an interactive session in which the new language may be chosen from a menu.

Options

-English
> Present interactive prompts in English.

-h Print a usage statement to standard output.

-langspec
> Specify the new system language on the command line, instead of interactively.

-Localized
> Present interactive prompts in the system's default language.

last

```
last [options] [users]
```

Lists information about current and previous login sessions, including username and duration of each session. Sessions are listed one per line, newest first. To view only sessions from select users, specify those usernames in *users*.

Options

-f file
> Read from log *file* instead of */var/log/wtemp*, the default.

-h host
> Report only on those sessions initiated from machine *host*.

-n Display only the first *n* lines of output.

-t tty
> Report only on those sessions initiated from device *tty*. To list Aqua logins, for example, specify *console* for *tty*.

launchctl

```
launchctl
```

```
launchctl { help | list | export | reloadttys | shutdown }
```

```
launchctl { start | stop } job…
```

```
launchctl { load | unload } [-w] pathname…
```

```
launchctl { stdout | stderr } pathname
```

```
launchctl { getenv | unsetenv } variable

launchctl setenv variable value

launchctl getrusage { self | children }

launchctl limit [{ core | cpu | data | filesize | maxfiles | maxproc | memlock |
rss | stack } [integer [integer]]]

launchctl umask [umask]

launchctl log [level level | { only | mask } level…]
```

Control utility for *launchd*. If called with no arguments, enters an interactive mode using the same set of subcommands as may be specified on the command line. You can use Control-D or Control-C to exit interactive mode.

Options

export
> Displays the shell commands necessary to export *launchd*'s environment variables.

getenv
> Displays the value of the specified *launchd* environment variable.

getrusage
> Displays resource utilization data for *launchd* or its child processes.

help
> Prints a usage statement to standard output.

limit
> With no further arguments, displays *launchd*'s resource limits. With one argument, displays the limit for the specified resource. If the resource name is followed by a number, both the hard and soft limits for the resource are set to the specified number. If the resource name is followed by two numbers, the soft limit is set to the first number, and the hard limit is set to the second number.

list
> Displays the jobs loaded by *launchd* and run by the invoking user. For information about system-wide jobs, this command must be invoked with superuser access.

load
> Loads the jobs into *launchd* associated with the specified configuration files, or directories containing configuration files. The -w flag makes the load persistent across reboots.

log
> With no further arguments, displays which *syslog* levels are logged by *launchd*. If *level* is specified, directs *launchd* to log that level and higher. If *only* is specified, directs *launchd* to log only the specified levels. If *mask* is specified, directs *launchd* to log all levels but those specified.

reloadttys
> Causes *launchd* to reread */etc/ttys*.

setenv
> Sets the value of the specified *launchd* environment variable.

shutdown
> Unloads all jobs in preparation for system shutdown.

start

Starts the specified job.

stderr

Redirects *launchd*'s standard error to the specified file.

stdout

Redirects *launchd*'s standard output to the specified file.

stop

Stops the specified job.

umask

Displays or sets the umask for *launchd*.

unload

Unloads the jobs from *launchd* associated with the specified configuration files, or directories containing configuration files. The *-w* flag makes the unload persistent across reboots.

unsetenv

Unsets the value of the specified *launchd* environment variable.

launchd

launchd [-h | -d | -s | -v | -x | *command*]

Introduced with Mac OS X Tiger (10.4), *launchd* is an automated process launcher, starting and stopping processes as needed. It's intended as a catch-all replacement for *init*, */etc/rc* and related scripts, *SystemStarter*, *register_mach_bootstrap_servers*, *cron*, *loginwindow* hooks run out of */etc/ttys*, and *watchdog* (although it hasn't yet displaced all of them). It is the first process started during the boot sequence, with a PID of 1.

Each job controlled by *launchd* is configured by an XML property list file located in either */System/Library/LaunchDaemons/* or */Library/LaunchDaemons/* (for system-wide daemon processes), or */System/Library/LaunchAgents/*, */Library/LaunchAgents/*, or *~/Library/LaunchAgents/* (for per-user processes).

launchd can be managed with the *launchctl* utility. Upon startup, it checks */etc/launchd.conf* or *~/.launchd.conf* for *launchctl* commands to execute, although the commands to load the daemon configuration files are currently located in */etc/rc*.

Options

-d   Causes *launchd* to run itself as a background process.

-h   Prints a limited usage statement to standard output.

-s   Boots the system in single-user mode. This flag is used when ⌘-S is held down on startup.

-v   Boots the system in verbose mode. This flag is used when ⌘-V is held down on startup.

-x   Boots the system in safe mode. This flag is used when Shift is held down on startup.

command

Starts an instance of *launchd* controlling a job given by the specified command line.

leave

`leave [[+]time]`

Sets a time to be reminded that it's "time to leave." *leave* will remind you with a message at the command prompt five minutes, and then one minute, before the specified time. You'll be reminded again at the specified time and then every minute after until you either log out of that shell session or kill *leave* with *kill -9 pid*. Specify the time in the *hhmm* format. Use + before *time* to specify a relative time, hours, and minutes from the current time. Without any arguments, *leave* prompts you to enter a time in the same format.

less

`less [options] [filename]`

less is a program for paging through files or other output. It was written in reaction to the perceived primitiveness of *more* (hence its name). A number may precede some commands.

Options

-[z]num

> Set number of lines to scroll to *num*. Default is one screenful. A negative *num* sets the number to *num* lines less than the current number.

+[+]command

> Run *command* on startup. If *command* is a number, jump to that line. The option ++ applies this command to each file in the command-line list.

-?   Print help screen. Ignore all other options; don't page through file.

-a, --skip-search-screen

> When searching, begin after last line displayed. (Default is to search from second line displayed.)

-b, --buffers=n

> Use *n* buffers for each file (default is 10). Buffers are 1 KB in size.

-B, --auto-buffers

> Don't automatically allocate buffers for data read from a pipe. If *-b* specifies a number of buffers, allocate that many. If necessary, allow information from previous screens to be lost.

-c, --clear-screen

> Redraw screen from top, instead of scrolling from the bottom.

-C, --CLEAR-SCREEN

> Same as *-c*, but clear the screen before redrawing.

-d, --dumb

> Suppress dumb-terminal error messages.

-e, --quit-at-eof

> Automatically exit after reaching EOF twice.

-E, --QUIT-AT-EOF

> Automatically exit after reaching EOF once.

-f, --force
Force opening of directories and devices; don't print warning when opening binaries.

-F, --quit-if-one-screen
Automatically exit if the file fits on one screen.

-g, --hilite-search
Highlight only string found by past search command, not all matching strings.

-G, --HILITE-SEARCH
Never highlight matching search strings.

-h, --max-back-scroll=num
Never scroll backward more than *num* lines at once.

-i, --ignore-case
Make searches case-insensitive, unless the search string contains uppercase letters.

-I, --IGNORE-CASE
Make searches case-insensitive, even when the search string contains uppercase letters.

-j, --jump-target=num
Position target line on line *num* of screen. Target line can be the result of a search or a jump. Count lines beginning from 1 (top line). A negative *num* is counted back from bottom of screen.

-k, --lesskey-file=file
Read *file* to define special key bindings.

-m, --long-prompt
Display a *more*-like prompt, including percent of file read.

-M Prompt more verbosely than with *-m*, including percentage, line number, and total lines.

-n, --line-numbers
Don't calculate line numbers. Affects *-m* and *-M* options and = and *v* commands (disables passing of line number to editor).

-N, --LINE-NUMBERS
Print line number before each line.

-o, --log-file=file
When input is from a pipe, copy output to *file* as well as to the screen. (Prompt for overwrite authority if *file* exists.)

-Ofile, --LOG-FILE=file
Similar to *-o*, but don't prompt when overwriting file.

-p, --pattern=pattern
At startup, search for first occurrence of *pattern*.

-P, --prompt=prompt
Sets the three preset prompt styles:

s   Set short, default prompt.

m   Set medium prompt (specified by *-m*).

M   Set long prompt (specified by *-M*).

w   Set message printed while waiting for data.

=   Set message printed by = command.

-q, --quiet, --silent
> Disable ringing of bell on attempts to scroll past EOF or before beginning of file. Attempt to use visual bell instead.

-Q, --QUIET, --SILENT
> Never ring terminal bell.

-r, --raw-control-chars
> Display "raw" control characters, instead of using ^x notation. Sometimes leads to display problems.

-s, --squeeze-long-lines
> Print successive blank lines as one line.

-S, --chop-long-lines
> Chop lines longer than the screen width, instead of wrapping.

-t, --tag=tag
> Edit file containing *tag*. Consult *./tags* (constructed by *ctags*).

-T, --tags-file=file
> With the *-t* option or *:t* command, read *file* instead of *./tags*.

-u, --underline-special
> Treat backspaces and carriage returns as printable input.

-U, --UNDERLINE-SPECIAL
> Treat backspaces and carriage returns as control characters.

-V, --version
> Display the lesser version number and a disclaimer.

-w, --hilite-unread
> Print lines after EOF as blanks instead of tildes (~).

-x, --tabs=n
> Set tab stops to every *n* characters. Default is 8.

-X, --no-init
> Don't send initialization and deinitialization strings from termcap to terminal.

-y, --max-forw-scroll=n
> Never scroll forward more than *n* lines at once.

Commands

Many commands can be preceded by a numeric argument, referred to as *number* in the command descriptions.

SPACE, ^V, f, ^F
> Scroll forward the default number of lines (usually one window).

z
> Similar to *SPACE*, but allows the number of lines to be specified, in which case it resets the default to that number.

RETURN, ^N, e, ^E, j, ^J
> Scroll forward. Default is one line. Display all lines, even if the default is more lines than the screen size.

d, ^D
> Scroll forward. Default is one-half the screen size. The number of lines may be specified, in which case the default is reset.

b, ^B, ESC-v
> Scroll backward. Default is one windowful.

w   Like *b*, but allows the number of lines to be specified, in which case it resets the default to that number.

y, ^Y, ^P, k, ^K
       Scroll backward. Default is one line. Display all lines, even if the default is more lines than the screen size.

u, ^U
       Scroll backward. Default is one-half the screen size. The number of lines may be specified, in which case the default is reset.

r, ^R, ^L
       Redraw screen.

R   Like *r*, but discard buffered input.

F   Scroll forward. When an EOF is reached, continue trying to find more output, behaving similarly to *tail -f*.

g, <, ESC-<
       Skip to a line. Default is 1.

G, >, ESC->
       Skip to a line. Default is the last one.

p, %
       Skip to a *position number* percent of the way into the file.

{   If the top line on the screen includes a *{*, find its matching *}*. If the top line contains multiple *{*s, use *number* to determine which one to use to find a match.

}   If the bottom line on the screen includes a *}*, find its matching *{*. If the bottom line contains multiple *}*s, use *number* to determine which one to use to find a match.

(If the top line on the screen includes a *(*, find its matching *)*. If the top line contains multiple *(*s, use *number* to determine which one to use to find a match.

)   If the bottom line on the screen includes a *)*, find its matching *(*. If the bottom line contains multiple *)*s, use *number* to determine which one to use to find a match.

[If the top line on the screen includes a *[*, find its matching *]*. If the top line contains multiple *[*s, use *number* to determine which one to use to find a match.

]   If the bottom line on the screen includes a *]*, find its matching *[*. If the bottom line contains multiple *]*s, use *number* to determine which one to use to find a match.

ESC-^F
       Behave like *{*, but prompt for two characters, which it substitutes for *{* and *}* in its search.

ESC-^B
       Behave like *}*, but prompt for two characters, which it substitutes for *{* and *}* in its search.

m   Prompt for a lowercase letter and then use that letter to mark the current position.

'   Prompt for a lowercase letter and then go to the position marked by that letter. There are some special characters:

' '   Return to position before last "large movement."

^   Beginning of file.

$ End of file.

^X^X
> Same as '.

/pattern
> Find next occurrence of *pattern*, starting at the second line displayed. Some special characters can be entered before *pattern*:

!   Find lines that don't contain *pattern*.

*   If current file doesn't contain *pattern*, continue through the rest of the files in the command-line list.

@   Search from the first line in the first file specified on the command line, no matter what the screen currently displays.

?pattern
> Search backward, beginning at the line before the top line. Treats *!*, ***, and *@* as special characters when they begin *pattern*, as */* does.

ESC-/pattern
> Same as */**.

ESC-?pattern
> Same as *?**.

n   Repeat last pattern search.

N   Repeat last pattern search, in the reverse direction.

ESC-n
> Repeat previous search command but as though it were prefaced by ***.

ESC-N
> Repeat previous search command but as though it were prefaced by *** and in the opposite direction.

ESC-u
> Toggle search highlighting.

:e [filename]
> Read in *filename* and insert it into the command-line list of filenames. Without *filename*, reread the current file. *filename* may contain special characters:

> **%**   Name of current file.

> **#**   Name of previous file.

^X^V, E
> Same as *:e*.

:n   Read in next file in command-line list.

:p   Read in previous file in command-line list.

:x   Read in first file in command-line list.

:d   Remove current from the list of files, effectively closing it.

t   Go to the next tag. See the *-t* option for details about tags.

T   Go to the previous tag.

:f, =, ^G
> Print filename, position in command-line list, line number on top of window, total lines, byte number, and total bytes.

-   Expects to be followed by a command-line option letter. Toggles the value of that option or, if appropriate, prompts for its new value.

-+ Expects to be followed by a command-line option letter. Resets that option to its default.

-- Expects to be followed by a command-line option letter. Resets that option to the opposite of its default, where the opposite can be determined.

_   Expects to be followed by a command-line option letter. Display that option's current setting.

+*command*
> Execute *command* each time a new file is read in.

q, :q, :Q, ZZ
> Exit.

v Not valid for all versions. Invoke editor specified by $VISUAL or $EDITOR, or *vi* if neither is set.

! [command]
> Not valid for all versions. Invoke $SHELL or *sh*. If *command* is given, run it and then exit. Special characters:

> %   Name of current file.

> #   Name of previous file.

> *!!*   Last shell command.

| mark-letter command
> Not valid for all versions. Pipe fragment of file (from first line on screen to *mark-letter*) to *command*. *mark-letter* may also be:

> ^   Beginning of file.

> $ End of file.

> *., newline*
> > Current screen is piped.

Prompts

The prompt interprets certain sequences specially. Those beginning with % are always evaluated. Those beginning with ? are evaluated if certain conditions are true. Some prompts determine the position of particular lines on the screen. These sequences require that a method of determining that line be specified. See the -P option and the manpage for more information.

---

ln

ln [options] *file1 file2*

ln [*options*] *files directory*

Creates pseudonyms (links) for files, allowing them to be accessed by different names. In the Finder, links appear and work as aliases. In the first form, link *file1* to *file2*, where *file2* is usually a new filename. If *file2* is an existing file, it is removed first; if *file2* is an existing directory, a link named *file1* is created in that directory. In the second form, create links in *directory*, each link having the same name as the file specified.

Options

-f   Force the link to occur (don't prompt for overwrite permission).

-i   Interactive mode. Asks for permission to overwrite if the target file exists. This is the default.

-n, -h

     Don't overwrite existing files.

-s   Create a symbolic link. This lets you link across filesystems and also see the name of the link when you run *ls -l*. (Otherwise, you have to use *find -inum* to find any other names a file is linked to.)

-v   Verbose mode. Show each file as it gets processed.

locate

```
locate pattern
```

Searches a database of filenames and prints matches. *, ?, [, and] are treated specially; / and . are not. Matches include all files that contain *pattern*, unless *pattern* includes metacharacters, in which case *locate* requires an exact match.

The locate database file is */var/db/locate.database*, which by default is updated as part of the *weekly* system maintenance cron job.

lock

```
lock [options]
```

Place a lock on the current shell session, preventing anyone from typing to the prompt without first entering a password or waiting until the end of the timeout period.

Options

-p   Use the user's system password instead of prompting to create a new one-time password.

-t timeout

     Unlock the prompt in *timeout* minutes instead of the default 15 minutes.

lockfile

```
lockfile [options] filenames
```

Creates semaphore file(s), used to limit access to a file. When *lockfile* fails to create some of the specified files, it pauses for eight seconds and retries the last one on which it failed. The command processes flags as they are encountered (i.e., a flag that is specified after a file won't affect that file).

Options

-sleeptime

     Time *lockfile* waits before retrying after a failed creation attempt. Default is eight seconds.

-!   Invert return value. Useful in shell scripts.

-l lockout_time
> Time (in seconds) after a lockfile was last modified at which it will be removed by force. See also *-s*.

-ml, -mu
> If the permissions on the system mail spool directory allow it or if *lockfile* is suitably setgid, it can lock and unlock your system mailbox with the options *-ml* and *-mu*, respectively.

-r retries
> Stop trying to create *files* after *retries* retries. The default is -1 (never stop trying). When giving up, remove all created files.

-s suspend_time
> After a lockfile has been removed by force (see *-l*), a suspension of 16 seconds takes place by default. (This is intended to prevent the inadvertent immediate removal of any lockfile newly created by another program.) Use *-s* to change the default 16 seconds.

---

logger

logger [*options*] [*messages*]

Logs messages to the system log (*/var/log/system.log*). Command-line messages are logged if provided. Otherwise, messages are read and logged, line-by-line, from the file provided via *-f*. If no such file is given, *logger* reads messages from standard input.

Options
-f file
> Read and log messages from *file*.

-i Log the PID of the *logger* process with each message.

-p priority
> Log each message with the given *priority*. Priorities have the form *facility.level*. The default is *user.notice*. See *syslog(3)* for more information.

-s Also log messages to standard error.

-t tag
> Add *tag* to each message line.

Example
Warn about upcoming trouble:

```
$ logger -p user.emerg 'Intruder Alert! Intruder Alert!'
```

---

look

look [*options*] *string* [*file*]

Looks through a sorted file and prints all lines that begin with *string*. Words may be up to 256 characters long. This program is potentially faster than *fgrep* because it relies on the *file* being sorted already, and can thus do a binary search through the file, instead of reading it sequentially from beginning to end.

With no *file*, *look* searches */usr/share/dict/words* (the spelling dictionary) with options -*df*. This can be a handy way to look up a word in the dictionary if you only know the start of the word. If you can't remember how to spell "carburetor," try *look carbur* to see the 12 words in the dictionary that start "carbur."

Options

-*d*   Use dictionary order. Only letters, digits, spaces, and tabs are used in comparisons.

-*f*   Fold case; ignore case distinctions in comparisons.

-*t char*
   Use *char* as the termination character, i.e., ignore all characters to the right of *char*.

lp

lp [*options*] [*files*]

Sends *files* to the printer. With no arguments, prints standard input. Part of the Common Unix Printing System (CUPS).

Options

-*c*   Copy *files* to print spooler; if changes are made to *file* while it is still queued for printing, the printout is unaffected. This option has no effect when used with a CUPS server, which performs in a similar manner already.

-*d dest*
   Send output to destination printer named *dest*.

-*E*   Force an encrypted connection if supported by the print server.

-*h host*
   Send print job to the print server *host*, *localhost* by default.

-*H action*
   Print according to the named *action*: *hold* (notify before printing), *resume* (resume a held request), *immediate* (print next; privileged users only).

-*i IDs*
   Override *lp* options used for request *IDs* currently in the queue; specify new *lp* options after -*i*. For example, change the number of copies sent.

-*m*   Send mail after files are printed (not supported in CUPS as of Version 1.1.15).

-*n number*
   Specify the *number* of copies to print.

-*o options*
   Set one or more printer options. CUPS documentation describing these options is included with Mac OS X and viewable via a web browser at *http://127.0.0.1:631/ sum. html#STANDARD_OPTIONS*.

-*P list*
   Print only the page numbers specified in *list*.

-*q n* Print request with priority level *n*, increasing from 1 to 100. The default is 50.

-*s*   Suppress messages.

-t title
> Use *title* for the print job name.

-u username
> Cancel jobs belonging to *username*.

Example

Print five copies of a formatted manpage:

```
$ man -t niutil | lp -n 5
```

lpc

lpc [*command*]

Controls line printer; CUPS version. If executed without a command, *lpc* generates a prompt (lpc>) and accepts commands from standard input.

Commands

?, help [commands]
> Get a list of commands or help on specific commands.

exit, quit
> Exit *lpc*.

status queue
> Return the status of the specified print queue.

lpq

lpq [*options*]

Shows the printer queue. Part of the Common Unix Printing System (CUPS).

Options

+interval
> Repeat the *lpq* command every *interval* seconds until the queue is empty.

-a   Show the jobs in the queues for all printers.

-E   Force an encrypted connection if supported by the print server.

-l   Be verbose.

-P printer
> Show queue for the specified *printer*.

lpr

lpr [*options*] *files*

Sends *files* to the printer spool queue. Part of the Common Unix Printing System (CUPS).

Options

-C, -J, -T title
  Use *title* for the print job name.

-E Force an encrypted connection if supported by the print server.

-l Assume print job is preformatted for printing and apply no further filtering. Same as *-o raw*.

-o options
  Set one or more printer options. CUPS documentation describing these options is included with Mac OS X and viewable via a web browser at *http://127.0.0.1:631/sum. html#STANDARD_OPTIONS*.

-p Print text files with pretty printing, adding a shaded header with date, time, job name, and page number. Same as *-o prettyprint*.

-P printer
  Output to *printer* instead of system default.

-r Remove the file upon completion of spooling.

-#num
  Print *num* copies of each listed file (100 maximum).

lprm

    lprm [options] [jobnum]

Removes a print job from the print spool queue. You must specify a job number or numbers, which can be obtained from *lpq*. Used with no arguments, *lprm* removes the current job. Part of the Common Unix Printing System (CUPS).

Options

-E Force an encrypted connection if supported by the print server.

-P printer
  Specify printer name. Normally, the default printer or printer specified in the PRINTER environment variable is used.

- Remove all jobs in the spool.

lpstat

    lpstat [options]

Prints the *lp* print queue status. With options that take a *list* argument, omitting the list produces all information for that option. *list* can be separated by commas or, if enclosed in double quotes, by spaces.

Options

-a [list]
  Show whether the *list* of printer or class names is accepting requests.

-c [list]
  Show information about printer classes named in *list*.

-d Show the default printer destination.

-E   Force an encrypted connection if supported by the print server.

-h *host*
:   Communicate with print server *host*, *localhost* by default.

-l   Show a long listing of classes, jobs, or printers when used before *-c*, *-o*, or *-p*, respectively.

-o *[list]*
:   Show job queues for printers in *list* or all printers if *list* isn't given.

-p *[list]*
:   Show the status of printers named in *list* or all printers if *list* isn't given.

-r   Show whether the print scheduler is on or off.

-R   Show the job's position in the print queue when used before *-o*.

-s   Summarize the print status (shows almost everything). Same as *-d -c -v*.

-t   Show all status information (reports everything). Same as *-r -d -c -v -a -p*.

-u *user*
:   Show request status for *user* or all users if user isn't given.

-v *[list]*
:   Show device associated with each printer named in *list* or all printers if *list* isn't given.

-W *completed|not-completed*
:   Only show completed or not completed print jobs, as appropriate. Option must appear before the *-o* option.

---

ls

```
ls [options] [names]
```

List contents of directories. If no *names* are given, list the files in the current directory. With one or more *names*, list files contained in a directory *name* or that match a file *name*. *names* can include filename metacharacters. The options let you display a variety of information in different formats. The most useful options include *-F*, *-R*, *-l*, and *-s*. Some options don't make sense together (e.g., *-u* and *-c*).

Options

-1   Print one entry per line of output.

-a   List all files, including the normally hidden files whose names begin with a period.

-A   List all files, including the normally hidden files whose names begin with a period. Don't include the . and .. directories.

-b   Print nonprintable characters with their C-style escape codes, such as \n for line feed and \t for tab. Characters without an escape code print with their octal values, such as \xxx.

-B   Print nonprintable characters with their octal codes, such as \xxx.

-c   List files by status change time (not creation/modification time).

-C   List files in columns (the default format).

-d   Report only on the directory, not its contents.

-e	Print the ACL for the file, if present.
-f	Print directory contents in exactly the order in which they are stored, without attempting to sort them.
-F	Flag filenames by appending / to directories, * to executable files, @ to symbolic links, | to FIFOs, = to sockets, and % to whiteouts.
-G	Enable colorized output.
-h	List sizes from the -l option with units: bytes, kilobytes, etc.
-H	Follow symbolic links.
-i	List the inode for each file.
-k	If file sizes are being listed, print them in kilobytes.
-l	Long format listing (includes permissions, owner, size, modification time, etc.).
-L	Used with -l. List the file or directory referenced by a symbolic link rather than the link itself.
-m	Print names across the screen, separated by commas.
-n	Used with -l. Displays GID and UID numbers instead of owner and group names.
-o	Used with -l. Shows file flags (see chflags).
-p	Mark directories by appending / to them.
-q	Show nonprinting characters as ? (the default when printing to the Terminal).
-r	List files in reverse order (by name or by time).
-R	Recursively list subdirectories as well as the specified (or current) directory.
-s	Print size of the files in blocks.
-S	Sort by file size, largest to smallest.
-t	Sort files according to modification time (newest first).
-T	Used with -l. Show complete time and date information.
-u	Sort files according to the file access time.
-x	List files in rows going across the screen.
-v	Don't edit nonprinting characters for output (the default when not printing to the Terminal).
-W	Show whiteouts when listing directories on mounted filesystems.

Examples

List all files in the current directory and their sizes; use multiple columns and mark special files:

    $ ls -asCF

List the status of directories /bin and /etc:

    $ ls -ld /bin /etc

List C-source files in the current directory, the oldest first:

    $ ls -rt *.c

Count the nonhidden files in the current directory:

    $ ls | wc -l

lsbom

```
lsbom [options] bomfile
```

Prints the contents of a binary *BOM* ("bill of materials") file (*bomfile*) in human-readable format. By default, *lsbom* prints a line of information for each file listed in the *BOM*, as in this example:

```
./Documents/Install Log.txt 100664 0/80 1182 4086739704
```

This line shows, in order, the plain file's pathname, permissions (modes) in octal format, owner and GIDs, size, and checksum. When listing symbolic links, *lsbom* reports the size and checksum of the link itself, and also lists the pathname of the linked file. Device file listings include the device number, but not the file size or checksum.

Options

-b   List only block devices.

-c   List only character devices.

-d   List only directories.

-f   List only files.

-l   List only symbolic links.

-m   When listing plain files, also display their modification dates.

-s   Print only the file pathnames.

-x   Don't show the permissions of directories and symbolic links.

-arch arch
> When listing fat binary files, show only the size and checksums of the code for chip type *arch*. Possible values for *arch* include *ppc*, *m68k*, *i386*, *hppa*, and *sparc*.

-p parameters
> Limit the content of each line as specified by *parameters*, which you can compose using any of the options in this list (but none more than once):

c   Show the checksum.

f   Show the filename.

F   Show the filename within quotes.

g   Show the GID.

G   Show the group name.

m   Show the octal file mode.

M   Show the symbolic file mode.

s   Show the file size.

S   Show the file size, formatted with commas.

t   Show the modification date in POSIX format (seconds since the epoch).

T   Show the modification date in human-readable format.

u   Show the UID.

U   Show the username.

/   Show the UID and GID, separated with a slash.

?   Show the username and group name, separated with a slash.

Examples

List the contents of *BOM* file *Installer.bom*:

    $ **lsbom Installer.bom**

List only the paths of the directories in the *BOM file*:

    $ **lsbom -s -d Installer.bom**

Format lines similar to those shown by the *ls -l* command:

    $ **lsbom -p MUGsTf Installer.bom**

lsof

lsof [*options*] [*pathname*]

Lists open files, including regular files, directories, special files, libraries, network files, and others. The following descriptions and examples cover *lsof*'s basic operation; for a complete description, refer to *lsof*'s manpage.

Used without arguments, *lsof* lists all files opened by all active processes. Used with *pathname*, *lsof* lists the open files in the given filesystem mount point. If *pathname* is a file, *lsof* lists any processes having the given file open.

Options

-a   Recognize all list options as joined with "and" instead of the default "or."

-b   Avoid *stat*, *lstat*, and *readlink* functions, since they may block.

-c chars
> List files opened by processes whose command names begin with characters *chars*. *chars* can contain a regular expression if put between slashes (/). You can further define the expression by following the closing slash with *b* to denote a basic expression, *i* to denote a case-insensitive expression, or *x* to denote an extended expression (the default).

+c width
> Print up to *width* characters of the command associated with a process. If *width* is 0, all characters are printed.

+d pathname
> List all open instances of the files and directories in *pathname*, including the directory *pathname* itself. This option doesn't search below the level of *pathname*, however.

+D pathname
> List all open instances of the files and directories in *pathname*, including directory *pathname* itself, searching recursively to the full depth of directory *pathname*.

-i [address]
> List all Internet files, or if specified, those with an Internet address matching *address*. Specify *address* as [*protocol*][@*host*][:*port*].

version
> Specify IP version; 4 for IPv4, the default. IPv6 is not supported in this version of *lsof*.

protocol
> Specify TCP or UDP.

host
> Specify a host by name or numerically.

port
> Specify a port number or service name.

-l   Print UID numbers, instead of login names.

-n   Prints IP addresses instead of doing reverse name lookups. May speed up output.

-p [pid]
> List files opened by processes whose IDs are specified in the comma-separated list *pid*.

+|-r [n]
> Operate in repeat mode. *lsof* lists open files as specified by the other options and then repeats the listing every 15 seconds (or *n* seconds, if specified). If *r* is prefixed with +, *lsof* repeats until the selection options produce no files to list. If *r* is prefixed with -, *lsof* repeats until the process is terminated with an interrupt or quit signal.

-u [user]
> List files opened by users whose login names or UIDs are in the comma-separated list *user*. You can also specify a user whose files aren't to be listed by prefixing *user* with ^.

Examples

List processes that have your home directory opened:

    $ lsof ~

List all open files in your home directory:

    $ lsof +D

List the files opened by processes whose names begin with "i" and whose owner is "bob":

    $ lsof -a -c i -u bob

List files using TCP port 80, repeating every two seconds until *lsof* is terminated:

    $ lsof -i TCP:80 -r 2

---

machine

machine

Returns the system's processor type. A returned value of ppc750 indicates a PowerPC G3 chip, and ppc7400 indicates a PowerPC G4, for example.

---

mailq

mailq [*option*]

Lists all messages in the *sendmail* mail queue. Equivalent to *sendmail -bp*.

Option
-v   Verbose mode.

---

mailstat

`mailstat [options] [logfile]`

Displays mail-arrival statistics. Parses a *procmail*-generated logfile and displays a summary about the messages delivered to all folders (total size, average size, etc.). The logfile is renamed as *logfile.old*, and a new *logfile* of size 0 is created.

Options

-k   Keep logfile intact.

-l   Long display format.

-m   Merge any errors into one line.

-o   Use the old logfile.

-s   Silent in case of no mail.

-t   Terse display format.

makekey

`makekey`

Produces *crypt* password hashes. This can be used to automatically populate a password database from known passwords, or to make hashes of prospective passwords that can be subjected to cracking attempts before being put into use.

Options/usage

makekey takes no command-line arguments. It accepts a character string on standard input, consisting of an eight-character password combined with a two-character *salt*, which is used to permute the DES password encryption algorithm. (Use *man crypt* for more information.) It prints a 13-character string to standard output, with the first two characters being the salt, and the other eleven characters being the password hash. The entire string is suitable for use as the password field in a standard Unix */etc/passwd*-format file or as the value of the passwd property in an Open Directory entry for a user employing Basic authentication.

Example

```
$ echo password12 | /usr/libexec/makekey
12CsGd8FRcMSM
```

man

`man [options] [section] [title]`

Displays information from the online reference manuals. *man* locates and prints the named *title* from the designated reference *section*.

Options

-a   Show all pages matching title.

-C filename
    Uses *filename* as the config file, instead of */usr/share/misc/man.conf*.

-d   Display debugging information. Suppress actual printing of manpages.

-f   Same as *whatis* command.

-h   Print help and exit.

-k   Same as *apropos* command.

-m systems
> Search *systems'* manpages. *systems* should be a comma-separated list.

-M path
> Search for manpages in *path*. Ignore -m option.

-p preprocessors
> Preprocess manpages with *preprocessors* before turning them over to *nroff, troff,* or *groff.* Always runs *soelim* first.

-P pager
> Select paging program *pager* to display the entry.

-S sections
> Define colon-separated list of *sections* to search.

-t   Format the manpage with *troff.*

-w   Print pathnames of entries on standard output.

Section names

Manpages are divided into sections, depending on their intended audience:

1   Executable programs or shell commands.

2   System calls (functions provided by the kernel).

3   Library calls (functions within system libraries).

4   Special files (usually found in */dev*).

5   File formats and conventions.

6   Games.

7   Macro packages and conventions.

8   System administration commands (usually only for a privileged user).

9   Kernel routines (nonstandard).

---

md5

md5 [*options*] [-s *string*] [*files*]

Calculates an *md5* checksum value of the text provided in *string, files,* or from standard input. By default, when *string* or *files* is given, md5 prints those values first, followed by the checksum.

Options

-s string
> Calculate a checksum of the text in *string.*

-p   Print the standard input followed by the checksum.

-q   Operate in quiet mode. Print only the checksum.

-r   Reverse the order of the output when string or files is given (checksum first).

-t   Run the built-in speed test, which calculates a checksum from 100 MB of data.

-x   Run the built-in test suite, which calculates checksums from seven short strings.

mDNS

```
mDNS [-E | -F | -A | -U | -N | -T | -M]

mDNS -B type domain

mDNS -L service_name _app_protocol._transport_protocol domain

mDNS -R service_name _app_protocol._transport_protocol domain port [string]...
```

A basic client for Bonjour multicast DNS (mDNS), primarily used for testing local mDNS service. When invoked with no arguments, it prints a usage statement to standard error. In most instances, the command doesn't return on its own, so you'll need to use Ctrl-C to break out.

When registering or looking up a name like *website._http._tcp.local.*, *website* is the *service_name*, *http* is the *app_protocol*, *tcp* is the *transport_protocol*, and *local* is the *domain*. For example, to register such a service:

```
% mDNS -R website _http._tcp local 80 "my web site"
```

Options

-A   Test mDNS by repeatedly adding, updating, and then deleting an HINFO resource record for *Test._testupdate._tcp.local.*.

-B   Browse for services (although this doesn't seem to work).

-E   Discover and list domains recommended for registration of services.

-F   Discover and list domains recommended for browsing of services.

-L   Look up a service, displaying its host address, port number, and TXT records if found.

-M   Test mDNS by registering a service (*Test._testdualtxt._tcp.local.*) with multiple TXT resource records.

-N   Test mDNS by registering a service (*Test._testupdate._tcp.local.*) with a large NULL resource record.

-R   Register a service.

-T   Test mDNS by registering a service (*Test._testlargetxt._tcp.local.*) with a large TXT resource record.

-U   Test mDNS by repeatedly updating a TXT resource record for *Test._testupdate._tcp.local.*.

mDNSResponder

```
mDNSResponder [-d]
```

The server for Bonjour multicast DNS (mDNS). It's started by the *mDNSResponder* startup item, creates a PID file in */var/run/*, and responds to TERM and INT signals by quitting cleanly.

Option

-d   Run in debug mode, preventing daemonization, although it doesn't appear to be particularly useful in this state.

mdcheckschema

mdcheckschema *filename(s)*

Validates the *mdimport* schema file specified to see if it can be parsed.

mdfind

mdfind [*-live*] [*-onlyin directory*] *query*

Searches the Spotlight metadata for items matching query, and returns a list of files for further manipulation.

Options

-0   Displays each entry followed by a null character instead of a linefeed. This is usually used for feeding into *xargs -0*.

-live
    After displaying the list of files, displays a count of files matching the query. The count is updated each time the count is updated. Use Control-C to cancel.

-onlyin dir
    Limit the directories searched to *dir*.

Common attributes

The following are attributes commonly set by the metadata indexer. These attributes are also used by the *mdls* command. You can use *mdimport -A* to list all attributes supported by indexers in your system.

kMDItemAttributeChangeDate
    The date and time that a metadata attribute was last changed.

kMDItemAudiences
    The intended audience of the file.

kMDItemAuthors
    The authors of the document.

kMDItemCity
    The document's city of origin.

kMDItemComment
    Comments regarding the document.

kMDItemContactKeywords
    A list of contacts associated with the document.

kMDItemContentCreationDate
    The document's creation date.

kMDItemContentModificationDate
    Last modification date of the document.

kMDItemContentType

The qualified content type of the document, such as *com.adobe.pdf* for PDF files and *com.apple.protected-mpeg-4-audio* for an Apple Advanced Audio Coding (AAC) files.

kMDItemContributors

Contributors to this document.

kMDItemCopyright

The copyright owner.

kMDItemCountry

The document's country of origin.

kMDItemCoverage

The scope of the document, such as a geographical location or a period of time.

kMDItemCreator

The application that created the document.

kMDItemDescription

A description of the document.

kMDItemDueDate

Due date for the item represented by the document.

kMDItemDurationSeconds

Duration (in seconds) of the document.

kMDItemEmailAddresses

Email addresses associated with this document.

kMDItemEncodingApplications

The name of the application, such as "Acrobat Distiller", that was responsible for converting the document in its current form.

kMDItemFinderComment

This contains any Finder comments for the document.

kMDItemFonts

Fonts used in the document.

kMDItemHeadline

A headline-style synopsis of the document.

kMDItemInstantMessageAddresses

IM addresses/screen names associated with the document.

kMDItemInstructions

Special instructions or warnings associated with this document.

kMDItemKeywords

Keywords associated with the document.

kMDItemKind

Describes the kind of document, such as "iCal Event."

kMDItemLanguages

Language of the document.

kMDItemLastUsedDate

The date and time the document was last opened.

kMDItemNumberOfPages

Page count of this document.

kMDItemOrganizations
> The organization that created the document.

kMDItemPageHeight
> Height of the document's page layout in points.

kMDItemPageWidth
> Width of the document's page layout in points.

kMDItemPhoneNumbers
> Phone numbers associated with the document.

kMDItemProjects
> Names of projects (other documents such as an iMovie project) that this document is associated with.

kMDItemPublishers
> The publisher of the document.

kMDItemRecipients
> The recipient of the document.

kMDItemRights
> A link to the statement of rights (such as a Creative Commons or old-school copyright license) that govern the use of the document.

kMDItemSecurityMethod
> Encryption method used on the document.

kMDItemStarRating
> Rating of the document (as in the iTunes "star" rating).

kMDItemStateOrProvince
> The document's state or province of origin.

kMDItemTitle
> The title.

kMDItemVersion
> The version number.

kMDItemWhereFroms
> Where the document came from, such as a URI or email address.

---

mdimport

mdimport [*options*] *file* | *directory*

Imports metadata from files or filesystem hierarchies.

Options

-A   Prints a list of all attributes currently supported and exits.

-d *level* | *category*
> Specifies debug level and categories. Valid *levels* are 1–4, and *category* can be *import-terse*, *import-input*, *import-output*, *import-warnings*, *import-verbose*, or *plugin-loading*. This option can be repeated.

-f   Force the files to be scanned, ignoring the rules for path filtering.

-I   Ignore Finder comments.

-L   Prints a list of all importers and exits.

-n   Don't actually set attributes on the file.

-p   Print performance information for the run. Seems to be identical to -V.

-r *importer*
      Reimport the files previously imported by *importer*.

-V   Print timing information for the run. Seems to be identical to -p.

-w *msecs*
      Wait for *msecs* milliseconds between scanning files.

-x   Print the schema file, then exit.

mdls

mdls [-name *attribute*] *filenames*

Displays the metadata tags for each of the *filenames*.

Options

-name *attribute*
      Only display the given attribute. This option is repeatable. See the *mdfind* entry
      for a list of common attributes.

-live
      After displaying the list of files, displays a count of files matching the query. The
      count is updated each time the count is updated. Use Control-C to cancel.

-onlyin *dir*
      Limit the directories searched to *dir*.

mdutil

mdutil [*options*] *volume*

Options

-p   Publishes the local copies of the metadata to their real drives.

-E   Erases the metadata for the volume. Mac OS X can then rebuild the data, if
      indexing is still on.

-i on | off
      Sets the indexing status for the volume.

-s   Show the indexing status of the volume.

merge

merge [*options*] *file1 file2 file3*

Performs a three-way file merge. *merge* incorporates all changes that lead from *file2* to
file3 and puts the results into *file1*. *merge* is useful for combining separate changes
to an original. Suppose *file2* is the original, and both *file1* and *file3* are modifications of *file2*. Then *merge* combines both changes. A conflict occurs if both *file1* and
file3 have changes in a common segment of lines. If a conflict is found, *merge*

normally outputs a warning and puts brackets around the conflict, with lines preceded by `<<<<<<<` and `>>>>>>>`. A typical conflict looks like this:

```
<<<<<<< file1
relevant lines from file1
=======
relevant lines from file3
>>>>>>> file3
```

If there are conflicts, the user should edit the result and delete one of the alternatives.

Options

-A Output conflicts using the -A style of *diff3*. This merges all changes leading from *file2* to *file3* into *file1*, and generates the most verbose output.

-e Don't warn about conflicts.

-E Output conflict information in a less verbose style than -A; this is the default.

-L *label*

Specify up to three labels to be used in place of the corresponding filenames in conflict reports. That is:

```
merge -L x -L y -L z file_a file_b file_c
```

generates output that looks as if it came from *x*, *y*, and *z* instead of from *file_a*, *file_b*, and *file_c*.

-p Send results to standard output instead of overwriting *file1*.

-q Quiet; don't warn about conflicts.

-V Print version number.

mkbom

```
mkbom [option] sourcedir bomfile
```

Creates a bill-of-materials, or *BOM* file. The new *BOM*, named in *bomfile*, lists the full contents of directory *sourcedir*. Included with each listing in the *BOM* is information about the listed file or directory, such as its permissions, size, and checksum. The Mac OS X Installer uses *BOMs* to determine what files to install, delete, or upgrade. See also *ditto* and *lsbom* for more information about working with *BOM* files.

Option

-s Create a simplified *BOM*, which includes only the pathnames of the listed files and directories.

mkdir

```
mkdir [options] directories
```

Creates one or more *directories*. You must have write permission in the parent directory to create a directory. See also *rmdir*. The default mode of the new directory is 0777, modified by the system or user's *umask*.

Options

-m Set the access *mode* for new directories. See *chmod* for an explanation of acceptable formats for *mode*.

-p Create intervening parent directories if they don't exist.

-v Verbose mode. Print directories as they're created.

Examples

Create a read-only directory named *personal*:

```
$ mkdir -m 444 personal
```

The following sequence:

```
$ mkdir work; cd work
$ mkdir junk; cd junk
$ mkdir questions; cd ../..
```

can be accomplished by typing this:

```
$ mkdir -p work/junk/questions
```

---

more

more [*options*] [*files*]

Displays the named *files* on a terminal, one screen at a time. See *less* for an alternative to *more*. Some commands can be preceded by a number.

Options

+*num*
    Begin displaying at line number *num*.

-*num*
    Set screen size to *num* lines.

+/*pattern*
    Begin displaying two lines before *pattern*.

-c Repaint screen from top instead of scrolling.

-d Display the prompt "Press space to continue, 'q' to quit" in response to illegal commands.

-f Count logical rather than screen lines. Useful when long lines wrap past the width of the screen.

-l Ignore form-feed (Control-L) characters.

-p Page through the file by clearing each window instead of scrolling. This is sometimes faster.

-r Force display of control characters, in the form ^x.

-s Squeeze; display multiple blank lines as one.

-u Suppress underline characters.

Commands

All commands in *more* are based on *vi* commands. An argument can precede many commands.

numSPACE
> Display next screen of text, or *num* more lines.

numz
> Display next lines of text, and redefine a screen to *num* lines. Default is one screen.

numRETURN
> Display *num* lines of text, and redefine a screen to *num* lines. Default is one line.

numd, ^D
> Scroll *num* lines of text, and redefine scroll size to *num* lines. Default scroll is 11 lines.

q, Q,
> Quit.

nums
> Skip forward *num* lines of text.

numf
> Skip forward *num* screens of text.

numb, ^B
> Skip backward *num* screens of text.

'
> Return to point where previous search began.

=
> Print number of current line.

/pattern
> Search for *pattern*, skipping to *num*th occurrence if an argument is specified.

n
> Repeat last search, skipping to *num*th occurrence if an argument is specified.

!cmd
> Invoke shell, and execute *cmd* in it.

v
> Invoke *vi* editor on the file, at the current line.

h
> Display the help information.

:n
> Skip to next file, skipping to *num*th file if an argument is specified.

:p
> Skip to previous file, skipping to *num*th file if an argument is specified.

:f
> Print current filename and line number.

.
> Re-execute previous command.

Examples

Page through *file* in "clear" mode and display prompts:

```
$ more -cd file
```

Format *doc* to the screen, removing underlines:

```
$ nroff doc | more -u
```

View the manpage for the *grep* command; begin near the word "BUGS" and compress extra whitespace:

```
$ man grep | more /BUGS -s
```

mount

mount [-t *type*]

mount [-d] [-f] [-r] [-u] [-v] [-w] { [-t *types*] -a | *special* | *mount_point* | [-o *mount_options*] *special mount_point*]

Integrates volumes on local storage devices and network file servers into the system's directory hierarchy.

The first form of the command merely lists currently mounted volumes.

The second form of the command mounts volumes, with one of four possible sets of arguments. The *-a* flag causes all filesystems (possibly limited to those of a certain *type*) listed in */etc/fstab* or in the */mounts* directory of an Open Directory domain to be mounted, with the options given in the configuration. If only *special* or *mount_point* is provided, the associated *fstab* or Open Directory entry is used to determine what's mounted. The final alternative specifies both *special* and *mount_point*, and a possible list of options.

Options

-*a*   Attempt to mount all filesystems listed in *fstab* or Open Directory, other than those marked with the *noauto* option.

-*d*   Disable the actual mount, but do everything else. May be useful when used with the *-v* flag in a troubleshooting situation.

-*f*   When using the *-u* flag and changing the status of a read-write filesystem to read-only, force the revocation of write access. Normally the change is denied if any files are open for writing at the time of the request.

-*o*   Take a comma-separated list of options, which may include *async*, *noauto*, *nodev*, *noexec*, *nosuid*, *union*, and others. See the *mount* manpage for details.

-*r*   Mount the filesystem for read-only access.

-*t*   Restrict the use of the command to filesystems of the specified types presented in a comma-separated list, which may include *hfs*, *ufs*, *afp*, *nfs*, or others.

-*u*   When used with *-o*, *-r*, or *-w*, change the status of a currently mounted filesystem to match the newly provided options.

-*v*   Enable verbose output.

-*w*   Mount the filesystem for read-write access.

special
>The form of this argument is particular to the type of filesystem being mounted, and could be a disk device name, a fixed string, or something involving a server name and directory. See the individual *mount_type* entries for details.

mount_point
>The directory on which the filesystem is mounted.

mount_afp

mount_afp [-i] [-o *mount_options*] afp:/[at]/[*username*[;AUTH=*auth_
method*][:*password*]@]*afp_server*[:*port_or_zone*]/*share_name mount_point*

Mounts Apple Filing Protocol (AFP) shares as filesystem volumes. It takes an AFP URL
and a mount point as arguments.

Options

-*i*   Prompt for password if not specified in the AFP URL.

-*o*   Takes -*o* options as listed in the *mount* manpage.

username
> The name to use for authentication to the AFP server. *username* may be null if the
> NO%20USER%20AUTHENT authentication method is used.

auth_method
> The   name   of   the   authentication   method   used.   Examples   include
> NO%20USER%20AUTHENT (no authentication required for guest-accessible shares),
> CLEARTXT%20PASSWRD (clear-text password), 2-WAY%20RANDNUM (two-way random
> number exchange), and CLIENT%20KRB%20V2 (Kerberos).

password
> The password to use for authentication. Note that specifying this on the
> command line exposes the password in a process listing.

afp_server
> The hostname or IP address of an AFP server.

port_or_zone
> A TCP port number if accessing the share over TCP/IP, or a zone name if
> accessing it over AppleTalk.

share_name
> The name of the AFP share you wish to access.

mount_point
> The directory on which the filesystem is mounted.

mount_autofs

mount_autofs [-f *server*:*pathname*] *mount_point*

Mounts an automounted filesystem on the specified mount point.

Options

-*f*   Specifies the share to be mounted.

server
> The hostname or IP address of a file server.

pathname
> The pathname of the share you wish to access.

mount_point
> The directory on which the filesystem will be mounted.

mount_cd9660

`mount_cd9660 [-e] [-g] [-j] [-r] [-s sector_num] device mount_point`

Mounts ISO-9660 CD-ROM filesystems into the directory hierarchy.

Options

-e   Enable extended attributes.

-g   Disable stripping version numbers from files, making all versions visible.

-j   Disable Joliet extensions.

-r   Disable Rockridge extensions.

-s   Start the filesystem at the specified sector (given in 2048-byte blocks). Normally this is determined automatically.

device
> The CD device filename, e.g., */dev/disk1s2*.

mount_point
> The directory on which the filesystem is mounted.

mount_cddafs

`mount_cddafs [-o mount_options] device mount_point`

Mounts CDDAFS audio CD filesystems into the directory hierarchy.

Options

-o   Take *-o* options as listed in the *mount* manpage.

device
> The CD device filename, e.g., */dev/disk1s2*.

mount_point
> The directory on which the filesystem is mounted.

mount_devfs

`mount_devfs [-o mount_options] devfs mount_point`

Mounts the *devfs* filesystem in */dev*, where block and character device special files exist.

Options

-o   Take *-o* options as listed in the *mount* manpage. Not normally used for *mount_devfs*.

mount_point
> The directory on which the filesystem is mounted, normally */dev*.

mount_fdesc

mount_fdesc [-o *mount_options*] fdesc *mount_point*

Mounts the *fdesc* filesystem in */dev*. It contains the *fd* subdirectory, which contains one entry for each file descriptor held open by the process reading the contents of the directory. It also contains *stdin*, *stdout*, and *stderr*, which are symlinks to *fd/0*, *fd/1*, and *fd/2*, respectively; and *tty*, a reference to the controlling terminal for the process.

Options

-o   Takes -o options as listed in the *mount* manpage. Normally includes the *union* option, which prevents mounting over and obscuring the *devfs* filesystem in */dev*.

mount_point
>The directory on which the filesystem is mounted, normally */dev*.

mount_ftp

mount_ftp [-o *mount_options*] [ftp://][*username*:*password*@]*ftp_server*:*port_num*[/ *pathname*] *mount_point*

Mounts FTP archives as filesystem volumes.

Options

-o   Take -o options as listed in the *mount* manpage.

username
>The login name to use with an FTP server that requires authentication.

password
>The password to use with an FTP server that requires authentication. Note that specifying this on the command line exposes the password in a process listing.

ftp_server
>The hostname or IP address of an FTP server.

port_num
>The port number on which the server offers FTP service.

pathname
>The path to the directory you wish to access on the FTP server, relative to the site's default FTP root directory (e.g., */Library/FTPServer/FTPRoot* on Mac OS X Server). Defaults to */*.

mount_point
>The directory on which the filesystem is mounted. It must be an absolute pathname.

mount_hfs

mount_hfs [-w] [-o *mount_options*] *device mount_point*

mount_hfs [-e] [-x] [-u *user_ID*] [-g *group_ID*] [-m *mode*] [-o *mount_options*] *device mount_point*

Mounts HFS and HFS+ filesystems into the directory hierarchy. The first form is applicable to HFS+ volumes, the second to HFS.

Options

-e   Set the character set encoding. Defaults to *Roman*.

-g   Set group ownership on files. Defaults to the mount point's group owner.

-m   Set the maximum permissions for files. The argument is an octal mode, as described in the *chmod* manpage.

-o   Take *-o* options as listed in the *mount* manpage.

-u   Set ownership on files. Defaults to the mount point's owner.

-w   Mount an HFS+ volume with its HFS wrapper, if one exists. An HFS wrapper is required for the volume to boot Mac OS 9.

-x   Disable execute permissions.

device
> The disk device filename, e.g., */dev/disk0s5*.

mount_point
> The directory on which the filesystem is mounted.

mount_msdos

mount_msdos [-l | -s | -9] [-W *filename*] [-L *locale*] [-u *user_ID*] [-g *group_ID*] [-m *mode*] [-o *mount_options*] *device 1q*

Mounts DOS FAT filesystems into the directory hierarchy.

Options

-9   Ignore files with Win95 long filenames and special attributes. This option may result in filesystem inconsistencies, so it's better to use *-s*.

-g   Set group ownership on files in the volume. Defaults to the mount point's group owner.

-l   List and generate long filenames and separate creation, modification, and access dates on files. This is the default if any long filenames exist in the volume's root directory, and neither *-s* nor *-9* have been specified.

-L   Set the locale for character set conversions. Defaults to *ISO 8859-1*.

-m   Set the maximum permissions for files in the volume. The argument is an octal mode, as described in the *chmod* manpage.

-o   Take *-o* options as listed in the *mount* manpage.

-s   Ignore and disable generation of long filenames and separate creation, modification, and access dates on files. This is the default if no long filenames exist in the volume's root directory and *-l* has not been specified.

-u   Set ownership on files in the volume. Defaults to the mount point's owner.

-W   Specify a file containing character set conversion tables.

device
> The disk device filename, e.g., */dev/disk0s5*.

mount_point
> The directory on which the filesystem is mounted.

mount_nfs

mount_nfs [*nfs_mount_options*] [-o *mount_options*] *nfs_server:pathname mount_point*

Mounts Network File System (NFS) exports as filesystem volumes. *mount_nfs* can take a large number of options, most of which offer knobs to tune the performance of NFS mounts. Only a few are described in the "Options" section; see the manpage for full details.

Options

-*b*   After an initial mount attempt fails, fork off a background process to continue trying the mount.

-*i*   Make the mount interruptible, so that processes failing to access the mount can be terminated, instead of getting stuck in an uninterruptible state waiting on I/O.

-*K*   Enable Kerberos authentication.

-*m*   Specify a Kerberos realm to use with the -*K* option. Takes a realm name as an argument.

-*o*   Takes -*o* options as listed in the *mount* manpage.

-*s*   Make the mount soft, so that processes failing to access the mount eventually receive an error, instead of getting interminably stuck waiting on I/O.

-*T*   Enable the use of TCP as the underlying network transport protocol, instead of the default UDP.

nfs_server
    The hostname or IP address of an NFS server.

pathname
    The pathname of the NFS export you wish to access.

mount_point
    The directory on which the filesystem is mounted.

mount_ntfs

mount_ntfs [-a] [-i] [-W *filename*] [-u *user_ID*] [-g *group_ID*] [-m *mode*]
[-o *mount_options*] *device mount_point*

Mounts NTFS filesystems into the directory hierarchy.

Options

-*a*   Filenames are mapped to DOS 8.3 format.

-*g*   Set group ownership on files in the volume. Defaults to the mount point's group owner.

-*i*   Cause filename lookups to be case insensitive.

-*m*   Set the maximum permissions for files in the volume. The argument is an octal mode, as described in the *chmod* manpage.

-*o*   Takes -*o* options as listed in the *mount* manpage.

-*s*   Turn on case sensitivity on name lookups.

-*u*   Set ownership on files in the volume. Defaults to the mount point's owner.

-W Specify a file containing character set conversion tables.

device
> The disk device filename, e.g., */dev/disk0s5*.

mount_point
> The directory on which the filesystem is mounted.

mount_smbfs

```
mount_smbfs { -h | -v }
mount_smbfs [-u username_or_ID] [-g groupname_or_ID] [-f mode] [-d mode]
[-I hostname_or_IP] [-n long] [-N] [-U username] [-W workgroup_name]
[-O c_user[:c_group]/s_user[:s_group]] [-M c_mode[/s_mode]] [-R num_retries]
[-T timeout]  [-o mount_options] [-x max_mounts] //
[workgroup;][username[:password]@]smb_server[/share_name] mount_point
```

Mounts Server Message Block (SMB) shares as filesystem volumes. It takes a share UNC and a mount point as arguments.

mount_smbfs can use the same configuration files used by *smbutil*: either *.nsmbrc* in the user's home directory or the global */usr/local/etc/nsmb.conf*, which overrides per-user files. The following example *.nsmbrc* demonstrates some of the available parameters:

```
[default]
username=leonvs
# NetBIOS name server
nbns=192.168.1.3

[VAMANA]
# server IP address
addr=192.168.1.6
workgroup=TEST

[VAMANA:LEONVS]
password= $$178465324253e0c07
```

The file consists of sections, each with a heading in brackets. Besides the [default] section, headings have a server name to which the parameters in the section apply, and can also include a username and a share name.

 Sections of the configuration file may not be read properly unless the hostnames and usernames in the section headings are rendered in uppercase characters.

All sections and parameter definitions in *.nsmbrc* are optional; everything can be specified right on the *mount_smbfs* command line. It may come in handy for providing passwords for automated connections, when prompting for a password (which is the most secure method of providing it) is impractical. The value of the password parameter can be a clear-text password, but in this example, it is derived from the output of *smbutil crypt password*. While that's better than clear text, don't trust the encryption too much, as it's fairly weak. Make sure you restrict permissions on *.nsmbrc* to prevent others from reading your passwords.

Options

-d   Specify directory permissions on the mounted volume, which default to the same as file permissions, plus an execute bit whenever a read bit is set. The argument is an octal mode, as described in the *chmod* manpage.

-f   Specify file permissions on the mounted volume, which default to the same as those set on the mount point. The argument is an octal mode, as described in the *chmod* manpage.

-g   Specify group ownership for files and directories on the mounted volume, which defaults to the same as that set on the mount point.

-h   Print a brief usage statement to standard error.

-I   Avoid NetBIOS name resolution, connecting directly to the hostname or IP address specified as an argument.

-M   Assign access rights to the SMB connection.

-n   With an argument of *long*, disable support for long filenames, restricting them to the "8.3" naming standard.

-N   Suppress the prompt for a password. Unless a password is specified in a configuration file, authentication will fail for nonguest users.

-o   Take *-o* options as listed in the *mount* manpage.

-O   Assign owner attributes to the SMB connection.

-R   Specify the number of times to retry a mount attempt. The default is 4.

-T   Specify the connection request timeout (in seconds). The default is 15.

-u   Specify ownership for files and directories on the mounted volume, which defaults to the same as that set on the mount point.

-U   Specify a username for authentication. This may also be part of the UNC.

-v   Print software version to standard error.

-W Specify an SMB workgroup or NT domain for authentication. This may also be part of the UNC.

-x   Automatically mount all shares from the SMB server. The argument specifies a maximum number of shares that *mount_smbfs* is willing to mount from a server, to forestall resource starvation when the server has a very large number of shares. If the server has more shares than *max_mounts*, the mount attempt is cancelled.

workgroup
> The name of the SMB workgroup or NT domain to use for authentication to the SMB server.

username
> The name to use for authentication to the SMB server.

password
> The password to use for authentication. Note that specifying this on the command line exposes the password in a process listing.

smb_server
> The NetBIOS name of an SMB server.

share_name
> The name of the SMB share you wish to access.

mount_point
> The directory on which the filesystem is mounted.

mount_synthfs

mount_synthfs [-o *mount_options*] synthfs *mount_point*

Mounts a *synthfs* filesystem, which is a simple mapping of memory into the filesystem hierarchy (i.e., the contents of a *synthfs* filesystem are contained in memory). While creation of files in the filesystem is prevented (in fact, you may cause the system to hang after attempting to create files), directory hierarchies are allowed. This could be used to set up transient mount points for other volumes on, for example, read-only media with a shortage of spare directories to serve as mount points (like an installation CD).

Options

-*o* Take -*o* options as listed in the *mount* manpage.

mount_point
   The directory on which the filesystem is mounted.

mount_udf

mount_udf [-e] [-o *mount_options*] *device mount_point*

Mounts Universal Disk Format (UDF) DVD-ROM filesystems into the directory hierarchy.

Options

-*e* Enable extended attributes.

-*o* Take -*o* options as listed in the *mount* manpage.

device
   The DVD device filename, e.g., */dev/disk1*.

mount_point
   The directory on which the filesystem is mounted.

mount_volfs

mount_volfs [-o *mount_options*] *mount_point*

Mounts the *volfs* filesystem in */.vol*. The *volfs* filesystem enables the Carbon File Manager API to map a file ID to a file, without knowing the BSD path to it. Thus, HFS aliases, which use file IDs, remain consistent, even if the targets of the aliases move around within the volume.

The */.vol* directory contains subdirectories named with numeric IDs, each associated with a volume on the system. While the directories appear empty if listed, with a file or directory ID, you can access any object on those volumes. A file ID is a unique number associated with each file on a volume (analogous to an inode number on a UFS-formatted filesystem) and can be viewed with the -*i* option of *ls*.

If you know a file's ID, you can access it as */.vol/vol_ID/file_ID*. If you know the ID of the directory the file is in, you can also access it as */.vol/vol_ID/dir_ID/filename*. The root directory of a volume always has a directory ID of 2, so you can map volume IDs to volumes with:

```
% cd /.vol/vol_ID/2; pwd
```

Options

-o   Take -o options as listed in the *mount* manpage. Not normally used for *mount_volfs*.

mount_point
    The directory on which the filesystem is mounted, normally */.vol*.

---

mount_webdav

mount_webdav [-afile_descriptor] [-o mount_options] webdav_server[:port] [/pathname] mount_point

Mounts directories from WebDAV-enabled servers as filesystem volumes.

Options

-a   Specify a file descriptor associated with a file containing authentication information. See the *mount_webdav* manpage for details.

-o   Take -o options as listed in the *mount* manpage.

webdav_server
    The hostname or IP address of a WebDAV server.

port
    The TCP port on which to access the server. Defaults to 80.

pathname
    The path to the directory you wish to access on the server, relative to the site's WebDAV root directory (e.g., */Library/WebServer/Documents* on Mac OS X Server). Defaults to */*.

mount_point
    The directory on which the filesystem is mounted.

---

mv

mv [option] sources target

Moves or renames files and directories. In Table 2-4, the source (first column) and target (second column) determine the result (third column).

Table 2-4. Sources, targets, and results for the mv command

Source	Target	Result
File	*name* (nonexistent)	Rename file to *name*.
File	Existing file	Overwrite existing file with source file.
Directory	*name* (nonexistent)	Rename directory to *name*.
Directory	Existing directory	Move directory to be a subdirectory of existing directory.
One or more files	Existing directory	Move files to directory.

mv doesn't preserve resource forks or HFS metadata when moving files that contain them. For such files, use *MvMac* instead.

Options

-*f*   Force the move, even if target file exists; suppress messages about restricted access modes. Overrides previous -*i* and -*n* options.

-*i*   Query user before removing files. Overrides previous -*f* and -*n* options.

-*n*   Don't overwrite existing target files. Overrides previous -*f* and -*i* options.

-*v*   Verbose; show files as they're being moved.

MvMac

MvMac ·*sources target*

Moves or renames files while preserving resource forks and HFS metadata. *MvMac* works like *mv*, but doesn't have any of *mv*'s options. It is not intended as a direct replacement for *mv*. *MvMac* is installed with the Xcode Tools into */Developer/Tools*. Since this directory isn't in the shell's search path by default, you might to need to specify *MvMac*'s pathname to invoke it.

netstat

netstat [*options*]

Shows network status. For all active sockets, prints the protocol, the number of bytes waiting to be received, the number of bytes to be sent, the port number, the remote address and port, and the state of the socket.

Options

-*A*   Show the address of any protocol control blocks associated with sockets.

-*a*   Show the state of all sockets, including server sockets (not displayed by default).

-*b*   Modify the -*i* option display by providing bytes in and bytes out.

-*d*   Modify the -*i* and -*w* options' display by providing dropped packets.

-*f address_family*
    Limit displayed information to the specified *address_family* where legitimate families are [*inet*, *inet6*, *unix*].

-*g*   Display group address (multicast routing) information.

-*I interface*
    Display information for the specified *interface*.

-*i*   Display state and packet transfer statistics for all autoconfigured interfaces.

-*L*   Display current listen queue sizes.

-*l*   Modify display of -*r* option to include *mtu* information. As a standalone option, prints full IPv6 address.

-*M core*
    Extract information from specified *core* file instead of */dev/kmem*.

-*m*   Display memory management statistics.

-N system
> Extract the name list from specified *system* instead of */kernel*.

-n   Display network addresses using dotted octet notation (i.e., 172.24.30.1).

-p protocol
> Display statistics about *protocol* (see */etc/protocols* for names and aliases).

-r   Display routing tables.

-s[s]
> Display per protocol statistics. Use of double *s* filters zero count statistics.

-W   Don't truncate addresses.

-w wait
> Display network statistics every *wait* seconds.

nice

`nice [option] [command [arguments]]`

Executes a *command* (with its *arguments*) with lower priority (i.e., be "nice" to other users). With no arguments, *nice* prints the default scheduling priority (niceness). If *nice* is a child process, it prints the parent process's scheduling priority. Niceness has a range of -20 (highest priority) to 20 (lowest priority).

Option

-n adjustment, -adjustment, --adjustment=adjustment
> Run *command* with niceness incremented by *adjustment* (1 to 20); default is 10. A privileged user can raise priority by specifying a negative *adjustment* (e.g., -5).

nicl

`nicl [options] datasource [command]`

Modifies entries in the NetInfo database. You can manipulate directories and properties with *nicl*. The *datasource* may be the path to a NetInfo directory (such as */_*) or the filesystem path of a NetInfo database (you must use the *-raw* option for this). Use *-raw* to work directly with the NetInfo database, such as */var/db/netinfo/local.nidb*. This is useful in cases when the NetInfo daemon is down (such as when you boot into single-user mode).

Options

-c   Create a new data source.

-p   Prompt for a password. You can use this instead of prefixing the command with *sudo*.

-P password
> Use the specified password.

-q   Be quiet.

-raw
> Indicates that the *datasource* is a filesystem path to a NetInfo database.

-ro   Open *datasource* as read-only.

-t Treat the domain as a tagged domain, which includes a machine name and a tagged NetInfo database.

-u user
Use the specified user's identity when running the command. You'll be prompted for a password.

-v Be verbose.

-x500
Use X.500 names (see the *nicl* manpage for more details).

Commands

-append path key val ...
Append a value to an existing property. The property is created if it doesn't already exist.

-copy path newparent
Copy the specified *path* to a new parent path.

-create path [key [val ...]]
Create a NetInfo directory specified by *path*.

-delete path [key [val ...]]
Destroy the specified path and all its contents. If you specify a key and/or value, only the specified key is deleted.

-domainname
Print the NetInfo domain name of *datasource*.

-echo string
Print a string to standard output. Only useful in scripts.

-flush
Flush the directory cache.

-history [<|=|> version]
With no options, prints the current version number of the database. With <, =, or > followed by a version number, prints a list of the directories that have been changed before, at, or after the given version number. Note that > and < are shell characters for redirection, so must be quoted, as in *nicl . -history ">" 300*. Without the quotes, this command would print the current version number into a file called *300*.

-insert path key val index
Operate like -append, but instead of placing the value at the end, it inserts it at the specified index.

-list path [key ...]
List all the NetInfo directories in the specified path. For example, to list all users, use *nicl / -list /users*.

-merge path key val ...
Operate like -append, but if the value already exists, it is not duplicated.

-move path newparent
Move the specified *path* to a new parent path.

-read path [key ...]
Display all the properties of the specified path. For example, to see root's properties, use *nicl / -read /users/ root*.

-rename path oldkey newkey
　　Rename a property.

-resync
　　Resynchronize NetInfo.

-rparent
　　Print the NetInfo parent of *datasource*.

-search arguments
　　Perform a search within the NetInfo database. For complete details, see the *nicl* manpage.

-statistics
　　Display NetInfo server statistics.

nidomain

nidomain *options*

Creates or destroys NetInfo databases. *nidomain* can also list which databases on a particular computer are serving which domains.

Options
-l [host]
　　List which domains are served by machine *host*, or the local host if *host* is not specified.

-m tag
　　Create a new local database to serve the NetInfo domain *tag*.

-d tag
　　Destroy the local database serving domain *tag*.

-c tag master/remotetag
　　Create the local database *tag*, cloned from the remote machine *master*'s database *remotetag*.

nidump

nidump [-T *timeout*] (-r *directory|format*) [-t] *domain*

Dumps NetInfo information in a flat-file format (such as the */etc/hosts* format) or in a raw format that uses a C-like syntax:

```
{
    "name" = ( "localhost" );
    "ip_address" = ( "127.0.0.1" );
    "serves" = ( "./local" );
}
```

Options
-T timeout
　　Specify a timeout in seconds.

-t Treat the domain as a tagged domain, which includes a machine name and a tagged NetInfo database. For example, *abbot/local* refers to the local NetInfo domain of the machine named abbot.

-r directory
Dump the directory in raw format. Directory should be a path to a NetInfo directory, such as */users/root* or */machines*.

format
Specify a format corresponding to a Unix flat file of the same name. Can be: *aliases, bootptab, bootparams, ethers, exports, fstab, group, hosts, networks, passwd, printcap, protocols, resolv.conf, rpc, services,* or *mountmaps*.

domain
Specify a NetInfo domain. For standalone machines, use a dot (.), which refers to the local domain.

nifind

nifind [*options*] *nidir* [*domain*]

Searches the root domain for the NetInfo directory *nidir* and returns the location and ID of the found directories. If *domain* is specified, searches the hierarchy only up to that domain.

Options

-a Search the entire NetInfo directory.

-n Don't search local directories.

-p Display the contents of the directories.

-T n Set the connection timeout to *n* seconds (default is 2).

-v Be verbose.

nigrep

nigrep *regx* [*option*]*domain* [*nidir*]

Searches the specified NetInfo domain using the regular expression *regx* and return the location and ID of the found directories. If *nidir* is specified, starts the search from that directory.

Option

-t Identify *domain* by a specified IP number or hostname and tag.

-T n Set the connection timeout to *n* seconds

niload

niload [-v] [-T *timeout*] [(-d|-m)] [(-p|-P *password*)]
[-u *user*] {-r *directory*|*format*} [-t] *domain*

Reads the Unix flat file format from standard input and loads it into the NetInfo database.

Options

-v   Select verbose mode.

-T timeout
>Specify a timeout in seconds.

-d   Specify that if a duplicate entry already exists, NetInfo deletes that entry before adding the new one. This can cause you to lose data if NetInfo is tracking information that isn't represented in the flat file. For example, if you dump the */users* directory to a flat *passwd* file format and load it back in with *niload -d*, you will lose the picture, hint, and sharedDir properties for every user on your system because the *passwd* file doesn't have a field for those properties. Most of the time, the *-m* option is what you want.

-m   Specify that if a duplicate entry already exists, *niload* will merge the changes. So, if you dump the */users* directory to a flat *passwd* file format, change a user's shell, and load that file back in with *niload*, NetInfo will keep the old shell. If you use the *-m* option, NetInfo will accept the new shell without the destructive side effects of the *-d* option.

-p   Prompt for a password. You can use this instead of prefixing the command with *sudo*.

-P password
>Use the specified password.

   If your shell history file is enabled, the *-P* option presents a security risk, since the password will be stored, along with the history of other shell commands. It is best to avoid using this option.

-u user
>Use the specified user's identity when running the command. You'll be prompted for a password.

-t   Treat the domain as a tagged domain, which includes a machine name and a tagged NetInfo database.

domain
>Specify a NetInfo domain.

directory
>Denotes a path to a NetInfo directory.

format
>Specify a format corresponding to a Unix flat file of the same name. Can be: *aliases*, *bootptab*, *bootparams*, *exports*, *fstab*, *group*, *hosts*, *networks*, *passwd*, *printcap*, *protocols*, *rpc*, or *services*.

---

nireport

nireport [-T *timeout*] [-t] *domain directory* [*property* ...]

Lists all NetInfo groups.

Options

-T timeout
> Specify a timeout in seconds.

-t Treat the domain as a tagged domain, which includes a machine name and a tagged NetInfo database.

domain
> Specify a NetInfo domain.

directory
> Denotes a path to a NetInfo directory.

property ...
> Specify one or more NetInfo properties; e.g., each user listed in the */users* directory has *name*, *passwd*, *uid*, and *gid* properties (as well as a few other properties). Every directory has a *name* property that corresponds to the directory name. For example, the */machines* directory's *name* property is machines.

You can use *nireport* to list any portion of the NetInfo directory. For example, to list the top-level directory, specify the local domain, the / directory, and the *name* property, as in *nireport . / name*.

---

niutil

niutil *command* [-T *timeout*] [(-p|-P *password*)] [-u *user*] [-R] [-t] *arguments*

Uses *niutil* to modify entries in the NetInfo database. You can manipulate directories and properties with *niutil*.

Options

-T timeout
> Specify a timeout in seconds.

-p Prompt for a password. You can use this instead of prefixing the command with *sudo*.

-P password
> Use the specified password.

-u user
> Use the specified user's identity when running the command. You'll be prompted for a password.

-R Retry the operation if the NetInfo server is busy.

-t Treat the domain as a tagged domain, which includes a machine name and a tagged NetInfo database.

Commands and arguments

niutil -create *options domain path*
> Create a NetInfo directory specified by *path*. For example, the first step in creating a user is to create the person's directory with *niutil -create . /users/ username*.

niutil -destroy *options domain path*
> Destroy the specified path and all its contents.

niutil -createprop options domain path propkey [val...]
> Create a property (specified by *propkey*) under the NetInfo directory specified by *path*. You can create a list by specifying multiple values.

niutil -appendprop options domain path propkey val...
> Append a value to an existing property. The property is created if it doesn't already exist.

niutil -mergeprop options domain path propkey val...
> This is like *-appendprop*, but if the value already exists, it is not added.

niutil -insertval options domain path propkey val index
> This is like *-appendprop*, but instead of placing the value at the end, it inserts it at the specified index.

niutil -destroyprop options domain path propkey...
> Delete the specified property. For an example, see the later section "Modifying a User."

niutil -destroyval options domain path propkey val...
> Delete one or more values from a property.

niutil -renameprop options domain path oldkey newkey
> Rename a property.

niutil -read options domain path
> Display all the properties of the specified path. For example, to see root's properties, use *niutil -read . /users/ root*.

niutil -list options domain path [propkey]
> List all the NetInfo directories in the specified path. For example, to list all users, use *niutil -list . /users*

niutil -readprop options domain path propkey
> Display the values of the specified property.

niutil -readval options domain path propkey index
> Display the value of the specified property at the given index. For example, to list the first member of the writers group, use *niutil -readval . /groups/writers users 0*.

niutil -rparent options domain
> Print the NetInfo parent of the specified domain.

niutil -resync options domain
> Resynchronize NetInfo.

niutil -statistics options domain
> Display NetInfo server statistics.

niutil -domainname options domain
> Print the NetInfo domain name of the specified domain.

notifyd

notifyd [-no_restart] [-no_startup] [-shm_pages *integer*]

The notification server for the API described in the *notify(3)* manpage. (Use *man 3 notify* to display this page.) Using the API, processes may post notifications associated with arbitrary names, and other processes can register to be informed of such notification events. (A name should follow the convention used for Java classes: the reversed DNS domain name associated with the responsible organization, followed by one or more segments; e.g., *com.apple.system.timezone*.) *notifyd* sets up the shared memory used for the *notify_register_check* call, and directly answers *notify_check* requests for other notification methods (signal, Mach port, and file descriptor).

It also reads a configuration file, */etc/notify.conf*. Each line begins with one of two keywords: reserve or monitor. The reserve keyword lays out access restrictions for portions of the namespace. The arguments are a name, a user and a group that "owns" the name, and a set of read and write permissions for the user, the group, and others, similar to those applied to files. For example, the following line:

```
reserve com.apple.system. 0 0 rwr-r-
```

states that any names starting with *com.apple.system.* are owned by UID 0 (*root*) and GID 0 (*wheel*), and that anyone can receive notifications for these names, but only *root* (the owner) can post notifications.

The monitor keyword takes a name and a filename as arguments. When the specified file is changed, a notification is posted for the name. For example, the following line from the stock */etc/notify.conf* can be used by processes wishing to keep track of time zone changes:

```
monitor com.apple.system.timezone /etc/localtime
```

Another use would be to monitor changes to a daemon's configuration file. When the file is changed, the daemon or another process could receive notification and cause the daemon to automatically reread the configuration.

notifyd is started as a bootstrap daemon, from */etc/mach_init.d/notifyd.plist* (processed by *register_mach_bootstrap_servers*). It responds to HUP or TERM signals by restarting (unless the *-no_restart* flag was used), thus rereading */etc/notify.conf*. Before *notifyd* exits, it sends notifications for all registered names; after it restarts, processes registered for notifications must register again, as their tokens become invalid.

Options

-no_restart
> Disable automatic restart. Normally, if *notifyd* is killed, it's restarted within a few seconds.

-no_startup
> Apparently prevents *notifyd* from issuing notifications, while using all available CPU time. The purpose of this option is unknown.

-shm_pages
> Specify the number of pages (i.e., units of 4096 bytes) to reserve for shared memory (although it appears to use about twice that). Defaults to 1.

nslookup

```
nslookup [-option...] [host_to_find | - [server ]]
```

Queries Internet domain nameservers. This command is deprecated, and users should turn to *dig* for their name lookup needs.

nslookup has two modes: interactive and noninteractive. Interactive mode allows the user to query nameservers for information about various hosts and domains or to print a list of hosts in a domain. Interactive mode is entered when either no arguments are provided (the default nameserver will be used), or the first argument is a hyphen and the second argument is the hostname or Internet address of a nameserver.

Noninteractive mode is used to print just the name and requested information for a host or domain. It is used when the name of the host to be looked up is given as the first argument. Any of the *keyword=value* pairs listed under the interactive *set* command can be used as an option on the command line by prefacing the keyword with a -. The optional second argument specifies a nameserver.

Options

All options under the *set* interactive command can be entered on the command line, with the syntax - *keyword[=value]*.

Interactive commands

exit
> Exit *nslookup*.

finger [name] [>|>>filename]
> Connect to finger server on current host, optionally creating or appending to *filename*.

help, ?
> Print a brief summary of commands.

host [server]
> Look up information for *host* using the current default server or using *server* if specified.

ls -[adhs] -[t querytype] domain [>|>>filename]
> List information available for *domain*, optionally creating or appending to *filename*. The -*a* option lists aliases of hosts in the domain. -*d* lists all contents of a zone transfer. -*h* lists CPU and operating system information for the domain. -*s* lists well-known services for the domain. -*t* lists all records of the specified type (see type table).

lserver domain
> Change the default server to *domain*. Use the initial server to look up information about *domain*.

root
> Change default server to the server for the root of the domain namespace.

server domain
> Change the default server to *domain*. Use the current default server to look up information about *domain*.

set keyword[=value]
> Change state information affecting the lookups. Valid keywords are:
>
> *all*
> > Print the current values of the frequently used options to *set*.
>
> *class=name(upper or lower class)*
> > Set query class to IN (Internet; default), CHAOS, HESIOD/HS, or ANY.
>
> *domain=name*
> > Change default domain name to *name*.
>
> *[no]debug*
> > Turn debugging mode on or off.
>
> *[no]d2*
> > Turn exhaustive debugging mode on or off.

[no]defname

    Append default domain name to a single-component lookup name.

[no]ignoretc

    Ignore truncate error.

[no]recurse

    Tell name server to query or not query other servers if it doesn't have the information.

[no]search

    With *defname*, search for each name in parent domains of current domain.

[no]vc

    Always use a virtual circuit when sending requests to the server.

port=port

    Connect to nameserver using *port*.

querytype=value

    See *type=value*.

retry=number

    Set number of retries to *number*.

root=host

    Change name of root server to *host*.

srchlist=domain-list

    Where *domain-list* is a maximum of six slash (/) separated domain names.

timeout=number

    Change timeout interval for waiting for a reply to *number* seconds.

type=value

    Change type of information returned from a query to one of:

    A

        Host's Internet address

    ANY

        Any available information

    CNAME

        Canonical name for an alias

    HINFO

        Host CPU and operating system type

    MD

        Mail destination

    MG

        Mail group member

    MINFO

        Mailbox or mail list information

    MR

        Mail rename domain name

    MX

        Mail exchanger

    NS

        Nameserver for the named zone

PTR
> Hostname or pointer to other information

SOA
> Domain start-of-authority

TXT
> Text information

UINFO
> User information

WKS
> Supported well-known services

ntp-wait

ntp-wait [-v] [-f] [-n *num_tries*] [-s *time*]

This is a Perl script that reports whether the local *ntpd* has synchronized yet. Returns 0 if synchronized, 1 if not.

Options

-f   Cause *ntp-wait* to return 1 if an indeterminate result is received from *ntpd*; otherwise, *ntp-wait* returns 0.

-n   Specify the number of times to try for a successful result before quitting. Defaults to 1000.

-s   Specify the number of seconds between tries. Defaults to 6.

-v   Enable verbose output to standard output.

ntptimeset

ntptimeset [-l] [-d]... [-v] [-s] [-c *filename*] [-u] [-S *integer*] [-V *integer*] [-t *timeout*] [-H] [-a *key_id*] [-e *delay*]

Synchronizes the system clock in a manner similar to *ntpdate*, but in a way that attempts to compensate for current, possibly degraded, network conditions.

Options

-a   Enable secure authentication with the key specified by the given identifier.

-c   Specify the location of the configuration file. Defaults to */etc/ntp.conf*.

-d   Enable debugging output.

-e   Specify the delay, in seconds, caused by authentication. Normally this is negligible.

-H   Simulate poor network conditions by dropping a proportion of network packets.

-l   Enable logging to *syslog*.

-s   Set the system clock. Otherwise, *ntptimeset* merely reports the clock's offset.

-S   Specify a minimum number of servers that must respond. Defaults to 3.

-t   Specify the time, in seconds, spent waiting for a server response. Defaults to 1.

-u   Use an unprivileged client port.

-*v*   Enable verbose output.

-*V*   Specify a minimum number of servers that must respond with a valid time. Defaults to 1.

nvram

nvram [-p] [-f *filename*] [*name*] [= *value*] ...

Modifies Open Firmware variables, which control the boot-time behavior of your Macintosh. To list all Open Firmware variables, use *nvram -p*. The Apple Open Firmware page is *http://bananajr6000.apple.com*.

To change a variable, you must run *nvram* as root or as the superuser. To set a variable, use *variable=value*. For example, to configure Mac OS X to boot verbosely, use *nvram boot-args=-v*. (Booting into Mac OS 9 or earlier resets this.) The table in this section lists Open Firmware variables. Some variables use the Open Firmware Device Tree notation (see the TechNotes available at the Apple Open Firmware page).

 Be careful changing the *nvram* utility, since incorrect settings can turn a G4 iMac into a $2,000 doorstop. If you render your computer unbootable, you can reset Open Firmware by zapping the PRAM. To zap the PRAM, hold down Option-⌘-P-R as you start the computer, and then release the keys when you hear a second startup chime.

Options

-*f filename*
    Read the variables to be set from *filename*, a text file of *name=value* statements.

-*d variable*
    Deletes Open Firmware variable *variable*.

-*p*   Display all Open Firmware variables.

Table 2-5. Open Firmware variables

Variable	Description
auto-boot?	The automatic boot settings. If true (the default), Open Firmware automatically boots an operating system. If false, the process stops at the Open Firmware prompt. Be careful using this with Old World (unsupported) machines and third-party graphics adapters because the display and keyboard may not be initialized until the operating system starts (in which case you won't have access to Open Firmware).
boot-args	The arguments that are passed to the boot loader.
boot-command	The command that starts the boot process. The default is mac-boot, an Open Firmware command that examines the boot-device for a Mac OS startup.
boot-device	The device to boot from. The syntax is *device*:[*partition*],*path*:*filename*, and a common default is hd:,\\: tbxi. In the path, \\ is an abbreviation for */System/Library/CoreServices*, and tbxi is the file type of the *BootX* boot loader. (Run */Developer/Tools/GetFileInfo* on *BootX* to see its type.)
boot-file	The name of the boot loader. (This is often blank because boot-command and boot-device are usually all that are needed.)
boot-screen	The image to display on the boot screen.

Table 2-5. (continued)Open Firmware variables

Variable	Description
boot-script	A variable that can contain an Open Firmware boot script.
console-screen	A variable that specifies the console output device, using an Open Firmware Device Tree name.
default-client-ip	An IP address for diskless booting.
default-gateway-ip	A gateway address for diskless booting.
default-mac-address?	See errata page at *http://www.oreilly.com/catalog/macpantherian*.
default-router-ip	A router address for diskless booting.
default-server-ip	An IP address for diskless booting.
default-subnet-mask	A default subnet mask for diskless booting.
diag-device	A private variable; not usable for security reasons.
diag-file	A private variable; not usable for security reasons.
diag-switch?	A private variable; not usable for security reasons.
fcode-debug?	A variable that determines whether the Open Firmware Forth interpreter displays extra debugging information.
input-device	The input device to use for the Open Firmware console.
input-device-1	A secondary input device (so you can have a screen and serial console at the same time). Use *scca* for the first serial port.
little-endian?	The CPU endian-ness. If true, initializes the PowerPC chip as little-endian. The default is false.
load-base	A private variable; not usable for security reasons.
mouse-device	The mouse device using an Open Firmware Device Tree name.
nvramrc	A sequence of commands to execute at boot time (if use-nvramc? is set to true).
oem-banner	A custom banner to display at boot time.
oem-banner?	The oem banner settings. Set to true to enable the oem banner. The default is false.
oem-logo	A 64-by-64 bit array containing a custom black-and-white logo to display at boot time. This should be specified in hex.
oem-logo?	The oem logo settings. Set to true to enable the oem logo. The default is false.
output-device	The device to use as the system console. The default is screen.
output-device-1	A secondary output device (so you can have everything go to both the screen and a serial console). Use *scca* for the first serial port.
pci-probe-mask	A private variable; not usable for security reasons.
ram-size	The amount of RAM currently installed. For example, 256 MB is shown as 0x10000000.
real-base	The starting physical address that is available to Open Firmware.
real-mode?	The address translation settings. If true, Open Firmware will use real-mode address translation. Otherwise, it uses virtual-mode address translation.
real-size	The size of the physical address space available to Open Firmware.
screen-#columns	The number of columns for the system console.
screen-#rows	The number of rows for the system console.
scroll-lock	Set by page checking output words to prevent Open Firmware text from scrolling off the top of the screen.
selftest-#megs	The number of MB of RAM to test at boot time. The default is 0.

Table 2-5. (continued)Open Firmware variables

Variable	Description
use-generic?	The device node naming settings. Specify whether to use generic device node names such as "screen," as opposed to Apple hardware code names.
use-nvramrc?	The command settings. If this is true, Open Firmware uses the commands in *nvramrc* at boot time.
virt-base	The starting virtual address that is available to Open Firmware.
virt-size	The size of the virtual address space Open Firmware.

od

od [-c] [-a] [-b] [-B] [-o] [-O] [-d] [-D] [-i] [-I] [-l] [-L] [-f] [-e]
[-F] [-h] [-x] [-H] [-X] [-v] [*filename*]

Prints the contents of a file to standard output in a variety of formats. (If no filename is specified, it acts on the contents of standard input.) The name is an acronym for *octal dump*, from its default behavior of displaying files as series of octal numbers.

od has been deprecated in favor of *hexdump*; in fact, the two binaries are hard-linked to the same data. However, traditional *od* syntax applies when invoked by that name. See the *hexdump* manpage for more.

Options

-a   Display content in 1-byte chunks of ASCII characters, hexadecimal numbers, and short strings representing control characters.

-b   Display content in 1-byte chunks of octal numbers.

-B   Display content in 2-byte chunks of octal numbers. This is the default.

-c   Display content in 1-byte chunks of ASCII characters, octal numbers, and escape sequences representing control characters. This is probably the most commonly used option.

-d   Display content in 2-byte chunks of unsigned decimal integers.

-D   Display content in 4-byte chunks of unsigned decimal integers.

-e   Display content in 8-byte chunks of decimal floating-point numbers.

-f   Display content in 4-byte chunks of decimal floating-point numbers.

-F   Same as -*e*.

-h   Display content in 2-byte chunks of hexadecimal numbers.

-H   Display content in 4-byte chunks of hexadecimal numbers.

-i   Display content in 2-byte chunks of signed decimal integers.

-I   Display content in 4-byte chunks of signed decimal integers.

-l   Same as -*i*.

-L   Same as -*I*.

-o   Same as -*B*.

-O   Display content in 4-byte chunks of octal numbers.

-v   Disable the suppression of duplicate lines, which are normally represented by a single asterisk.

-x   Same as *-h*.

-X   Same as *-H*.

---

open

open *file*

open [-a *application*] *file*

open [-e] *file*

The *open* command can be used to open files and directories, and to launch applications from the Terminal application.

Options

-a application

> Use *application* to open the file.

-b identifier

> Specifes the application to open the file with, as identified with *identifier*. For example, to open a CSV-format file *names.csv* with Excel, use *open -b com.microsoft.Excel names.csv*.

-e file

> Force the use of Mac OS X's TextEdit application to open the specified *file*.

-f   Read input from standard input and open the text in TextEdit.

-t file

> Open *file* with the default text editor, which may not be TextEdit.

Examples

To open a directory in the Finder, use *open*, followed by the name of the directory. For example, to open the current directory, type:

> `$ open .`

To open your Public folder in the Finder:

> `$ open ~/Public`

To open the */Applications* folder in the Finder:

> `$ open /Applications`

To open an application, you need only its name. For example, you can open Xcode (*/Developer/Applications*) with this command:

> `$ open -a Xcode`

You aren't required to enter the path for the application—only its name—even if it is a Classic application. The only time you are required to enter the path is if you have two different versions of an application with similar names on your system.

You can also supply a filename argument with the *-a* option, which launches the application and opens the specified file with that application. You can use this option to open a file with something other than the application with which it's associated. For example, to open an XML file in Xcode instead of the default text editor, TextEdit, you can use the following command:

> `$ open -a Xcode data.xml`

To open multiple files, you can use wildcards:

```
$ open *.c
```

To force a file to be opened with TextEdit, use *-e*:

```
$ open -e *.c
```

The *-e* option opens only files in the TextEdit application; it can't open a file in another text editor, such as BBEdit. If you want to use TextEdit on a file that's owned by an administrator (or root), *open -e* won't work. You need to specify the full executable path, as in:

```
$ sudo /Applications/TextEdit.app/Contents/MacOS/TextEdit filename
```

opendiff

opendiff *file1 file2* [-ancestor *ancestor_file*] [-merge *merge_file*]

Opens the two designated files in the FileMerge application.

Options

-ancestor
Compare the two files against a common ancestor file.

-merge
Merge the two files into a new file.

open-x11

open-x11 *app_name...*

Starts specified X Window System applications using the X11 application.

Option

app_name
The name of an executable X11 application. Those delivered with Mac OS X are in */usr/X11R6/bin/*. If located in a standard directory, the application pathname is not required.

osacompile

osacompile [-l *language*] [-e *command*] [-o *name*] [-d] [-r *typeid*] [-t *type*]
[-c *creator*] [*file...*]

Compiles into a new script file one or more text or compiled OSA script files or standard input.

Options

-c creator
Assign the four-character file-creator code *creator* to the new script (the default is *osas*).

-e command

Use *command* as a line of script to be compiled. You can use more than one *-e* option; each will specify a new line of script.

-d Use the dictionary from the application *pathname* when compiling.

-i pathname

Use the dictionary from the application *pathname* when compiling.

-l OSAlang

Use OSA language *OSAlang* instead of the default AppleScript. Use the *osalang* command (described later in this chapter) to get information on all the system's OSA languages.

-o name

Use *name* as a filename for the new script instead of the default *a.scpt*.

-r type:id

Place the resulting script in the resource fork of the output file, in the resource specified by *type:id*.

-s Make the new applet or droplet be a stay-open applet.

-t type

Assign the four-character file-type code *type* to the new script (the default is *osas*).

-u Make the new applet or droplet use a startup screen.

-x Save file as execute only. This doesn't produce an applet, but a compiled script file that can't be viewed in Script Editor.

Examples

Use the filename *newscript* for a new script file, compiled from the source in *scripttext. txt*:

```
$ osacompile -o newscript scripttext.txt
```

Compile the file *scripttext.txt* into a compiled script called *newscript* (assuming that a JavaScript OSA scripting component exists on the system):

```
$ osacompile -l JavaScript rawscript.txt
```

osalang

osalang [*options*]

Lists the computer's installed OSA-compliant languages (i.e., languages that use Apple Events to communicate among applications). In the newness of Mac OS X, this command may only return "AppleScript" and "Generic Scripting System."

Options

-d Print only the default language.

-l List the name and description for each installed language.

-L List the name and a longer description for each installed language.

osascript

osascript [*options*] [*files*]

Executes an OSA script from *files*, or from standard input if *files* isn't specified.

Options

-e command
> Use *command* as a line of script to be compiled. You can use more than one *-e* option; each specifies a new line of script.

-l OSAlang
> Use OSA language *OSAlang* instead of the default AppleScript. Use the *osalang* command (described previously) to get information on all the system's OSA languages.

-s options
> Provide output as specified in *options* with one or more of these flags:
>
> *h*   Human readable (default)
>
> *s*   Recompilable source
>
> *e*   Send errors to standard error (default)
>
> *o*   Send errors to standard output

Examples

To run a script that displays a dialog window from the Finder, first run *osascript* with no arguments, which allows you to enter the script into standard input:

```
$ osascript
tell app "Finder"
activate
display dialog "Mac OS X Rules!"
end tell
```

Press Ctrl-D to send an EOF, at which point *osascript* executes the script and prints the value returned:

```
button returned:OK
```

Run with the *-s s* option, the output is better formatted for subsequent parsing:

```
$ osascript -s s
tell app "Finder"
activate
display dialog "Mac OS X Rules!"
end tell
{button returned:"OK"} or argument/switch mismatch
```

passwd

passwd [-i *infosystem*] [-l *location*] [*username*]

Sets a user password in the designated directory service.

Options

-i   Specify the directory service to use, which may be *file*, *netinfo* (the default), *nis*, or *opendirectory*.

-l   Depending on the directory service being used, it's either a filename (defaults to */etc/master.passwd*), a NetInfo domain name or server/tag combo, a NIS domain name, or an Open Directory node name.

username
> Designate whose password will be set. It defaults to that of the user running the command.

---

paste

paste [*options*] *files*

Merges corresponding lines of one or more *files* into vertical columns, separated by a tab. See also *cut*, *join*, and *pr*.

Options

-     Replace a filename with the standard input.

-d'*char*'
> Separate columns with *char* instead of a tab. *char* can be any regular character or the following escape sequences:

> You can separate columns with different characters by supplying more than one *char*:

\n   Newline

\t   Tab

\   Backslash

\0   Empty string

-s   Merge subsequent lines from one file.

Examples

Create a three-column file from files *x*, *y*, and *z*:

    $ **paste** *x y z* > *file*

List users in two columns:

    $ **who | paste - -**

Merge each pair of lines into one line:

    $ **paste -s -d"\t\n" list**

---

pax

pax [*options*] [*patterns*]

Portable Archive Exchange program. When members of the POSIX 1003.2 working group couldn't standardize on either *tar* or *cpio*, they invented this program. (See also *cpio* and *tar*.) Note that until native drivers for tape drives exist for Mac OS X, *pax* can't write to tape. Note also that *pax* doesn't preserve resource forks or HFS meta-data when copying files that contain them.

pax operates in four modes, depending on the combinations of *-r* and *-w*:

List mode
No *-r* and no *-w*. List the contents of a *pax* archive. Optionally, restrict the output to filenames and/or directories that match a given pattern.

Extract mode
-r only. Extract files from a *pax* archive. Intermediate directories are created as needed.

Archive mode
-w only. Archive files to a new or existing *pax* archive. The archive is written to standard output; it may be redirected to an appropriate tape device if needed for backups.

Pass-through mode
-r and *-w*. Copy a directory tree from one location to another, analogous to *cpio -p*.

Options

Here are the options available in the four modes:

```
None:     c d f     n   s   v                 U G   T
-r:       c d f i k n o p s u v D       Y Z E U G   T
-w:     a b   d f i     o   s t u v x H L P X   U G B T
-rw:        d   i k l n   p s t u v D H L P X Y Z U G   T
```

-a   Append files to the archive. This may not work on some tape devices.

-b size
Use *size* as the blocksize, in bytes, of blocks to be written to the archive.

-c   Complement. Match all file or archive members that don't match the patterns.

-d   For files or archive members that are directories, extract or archive only the directory itself, not the tree it contains.

-f archive
Use *archive* instead of standard input or standard output.

-i   Interactively rename files. For each file, *pax* writes a prompt to */dev/tty* and reads a one-line response from */dev/tty*. The responses are as follows:

Return
Skip the file.

A period
Take the file as is.

New name
Anything else is taken as the new name to use for the file.

EOF
Exit immediately with a nonzero exit status.

-k   Don't overwrite existing files.

-l   Make hard links. When copying a directory tree (*-rw*), make hard links between the source and destination hierarchies wherever possible.

-n   Choose the first archive member that matches each pattern. No more than one archive member will match for each pattern.

-o options

    Reserved for format-specific options specified by the *-x* option.

-p privs

    Specify one or more privileges for the extracted file. *privs* specify permissions or other characteristics to be preserved or ignored.

    a   Don't preserve file-access times.

    e   Retain the user and GIDs, permissions (mode), and access and modification time.

    m   Don't preserve the file modification time.

    o   Retain the user and group ID.

    p   Keep the permissions (mode).

    -r   Read an archive and extract files.

-s replacement

    Use *replacement* to modify file or archive member names. This is a string of the form - *s/old/new/[gp]*. This is similar to the substitution commands in *ed*, *ex*, and *sed*. *old* is a regular expression, and *new* may contain & to mean the matched text and \n for subpatterns. The trailing *g* indicates the substitution should be applied globally. A trailing *p* causes *pax* to print the resulting new filename. Multiple *-s* options may be supplied. The first one that works is applied. Any delimiter may be used, not just /, but in all cases, it is wise to quote the argument to prevent the shell from expanding wildcard characters.

-t   Reset the access time of archived files to what they were before being archived by *pax*.

-u   Ignore files older than preexisting files or archive members. The behavior varies based on the current mode:

    Extract mode

        Extract the archive file if it is newer than an existing file with the same name.

    Archive mode

        If an existing file with the same name as an archive member is newer than the archive member, supersede the archive member.

    Pass-through mode

        Replace the file in the destination hierarchy with the file in the source hierarchy (or a link to it) if the source hierarchy's file is newer.

-v   In list mode, print a verbose table of contents. Otherwise, print archive member names on standard error.

-w   Write files to standard output in the given archive format.

-x format

    Use the given format for the archive. The value of *format* is either *cpio* or *ustar*. The details of both formats are provided in the IEEE 1003.1 (1990) POSIX standard. The two formats are mutually incompatible; attempting to append using one format to an archive while using the other is an error.

-B   Set the number of bytes that can be written to one archive volume. This option can be used only by a device that supports an end-of-file read condition such as a file or tape drive. This option shouldn't be used with a floppy or hard disk.

-D   The file inode change time is checked to see if it is a newer version of the file.

-E limit

> Set the number of read errors that can occur before *pax* will stop. *limit* can be from 0 to *none*. 0 causes *pax* to stop after the first read error; *none* keeps *pax* from stopping on any amount of errors. Caution should be used with *none*, as it can put *pax* into an infinite loop if the archive is severely flawed

-G   The group is used to select the file. To select by group number instead of group name, use a # in front of the number; to escape the #, use \.

-H   If any of the pathnames given in the command line are symbolic links, follow only those links.

-L   Follow all symbolic links.

-P   Don't follow symbolic links. This is the default.

-T [from_date][,to_date][/[c][m]]

> Use either file modification date[*m*] or inode change time[*c*] to select files in a specified date range. The options *c* and *m* can be used together. The default option is *m*.

-U   The user is used to select the file. To select by UID instead of username, place a # in front of the number; to escape the #, use \.

-X   When traversing directory trees, don't cross into a directory on a different device (the *st_dev* field in the *stat* structure, see *stat(2)*; similar to the *-mount* option of *find*).

-Y   Similar to the *-D* option, with the exception that *pax* checks the inode change time after it has completed the filename modifications and a pathname has been generated.

-Z   Similar to the *-u* option, with the exception that *pax* checks the modification time after it has completed the filename modifications and a pathname has been generated.

Example

Copy a home directory to a different directory (presumably on a bigger disk):

```
$ cd /Users
$ pax -r -w chuck/newhome
```

pbcopy

pbcopy [-help] [-pboard (general | find | font | ruler)]

Copies standard input to the pasteboard buffer. The Clipboard is used to implement GUI copy, cut, and paste operations; drag-and-drop operations; and the Cocoa Services menu.

Options

-help

> Print a usage statement to standard output.

-pboard name

> Specify the *name* of the pasteboard to use: either the name used for general copying and pasting or a special-purpose pasteboard used for holding *find*, *font*, or *ruler* settings. Defaults to *general*.

pbpaste

```
pbpaste[-help] [-pboard ( general | find | font | ruler }]
[-Prefer { ascii | rtf | ps }]
```

Prints the contents of the Clipboard to standard output. The combination of *pbcopy* and *pbpaste* may be an interesting tool to use in scripting. However, the Clipboard can be modified by other processes at any time, which limits the tool's actual usefulness.

Options

-help
> Print a usage statement to standard output.

-Prefer format
> Specify the output format to use if the desired format (*ascii*, *rtf*, or *ps* for ASCII, Rich Text Format, or PostScript, respectively) is available in the Clipboard.

-pboard name
> Specify the *name* of the pasteboard to use: either the name used for general copying and pasting or a special-purpose pasteboard used for holding *find*, *font*, or *ruler* settings. Defaults to *general*.

pdisk

```
pdisk
```

```
pdisk device { -diskSize | -isDiskPartitioned | -dump | -blockSize |-initialize }
```

```
pdisk device { -partitionEntry | -partitionName | -partitionType | -partitionBase
| -partitionSize | -deletePartition } part_num
```

```
pdisk device { -setWritable | -setAutoMount } part_num { 0 | 1 }
```

```
pdisk device -makeBootable part_num boot_addr boot_bytes load_addr goto_addr
```

```
pdisk device -createPartition part_name part_type part_base part_size
```

```
pdisk device -splitPartition part_num part1_size part2_name part2_type
```

```
pdisk device -getPartitionOfType part_type instance_num
```

```
pdisk device -getPartitionWithName part_name instance_num
```

Provides control over Apple partition maps on disk devices in Macintosh systems.

Options

-a, --abbr
> Turn on abbreviation mode. For example, *Apple_HFS* displays as *HFS*.

-blockSize
> Print the block size of the specified device, in bytes, to standard output.

-c, -compute_size
> Toggle the "compute size" flag, where partition sizes are computed, not taken from the partition map.

-createPartition
> Add a partition to the partition map with the specified name, type (such as *Apple_HFS* or *Apple_UFS*), base (i.e., starting block number), and size (in blocks).

-d, --debug
> Toggle the debug flag. When in interactive mode, some extra commands are enabled, including commands to display block contents and partition map data structures.

-deletePartition
> Delete the specified partition from the partition map.

-dump
> Print the partition map on the specified device to standard output.

-f, --fname
> Toggle the "show filesystem name" flag. This should cause *pdisk* to display HFS volume names *rather* than names taken from the partition map, but it doesn't appear to make a difference.

-getPartitionOfType
> Print the number of a partition with the specified type to standard output. An *instance_num* of 0 refers the lowest-numbered partition of the specified type, 1 refers to the second partition of that type, etc.

-getPartitionWithName
> Print the number of a partition with the specified name to standard output. An *instance_num* of 0 refers the lowest-numbered partition with the specified name, 1 refers to the second partition of that name, etc.

-h, --help
> Prints a usage statement to standard error.

-i, --interactive
> Enters interactive mode, where menus of single-character commands are available. If a device name is provided as an argument, the set of available commands differs, offering more control over partitions on the device. Interactive commands that take arguments will prompt for any that are missing.

-initialize
> Create a partition map on the device.

-isDiskPartitioned
> Return 0 if the device has an Apple partition map on it, 1 if not.

-partitionEntry
> Print a line to standard output containing the name, type, base, and size of the specified partition.

-partitionName
> Print the name of the specified partition to standard output.

-partitionSize
> Print the size of the specified partition, in blocks, to standard output.

-partitionType
> Print the type of the specified partition to standard output.

-r, --readonly
> Toggles the read-only flag. When in read-only mode, changes to the partition map are disallowed.

-setAutoMount

Set (1) or clear (0) the automount bit on a partition. This is unused by Mac OS X.

-setWritable

Set (1) or clear (0) the writable bit on a partition.

-splitPartition

Split an existing partition in two. The arguments include the size (in blocks) of the first partition formed from the split, and the name and type of the second partition.

`device`

The disk device filename, e.g., */dev/disk0*.

periodic

`periodic` *name*

Serves as a method of organizing recurring administrative tasks. *periodic* is used in conjunction with the *cron* facility, called by the following three entries from */etc/crontab*:

```
1   3   *   *   *   root   periodic daily
15  4   *   *   6   root   periodic weekly
30  5   1   *   *   root   periodic monthly
```

The facility is controlled by the */etc/defaults/periodic.conf* file, which specifies its default behavior. *periodic* runs all the scripts that it finds in the directory specified in *name*. If *name* is an absolute pathname, there is no doubt as to which directory is intended. If simply a name—such as *daily*—is given, the directory is assumed to be a subdirectory of */etc/periodic* or of one of the alternate directories specified in the configuration file's *local_periodic* entry.

periodic can also be executed from the command line to run the administrative scripts manually. For example, to run the daily script, run *periodic* as root using *daily* as its argument:

```
$ sudo periodic daily
```

The configuration file contains several entries for valid command arguments that control the location and content of the reports that *periodic* generates. Here are the entries related to daily:

```
# Daily options
...
daily_output="/var/log/daily.out"    Append report to a file
daily_show_success="YES"             Include success messages
daily_show_info="YES"                Include informational messages
daily_show_badconfig="NO"            Exclude configuration error
messages.
```

ping

`ping` [*options*] *host*

Confirms that a remote host is online and responding. *ping* is intended for use in network testing, measurement, and management. Because of the load it can impose on the network, it is unwise to use *ping* during normal operations or from automated scripts.

For a full list of options, see the *ping* manpage.

Options

-a Beeps whenever a packet is received.

-c count
Stop after sending (and receiving) *count* ECHO_RESPONSE packets.

-d Set the SO_DEBUG option on the socket being used.

-f Flood *ping*-output packets as fast as they come back or 100 times per second, whichever is more. This can be very hard on a network and should be used with caution; only a privileged user may use this option.

-i wait
Send a packet every *wait* seconds. Default is to wait 1 second between each packet. *wait* must be a positive integer value. Cannot be used with the *-f* option.

-l preload
Send *preload* number of packets as fast as possible before changing to default packet dispatch frequency. High packet losses are to be expected during preload delivery.

-n Only show host IP addresses, not hostnames.

-o Stop after one reply packet.

-p digits
Specify up to 16-pad bytes to fill out packet sent. This is useful for diagnosing data-dependent problems in a network. The 32 most significant hexidecimal *digits* are used for the pattern. For example, *-p ff* causes the sent packet to be filled with all 1s, as does:

```
-p ffffffffffffffffffffffffffffff0001
```

-q Quiet output; nothing is displayed except the summary lines at startup time and when finished.

-r Bypass the normal routing tables and send directly to a host on an attached network.

-R Set the IP record route option, which stores the route of the packet inside the IP header. The contents of the record route will be printed if the *-v* option is given and will be set on return packets if the target host preserves the record route option across echoes or the *-l* option is given.

-s packetsize
Specify number of data bytes to be sent. Default is 56, which translates into 64 ICMP data bytes when combined with the 8 bytes of ICMP header data. Maximum *packetsize* is $8192(2^{13}) - 8 = 8184$.

-t seconds
Time out after *seconds* seconds, no matter how many packets have been received.

-v Verbose; list ICMP packets received other than *ECHO_RESPONSE*.

pl

pl [-input *input_binary_file* | -output *output_binary_file*]

Translates XML property list files into the more compact and readable key/value NeXT format. Also translates between this and a serialized binary format, in either direction. XML is read from standard input, NeXT-format data is read from standard input and written to standard output, and serialized binary data is read from and written to files specified with arguments.

This command has been deprecated. You should use *plutil* instead.

Options
-input
> Specify a serialized binary file as input.

-output
> Specify a serialized binary file as output.

plutil

plutil [-lint] [-convert [xml1 | binary1]] *filenames*

Checks property list files for validity, or converts property list files between XML and binary formats. Files are converted in place, unless the *-o* option is used.

Options
-lint
> Check the file for errors. This is the default action.

-convert format
> Converts the file to *format*, where *format* is *XML1* or *binary1*.

-o target
> Sends converted data to file *target*. Can only be used with a single input file.

-e ext
> Uses *ext* as the extension for the converted file.

pmset

pmset [-a | -b | -c] *action(s)*

Modifies the system's power management settings. *pmset* is a command-line alternative to the Energy Saver System Preferences. The settings apply system wide and across reboots. Therefore, *pmset* requires root privileges to run.

Options
-a Use the settings that follow for all modes (the default).

-b Use the settings that follow this flag when only the battery is in use.

-c Use the settings that follow this flag only when the power adapter is plugged in.

-g subsystem
> Display current settings of subsystem, where subsystem is one of:

cap
> Capabilities of the machine

disk
> Settings on disk

sched
> Scheduled events

ups
> UPS thresholds

ps
> Battery and UPS status

pslog
> Continuous log of power sources

-u   Use the settings that follow this flag only when running off a UPS.

Actions

acwake 1 | 0
> Wake when the power source is changed.

autorestart 1 | 0
> Restart automatically after power loss.

disksleep n
> Spin down the hard drive after *n* minutes of idle time.

displaysleep n
> Dim the display after *n* minutes of idle time.

dps 1 | 0
> Change processor speed based on load.

halfdim 1 | 0
> Dim the screen to halfway between full brightness and off.

lessbright 1 | 0
> Dim the screen slightly when using this power source.

lidwake 1 | 0
> Wake when the laptop lid is opened.

powerbutton 1 | 0
> Sleep when the power button is pressed.

reduce 1 | 0
> Reduce processor speed (1), or set to highest (0).

ring 1 | 0
> Wake on modem ring

sleep n
> Put the computer to sleep after *n* minutes of idle time.

sms 1 | 0
> Park the heads when sudden changes in motion are detected.

womp 1 | 0
> Set the wake on magic packet ("wake for network administrator access") to on (1) or off (0).

Examples

Set the system to dim the display after three minutes and go to sleep after 10 minutes when using the battery:

```
$ pmset -b dim 3 sleep 10
```

Set both the battery-only and power adapter settings at once:

```
$ pmset -b dim 3 sleep 10 slower 1 -c dim 20

sleep 60 slower 0
```

---

pr

pr [*files*]

Converts a text file or files to a paginated, columned version, with headers. If - is provided as the filename, read from standard input.

Options

+*beg_pag*
>   Begin printing on page *beg_pag*.

-*num_cols*
>   Print in *num_cols* number of columns, balancing the number of lines in the columns on each page.

-*a*   Print columns horizontally, not vertically.

-*d*   Double space.

-*e*[*tab-char*[*width*]]
>   Convert tabs (or *tab-chars*) to spaces. If *width* is specified, convert tabs to *width* characters (default is 8).

-*F*   Separate pages with formfeeds, not newlines.

-*f*   Same as -*F*, but pause before printing the first page to the screen.

-*h header*
>   Use *header* for the header instead of the filename.

-*i*[*out-tab-char*[*out-tab-width*]]
>   Replace spaces with tabs on output. Can specify alternative tab character (default is tab) and width (default is 8).

-*l lines*
>   Set page length to *lines* (default 66). If *lines* is less than 10, omit headers and footers.

-*m*   Print all files, one file per column.

-*n*[*delimiter*[*digits*]]
>   Number columns, or, with the -*m* option, number lines. Append *delimiter* to each number (default is a tab) and limit the size of numbers to *digits* (default is 5).

-*o offset*
>   Set left margin to *offset*.

-*p*   Pause before each page, if output is to a terminal.

-*r*   Continue silently when unable to open an input file.

-s[delimiter]
> Separate columns with *delimiter* (default is a tab) instead of spaces.

-t   Suppress headers, footers, and fills at end of pages.

-v   Convert unprintable characters to octal backslash format.

-w page_width
> Set the page width to *page_width* characters for multicolumn output. Default is 72.

printenv

printenv [*variables*]

Prints values of all environment variables or, optionally, only the specified *variables*.

ps

ps [*options*]

Reports on active processes. Note that you don't need to include a - before options. In options, *list* arguments should either be separated by commas or be put in double quotes.

Options

a   List all processes, not just yours.

c   List the command name without the path.

e   Include environment.

h   Include a header with each page of information.

j   List information for keywords: user, pid, ppid, pgid, sess, jobc, state, tt, time, and command.

L   List all keywords.

l   List information for keywords: uid, pid, ppid, cpu, pri, nice, vsz, rss, wchan, state, tt, time, and command.

M   List each tasks threads.

m   Sort by memory usage.

O   Append the *keywords* that are in a list after the PID. The title of the *keyword* can be changed by using an = sign after the *keyword*. (*keyword=newtitle*)

o   Same as *O* except it uses only the supplied keywords for the output of *ps*.

p   List information for the supplied PID.

r   List by CPU rather than by PID.

S   Include child processes' CPU time and page faults.

T   List information for standard input process.

ttty
> Display only processes running on *tty*.

U   List processes belonging to username.

u	List information for keywords: user, pid, %cpu, %mem, vsz, rss, tt, state, start, time, and command. The listing will be as if the *-r* option was supplied to *ps*.
v	List information for keywords: pid, state, time, sl, re, pagein, vsz, rss, lim, tsiz, %cpu, %mem, and command. The listing will be as if the *-m* option was supplied to *ps*.
w	Wide format. Don't truncate long lines.
x	Include processes without an associated terminal.

Keywords

If there is an alias for the keyword, it's listed next to it.

Table 2-6. Keywords for use with the ps command

Keyword	Description
%cpu, pcpu	Percentage of CPU used
%mem, pmem	Percentage of memory used
acflag, acflg	Accounting flag
command	Command and arguments
cpu	Short-term factor of CPU use
flags, f	Hexadecimal representation of process flags
inblk, inblock	Total amount of blocks read
jobc T	Count for job control
ktrace	Tracing flags
ktracep	Tracing vnode
lim	Limit of memory usage
logname	Username of user that started the command
lstart	Start time
majflt, pagein	Page fault totals
minflt	Page reclaim totals
msgrcv	Messages received total
msgsnd	Messages sent total
nice, ni	Value of nice
nivcsw	Involuntary context switches total
nsigs, nsignals	Signals taken total
nswap	Swap in/out totals
nvcsw	Voluntary context switch totals
nwchan	Wait channel
oublk, oublock	Blocks written total
p_ru	Amount of resources used out of resources used
padd	Address of swap
pgid	Group number for the process
pid	ID number of the process
poip	Progress of current pageouts
ppid	ID number of the parent process
pri	Scheduling priority

Table 2-6. Keywords for use with the ps command (continued)

Keyword	Description
re	Core residency time
rgid	The real GID
rlink	Reverse link on run queue
rss	Resident set size
rsz	Resident set size + (text size/text use count) (alias rssize)
rtprio	Priority in real time
ruid	ID of the real user
ruser	Name of the user
sess	Pointer for the session
sig, pending	Signals that are pending
sigcatch, caught	Signals that have been caught
sigignore, ignored	Signals that have been ignored
sigmask, blocked	Signals that have been blocked
sl	Sleep time
start	Start time
state, stat	State of symbolic process
svgid	An executable setgid's saved GID
svuid	An executable setuid's saved UID
tdev	Device number of the control terminal
time, cputime	Total of user and system CPU time
tpgid	GID of the control terminal process
tsess	Pointer session of the control terminal
tsiz	Size of the text
tt	Name of control terminal
tty	The control terminal's full name
uprocp	Pointer of the process
ucomm	Accounting name
uid	ID of the user
upr, usrpri	The scheduling priority after a system call as been made
user	Name of the user from UID
vsz, vsize	Listed in kilobytes the virtual size
wchan	Wait channel
xstat	Status of a zombie or stopped process; exit or stop

pwd

pwd [*options*]

Prints the full pathname of the current working directory.

Options

-L   Write the full pathname of the current working directory without resolving symbolic links.

-P   Write the full pathname of the current working directory with resolving symbolic links (-P is the default behavior).

quota

quota [*options*]

Displays the disk limits for the current user, or the current user's group, or other users and groups if the user is the superuser.

Options

-g [*group*]
    Display quotas for the specified *group*, if the user is a member of that group. If *group* is not specified, list all groups for which the user is a member. If the user is super-user, any *group*'s quotas may be listed.

-q   Quiet mode. Only displays a message if the user is over quota. This is useful for login scripts.

-u *user*
    Display quotas for user. May only be used by the superuser.

-v   Display quotas even on filesystems where no storage is allocated. This option takes precedence over -q.

rcp

rcp [*options*] *file1 file2*

rcp [*options*] *file... directory*

Copies files between two machines. Each *file* or *directory* is either a remote filename of the form *rname@rhost:path* or a local filename.

rcp doesn't preserve resource forks or metadata when copying files that contain them.

Options

-K   Suppress all Kerberos authentication.

-k   Attempt to get tickets for remote host; query *krb_realmofhost* to determine realm.

-p   Preserve modification times and modes of the source files.

-r   If any of the source files are directories, *rcp* copies each subtree rooted at that name. The destination must be a directory.

-x   Turn on DES encryption for all data passed by *rcp*.

reboot

```
reboot [options]
```

Prepares the system, terminates all processes, and then reboots the operating system. During preparation, all filesystem caches are flushed and running processes are sent a SIGTERM followed by SIGKILL.

Options

-l   Don't log the halt via syslog (i.e., *mach_kernel*, syncing disks, etc.).

-n   Don't flush filesystem caches. Should not be used indiscriminately.

-q   The filesystem caches are flushed but the system is otherwise halted ungracefully. Should not be used indiscriminately.

register_mach_bootstrap_servers

```
register_mach_bootstrap_servers config_source
```

Registers a Mach port with the bootstrap task of *mach_init* on behalf of a specified daemon. (A Mach *task* is analogous to a process that runs within the kernel of Mac OS X; a *port* is used to communicate between tasks.) When another task sends a request to the bootstrap task for access to a port, *mach_init* starts up the associated daemon if necessary.

This serves as a replacement for certain startup items. Instead of launching services from */System/Library/StartupItems/* (processed by *SystemStarter*), files in */etc/mach_init.d/* are processed by *register_mach_bootstrap_servers*, which is called from */etc/rc*. (Per-user services are started by the login window application, which uses *register_mach_bootstrap_servers* to process */etc/mach_init_per_user.d/*.) One advantage of this over startup items is that a daemon can be run only when needed, if another process needs to communicate with it, thus reducing resource consumption.

Options

config_source
    Either an XML property list (*.plist*) file, or a directory containing such files. Each file is usually named after the associated daemon, and contains some of the following keys:

    command
        The path to the server executable. This is a required key.

    isKUNCServer
        Specify whether the daemon is *kuncd*, the Kernel-User Notification Center server, used by the kernel to communicate with users. Defaults to false.

    OnDemand
        Specify whether the daemon should only be started when it first receives a request for its bootstrap port. If set to false, the daemon is started immediately. Defaults to true.

ServiceName
> An identifier for the service. The name should follow the convention used for Java classes: the reversed DNS domain name associated with the responsible organization, followed by one or more segments specifically identifying the service (e.g., *com.apple.DirectoryService*). This is a required key.

username
> The user under which the daemon is started.

renice

```
renice [priority] [options] [target]
```

Controls the scheduling priority of various processes as they run. May be applied to a process, process group, or user (*target*). A privileged user may alter the priority of other users' processes. *priority* must, for ordinary users, lie between 0 and the environment variable PRIO_MAX (normally 20), with a higher number indicating increased niceness. A privileged user may set a negative priority, as low as PRIO_MIN, to speed up processes.

Options

+num
> Specify number by which to increase current priority of process, rather than an absolute priority number.

-num
> Specify number by which to decrease current priority of process, rather than an absolute priority number.

-g   Interpret *target* parameters as process GIDs.

-p   Interpret *target* parameters as PIDs (default).

-u   Interpret *target* parameters as usernames.

rev

```
rev [files]
```

Prints each line of each specified file. The order of the characters in each line is reversed. If no file is specified, *rev* reads from standard input.

rlogin

```
rlogin rhost [options]
```

Remote login. *rlogin* connects the terminal on the current local host system to the remote host system *rhost*. The remote terminal type is the same as your local terminal type. The terminal or window size is also copied to the remote system if the server supports it.

Options

-8   Allow an 8-bit input data path at all times.

-d   Debugging mode.

-e char
> Specify escape character *char* (default is ~).

-E   Don't interpret any character as an escape character.

-k   Attempt to get tickets from remote host, requesting them in the realm as determined by *krb_realm-ofhost*.

-K   Suppress all Kerberos authentication.

-l username
> Specify a different *username* for the remote login. Default is the same as your local username.

-L   Allow *rlogin* session to be run without any output postprocessing (i.e., run in *litout* mode).

---

rm

```
rm [options] files
```

Deletes one or more *files*. To remove a file, you must have write permission in the directory that contains the file, but you need not have permission on the file itself. If you don't have write permission on the file, you will be prompted (y or n) to override.

Note that on symbolic links, *rm* removes the link, not the target file.

If any of the files you're removing begin with a dash, put a -- in front of them. For instance, if you create a file called *-f* (dash eff), use *rm -- -f* to remove it.

Options

--   All options following are filenames, not options.

-d   Remove directories, even if they are not empty.

-f   Remove write-protected files without prompting.

-i   Prompt for y (remove the file) or n (don't remove the file).

-P   Cause *rm* to overwrite files three different times before deleting them.

-r, -R
> If *file* is a directory, remove the entire directory and all its contents, including subdirectories. This option can be dangerous.

-v   Turn on verbose mode. *rm* prints the name of each file before removing it.

-W   Undelete files on a union filesystem that whiteouts have been applied over.

If any of the files you're removing begin with a dash, put a -- in front of them. Say you create a file called *-x*:

```
$ ls > -x
$ rm -x
rm: invalid option -- x
Try `rm --help' for more information.
```

The *-x* is taken as an option to *rm*. Instead, put the -- in front:

```
$ rm -- -x
```

rmdir

```
rmdir [options] directories
```

Deletes the named *directories* (not the contents). *directories* are deleted from the parent directory and must be empty (if not, *rm -r* can be used instead). See also *mkdir*.

Option

-p   Remove *directories* and any intervening parent directories that become empty as a result; useful for removing subdirectory trees.

rsync

```
rsync [options] source destination
```

Transfers files from *source* to *destination*. *rsync* is a synchronization system that uses checksums to determine differences (instead of relying on modification dates) and does partial file transfers (transferring only the differences instead of the entire files).

rsync can use a remote shell (*rsh* by default) as a transport, in which case the remote host must have *rsync* installed as well. You can use a remote shell like *ssh* instead of the default by specifying that in *options*.

You can also use *rsync* without a remote shell, in which case *rsync* requires that the remote host run an *rsync* server daemon. For details on the advanced features of *rsync*, including running an *rsync* server, refer to *rsync*'s manpage. The following descriptions and examples cover *rsync*'s basic operation.

rsync doesn't preserve resource forks or HFS metadata when copying files that contain them.

The *rsync source* and *destination* arguments can be specified in several ways, as shown in Table 2-7.

Table 2-7. rsync source and destination arguments

Source	Destination	Description
srcpath [...]	[user@]host:destpath	Transfer local directory srcpath to remote directory destpath.[a]
[user@]host:srcpath	destpath	Transfer remote directory srcpath to local directory destpath.[a]
[user@]host:srcpath		List contents of srcpath without transferring anything.[a]
srcpath [...]	[user@]host::destpath	Transfer local directory srcpath to remote directory destpath.[b]
[user@]host::srcpath	[destpath]	Transfer remote directory srcpath to local directory destpath, or list srcpath if destpath is not specified.[b]
rsync://[user@]host[:port]:/ srcpath	[destpath]	Transfer remote directory srcpath to local directory destpath, or list srcpath if destpath is not specified.[b]
srcpath [...]	destpath	Transfer local directory srcpath to local directory destpath.

a Uses a remote shell as the transport and requires *rsync* on the remote host.
b Doesn't use a remote shell but requires an *rsync* server running on the remote host. Note the double colons (::), except for the URL format.

Selected options

-a, --archive

Copy *source* recursively and save most file metadata in the copies, including owner, group, permissions, and modification times. Also copies symlinks (but not hard links). Equivalent to using *-rlptgoD*.

-b, --backup

If a file in *source* already exists in *destination*, make a backup copy before overwriting. Name the backup file by appending ~ to the original filename.

-D, --devices

Copy any character and block device files in *source* to *destination*.

--delete

Delete any files in destination that aren't in source.

-e command, --rsh=command

Use the remote shell *command* as the transport instead of the default *rsh*. The usual alternative is *ssh*.

--existing

Don't add any new files to *destination*; update only what's there with any newer versions in *source*.

--exclude=pattern

Exclude from transfer those files in *source* that match *pattern*. See *rsync*'s manpage for details on constructing exclude patterns.

-g, --group

Preserve the groups of the source files in the copies.

-I, --ignore-times

Transfer source files that have the same name, length, and date stamp as files in destination. The default behavior is to skip transfer of such files.

-l, --links

Copy any symbolic links in source to destination.

-o, --owner

Preserve the owners of the source files in the copies.

-p, --perms

Preserve the permissions of the source files in the copies.

--partial

Don't remove partially transferred files from *destination*. If a transfer is interrupted, this option allows a retried transfer to resume from where the failed attempt ended, instead of starting again from the beginning.

-r, --recursive

Copy recursively. If any of the source files are directories, *rsync* copies each subtree rooted at that name.

-t, --times

Preserve the modification times of the source files in the copies. Use this option whenever you want identical files excluded from subsequent transfers to the same directory.

-u, --update

Don't transfer a file if it has a newer copy already existing in destination.

-v, --verbose

> Be verbose. Add *v*s for increased verbosity.

-z, --compress

> Compress data before transfer, which helps decrease transfer time over slower connections.

Examples

Transfer the entire local *~/Documents* directory into the folder named *Backups* on the machine at 192.168.2.56, using *rsh* as the transport:

```
$ rsync ~/Documents fred@192.168.2.56:Backups
```

Perform the same transfer using the archive and compress options as well as *ssh* as the transport:

```
$ rsync -aze ssh ~/Documents fred@192.168.2.56:Backups
```

A trailing slash on the source pathname causes *rsync* to transfer only the *contents* of that directory into the destination directory. This example transfers the contents of the remote */Backups/Documents* directory in the local *~/Temp* directory:

```
$ rsync -aze ssh fred@192.168.2.56:Backups/Documents/ ~/Temp
```

---

say

say [-v *voice*] [-o *out*.aiff] [-f *file* | *string* . . .]

Uses Mac OS X's Speech Synthesis manager to speak the *file* or *string* using the default voice set in the Speech preference panel (System Preferences → Speech → Text to Speech → System Voice).

Options

string

> Text to be spoken using the default system voice; for example:
>
> ```
> $ say "I love Mac OS X"
> ```
>
> Notice how the system pronounces the "X" of "Mac OS X" as "ten."

-f file

> Specify a *file* to be read as input and spoken using the default system voice; for example:
>
> ```
> $ say -f filename.txt
> ```

-v voice

> Use the specified voice instead of the default system voice; for example
>
> ```
> $ say -v Fred "I love Mac OS X"
> ```
>
> This uses the Fred *voice* to speak the *string*, "I love Mac OS X." The list of voices can be found in the Speech → Default Voices preference panel.

-o out.aiff

> Output the spoken text as an AIFF sound file; for example,
>
> ```
> $ say -o ~/Desktop/iheartmosx.aiff -v Fred "I love Mac OS X"
> ```
>
> This command uses the *voice* Fred to speak the *string* "I love Mac OS X," and save it as a sound file named *iheartmosx.aiff* on the Desktop. When outputting a sound file, the *-o* option *must* immediately follow the *say* command.

scp

scp [*options*] *file1 file2*

scp [*options*] *file... directory*

Securely copies files between two machines, using *ssh* as the transport. Each *file* or *directory* is either a remote filename of the form *rname@rhost:path* or a local filename.

scp doesn't preserve resource forks or metadata when copying files that contain them.

Options

-B   Run in batch mode; don't prompt for passwords.

-c *cipher*
> Use the specified type of encryption, either *blowfish*, *des*, or *3des*. (*3des* is the default.)

-C   Turn on compression.

-E   Preserves extended attributes, resource forks, and ACLs. Both ends of the connection must be running Mac OS X 10.4 or higher.

-F *filename*
> Use specified ssh configuration file.

-i *keyfile*
> Specify an identity file to use for authentication. The default is *$HOME/.ssh/identity*.

-o *keyword*
> Set configuration keyword, in the same format as the SSH config file.

-p   Preserve modification times and modes of the source files.

-P *port*
> Select port number to connect to. Note that this is a capital -*P*, not a lowercase -*p* as in *ssh*.

-q   Run in quiet mode, with no progress bar.

-r   If any of the source files are directories, *scp* copies each subtree rooted at that name. The destination must be a directory.

-S *pathname*
> Use the local *ssh* executable located at *pathname*.

-v   Be verbose.

-1   Force use of SSH1.

-2   Force use of SSH2.

-4   Use only IPv4 addresses.

-6   Use only IPv6 addresses.

screencapture

screencapture [-i [-s | -w | -W] | -m] [-x] { -c | *pathname* ...}

Saves the contents of the screen to a PDF file or to the Clipboard. Unless using the -*i* option to start an interactive screen capture, the contents of the entire display are captured.

Options

-c   Save screenshot to the Clipboard for later pasting.

-C   Capture the cursor, too.

-i   Initiate interactive screen capture. The mouse is used to select a region of the screen to capture. Pressing the spacebar toggles between this mouse selection mode and a window selection mode, in which clicking on a window captures the portion of the screen taken up by that window. Pressing the Control key saves the screenshot to the Clipboard. Pressing the Escape key cancels the interactive screen capture.

-m   Capture only the main display, if multiple displays are in use.

-s   Disable window selection mode in an interactive screen capture; only mouse selection is allowed.

-S   Capture the screen, not the window, even in window capture mode.

-w   Disable mouse selection mode in an interactive screen capture; only window selection is allowed.

-W   Start an interactive screen capture in window selection mode instead of mouse selection mode.

-x   Disable sound effects.

pathname
   The name of a file in which to save the screenshot. You should terminate the filename with a *.pdf* extension.

---

script

```
script [option] [file]
```

Forks the current shell and makes a typescript of a terminal session. The typescript is written to *file*. If no *file* is given, the typescript is saved in the file *typescript*. The script ends when the forked shell exits, usually with Control-D or *exit*.

Option

-a   Append to file or typescript instead of overwriting the previous contents.

---

scselect

```
scselect [[-n] location]
```

Changes active network location. With no arguments, a usage statement and a list of defined locations (or "sets") is printed to standard output, along with an indication of which location is currently active. Locations can be referred to by name or by integer ID.

Option

-n   Change the active network location, but don't apply the change.

scutil

```
scutil [-v] [-p]

scutil [-v] [-d] -r { hostname | IP_addr [IP_addr] }

scutil [-v] -w key [-t timeout]

scutil [-v] --get { ComputerName | LocalHostName }

scutil [-v] --set { ComputerName | LocalHostName } [hostname]
```

Provides control of the System Configuration framework's dynamic store. It's used to open an interactive session with *configd*, in which various commands are available to view and modify System Configuration keys.

As a quick example of interactive use, try this:

1. Invoke *scutil*. You will be placed at the *scutil* prompt.
2. Enter **open** to open the session with *configd*.
3. Enter **list**. You will see a set of keys, some of which are provided by the System Configuration framework (such as the keys in the File: domain), some of which are obtained from */Library/Preferences/SystemConfiguration/preferences.plist* (the Setup: keys), and some of which are published by the configuration agents (the State: keys).
4. Enter **show State:/Network/Global/DNS** to display the DNS dictionary. You should see a list of DNS servers and search domains configured on your system.
5. Enter **close**, then **quit**.

Options

-d   Enable debugging output to standard error.

--dns
    Display DNS configuration.

--get pref
    Print the system's computer name (use *pref* of *LocalHostName*) or Bonjour hostname (*ComputerName*) to standard output.

-p   Enable a private API with additional commands, including *lock*, *unlock*, *touch*, *snapshot*, *n.file*, *n.signal*, *n.wait*, and *n.callback*.

--proxy
    Display proxy configuration.

-r *nodename*
    Determine how the specified node (given as a hostname or an IP address) would be reached, printing the result to standard output. Possibilities include *Reachable*, *Directly Reachable Address* (the address is on the local network), and *Local Address* (the address resolves to the host on which the command is run). For systems with more than one network interface, two arguments may be given, where the first is the system's local address, and the second is the remote address. Note that this doesn't determine whether a machine at the specified address is currently active, only whether that address is reachable.

--set pref name
> Set the system's computer name or Bonjour hostname. If the new hostname isn't specified on the command line, it's taken from standard input.

-*t* Specify the timeout to wait for the presence of a data store key, in seconds. Defaults to 15.

-*v* Enable verbose output to standard error.

-*w* Exit when the specified key exists in the data store or until the timeout has expired.

Commands

scutil enters interactive mode when invoked with no arguments.

add key [temporary]
> Add a key to the data store with the value of the current dictionary. The *temporary* keyword causes it to be flushed when the session to *configd* is closed.

close
> Close a session with *configd*.

d.add key [| ? | #] value...*
> Add an entry to the current dictionary. The optional type specifier can designate the values as arrays (*), Booleans (?), or numbers (#).

d.init
> Create an empty dictionary.

d.remove key
> Remove the specified key from the current dictionary.

d.show
> Display the contents of the current dictionary.

exit
> Exit the *scutil* session.

f.read file
> Read prepared commands from a file.

get key
> Cause the value of the specified key to become the current dictionary.

help
> Print a list of available commands.

list [regex]
> List keys in the System Configuration data store. A regular expression may be specified to restrict which keys are listed.

lock
> Prevent changes to the data store by other processes.

n.add key [pattern]
> Request notification of changes to the specified key or to keys matching a regular expression (when the *pattern* argument is used).

n.callback [verbose]
> Send notifications via a callback function defined in the *scutil* code. This isn't particularly useful without modifying the source code.

n.cancel
> Cancel *n.watch* settings.

n.changes
> List changed keys that have been marked with notification requests and reset the state of notification.

n.file [identifier]
> Send notifications to a file descriptor. After issuing this command, the prompt returns only after a notification is received.

n.list [pattern]
> List keys upon which notification requests have been set. With the *pattern* argument, lists notification requests for keys matching regular expressions.

n.remove key [pattern]
> Remove notification requests for the specified key or regular expression (when the *pattern* argument is used).

n.signal signal [process_ID]
> Send notifications by signaling a process. If a PID isn't specified, the signal is sent to the *scutil* process. The signal is specified either as a name or a number (as described in the *kill* manpage).

n.wait
> Send notifications via Mach messaging.

n.watch [verbose]
> Cause changes to keys marked with notification requests to issue immediate notices, obviating the need to use *n.changes* to notice that the change has occurred.

notify key
> Send a notification for the specified key.

open
> Open a session with *configd*.

q   Exit the *scutil* session.

quit
> Exit the *scutil* session.

remove key
> Remove the specified key from the data store.

set key
> Set the specified key to the value of the current dictionary.

show key [pattern]
> Same as *get key*, followed by *d.show*.

snapshot
> Save current store and session data to XML property lists in */var/tmp/*.

touch key
> "Touch" the specified key, spurring notifications as if it had changed, but leaving it unaltered.

unlock
> After issuing a *lock* command, allow other processes to make changes to the data store.

sdiff

sdiff [*options*] *file1 file2*

Compares two files to find differences and interactively merges them. Without the *-o* option, *sdiff* behaves like *diff-side-by-side*.

Options

-a, --text
> Treat all files as text files. Useful for checking to see if binary files are identical.

-b, --ignore-space-change
> Ignore repeating blanks and end-of-line blanks; treat successive blanks as one.

-B, --ignore-blank-lines
> Ignore blank lines in files.

-d, --minimal
> Ignore segments of numerous changes and output a smaller set of changes.

-E, --ignore-tab-expansion
> Ignore changes based on expanding tabs.

-H, speed-large-files
> Speed output of large files by scanning for scattered small changes; long stretches with many changes may not show up.

--help
> Print brief usage message.

-i, --ignore-case
> Ignore case in text comparison. Upper- and lowercase are considered the same.

-I regexp, --ignore-matching-lines=regexp
> Ignore lines in files that match the regular expression *regexp*.

-l, --left-column
> For two-column output (*-y*), show only left column of common lines.

-o outfile, --output=outfile
> Send identical lines of *file1* and *file2* to *outfile*; print line differences and edit *outfile* by entering, when prompted, the following commands:
>
> | | |
> |---|---|
> | *e* | Edit an empty file. |
> | *e b* | Edit both left and right columns. |
> | *e l* | Edit left column. |
> | *e r* | Edit right column. |
> | *l* | Append left column to *outfile*. |
> | *q* | Exit the editor. |
> | *r* | Append right column to *outfile*. |
> | *s* | Silent mode; don't print identical lines. |
> | *v* | Turn off "silent mode." |

-s, --suppress-common-lines
> For two-column output (*-y*), don't show common lines.

--strip-trailing-cr
> Strip trailing carriage return from input.

-t, --expand-tabs
> Produce output with tabs expanded to spaces to line up tabs properly in output.

-v, --version
> Print version number of this version of *sdiff*.

-W, --ignore-all-space
> Ignore all whitespace in files for comparisons.

-wn, --width=n
> For two-column output (*-y*), produce columns with a maximum width of *n* characters. Default is 130.

Example

Show differences using 80 columns and ignore identical lines:

```
$ sdiff -s -w80 list.1 list.2
```

---

sed

sed [*options*] [*files*]

Streams editor. Edits one or more *files* without user interaction. For more information on *sed*, see *sed and awk* (O'Reilly). The *-e* and *-f* options may be provided multiple times, and they may be used with each other.

Options

-a   Treat all files as text and compare them.

-e instruction
> Apply the editing *instruction* to the files.

-E   Use extended regular expressions.

-f script
> Apply the set of instructions from the editing *script*.

-i extension
> Edit files in place, saving the original files with *extension* appended. If *extension* is not specified, no backups are made.

-n   Suppress default output.

---

service

service --list

service { --test-if-available | --test-if-configured-on } *service*

service *service* { start | stop }

A shell script used to list, start, and stop network services. Primarily, this is an interface to services managed by *xinetd*, but it also includes support for Postfix (with a service name of *smtp*) and for receipt of faxes (*fax-receive*).

Options

--list
> Print a list of services available for management to standard output.

--test-if-available
> Return 0 if the specified service is available on the system; 1 if not.

--test-if-configured-on
> Return 0 if the specified service is currently configured to run; 1 if not.

SetFile

SetFile [*options*] *files*

Sets the HFS+ file attributes (metadata) of *files*. *SetFile* is installed with the Xcode Tools (*/Developer/Tools*). Since this directory isn't in the shell's search path by default, you might to need to specify *SetFile*'s pathname to invoke it. See also *GetFileInfo*.

Options

-a attribute
> Set those file attributes that toggle on or off (sometimes called "Finder flags"). To set an attribute, provide that attribute's letter as uppercase in *attribute*. To unset an attribute, provide the letter in lowercase. You can specify multiple attributes at once; any not specified will retain their current setting in *files*. Refer to Table 2-8 for the specific attributes.

Table 2-8. Attributes for use with SetFile's -a option

Attribute	Set | unset	Meaning
Alias	*A | a*	File is/isn't an alias.
Bundle	*B | b*	File has/hasn't a bundle resource.
Custom Icon	*C | c*	File has/hasn't a custom icon.
Desktop Item	*D | d*	File is/isn't on the Desktop.
Extension	*E | e*	Filename extension is/isn't hidden.
Inited	*I | i*	File is/isn't init'ed.
Locked	*L | l*	File is/isn't locked.
Shared	*M | m*	Multiple users can/can't run file at once (applies to application files).
INIT	*N | n*	File has/hasn't INIT resource.
System	*S | s*	File is/isn't a system file (locks name).
Stationary	*T | t*	File is/isn't a stationary file.
Invisible	*V | v*	File is/isn't invisible to Finder.

-c creator
> Set the file's four-character creator code to *creator*.

-d date
> Set the file's creation date to *date*. Specify *date* in this format: "*mm/dd[yy]yy* [*hh:mm*[:*ss*] [AM | PM]]". Enclose *date* in quotes if it contains spaces.

-m date
> Set the file's modification date to *date*, specified as for *-d*.

-t type
> Set the file's four-character type code to *type*.

Example

Set the attributes of all files in the working directory whose names end with "jpg" to those of an unlocked GraphicConverter JPEG file, and give them all the same creation date:

```
$ /Developer/Tools/SetFile -a l -c GKON -t JPEG - d ↵
"07/01/05  00:00" *jpg
```

sftp

sftp [*options*] [*hostname*]

sftp [*user@*]*hostname*:[*pathname*]

Secure FTP. Transfers files to and from remote network site *hostname* using *ssh* as the transport. Once an *sftp* connection is made, *sftp* becomes interactive, prompting the user for a command. Type *help* to see a list of known commands.

If *pathname* is a directory, it becomes the initial remote working directory once the connection is made. If *pathname* is a file, *sftp* transfers that file into the local working directory, closes the connection, and exits without entering interactive mode.

Options

-b filename
> Run in batch mode, reading commands from *filename* instead of standard input.

-B buffersize
> Use a buffer size of *buffersize* bytes when transferring files instead of the default 32768 bytes.

-C   Turn on compression.

-F filename
> Use specified *ssh* configuration file.

-o keyword
> Set configuration keyword.

-P sftp-server_path
> Connect to the local *sftp-server* program at *sftp-server_path*, instead of using *ssh* (for debugging purposes). The default location for the program on Mac OS X is */usr/libexec/sftp-server*.

-R n
> Allow up to *n* outstanding requests, instead of the default, 16.

-s subsystem
> Invoke remote subsystem.

-S pathname
> Use local *ssh* executable located at *pathname*.

-v   Be verbose.

-1   Attempt a Version 1 connection.

showmount

showmount [-a | -d | -e] [-3] [*nfs_server*]

Queries the NFS mount daemon, *mountd*, to show which clients have mounted which directories from the NFS server. Called without flags, *showmount* prints a list of NFS client IP addresses to standard output; *nfs_server* defaults to *localhost*.

Options

-3   Use NFS Version 3.

-a   List clients with the exports they're mounting, in the form *IP_addr:pathname*.

-d   List exports that are mounted on clients, instead of client IP addresses.

-e   Print the server's list of NFS exports to standard output.

shutdown

shutdown [*options*] *when* [*message*]

Terminates all processing. *when* may be a specific time (in *hh:mm* format), a number of minutes to wait (in *+m* format), or *now*. A broadcast *message* notifies all users to log off the system. Processes are signaled with SIGTERM, to allow them to exit gracefully. Only privileged users can execute the *shutdown* command. Broadcast messages, default or defined, are displayed at regular intervals during the grace period; the closer the shutdown time, the more frequent the message.

Options

-h   Halt the system when shutdown is complete.

-k   Print the warning message, but suppress actual shutdown.

-o [*-n*]
      Execute *halt* or *reboot* instead of calling *init*. Passing *-n* also prevents a file cache flush.

-r   Reboot the system when shutdown is complete.

sips

sips [-h | --help | -H | --helpProperties]

sips [--debug] { -g | --getProperty } *property image_or_profile_filename*...

sips [--debug] { -x | --extractProfile } *profile_filename image_filename*...

sips [--debug] { -X | --extractTag } *tag tag_filename profile_filename*...

sips [--debug] { -v | --verify } *profile_filename*...

sips [--debug] { -s | --setProperty } *property value* [--out *filename*] *image_or_profile_filename*...

sips [--debug] { -d | --deleteProperty } *property* [--out *filename*] *image_or_profile_filename*...

```
sips [--debug] { -r | --rotate } degrees [--out filename] image_filename...

sips [--debug] { -f | --flip } { horizontal | vertical } [--out filename]
image_filename...

sips [--debug] { -c | --cropToHeightWidth | -p | --padToHeightWidth | -z
|resampleHeightWidth } height_pixels width_pixels [--out filename] image_
filename...

sips [--debug] { -Z | --resampleHeightWidthMax | --resampleHeight |
--resampleWidth } pixels [--out filename] image_filename...

sips [--debug] { -i | --addIcon } [--out filename] image_filename...

sips [--debug] { -e | --embedProfile | -E | --embedProfileIfNone | -m |
--matchTo } profile_filename [--out filename] image_filename...

sips [--debug] { -M | --matchToWithIntent } profile_filename { absolute |
relative | perceptual | satuation } [--out filename] image_filename...

sips [--debug] --deleteTag tag [--out filename] profile_filename...

sips [--debug] --copyTag src_tag dst_tag [--out filename] profile_filename...

sips [--debug] --loadTag tag tag_filename [--out filename] profile_filename...

sips [--debug] --repair [--out filename] profile_filename...
```

The Scriptable Image Processing System (SIPS) tool can manipulate images and
ColorSync profiles from the command line.

> ColorSync profiles are International Color Consortium (ICC) files
> that characterize the color properties of different devices, so that
> accurate color matching can be performed between them. There are
> ColorSync profiles located under */System/Library/ColorSync/Profiles/*,
> */Library/ColorSync/Profiles/*, */Library/Printers/*, and */Library/Image
> Capture/Devices/*, among other places. For more on ColorSync, see
> *http://www.apple.com/macosx/features/colorsync/*.

Options

-c | --cropToHeightWidth
Crop an image to the specified size (in pixels). The image is cropped equally from
both top and bottom, and from both sides.

--copyTag
Copy the value of a tag in a ColorSync profile to another tag in the same profile.

-d | --deleteProperty
Delete the specified property. A list of possible properties may be obtained with
sips -H.

--debug
Enable debugging output.

--deleteTag
Delete the specified tag from a ColorSync profile.

-e | --embedProfile
Embed the specified ColorSync profile into the image.

-E | --embedProfileIfNone

Embed the specified ColorSync profile into the image only if another profile is not already embedded.

-f | --flip

Flip an image in the specified direction.

-g | --getProperty

Print the value of the specified property to standard output. A list of possible properties may be obtained with *sips -H*.

-h | --help

Print a usage message to standard output.

-H | --helpProperties

Print a list of image and profile properties to standard output.

-i | --addIcon

Add an icon for an image file to its resource fork, which is used in Finder previews.

--loadTag

Copy the value of a tag from a file to a ColorSync profile. (This is the opposite of *--extractTag*.)

-m | --matchTo

Match an image to the specified ColorSync profile.

-M | --matchToWithIntent

Match an image to the specified ColorSync profile with the given rendering intent. (Note the misspelled *satuation*; this is a typo in the *sips* code.)

--out

Specify the filename of the modified image file. By default, *sips* modifies the file in place; this option lets you save the modified file under a different name, leaving the original unchanged.

-p | --padToHeightWidth

Pad an image with blank space to the specified size (in pixels). The image is padded equally on both top and bottom, and on both sides.

-r | --rotate

Rotate an image the specified number of degrees clockwise.

--repair

Attempt to repair a malformed *desc* tag in a ColorSync profile. This is the same as the Repair operation under Profile First Aid in the ColorSync Utility application.

--resampleHeight

Stretch or compress an image to the specified height (in pixels).

--resampleWidth

Stretch or compress an image to the specified width (in pixels).

-s | --setProperty

Set a property to the specified value. A list of possible properties may be obtained with *sips -H*.

-v | --verify

Verify the syntax of a ColorSync profile. This is the same as the Verify operation under Profile First Aid in the ColorSync Utility application.

-x | --extractProfile
>	Copy an embedded ColorSync profile from an image to a file with the specified name.

-X | --extractTag
>	Copy the value of a tag (such as *desc*) from a ColorSync profile to a file with the specified name.

-z | --resampleHeightWidth
>	Stretch or compress an image to the specified size (in pixels).

-Z | --resampleHeightWidthMax
>	Stretch or compress an image while maintaining the aspect ratio. The largest dimension (height or width) is set to the specified size (in pixels).

Examples

Show the properties of a ColorSync profile (similar to what's displayed under the Profiles tab of the ColorSync Utility application):

```
$ sips -g all /Library/ColorSync/Profiles/WebSafeColors.icc
/Library/ColorSync/Profiles/WebSafeColors.icc
  size: 10644
  cmm: appl
  version: 2.2.0
  class: nmcl
  space: RGB
  pcs: Lab
  creation: 2003:07:01 00:00:00
  platform: APPL
  quality: normal
  deviceManufacturer: 0
  deviceModel: 0
  deviceAttributes0: 0
  deviceAttributes1: 0
  renderingIntent: perceptual
  creator: appl
  md5: 14487F1ED8F8947B15F6682BFCF21E00
  description: Web Safe Colors
  copyright: Copyright 2001 - 2003 Copyright Apple Computer Inc., all
rights reserved.
```

Convert a TIFF to a JPEG from the command line (also works for PNG, GIF, PICT, BMP, and other image formats):

```
$ sips -s format jpeg --out sample.jpeg sample.tiff
```

slogin

See *ssh*. (The *slogin* command file is a symbolic link to the *ssh* executable.)

slp_reg

    slp_reg -l

    slp_reg { -r | -d } URL [-a attribute_list]

Communicates with *slpd* to register services with the Service Location Protocol. Services are designated by SLP URLs.

Options

-*a*   Specify an SLP attribute list.

-*d*   Deregister the given service.

-*l*   List registered services. This option is currently unimplemented.

-*r*   Register the given service.

softwareupdate

    softwareupdate [-h | --help | -l | --list]

    softwareupdate { -i | --install | -d | --download } { -a | --all | -r |
    --req | package? }

    softwareupdate --ignored { none | add package ? | remove { -a | --all |
    package ? } }

    softwareupdate --schedule { on | off }

A command-line version of the Software Update application, this checks for and installs Apple software updates. When invoked without arguments, it prints a usage statement to standard output.

Options

-*d, --download*
> Download the specified update packages to the directory specified in Internet Preferences (now part of Safari's General preferences), but don't install them. The arguments are the same as the *-i* or *--install* option. This is useful when downloading updates for clients of a Network Install server.

-*h, --help*
> Print a usage statement to standard output.

-*i, --install*
> Install the specified update packages: either an explicit list of packages (with names as given by the *-l* or *--list* flag), all uninstalled packages (*-a* or *--all*), or only those packages listed as required (*-r* or *--req*).

-*l, --list*
> Print a list of uninstalled updates to standard output, including package name, version number, size, and whether a reboot is required after the install.

--ignored
> Add or remove packages to or from the list of those ignored for the system.

--reset-ignored
> Clear the list of ignored packages.

--schedule
> Turn automatic checks for updates on or off.

sort

sort [*options*] [*files*]

Sorts the lines of the named *files*. Compare specified fields for each pair of lines, or, if no fields are specified, compare them by byte, in machine collating sequence. See also *uniq*, *comm*, and *join*.

Options

-b   Ignore leading spaces and tabs.

-c   Check whether *files* are already sorted, and if so, produce no output.

-d   Sort in "phone directory" order, ignoring all characters except letters, digits, and blanks.

-f   Fold; ignore uppercase/lowercase differences.

-i   Ignore nonprinting characters (those outside ASCII 32 (space) to 126 (tilde)).

-m   Merge (i.e., sort as a group) input files.

-M   Attempt to treat the first three characters as a month designation (JAN, FEB, etc.). In comparisons, treat JAN < FEB and any valid month as less than an invalid name for a month.

-n   Sort in arithmetic order.

-o*file*
> Put output in *file*.

-r   Reverse the order of the sort.

-tc Separate fields with *c* (default is a tab).

-u   Identical lines in input file appear only one (unique) time in output.

-z*recsz*
> Provide *recsz* bytes for any one line in the file. This option prevents abnormal termination of *sort* in certain cases.

+n [-m]
> Skip *n* fields before sorting, and sort up to field position *m*. If *m* is missing, sort to end of line. Positions take the form *a.b*, which means character *b* of field *a*. If *.b* is missing, sort at the first character of the field.

-k n[,m]
> Similar to +. Skip *n*-1 fields and stop at *m*-1 fields (i.e., start sorting at the *n*th field, where the fields are numbered beginning with 1).

-T *tempdir*
> Directory pathname to be used for temporary files.

Examples

List files by decreasing number of lines:

> `$ wc -l * | sort -r`

Alphabetize a list of words, remove duplicates, and print the frequency of each word:

> `$ sort -fd wordlist | uniq -c`

---

split

`split [option] [infile] [outfile]`

Splits *infile* into equal-sized segments. *infile* remains unchanged, and the results are written to *outfileaa*, *outfileab*, and so on. (Default is *xaa*, *xab*, etc.). If *infile* is (or missing and default *outfile* is used), standard input is read.

Options

-n, -l n
> Split *infile* into *n*-line segments (default is 1000).

-b n[km]
> Split *infile* into *n*-byte segments. Alternate blocksizes may be specified:

k   1 kilobyte

m   1 megabyte

-    Take input from the standard input.

Examples

Break *bigfile* into 1000-line segments:

> `$ split bigfile`

Join four files, then split them into 10-line files named *new.aa*, *new.ab*, and so on. Note that without the -, *new.* is as a nonexistent input file:

> `$ cat list[1-4] | split -10 - new.`

SplitForks

`SplitForks { -u | -s | [-v] pathname }`

Copies the resource fork and HFS attributes from a file named *filename* into a separate file named *._filename*, equivalent to an AppleDouble Header file. The original file retains the resource fork and HFS metadata as well.

If *pathname* refers to a file, that file's resource fork and metadata are split out. If *pathname* is a directory, *SplitForks* does a recursive descent into the directory, working on every file within it.

FixupResourceForks undoes the actions of *SplitForks*.

Options

-s   Strip resource fork from source after splitting. By default, the resource fork is left in the file.

-u   Print a usage statement to standard output.

-v   Enable verbose output.

---

spray

spray [*options*]

Similar to *ping*, *spray* sends RPC packets to a host and determines how many were received and their transit time. *spray* can cause a lot of network traffic, so use it cautiously.

Options

-c count
> Specify *count* packets to send.

-d delay
> Allow for *delay* microseconds between each packet.

-l length
> Set the RPC call message packet length to *length* bytes. Because all values are not possible, *spray* rounds to the nearest possible value.

srm

srm [*option*] *file*

Securely removes files or directories by overwriting, renaming, and truncating before unlinking. This prevents other users from undeleting or recovering any information about the file from the command line. *srm* is the brute force behind the Finder's Secure Empty Trash option.

srm can't remove write-protected files owned by another user, regardless of the permissions on the directory containing the file.

Options

-f, --force
> Ignore nonexistent files, and never prompt.

-i, --interactive
> Prompt before files are deleted.

-r, -R, --recursive
> Recursively remove the files of directories.

-s, --simple
> Delete the file, but only overwrite the file with a single pass.

-m, --medium
> Overwrite the file with seven U.S. Department of Defense-compliant passes (0xF6, 0x00, 0xFF, random, 0x00, 0xFF, random).

-z, --zero
> After overwriting, zero blocks used by file.

-n, --nounlink
> Overwrite the file, but don't rename or unlink it.

-v, --verbose
> Display what is being done.

--help
> Display help file information for the *srm* command.

--version
> Display the version information for *srm*.

---

ssh

ssh [-l *user*] *host* [*commands*]

ssh [*options*] [*user@*]*host*

The Secure Shell, *ssh* is a secure replacement for the *rsh*, *rlogin*, and *rcp* programs. *ssh* uses strong public-key encryption technologies to provide end-to-end encryption of data. There may be licensing/patent issues restricting the use of the software in some countries.

Options

-a Turn off authentication agent connection forwarding.

-A Turn on authentication agent connection forwarding.

-b interface
> Use the specified network interface (on a multiple interface machine).

-c cipher
> Use the specified type of encryption, either *blowfish*, *des*, or *3des*. *3des* is the default.

-C Turn on compression.

-D port
> Behave like a SOCKS4 server, listening on port *port*.

-ec Specify escape character *c*. Use the word "none" to disable any escape character.

-f Send *ssh* to the background.

-F filename
> Use specified configuration file.

-g Accept connections to local forward ports from remote hosts.

-i keyfile
> Specify an identity file to use for authentication. The default is *$HOME/.ssh/identity*.

-I device
> Used smartcard *device*.

-k Turn off Kerberos ticket forwarding.

-l user
> Log in as *user*.

-L listenport:targethost: targetport
> Set up port forwarding from local host to a target host. For example, to listen on port 8143 locally, and have it forwarded to *imap.example.com* on port 143, use *-L 8143:imap.example.com:143*.

-m algorithm
> Use specified MAC algorithm(s).

-n   Don't allow reading from STDIN. For use when *ssh* is running in the background.

-N   Turn off remote command execution.

-o keyword
     Set configuration keyword.

-p port
     Connect to remote host on port *port*.

-P   Use a nonprivileged port for outgoing connections.

-q   Run in quiet mode.

-R port1:host2: port2
     Set up port forwarding from a remote host to a local host. See *-L*, but in reverse.

-s subsystem
     Invoke remote subsystem.

-t   Turn on pseudo-*tty* distribution.

-T   Turn off pseudo-*tty* distribution.

-v   Be verbose.

-x   Turn off X11 forwarding.

-X   Turn on X11 forwarding.

-Y   Turn on trusted X11 forwarding.

-1   Attempt a Version 1 connection.

-2   Attempt a Version 2 connection.

-4   Use only IPv4 addresses.

-6   Use only IPv6 addresses.

---

strings

strings [*options*] *files*

Searches object or binary files for sequences of four or more printable characters that end with a newline or null.

Options

-a   Search entire file, not just the initialized data portion of object files. Can also specify this option as -.

-o   Display the string's offset position before the string.

-t format
     Prepend each line of output with its byte offset. The offset is displayed in octal if *format* is *o*, decimal for *d*, and hex for *x*. You must specify *format*; there is no default.

-num
     Minimum string length is *num* (default is 4). Can also specify this option as *-n*.

stty

stty [*options*] [*modes*]

Sets terminal I/O options for the current device. Without options, *stty* reports the terminal settings, where a ^ indicates the Control key, and ^' indicates a null value. Most modes can be switched using an optional preceding dash (-, shown in brackets). The corresponding description is also shown in brackets. As a privileged user, you can set or read settings from another device using the syntax:

stty [*options*] [*modes*] < *device*

stty is one of the most complicated Unix commands. The complexity stems from the need to deal with a large range of conflicting, incompatible, and nonstandardized terminal devices—everything from printing teletypes to CRTs to pseudoterminals for windowing systems. Only a few of the options are really needed for day-to-day use. *stty sane* is a particularly valuable one to remember.

Options

-*a*   Report all option settings.

-*e*   Report current settings in BSD format.

-*f file*
        Use file instead of standard input.

-*g*   Report current settings in *stty* format.

Control modes

0   Hang upconnection (set the baud rate to zero).

n   Set terminal baud rate to *n* (e.g., 19200).

[-]clocal
        [Enable] disable modem control.

[-]cread
        [Disable] enable the receiver.

[-]crtscts
        [Disable] enable output hardware flow control using RTS/CTS.

csn
        Select character size in bits (5 *n* 8).

[-]cstopb
        [One] two stop bits per character.

[-]hup
        [Don't] hang up connection on last close.

[-]hupcl
        Same as *[-]hup*.

ispeed n
        Set terminal input baud rate to *n*.

[-]loblk
        [Don't] block layer output. For use with *shl*; obsolete.

ospeed n
        Set terminal output baud rate to *n*.

[-]parenb
> [Disable] enable parity generation and detection.

[-]parext
> [Disable] enable extended parity generation and detection for mark and space parity.

[-]parodd
> Use [even] odd parity.

speed num
> Set *ispeed* and *opseed* to the same *num*.

Input modes

[-]brkint
> [Don't] signal INTR on break.

[-]icrnl
> [Don't] map carriage return (^M) to newline (^J) on input.

[-]ignbrk
> [Don't] ignore break on input.

[-]igncr
> [Don't] ignore carriage return on input.

[-]ignpar
> [Don't] ignore parity errors.

[-]imaxbel
> [Don't] echo BEL when input line is too long.

[-]inlcr
> [Don't] map newline to carriage return on input.

[-]inpck
> [Disable] enable input parity checking.

[-]istrip
> [Don't] strip input characters to seven bits.

[-]iuclc
> [Don't] map uppercase to lowercase on input.

[-]ixany
> Allow [only XON] any character to restart output.

[-]ixoff
> [Don't] send START/STOP characters when the queue is nearly empty/full.

[-]ixon
> [Disable] enable START/STOP output control.

[-]parmrk
> [Don't] mark parity errors.

Output modes

[-]ocrnl
> [Don't] map carriage return to newline on output.

[-]olcuc
> [Don't] map lowercase to uppercase on output.

[-]onlcr
> [Don't] map newline to carriage return-newline on output.

[-]onlret
> [Don't] perform carriage return after newline.

[-]onocr
> [Don't] output carriage returns at column zero.

[-]opost
> [Don't] postprocess output; ignore all other output modes.

[-]oxtabs
> [Don't] on output expand tabs to spaces.

Local modes

[-]echo
> [Don't] echo every character typed.

[-]echoctl
> [Don't] echo control characters as ^char, DEL as ^?.

[-]echoe
> [Don't] echo ERASE character as BS-space-BS string.

[-]echok
> [Don't] echo newline after KILL character.

[-]echoke
> [Don't] erase entire line on line kill.

[-]echonl
> [Don't] echo newline (^J).

[-]echoprt
> [Don't] echo erase character as \retcaeahc/. Used for printing terminals.

[-]flusho
> Output is [not] being flushed.

[-]icanon
> [Disable] enable canonical input (ERASE and KILL processing).

[-]iexten
> [Disable] enable extended functions for input data.

[-]isig
> [Disable] enable checking of characters against INTR, QUIT, and SWITCH.

[-]lfkc
> Same as *[-]echok*. Obsolete.

[-]noflsh
> [Enable] disable flush after INTR, QUIT, or SWITCH.

[-]pendin
> [Don't] retype pending input at next read or input character.

[-]stappl
> [Line] application mode on a synchronous line.

[-]stflush
> [Disable] enable flush on synchronous line.

[-]stwrap
> [Enable] disable truncation on synchronous line.

[-]tostop
> [Don't] send SIGTTOU when background processes write to the terminal.

[-]altwerase
> [Don't] use a different erase algorithm when processing WERASE characters.

[-]mdmbuf
> Carrier Detect condition determines flow control output if on. If off, low Carrier Detect writes, return an error.

[-]xcase
> [Don't] change case on local output.

Control assignments

ctrl-char c
> Set control character to *c*. *ctrl-char* is one of the following: *dsusp, eof, eol, eol2, erase, intr, kill, lnext, quit, reprint, start, status, stop, susp, switch,* or *werase*.

min n
> With *-icanon*, *n* is the minimum number of characters that will satisfy the *read* system call until the timeout set with *time* expires.

time n
> With *-icanon*, *n* is the number of tenths of seconds to wait before a *read* system call times out. If the minimum number of characters set with *min* is read, the *read* can return before the timeout expires.

Combination modes

[-]evenp
> Same as *[-]parenb* and *cs7[8]*.

ek Reset ERASE and KILL characters to # and @.

[-]nl
> [Un] set *icrnl* and *onlcr*. *-nl* also unsets *inlcr, igncr, ocrnl,* and *onlret*.

[-]oddp
> Same as *[-]parenb, [-]parodd,* and *cs7[8]*.

[-]parity
> Same as *[-]parenb* and *cs7[8]*.

[-]raw
> [Disable] enable raw input and output (no ERASE, KILL, INTR, QUIT, EOT, SWITCH, or output postprocessing).

sane
> Reset all modes to reasonable values.

tty Line discipline is set to TTYDISC.

[-]crt
> [Don't] set all CRT display modes.

[-]kerninfo
> [Don't] allow a STATUS character to display system information.

columns num, cols *num*
> Terminal size is set to *num* columns.

rows num
> Terminal size is set to *num* rows.

dec
> Digital Equipment Corporation mode set.

[-]extproc
> Terminal hardware is [is not] doing some of the terminal processing.

size
> Terminal size is output as row number and column number.

---

su

su [*option*] [*user*] [*shell_args*]

Creates a shell with the effective user ID *user*. If no *user* is specified, creates a shell for a privileged user (that is, becomes a superuser). Enter **EOF** to terminate. You can run the shell with particular options by passing them as *shell_args* (e.g., if the shell runs *sh*, you can specify *-c command* to execute *command* via *sh* or *-r* to create a restricted shell).

Options

-c command
> Execute *command* in the new shell and then exit immediately. If *command* is more than one word, it should be enclosed in quotes—for example:
>
> > $ **su -c 'find / -name *.c -print' nobody**

-f If the shell is *csh* or *tcsh*, this suppresses the reading of the *.cshrc* file.

-l Go through the entire login sequence (i.e., change to user's environment).

-m Don't reset environment variables.

---

sudo

sudo [*options*] *command*

Executes a command as the superuser or as another user on the system. Before *sudo* executes *command*, it prompts for the current account password (not root's). This lets a system administrator allow privileged processes without knowing the root password.

sudo determines authorized users by consulting the file */etc/sudoers*. If the current user account is listed in */etc/sudoers* and is authorized there to run *command*, that user can then run subsequent *sudo* commands without being prompted for a password. However, if five minutes (the default value) passes between *sudo* commands, the user is prompted again for a password at the next *sudo* attempt and given another five minute window.

By default, Mac OS X includes the *admin* group in the *sudoers* file and gives that group authorization to run any command with *sudo*. Mac OS X accounts given administrator privileges become members of the *admin* group and thereby receive complete *sudo* privileges.

Note that the file */etc/sudoers* must not be edited directly. Instead, use the *visudo* command.

All attempts to use the *sudo* command are logged to the system log.

Options

-*b*   Run *command* in the background, but don't allow use of shell job control to manipulate the process.

-*h*   Print a usage statement.

-*H*   Set the HOME environment variable to the target user's home directory path. By default, *sudo* doesn't modify HOME.

-*k*   Kill the timestamp by setting it past the default timeout value. A password is not needed to use this option.

-*K*   Kill the timestamp by removing it. A password doesn't need to be supplied.

-*l*   List the commands that the current user is authorized to run with *sudo*.

-*L*   List all option settings that can be used in the "Defaults" section of the *sudoers* file.

-*p prompt*

    Use *prompt* instead of the default password prompt. Within *prompt*, you can use the following special sequences:

    %h   Local hostname

    %H   Local hostname, fully qualified

    %u   Username of the invoking user

    %U   Username of the user the command is being run as

    %%   A single percent sign

-*P*   Preserve the user's group vector instead of changing it to that of the target user.

-*s*   Begin a shell session as root or user, if -*u* is specified.

-*S*   Read password from standard input instead of prompting for it.

-*u user*

    Run the command as *user*, specified by either name or UID.

-*v*   Reset the timestamp, giving the user a new five-minute window to use *sudo* without being prompted for a password.

-*V*   Print the version number. When run by *root*, also list the options used at *sudo*'s compilation.

--   Stop processing command-line arguments. This option makes the most sense when run with -*s*.

Examples

These examples assume that an appropriate *sudoers* file is in place. Refer to the *sudoers* manpage for more information on modifying the file.

List an otherwise protected directory:

    `$ sudo ls /Users/quinn`

Edit the *hostconfig* file:

    `$ sudo vi /etc/hostconfig`

Edit another user's *.login* file:

    `$ sudo -u max vi ~quinn/.login`

sw_vers

sw_vers [*option*]

Displays the product name, version, and build version for the OS.

Options
-productName
> Display the name of the operating system, resulting in Mac OS X.

-productVersion
> Display the version number of the operating system.

-buildVersion
> Display the build number of the operating system.

Example
Display the version information for your system:

```
$ sw_vers
ProductName:    Mac OS X
ProductVersion: 10.4.2
BuildVersion:   8C46
```

systemkeychain

systemkeychain [-v] [-f] -C [*password*]

systemkeychain [-v] -t

systemkeychain [-v] [-c] [-k *dest_keychain*] -s *keychain*

Creates and manages the system Keychain, */Library/Keychains/System.keychain*. (It also creates */var/db/SystemKey*, which presumably contains a randomly generated Keychain password in encrypted form.) This Keychain is used by system processes that run as *root*, such as daemons and boot processes, and is created automatically by the *SecurityServer* startup item.

Options
-c   Create the destination Keychain if it doesn't already exist.

-C   Create a new system Keychain, unless one already exists. The Keychain password can be specified with an optional argument.

-f   Force an overwrite of an existing system Keychain when creating a new one.

-k   Instead of adding a key to the system Keychain, add it to the specified destination Keychain.

-s   Add a key to the system Keychain that can be used to unlock the specified Keychain.

-t   Unlock the system Keychain.

-v   Enable verbose output.

system_profiler

```
system_profiler [-usage] | [-listDataTypes]

system_profiler [-xml] [dataType1 ... dataTypeN]

system_profiler [-xml] [-detailLevel -n]
```

Reports on the hardware and software of the system. Performs the same function as the System Profiler utility (*/Applications/Utilities*), except from the command line. This command replaces the *AppleSystemProfiler* command from Mac OS X 10.2 (Jaguar), located in */usr/sbin*.

Options

The following options are available:

-detailLevel -level
> Specify the level of detail for the report with *level* being one of:
>
> *short*
>> Short report
>
> *basic*
>> Basic hardware and network information
>
> *full* All available information

-listDataTypes
> List the available datatypes for the system.

-usage
> Display usage information and examples.

-xml
> Generate a report in XML format. The file will have a *.spx* file extension, which can be opened with the System Profiler.

Examples

Generate the standard System Profiler report and display it in the Terminal:

> `$ system_profiler`

Show a listing of the available datatypes:

> `$ system_profiler -listDataTypes`

Generate a report containing information about a specific datatype:

> `$ system_profiler dataTypeName`

Generate an XML file containing a report that can be opened by the System Profiler utility and save it to the Desktop:

> `$ system_profiler -xml > ~/Desktop/SysReport.spx`

SystemStarter

```
SystemStarter [options] [action [service]]
```

Utility to control the starting, stopping, and restarting of system services. The services that can be affected are described in the */Library/StartupItems* and */System/Library/StartupItems/* paths.

The action and service arguments are optional. If no service argument is specified, all startup items will be affected. When a specific startup item is given, that item and all the items on which it depends, or that are dependent on it, will be affected.

Currently, *rc* calls *SystemStarter* at boot time. Because *SystemStarter* may eventually take over the role of *rc*, it's advisable to create custom startup items rather than continue to modify *rc*.

Options

-g   Graphical startup.

-v   Verbose startup.

-x   Safe mode startup (a basic startup that only runs Apple items).

-r   Keep running after last startup item completes (in graphical startup only).

-d   Print debugging output.

-D   Print debugging output and shows dependencies.

-q   Quiet mode that silences debugging output.

-n   A pretend run mode that doesn't actually perform actions on any items.

tab2space

tab2space { -h | -help }

tab2space [-crlf | -cr | -lf | -dos | -mac | -unix] [-t*integer* | -tabs] [*input_file* [*output_file*]]

Converts tabs to spaces in text files, and also converts line endings.

Options

-cr   Converts line endings to carriage return (CR) characters, which is the standard for Mac OS.

-crlf
        Converts line endings to CR/LF combinations, which is the standard for DOS and Windows. This is the default for *tab2space*.

-dos
        Same as -crlf.

-h, -help
        Prints a usage statement to standard output.

-lf   Converts line endings to linefeed (LF) characters, which is the standard for Unix.

-mac
        Same as -cr.

-t   Converts tabs to the specified number of spaces. Defaults to 4.

-tabs
        Disables conversion of tabs to spaces.

-unix
        Same as -lf.

input_file
> The file on which *tab2space* operates. If no *input_file* is specified, the command operates on standard input, and sends converted text to standard output.

output_file
> The file to which *tab2space* sends converted output. Defaults to standard output.

tail

`tail [options] [file]`

Prints the last 10 lines of the named file. Uses either -*f* or -*r*, but not both.

Options

-*f*   Don't quit at the end of file; "follow" file as it grows. End with an INTR (usually ^C).

-*F*   Behaves the same as the -*f* option with the exception that it checks every five seconds to see if the filename has changed. If it has, it closes the file and opens the new file.

-*r*   Copy lines in reverse order.

-*c n*
> Begin printing at *n*th byte from the end of file.

-*b n*
> Begin printing at *n*th block from the end of file.

-*n n*
> Start at *n*th line from the end of file. -*n* is the default and doesn't need to be specified.

[+/-]
> To start from the beginning of the file, use + before *num*. The default is to start from the end of the file; this can also be done by using a - before *num*.

Examples

Show the last 20 lines containing instances of .*Ah*:

```
$ grep '\.Ah' file | tail -20
```

Continually track the system log:

```
$ tail -f /var/log/system.log
```

Show the last 10 characters of variable name:

```
$ echo "$name" | tail -c -10
```

Reverse all lines in *list*:

```
$ tail -r list
```

talk

`talk user [@hostname] [tty]`

Exchanges typed communication with another *user* who is on the local machine or on the machine *hostname*. *talk* might be useful when you're logged in via modem and need something quickly, making it inconvenient to telephone or send email. *talk* splits your screen into two windows. When a connection is established, you type in the top half while *user*'s typing appears in the bottom half. Type ^L to redraw the screen and ^C (or interrupt) to exit. If *user* is logged in more than once, use *tty* to specify the terminal line. The *user* needs to have used *mesg y*.

Notes

Please note the following:

- There are different versions of *talk* that use different protocols; interoperability across different Unix systems is very limited.

- *talk* is also not very useful if the remote user you are "calling" is using a windowing environment, because there is no way to know which *tty* to use to get the user's attention. The connection request can easily show up in an iconified window! Even if you know the remote *tty*, the called party must have done a *mesg y* to accept the request.

---

tar

tar [*options*] [*tarfile*] [*files*]

Copies *files* to or restores *files* from an archive medium. If any *files* are directories, *tar* acts on the entire subtree. Options need not be preceded by a dash (-), although they may be. Note that until native drivers for tape drives exist for Mac OS X, *tar* can't write to tape. Note also that *tar* doesn't preserve resource forks or metadata when copying files that contain them.

For a complete list of *tar*'s options, please see the manpage.

Command options

You must use exactly one of these, and it must come before any other options:

c   Create a new archive.

r, u Append *files* to the end of an existing archive.

t   Print the names of *files* if they are stored on the archive (if *files* aren't specified, print names of all files).

x   Extract *files* from an archive (if *files* aren't specified, extract all files).

Selected options

-b   Set block size to 512 bytes.

-e   If there is an error, stop.

-f arch
       Store files in or extract files from archive *arch*. The default is */dev/rst0*. Because Mac OS X has no native tape drive support, *tar* produces an error unless the *-f* option is used.

-h   Dereference symbolic links.

-m   Don't restore file modification times; update them to the time of extraction.

-O   Create non-POSIX archives.

-o   Don't create archives with directory information that v7 *tar* can't decode.

-*p*   Keep ownership of extracted files the same as that of original permissions.

-*s regex*

    Using *ed*-style regular expressions, change filenames in the archive.

-*v*   Verbose; print filenames as they are added or extracted.

-*w*   Rename files with user interaction.

-*z*   Compress files with *gzip* before archiving them, or uncompress them with *gunzip* before extracting them.

-*C*   *cd* to *directory* before beginning *tar* operation.

-*H*   If any of the pathnames given in the command line are symbolic links, follow only those links.

-*L*   Follow all symbolic links.

-*P*   Don't remove initial slashes (/) from input filenames.

-*X*   Mount points will not be crossed.

-*Z*   Compress files with *compress* before archiving them, or uncompress them with *uncompress* before extracting them.

Examples

Create an archive of */bin* and */usr/bin* (*c*), show the command working (*v*), and write to the file in your home directory, *~/archive.tar*:

    $ **tar cvf ~/archive.tar /bin /usr/bin**

List the file's contents in a format like *ls -l*:

    $ **tar tvf ~/archive.tar**

Extract only the */bin* directory from *archive.tar* to the current directory:

    $ **tar xvf ~/archive.tar bin**

---

tee

tee [*options*] *files*

Accepts output from another command and sends it both to the standard output and to *files* (like a T-shaped pipe for water, or a fork in a road).

Options

-*a*   Append to *files*; don't overwrite.

-*i*   Ignore interrupt signals.

Example

View listing and save for later:

    $ **ls -l | tee savefile**

telnet

telnet [*options*] [*host* [*port*]]

Accesses remote systems. *telnet* is the user interface that communicates with another host using the Telnet protocol. If *telnet* is invoked without *host*, it enters command mode, indicated by its prompt, telnet>, and accepts and executes the commands listed after the following options. If invoked with arguments, *telnet* performs an *open* command (shown in the following list) with those arguments. *host* indicates the host's official name. *port* indicates a port number (default is the Telnet port).

Use of *telnet* has mostly been replaced by *ssh* for use as a terminal program, since *telnet* sends its traffic across the network in plain text. However, it can still be useful for debugging transactions on arbitrary ports with servers and services.

Options

-*a*   Automatic login into the remote system.

-*b alias*

Used to connect to an *alias* setup by *ifconfig* or another interface as the local address to bind to.

-*c*   Tell *telnet* not to use a user's *.telnetrc* file.

-*d*   Turn on socket-level debugging.

-*e [escape_char]*

Set initial *telnet* escape character to *escape_char*. If *escape_char* is omitted, there will be no predefined escape character.

-*k*   Attempt to get tickets for remote host; query *krb_realmofhost* to determine realm.

-*l user*

When connecting to remote system, and if remote system understands ENVIRON, send *user* to the remote system as the value for variable USER.

-*n tracefile*

Open *tracefile* for recording the trace information.

-*r*   Emulate *rlogin*. The default escape character is a tilde (~); an escape character followed by a dot causes *telnet* to disconnect from the remote host; a ^Z instead of a dot suspends *telnet*; and a] (the default *telnet* escape character) generates a normal *telnet* prompt. These codes are accepted only at the beginning of a line.

-*x*   Use encryption if possible.

-*8*   Request 8-bit operation.

-*E*   Disable the escape character functionality.

-*F*, -*f*

Forward Kerberos authentication criteria if Kerberos is being used.

-*K*   Disable automatic login to remote systems

-*L*   Specify an 8-bit data path on output.

-*S tos*

Set the IP type-of-service (TOS) option for the Telnet connection to the value *tos*.

-*X type*

Turn off the *type* of authentication.

Commands

Control-Z

Suspend *telnet*.

! [command]

Execute a single command in a subshell on the local system. If *command* is omitted, an interactive subshell will be invoked.

? [command]

Get help. With no arguments, print a help summary. If a *command* is specified, print the help information for just that command.

auth argument ...

Control information sent through the TELNET AUTHENTICATION option.

disable type

Authentication *type* is turned off.

enable type

Authentication *type* is turned on.

status

Status of authentication type is displayed.

close

Close a Telnet session and return to command mode.

display argument ...

Display all, or some, of the *set* and *toggle* values.

encrypt arguments ...

Control information sent through the TELNET ENCRYPT option.

disable type [input|output]

Encryption *type* is turned off.

enable type [input|output]

Encryption *type* is turned on.

start [input|output]

Encryption is turned on if it can be. If neither input nor output is given, both will be started.

status

Encryption status is displayed.

stop [input|output]

Encryption is turned off. If neither input nor output is given, both are stopped.

type type

Encryption *type* is set.

environ [arguments [...]]

Manipulate variables that may be sent through the TELNET ENVIRON option. Valid arguments for *environ* are:

?

Get help for the *environ* command.

define variable value

Define *variable* to have a value of *value*.

undefine variable
> Remove *variable* from the list of environment variables.

export variable
> Mark *variable* to have its value exported to the remote side.

unexport variable
> Mark *variable* to not be exported unless explicitly requested by the remote side.

list Display current variable values.

logout
> If the remote host supports the *logout* command, close the *telnet* session.

mode [type]
> Depending on state of Telnet session, *type* is one of several options:

> *?*   Print out help information for the *mode* command.

> *character*
>> Disable TELNET LINEMODE option, or, if remote side doesn't understand the option, enter "character-at-a- time" mode.

> *[-]edit*
>> Attempt to [disable] enable the EDIT mode of the TELNET LINEMODE option.

> *[-]isig*
>> Attempt to [disable] enable the TRAPSIG mode of the LINEMODE option.

> *line*
>> Enable LINEMODE option, or, if remote side doesn't understand the option, attempt to enter "old line-by-line" mode.

> *[-]softtabs*
>> Attempt to [disable] enable the SOFT_TAB mode of the LINEMODE option.

> *[-]litecho*
>> [Disable] enable LIT_ECHO mode.

open[-l user] host [port]
> Open a connection to the named *host*. If no *port* number is specified, attempt to contact a Telnet server at the default port.

quit Close any open Telnet session and then exit *telnet*.

status
> Show current status of *telnet*. This includes the peer you are connected to, as well as the current mode.

send arguments
> Send one or more special character sequences to the remote host. Following are the arguments that may be specified:

> *?*   Print out help information for *send* command.

> *abort*
>> Send Telnet ABORT sequence.

> *ao*
>> Send Telnet AO sequence, which should cause the remote system to flush all output from the remote system to the user's terminal.

> *ayt*
>> Send Telnet AYT (Are You There) sequence.

brk

    Send Telnet BRK (Break) sequence.

do cmd

dont cmd

will cmd

wont cmd

    Send Telnet DO *cmd* sequence, where *cmd* is a number between 0 and 255 or a symbolic name for a specific *telnet* command. If *cmd* is *?* or *help*, this command prints out help (including a list of symbolic names).

ec

    Send Telnet EC (Erase Character) sequence, which causes the remote system to erase the last character entered.

el

    Send Telnet EL (Erase Line) sequence, which causes the remote system to erase the last line entered.

eof

    Send Telnet EOF (End Of File) sequence.

eor

    Send Telnet EOR (End Of Record) sequence.

escape

    Send current Telnet escape character (initially ^).

ga

    Send Telnet GA (Go Ahead) sequence.

getstatus

    If the remote side supports the Telnet STATUS command, *getstatus* sends the subnegotiation request that the server sends to its current option status.

ip

    Send Telnet IP (Interrupt process) sequence, which causes the remote system to abort the currently running process.

nop

    Send Telnet NOP (No operation) sequence.

susp

    Send Telnet SUSP (Suspend process) sequence.

synch

    Send Telnet SYNCH sequence, which causes the remote system to discard all previously typed (but not read) input.

set argument value

unset argument value

    Set any one of a number of *telnet* variables to a specific value or to True. The special value off disables the function associated with the variable. *unset* disables any of the specified functions. The values of variables may be interrogated with the aid of the *display* command. The variables that may be specified are:

?   Display legal *set* and *unset* commands.

ayt

    If *telnet* is in LOCALCHARS mode, this character is taken to be the alternate AYT character.

echo

> This is the value (initially ^E) that, when in "line-by-line" mode, toggles between doing local echoing of entered characters and suppressing echoing of entered characters.

eof

> If *telnet* is operating in LINEMODE or in the old "line-by-line" mode, entering this character as the first character on a line causes the character to be sent to the remote system.

erase

> If *telnet* is in LOCALCHARS mode or operating in the "character-at-a-time" mode, then when this character is entered, a Telnet EC sequence is sent to the remote system.

escape

> This is the Telnet escape character (initially ^[), which causes entry into the Telnet command mode when connected to a remote system.

flushoutput

> If *telnet* is in LOCALCHARS mode, and the *flushoutput* character is entered, a Telnet AO sequence is sent to the remote host.

forw1

> If Telnet is in LOCALCHARS mode, this character is taken to be an alternate end-of- line character.

forw2

> If Telnet is in LOCALCHARS mode, this character is taken to be an alternate end-of- line character.

interrupt

> If Telnet AO is in LOCALCHARS mode, and the *interrupt* character is entered, a Telnet IP sequence is sent to the remote host.

kill

> If Telnet IP is in LOCALCHARS mode and operating in the "character-at-a-time" mode, then when this character is entered, a Telnet EL sequence is sent to the remote system.

lnext

> If Telnet EL is in LINEMODE or in the old "line-by-line" mode, then this character is taken to be the terminal's *lnext* character.

quit

> If Telnet EL is in LOCALCHARS mode, and the *quit* character is entered, a Telnet BRK sequence is sent to the remote host.

reprint

> If Telnet BRK is in LINEMODE or in the old "line-by- line" mode, this character is taken to be the terminal's *reprint* character.

rlogin

> Enable rlogin mode. Same as using -r command-line option.

start

> If the Telnet TOGGLE-FLOW-CONTROL option is enabled, this character is taken to be the terminal's *start* character.

stop

> If the Telnet `TOGGLE-FLOW-CONTROL` option is enabled, this character is taken to be the terminal's *stop* character.

susp

> If Telnet is in `LOCALCHARS` mode, or if the `LINEMODE` is enabled and the *suspend* character is entered, a Telnet SUSP sequence is sent to the remote host.

tracefile

> The file to which output generated by *netdata* is written.

worderase

If Telnet BRK is in `LINEMODE` or in the old "line-by- line" mode, this character is taken to be the terminal's *worderase* character. Defaults for these are the terminal's defaults.

slc [state]

Set the state of special characters when Telnet `LINEMODE` option has been enabled.

?   List help on the *slc* command.

check

> Verify current settings for current special characters. If discrepancies are discovered, convert local settings to match remote ones.

export

> Switch to local defaults for the special characters.

import

> Switch to remote defaults for the special characters.

toggle arguments [...]

Toggle various flags that control how Telnet responds to events. The flags may be set explicitly to `true` or `false` using the *set* and *unset* commands listed previously. The valid arguments are:

?   Display legal *toggle* commands.

autoflush

> If *autoflush* and `LOCALCHARS` are both `true`, then when the *ao* or *quit* characters are recognized, Telnet refuses to display any data on the user's terminal until the remote system acknowledges that it has processed those Telnet sequences.

autosynch

> If *autosynch* and `LOCALCHARS` are both `true`, then when the *intr* or *quit* characters are entered, the resulting Telnet sequence sent is followed by the Telnet `SYNCH` sequence. The initial value for this *toggle* is `false`.

binary

Enable or disable the Telnet `BINARY` option on both the input and the output.

inbinary

Enable or disable the Telnet `BINARY` option on the input.

outbinary

Enable or disable the Telnet `BINARY` option on the output.

crlf

> If this *toggle* value is true, carriage returns are sent as `CR-LF`. If it is false, carriage returns are sent as `CR-NUL`. The initial value is `false`.

crmod
> Toggle carriage return mode. The initial value is false.

debug
> Toggle socket level debugging mode. The initial value is false.

localchars
> If the value is true, then *flush*, *interrupt*, *quit*, *erase*, and *kill* characters are recognized locally, and then transformed into appropriate Telnet control sequences. Initial value is true.

netdata
> Toggle display of all network data. The initial value is false.

options
> Toggle display of some internal *telnet* protocol processing that pertains to Telnet options. The initial value is false.

prettydump
> When *netdata* is enabled, and if *prettydump* is enabled, the output from the *netdata* command is reorganized into a more user-friendly format, spaces are put between each character in the output, and an asterisk precedes any Telnet escape sequence.

skiprc
> Toggle whether to process ~/.telnetrc file. The initial value is false, meaning the file is processed.

termdata
> Toggle printing of hexadecimal terminal data. Initial value is false.

Verbose_enrypt
> When encryption is turned on or off, Telnet displays a message.

z Suspend *telnet*; works only with *csh*.

---

test

    test expression [expression]

Also exists as a built-in in most shells.

Evaluates an *expression* and, if its value is true, returns a zero exit status; otherwise, returns a nonzero exit status. In shell scripts, you can use the alternate form [expression]. This command is generally used with conditional constructs in shell programs.

File testers

The syntax for all of these options is *test option file*. If the specified file doesn't exist, the testers return false. Otherwise, they test the file as specified in the option description.

-b Is the file block special?

-c Is the file character special?

-d Is the file a directory?

-e Does the file exist?

-f Is the file a regular file?

-g   Does the file have the *set-group-ID* bit set?

-G   Is the file owned by the process's effective GID?

-k   Does the file have the sticky bit set?

-L   Is the file a symbolic link?

-n   Is the string of nonzero length?

-O   Is the file owned by the process's effective UID?

-p   Is the file a named pipe?

-r   Is the file readable by the current user?

-s   Is the file nonempty?

-S   Is the file a socket?

-t *[file-descriptor]*
     Is the file associated with *file-descriptor* (or 1, which is standard output, by default) connected to a terminal?

-u   Does the file have the *set-user-ID* bit set?

-w   Is the file writable by the current user?

-x   Is the file executable?

File comparisons

The syntax for file comparisons is *test file1 option file2*. A string by itself, without options, returns true if it's at least one character long.

-nt Is *file1* newer than *file2*? Check modification, not creation, date.

-ot Is *file1* older than *file2*? Check modification, not creation, date.

-ef Do the files have identical device and inode numbers?

String tests

The syntax for string tests is *test option string*.

-z   Is the string 0 characters long?

-n   Is the string at least 1 character long?

= *string*
     Are the two strings equal?

!= *string*
     Are the strings unequal?

<   Does *string1* come before *string2*, based on their ASCII values?

>   Does *string1* come after *string2*, based on their ASCII values?

Expression tests

Note that an expression can consist of any of the previous tests.

! *expression*
     Is the expression false?

expression -a expression
     Are the expressions both true?

expression -o expression
     Is either expression true?

Integer tests

The syntax for integer tests is *test integer1 option integer2*. You may substitute *-l string* for an integer; this evaluates to *string*'s length.

-eq Are the two integers equal?

-ne Are the two integers unequal?

-lt Is *integer1* less than *integer2*?

-le Is *integer1* less than or equal to integer2?

-gt Is *integer1* greater than *integer2*?

-ge Is *integer1* greater than or equal to *integer2*?

---

tftp

    tftp [host [port]]

User interface to the TFTP (Trivial File Transfer Protocol), which allows users to transfer files to and from a remote machine. The remote *host* may be specified, in which case *tftp* uses *host* as the default host for future transfers.

Commands

Once *tftp* is running, it issues the prompt:

    tftp>

and recognizes the following commands:

? [command-name...]
> Print help information.

ascii
> Shorthand for *mode ASCII*.

binary
> Shorthand for *mode binary*.

connect hostname [port]
> Set the *hostname*, and optionally the *port*, for transfers.

get filename

get remotename localname

get filename1 filename2 filename3...filenameN
> Get a file or set of files from the specified remote sources.

mode transfer-mode
> Set the mode for transfers. *transfer-mode* may be ASCII or binary. The default is ASCII.

put filename

put localfile remotefile

put filename1 filename2...filenameN remote-directory
> Transfer a file or set of files to the specified remote file or directory.

quit
> Exit *tftp*.

rexmt retransmission-timeout
> Set the per-packet retransmission timeout, in seconds.

---

status

Print status information: whether *tftp* is connected to a remote host (i.e., whether a host has been specified for the next connection), the current mode, whether verbose and tracing modes are on, and the values for retransmission timeout and total transmission timeout.

timeout total-transmission-timeout

Set the total transmission timeout, in seconds.

trace

Toggle packet tracing.

verbose

Toggle verbose mode.

tiff2icns

`tiff2icns [-noLarge]` *input_filename* `[`*output_filename*`]`

Converts TIFF image files to Apple icon (ICNS) files. If *output_filename* is not specified, the output file receives the same name as the input file, with the filename extension changed to *.icns*.

Option

-noLarge

Prevent the creation of the highest resolution icons (128 × 128 pixels).

tiffutil

`tiffutil { -dump | -info | -verboseinfo }` *input_file...*

`tiffutil { -extract` *number* `| -jpeg [-f`*N*`] | -lzw | -none |-packbits }` *input_file*
`[-out` *output_file*`]`

`tiffutil -cat` *input_file...* `[-out` *output_file*`]`

Manipulates TIFF image files.

Options

-cat

Concatenate multiple input files.

-dump

Print a list of all tags in the input file to standard output.

-extract

Extract an individual image from the input file, with 0 designating the first image in the file.

-f   Specify the compression factor to use with JPEG compression. The value can range from 1 to 255. The default is 10.

-info

Print information about images in the input file to standard output.

-jpeg

Specify the use of JPEG compression when producing the output file.

-lzw

Specify the use of Lempel-Ziv-Welch compression when producing the output file.

-none

Specify the use of no compression when producing the output file.

-out

Specify the name of the output file; defaults to *out.tiff*.

-packbits

Specify the use of PackBits compression when producing the output file.

-verboseinfo

Print lots of information about images in the input file to standard output.

time

```
time [option] command [arguments]
```

Executes a *command* with optional *arguments* and prints the total elapsed time, execution time, process execution time, and system time of the process (all in seconds). Times are printed on standard error.

Options

-l   Prints the detailed contents of the internal usage structure, such as memory sizes, page faults, and swap counts.

-p   Print the real, user, and system times with a single space separating the title and the value, instead of a tab.

top

```
top [options] [number]
```

Full screen, dynamic display of global and per-process resource usage by descending PID order.

Options

number

top limits the total processes displayed to *number*.

-c mode

Display counts in the specified *mode*, which is one of the following:

a   Cumulative event counting mode. Counts are cumulative from top start time. *-w* and *-k* are superseded and ignored while *-ca* is in effect.

d   Delta event counting mode. Counts are deltas relative to a previous sample. *-w* and *-k* are superseded and ignored while *-cd* is in effect.

e   Absolute event counting mode. Counts are absolute values from process start times. *-w* and *-k* are superseded and ignored while *-ce* is in effect.

n   Non-event mode. CPU usage is calculated from previous sample.

-F   Don't calculate on shared libraries. This greatly decreases *top*'s system load.

-l samples

> Logging mode. Change display mode from periodic full screen updating to a sequential line mode output suitable for output redirection. The number of sequential snapshots is specified as *samples*.

-n num

> Limit to showing top *num* processes.

-o order

> Display processes sorted by order. If preceded by a plus or minus sign, sort in ascending or descending order, respectively.

> *command*Command name.

> *cpu*
>> CPU usage.

> *pid*
>> Process ID.

> *prt* Number of Mach ports.

> *reg* Number of memory regions.

> *rprvt*
>> Resident private address space size.

> *rshrd*
>> Resident shared address space size.

> *rsize*
>> Resident memory size.

> *th* Number of threads.

> *time*
>> Execution time.

> *uid*
>> User ID.

> *username*
>> User name.

> *vprvt*
>> Private address space size.

> *vsize*
>> Total memory size.

-O order

> Specify second sort order. See *-o* for *order*'s values.

-R Do not traverse memory object map for each process. This decreases *top*'s system load.

-s interval

> Sampling interval. Default one second sample interval is replaced by *interval*.

-S Display information about swap usage.

-t Translate UIDs to usernames.

-u Sort processes by decreasing CPU usage instead of by descending PID order.

-w Change the memory map and memory size parameters for all processes from counts to deltas, and add a VPRVT column.

touch

touch [*options*] *files*

For one or more *files*, updates the access time and modification time (and dates) to the current time and date. *touch* is useful in forcing other commands to handle files a certain way; e.g., the operation of *make*, and sometimes *find*, relies on a file's access and modification time. If a file doesn't exist, *touch* creates it with a file size of 0.

Options

-*a*   Update only the access time.

-*c*   Don't create any file that doesn't already exist.

-*f*   Try to update even if you don't have permissions.

-*m*   Update only the modification time.

-*r file*
       Change times to be the same as those of the specified *file*, instead of the current time.

-*t time*
       Use the time specified in *time* instead of the current time. This argument must be of the format *[[cc]yy]mmddhhmm[.ss]*, indicating optional century and year, month, date, hours, minutes, and optional seconds.

---

tr

tr [*options*] [*string1* [*string2*]]

Translates characters; copies standard input to standard output, substituting characters from *string1* to *string2*, or deleting characters in *string1*.

Options

-*c*   Complement characters in *string1* with respect to ASCII 001-377.

-*d*   Delete characters in *string1* from output.

-*s*   Squeeze out repeated output characters in *string2*.

-*u*   Guarantee that any output is unbuffered.

Special characters

Include brackets ([ ]) where shown.

\a   ^G (bell).

\b   ^H (backspace).

\f   ^L (form feed).

\n   ^J (newline).

\r   ^M (carriage return).

\t   ^I (tab).

\v   ^K (vertical tab).

\nnn Character with octal value *nnn*.

\\   Literal backslash.

char1-char2
> All characters in the range *char1* through *char2*. If *char1* doesn't sort before *char2*, produce an error.

[*char1-char2*]
> Same as *char1-char2* if both strings use this.

[*char**]
> In *string2*, expand *char* to the length of *string1*.

[*char*number*]
> Expand *char* to number occurrences. [x*4] expands to xxxx, for instance.

[:*class*:]
> Expand to all characters in *class*, where *class* can be:

> *alnum*
>> Letters and digits

> *alpha*
>> Letters

> *blank*
>> Whitespace

> *cntrl*
>> Control characters

> *digit*
>> Digits

> *graph*
>> Printable characters except space

> *lower*
>> Lowercase letters

> *print*
>> Printable characters

> *punct*
>> Punctuation

> *space*
>> Whitespace (horizontal or vertical)

> *upper*
>> Uppercase letters

> *xdigit*
>> Hexadecimal digits

[=*char*=]
> The class of characters in which *char* belongs.

Examples

Change uppercase to lowercase in a file:

```
$ cat file | tr '[A-Z]' '[a-z]'
```

Turn spaces into newlines (ASCII code 012):

```
$ tr ' ' '\012' < file
```

Strip blank lines from *file* and save in *new.file* (or use 011 to change successive tabs into one tab):

> $ **cat** *file* **|** **tr -s "" "\012" > new.file**

Delete colons from *file*; save result in *new.file*:

> $ **tr -d : <** *file* **> new.file**

---

traceroute

traceroute [*options*] *host* [*packetsize*]

Traces the route taken by packets to reach network host. *traceroute* attempts tracing by launching UDP probe packets with a small TTL (time to live), then listening for an ICMP "time exceeded" reply from a gateway. *host* is the destination hostname or the IP number of host to reach. *packetsize* is the packet size in bytes of the probe datagram. Default is 38 bytes.

Options

-*d*   Turn on socket-level debugging.

-*f ttl*
> Set the TTL for the first probe packet.

-*F*   Set the "don't fragment" bit.

-*g gateway*
> Set a loose gateway.

-*i interface*
> Specify the interface for outgoing packets.

-*m max_ttl*
> Set maximum time-to-live used in outgoing probe packets to *max-ttl* hops. Default is 30 hops.

-*n*   Show numerical addresses; don't look up hostnames. (Useful if DNS is not functioning properly.)

-*p port*
> Set base UDP port number used for probe packets to *port*. Default is (decimal) 33434.

-*P prototype*
> Specify the protocol to use: *UDP*, *TCP*, *GRE* or *ICMP*.

-*q n* Set number of probe packets for each time-to-live setting to the value *n*. Default is 3.

-*r*   Bypass normal routing tables and send directly to a host on an attached network.

-*s src_addr*
> Use *src_addr* as the IP address that will serve as the source address in outgoing probe packets.

-*t tos*
> Set the type-of-service in probe packets to *tos* (default 0). The value must be a decimal integer in the range 0 to 255.

-*v*   Verbose; received ICMP packets (other than TIME_EXCEEDED and PORT_UNREACHABLE) will be listed.

-w wait
> Set time to wait for a response to an outgoing probe packet to *wait* seconds (default is three seconds).

-z msecs
> Specify the number of milliseconds to wait between probes.

true

true

A null command that returns a successful (0) exit status. See also *false*.

tset

tset [*options*] [*type*]

Sets terminal modes. Without arguments, the terminal is reinitialized according to the TERM environment variable. *tset* is used in startup scripts (*.profile* or *.login*). *type* is the terminal type; if preceded by a *?*, *tset* prompts the user to enter a different type, if needed. Press the Return key to use the default value, *type*.

Options

-q, - Print terminal name on standard output; useful for passing this value to TERM.

-ec Set erase character to *c*; default is ^H (backspace).

-ic Set interrupt character to *c*; default is ^C.

-I Don't output terminal initialization setting.

-kc Set line-kill character to *c*; default is ^U.

-m[port[baudrate]:type]
> Declare terminal specifications. *port* is the port type (usually *dialup* or *plugboard*). *tty* is the terminal type; it can be preceded by ? as above. *baudrate* checks the port speed and can be preceded by any of these characters:

> \>   Port must be greater than *baudrate*.

> <   Port must be less than *baudrate*.

> @   Port must transmit at *baudrate*.

> !   Negate a subsequent >, <, or @ character.

> ?   Prompt for the terminal type. With no response, use the given type.

-Q Don't print "Erase set to" and "Kill set to" messages.

-r Report the terminal type.

-s Return the values of TERM assignments to the shell environment. This is commonly done via *eval \'tset -s\'* (in the C shell, surround this with the commands *set noglob* and *unset noglob*).

-V Print the version of *ncurses* being used.

Examples

Set TERM to wy50:

```
$ eval `tset -s wy50`
```

Prompt user for terminal type (default is vt100):

```
$ eval `tset -Qs -m '?vt100'`
```

Similar to above, but the *baudrate* must exceed 1200:

```
$ eval `tset -Qs -m '>1200:?xterm'`
```

Set terminal via modem. If not on a dial-in line, ?$TERM causes *tset* to prompt with the value of $TERM as the default terminal type:

```
$ eval `tset -s -m dialup:'?vt100' "?$TERM"`
```

tty

tty [*option*]

Prints the device name for your terminal. This is useful for shell scripts and commands that need device information. *tty* exits 0 if the standard input is a terminal, 1 if the standard input is not a terminal, and >1 if an error occurs.

Option

-s   Suppress the terminal name.

umount

umount [-f] [-v] [-t *types*] { -a | -A | -h *hostname* }

umount [-f] [-v] { *special* | *mount_point* }

Removes mounted volumes from the directory hierarchy.

Options

-a   Unmount all filesystems listed in *fstab* or Open Directory.

-A   Unmount all currently mounted filesystems, other than root's.

-f   Attempt to force the unmount.

-h   Unmount all filesystems currently mounted from the specified server.

-t   Restrict the use of the command to filesystems of the specified types presented in a comma-separated list, which may include *hfs*, *ufs*, *afp*, *nfs*, or others.

-v   Enable verbose output.

special
    The form of this argument is particular to the type of filesystem being mounted and can be a disk device name, a fixed string, or something involving a server name and directory. See the individual *mount_type* entries for details.

mount_point
    The directory on which the filesystem is mounted.

uname

uname [*options*]

Prints information about the machine and operating system. Without options, prints the name of the operating system.

Options

-*a*   Combine all the system information from the other options.

-*m*   Print the hardware the system is running on.

-*n*   Print the machine's hostname.

-*p*   Print the type of processor.

-*r*   Print the release number of the kernel.

-*s*   Print the name of the operating system.

-*v*   Print build information about the kernel.

uncompress

uncompress [*option*] [*files*]

Restores the original file compressed by *compress*. The .Z extension is implied, so it can be omitted when specifying *files*.

The -*b*, -*c*, -*f*, and -*v* options from *compress* are also allowed. See *compress* for more information.

unexpand

unexpand [*options*] [*files*]

Converts strings of initial whitespace, consisting of at least two spaces and/or tabs to tabs. Reads from standard input if given no file or a given file named -. See also *expand*.

Option

-*a*   Convert all, not just initial, strings of spaces and tabs.

-*t tab1,tab2,...,tabn*
       Set tab stops at *tab1*, *tab2*, etc. If only *tab1* is specified, sets tab stops every *tab1* spaces.

uniq

uniq [*options*] [*file1* [*file2*]]

Removes duplicate adjacent lines from sorted *file1*, sending one copy of each line to *file2* (or to standard output). Often used as a filter. Specify only one of -*c*, -*d*, or -*u*. See also *comm* and *sort*.

Options

-c   Print each line once, counting instances of each.

-d   Print duplicate lines once, but no unique lines.

-f n Ignore the first *n* fields of a line. Fields are separated by spaces or by tabs.

-s n Ignore the first *n* characters of a field.

-u   Print only unique lines (no copy of duplicate entries is kept).

-n   Ignore the first *n* fields of a line. Fields are separated by spaces or by tabs.

+n   Ignore the first *n* characters of a field. Both [-/+]*n* have been deprecated but are still in this version.

Examples

Send one copy of each line from *list* to output file *list.new* (*list* must be sorted):

        $ uniq list list.new

Show which names appear more than once:

        $ sort names | uniq -d

Show which lines appear exactly three times:

        $ sort names | uniq -c | awk '$1 == 3'

---

units

units [*options*]

Interactively supply a formula to convert a number from one unit of measure to another. A complete list of the units can be found in */usr/share/misc/units.lib*.

Options

-f *filename*
        Use the units data in *filename*.

-q   The prompts for "you have" and "you want" won't appear.

-v   The version of *units* is listed.

[*have-unit want-unit*]
        A unit conversion can be entered from the command line instead of using the interactive interface.

---

unzip

unzip [-v]

unzip -Z [-v] [-M] [-s | -m | -l | -1] [-T] *archive_filename* [*pathname*...] [-x *pathname*...]

unzip -Z [-v] [-M] [-2] [-h] [-t] [-z] *archive_filename* [*pathname*...] [-x *pathname*...]

unzip [-q[q] | -v] [-M] [-l | -t | -z | -p | -c [-a[a]]] [-b] [-C] *archive_filename* [*pathname*...] [-x *pathname*...]

```
unzip [-q[q] | -v] [-M] [-f | -u] [-a[a] | -b] [-C] [-L] [-j] [-V] [-X] [-n | -o]
[-d directory] archive_filename [pathname...] [-x pathname...]
```

Lists or extracts files from a ZIP archive (such as one created by the *zip* command). If the name of the archive file ends in *.zip*, that extension need not be specified in *archive_filename*. If *pathname* arguments are given, only archive items matching those arguments are processed; otherwise, *unzip* lists or extracts all items in the archive. When called with no arguments, it prints a usage statement to standard output.

Options

-a Convert text files in the archive to native format. For instance, it translates DOS linefeeds to Unix linefeeds on Mac OS X. When doubled (*-aa*), it attempts to convert all files, whether text or binary.

-b Treat all files as binary, so that no text conversions are attempted.

-c Extract file data to standard output.

-C Use case-insensitive matching of *pathname* arguments to archive items.

-d Extract files into the given directory. Otherwise, files are extracted into the current working directory.

-f Extract files only if they already exist, and if the modification timestamps in the archive are more recent than those on disk.

-j Discard the paths of archived files, so that all files are extracted into the same directory.

-l List archive contents, along with sizes, modification timestamps, and comments. More information is printed if *-v* is also used.

-L Convert filenames to lowercase if they were archived from a single-case filesystem (such as FAT). When doubled (*-LL*), all filenames are converted to lowercase.

-M Display output a page at a time.

-n Never overwrite existing files when extracting. By default, *unzip* prompts the user if an existing file would be overwritten.

-o Overwrite existing files when extracting, without prompting.

-p As *-c*, except that text conversions aren't allowed.

-q Minimize output. When doubled (*-qq*), produces even less output.

-t Perform a CRC check on archive items to determine if they have changed since being archived.

-u As *-f*, but also extract files that don't already exist on the disk.

-v Enable verbose output. If it's the only argument, print version information, compile settings, and environment variable settings to standard output.

-V For items archived on a VMS system, this retains file version numbers in filenames.

-x Exclude the files specified by the additional *pathname* arguments, which usually include wildcards to match filenames of a certain pattern.

-X Restore owner and group information for extracted files. Successful use of this flag will most likely require superuser privileges.

-z Print comments stored in the archive file to standard output.

-Z Provide more control over information displayed to standard output about archive contents. Any options following *-Z* are passed to *zipinfo*. You may also simply call *zipinfo* directly rather than through *unzip*.

Examples

List the contents of a ZIP archive:

```
$ unzip -lv whizprog.zip
```

Extract C source files in the main directory, but not in subdirectories:

```
$ unzip whizprog.zip '*.[ch]' -x '*/*'
```

uptime

uptime

Prints the current time, amount of time the system has been up, number of users logged in, and the system-load averages over the last 1, 5, and 15 minutes. This output is also produced by the first line of the *w* command.

users

users [*file*]

Prints a space-separated list of each login session on the host. Note that this may include the same user multiple times. Consult *file* or, by default, */var/run/utmp*.

uudecode

uudecode [*options*] [*file*]

Reads a uuencoded file and recreates the original file with the permissions and name set in the file (see *uuencode*).

Options

-*c*   Decode multiple files from the input, if possible.

-*i*   Do not overwrite files.

-*o* *filename*
        Send output to *filename* instead of standard output.

-*p*   Decode file to standard output

-*s*   Do not strip pathname. By default, uudecode strips the path of any decoded files.

uuencode

uuencode [-m] [-o *output*] [*file*] *filleame*

Encodes a binary file. The encoding uses only printable ASCII characters and includes the permissions and *name* of the file. When *file* is reconverted via *uudecode*, the output is saved as *name*. If the *file* argument is omitted, *uuencode* can take standard input, so a single argument is taken as the name to be given to the file when it is decoded.

uuencode doesn't preserve resource forks or metadata when copying files that contain them.

Options

-m Use Base64 encoding instead of uuencoding.

-o filename
> Send output to *filename* instead of standard output.

Examples

It's common to encode a file and save it with an identifying extension, such as *.uue*. This example encodes the binary file *flower12.jpg*, names it *rose.jpg*, and saves it to a *.uue* file:

```
$ uuencode flower12.jpg rose.jpg > rose.uue
```

Encode *flower12.jpg* and mail it:

```
$ uuencode flower12.jpg flower12.jpg | mail me@oreilly.com
```

---

uuidgen

uuidgen

Sends to standard output a generated Universally Unique Identifier (UUID). A UUID is a 128-bit value guaranteed to be unique. This is achieved by combining a value unique to the computer, such as the MAC Ethernet address, and a value representing the number of 100-nanosecond intervals since a specific time in the past.

---

vi

vi [*options*] [*files*]

A screen-oriented text editor based on *ex*. See Chapter 7 for more information on *vi* and *ex*. Options *-c*, *-C*, *-L*, *-r*, *-R*, and *-t* are the same as in *ex*.

Options

-c command
> Enter *vi* and execute the given *vi command*.

-e Edit in *ex* mode.

-F Don't make a temporary backup of the entire file.

-l Run in LISP mode for editing LISP programs.

-r file
> Recover and edit *file* after an editor or system crash.

-R Read-only mode. Files can't be changed.

-S No other programs can be run; *vi* is put in secure edit mode.

-s This option works only when *ex* mode is being used. It enters into batch mode.

-t tag
> Edit the file containing *tag* and position the editor at its definition.

-wn Set default window size to *n*; useful when editing via a slow dial-up line.

+ Start *vi* on last line of file.

+n Start *vi* on line *n* of file.

+/pat
>Start *vi* on line containing pattern *pat*. This option fails if *nowrapscan* is set in your *.exrc* file.

view

```
view [options] [files]
```
Same as *vi -R.*

visudo

```
visudo [options]
```
Edits *sudo*'s control file *sudoers* in the *vi* editor. Using *visudo* instead of editing directly prevents two users from performing edits at once. Also, *visudo* will not save edits to *sudoers* if they are not syntactically correct.

-c Syntax check on the file's contents, without editing. Exits with 0 if it's valid, or 1 if not.

-f filename
>Specifies an alternate location for the *sudoers* file.

-q Quiet mode. When used with *-c*, do not print errors.

-s Strict checking. An alias used before it is defined is an error.

-V Print the version number.

vm_stat

```
vm_stat [interval]
```
Displays Mach virtual memory statistics. The default view, without a specified interval, shows accumulated statistics. If *interval* is specified, *vm_stat* lists the changes in each statistic every *interval* seconds, showing the accumulated statistics for each item in the first line.

vmmap

```
vmmap [options] PID
```
Displays the virtual memory regions associated with *PID*. *vmmap* displays the starting address, region size, read/write permissions for the page, sharing mode for the page, and the page purpose. This can be useful information for programmers especially, who often need to understand the memory allocation of a given process.

Options

-allSplitLibs
>Print information about all shared system split libraries, even if they have not been loaded.

-d seconds
> Display the difference between two snapshots taken *seconds* seconds apart.

-interleaved
> Print regions in address order, instead of grouping writable and non-writable regions.

-pages
> Print sizes in pages, not kilobytes.

-resident
> Show resident memory as well as virtual.

-submap
> Print information about submaps.

-w, -wide
> Display wide output.

vndevice

vndevice { attach | shadow } *device pathname*

vndevice detach *device*

Attaches or detaches a virtual device node to or from a disk image file. (Note that the functionality of *vndevice* is incorporated within *hdiutil*.) Modifications to data on the attached disk image will instead be written to the virtual node, or *shadow image*, and subsequent access to that data will be from the shadow. This allows effective read/write access to data on a disk image that shouldn't or can't be modified.

Options

attach
> Attach a device node to a disk image designated by *pathname*.

detach
> Detach a device node from a disk image.

shadow
> Associate an attached device node to a shadow disk image designated by *pathname*.

device
> The device node filename, e.g., */dev/vn0*.

Examples

Create a disk image, attach a virtual device node to it, and mount it:

```
$ hdiutil create test.dmg -volname test -size 5m -fs HFS+ -layout NONE
$ sudo vndevice attach /dev/vn0 test.dmg
$ mkdir mount_point
$ sudo mount -t hfs /dev/vn0 mount_point
```

Wait a minute, and then:

```
$ touch mount_point/test_file
$ ls -l test.dmg
```

Note that the modification time on the disk image is current, reflecting the change you made by creating a test file.

Now set up shadowing. Unmount the volume first, then create the shadow disk image, attach the virtual node to it, and mount it again:

```
$ sudo umount /dev/vn0
$ hdiutil create shadow.dmg -volname shadow -size 5m -fs HFS+ -layout NONE
$ sudo vndevice shadow /dev/vn0 shadow.dmg
$ sudo mount -t hfs /dev/vn0 mount_point
```

Wait a minute, and then:

```
$ rm mount_point/test_file
$ ls -l test.dmg; ls -l shadow.dmg
```

The modification time on the test image wasn't updated, but the shadow image reflects the change you just made, indicating that writes are being passed through to the shadow.

Finish up by unmounting the volume and detaching the virtual node:

```
$ sudo umount /dev/vn0
$ sudo vndevice detach /dev/vn0
```

vsdbutil

vsdbutil { -a | -c | -d } *pathname*

vsdbutil -i

Enables or disables the use of permissions on a disk volume. This is equivalent to using the "Ignore Privileges" checkbox in the Finder's Info window for a mounted volume. The status of permissions usage on mounted volumes is stored in the permissions database, */var/db/volinfo.database*.

Options

-*a*   Activate permissions on the volume designated by *pathname*.

-*c*   Print the status of permissions usage on the volume designated by *pathname* to standard output.

-*d*   Deactivate permissions on the volume designated by *pathname*.

-*i*   Initialize the permissions database to include all mounted HFS and HFS+ volumes.

w

w [*options*] [*user*]

Prints summaries of system usage, currently logged-in users, and what they are doing. *w* is essentially a combination of *uptime*, *who*, and *ps -a*. Display output for one user by specifying *user*.

Options

-*d*   Dumps all processes, rather than just top-level ones.

-*h*   Suppress headings and *uptime* information.

-*i*   List by idle time.

-M file
>   Use data from the supplied *file*.

-N sysname
>   Use data from the supplied *sysname*.

-n   List IP address as numbers.

wall

```
wall [file]
```

Writes to all users. *wall* reads a message from the standard input until an end-of-file. It then sends this message to all users currently logged in, preceded by "Broadcast Message from...." If *file* is specified, read input from that, rather than from standard input.

Option

-g group
>   Sends the output only to users in group *group*. This option may be repeated.

wc

```
wc [options] [files]
```

Prints byte, character, word, and line counts for each file. Prints a total line for multiple *files*. If no *files* are given, reads standard input. See other examples under *ls* and *sort*.

Options

-c   Print byte count only.

-l   Print line count only.

-m   Print character count only.

-w   Print word count only.

Examples

Count the number of users logged in:

```
$ who | wc -l
```

Count the words in three essay files:

```
$ wc -w essay.[123]
```

Count lines in the file named by variable $file (don't display the filename):

```
$ wc -l < $file
```

whatis

```
whatis keywords
```

Searches the short manpage descriptions in the *whatis* database for each *keyword* and prints a one-line description to standard output for each match. Like *apropos*, except that it searches only for complete words. Equivalent to *man -f*.

whereis

whereis *files*

Checks the standard binary directories for the specified programs, printing out the paths of any it finds.

Compatibility

The historic flags and arguments for the *whereis* utility are no longer available in this version.

which

which [*commands*]

Lists which files are executed if the named *commands* are run as a command. *which* reads the user's *.cshrc* file (using the *source* built-in command), checking aliases and searching the path variable. Users of the Bourne or Korn shells can use the built-in *type* command as an alternative.

Example

```
$ which file ls
/usr/bin/file
ls:      aliased to ls -sFC
```

who

who [*options*] [*file*]

Displays information about the current status of the system. With no options, lists the names of users currently logged into the system. An optional system file (default is */var/run/utmp*) can be supplied to give additional information. *who* is usually invoked without options, but useful options include *am i* and *-u*. For more examples, see *cut*, *line*, *paste*, *tee*, and *wc*.

Options

-*H*   Print headings.

-*m*   Report only about the current terminal.

=*q*   List names and number of users in columns.

-*T*   Report whether terminals are writable (+), not writable (-), or unknown (?).

-*u*   Report terminal usage (idle time). A dot (.) means less than one minute idle; *old* means more than 24 hours idle.

am i Print the username of the invoking user. (Similar to results from *id*.)

Example

This sample output was produced at 1:55 p.m. on January 15:

```
$ who -uH
USER    LINE    WHEN        IDLE    FROM
chuck   console Jan 14 19:55 18:01
```

```
chuck    ttyp1    Jan 15 13:11    .
chuck    ttyp2    Jan 15 13:55    .
```

The output shows that the user *chuck* has been idle for 18 hours and 1 minute (18:01, under the IDLE column).

---

whoami

whoami

Prints current UID. Equivalent to *id -un*.

---

whois

whois [*option*] *name*

Queries the Network Information Center (NIC) database to display registration records matching *name*. Multiple *names* need to be separated by whitespace. The special *name* "help" returns more information on the command's use.

Options

-a   Use the American Registry for Internet Numbers (ARIN) database.

-A   Use the Asia/Pacific Network Information Center (APNIC) database.

-b   Use the Network Abuse Clearinghouse database.

-c *countrycode*
    Check country-specific *whois* server at *countrycode.whois-servers.net*.

-d   Use the U.S. Department of Defense database for *.mil*.

-g   Use the U.S. non-military federal government database for *.gov*.

-h *host*
    Specify a different *whois* server, *host*, to query. The default is *whois.internet.net*.

-i   Use the Network Solutions Registry for Internet Numbers database.

-I   Use the Internet Assigned Numbers Authority (IANA) database.

-l   Use the Latin American and Caribbean IP address Regional Registry (LACNIC) database.

-m   Use the Route Arbiter Database (RADB) database.

-p *port*
    Connect to the *whois* server on *port*.

-r   Use the R'eseaux IP Europ'eens (RIPE) database.

-6   Use the IPv6 Resource Center (6bone) database.

---

write

write *user* [*tty*] *message*

Initiates or responds to an interactive conversation with *user*. A *write* session is terminated with EOF. If the user is logged into more than one terminal, specifies a *tty* number. See also *talk*; use *mesg* to keep other users from writing to your terminal.

xargs

xargs [*options*] *command*

Executes *command* (with any initial arguments) but reads remaining arguments from standard input instead of specifying them directly. *xargs* passes these arguments in several bundles to *command*, allowing *command* to process more arguments than it could normally handle at once. The arguments are typically a long list of filenames (generated by *ls* or *find*, for example) that get passed to *xargs* via a pipe.

Options

-0   Expect filenames to be terminated by NULL instead of whitespace. Don't treat quotes or backslashes specially.

-*E str*
    Use *str* as EOF.

-*I replstr*
    Specifies *replstr* as the string to be replaced in command with each input line.

-*J replstr*
    Like -*I*, but input lines are joined together, separated by spaces, to replace *replstr*.

-*L lines*
    Call command once for each *lines* lines.

-*n args*
    Allow no more than *args* arguments on the command line. May be overridden by -*s*.

-*R replacements*
    Specify the maximum number of arguments that will be replaced by -*I*.

-*s max*
    Allow no more than *max* characters per command line.

-*t*   Verbose mode. Print command line on standard error before executing.

-*x*   If the maximum size (as specified by -*s*) is exceeded, exit.

Examples

Search for pattern in all files on the system, including those with spaces in their names:

    $ **find / -print0 | xargs -0 grep pattern > out &**

Run *diff* on file pairs (e.g., *f1.a* and *f1.b*, *f2.a* and *f2.b...*):

    $ **echo $* | xargs -n2 diff**

The previous line would be invoked as a shell script, specifying filenames as arguments. Display *file*, one word per line (same as *deroff -w*):

    $ **cat file | xargs -n1**

yes

yes [*strings*]

Prints the command-line arguments, separated by spaces and followed by a newline, until killed. If no arguments are given, print y followed by a newline until killed. Useful in scripts and in the background; its output can be piped to a program that issues prompts.

zcat

zcat [*options*] [*files*]

Reads one or more *files* that have been compressed with *gzip* or *compress* and writes them to standard output. Reads standard input if no *files* are specified or if - is specified as one of the files; ends input with EOF. *zcat* is identical to *gunzip -c* and takes the options *-fhLV* described for *gzip/gunzip*.

zcmp

zcmp [*options*] files

Reads compressed files and passes them, uncompressed, to the *cmp* command, along with any command-line options. If a second file is not specified for comparison, looks for a file called *file.gz*.

zdiff

zdiff [*options*] *files*

Reads compressed files and passes them, uncompressed, to the *diff* command, along with any command-line options. If a second file is not specified for comparison, looks for a file called *file.gz*.

zgrep

zgrep [*options*] [*files*]

Uncompresses files and passes to *grep*, along with any command-line arguments. If no files are provided, reads from (and attempts to uncompress) standard input. May be invoked as *zegrep* or *zfgrep*; in those cases, invokes *egrep* or *fgrep*.

zip

```
zip [-h | -v]
```

```
zip [-q | -v] [-T] [-0 | -1 | -9] [-F[F]] [-o] [-f | -u] [-g] [-b directory]
[-J] archive_filename
```

```
zip [-q | -v] [-T] [-0 | -1 | -9] [-r [-D]] [-m] [-t MMDDYY] [-o] [-c] [-z]
[-X] [-j] [-k] [-1[1]] [-y] [-n suffix[:suffix]...] [ -f | -u] [-d] [-g]
[-b directory] [-A] archive_filename { pathname... | -@ } [{ -i | -x }
pathname...]
```

The files given by the *pathname* arguments are collected into a single archive file with some metadata (as with *tar*), where they are compressed using the PKZIP algorithm. The archive file is named with a *.zip* extension unless another extension is specified. If pathname is given as -, data to be archived and compressed is read from standard input; if *archive_filename* is -, the ZIP archive data is written to standard output instead of to a file. If *archive_filename* already exists, then the specified files are added to or updated in the existing archive. When called with no arguments, it prints a usage statement to standard output.

Unlike the creation of ZIP archives from the Finder, *zip* doesn't preserve resource or attribute forks.

Options

-b *path*

When updating an existing archive, specify *path* as the directory in which the new archive is temporarily stored before being copied over the old. Normally the temporary file is created in the current directory.

-c   Prompt for one-line comments associated with each file in the archive.

-d   Remove files from an existing archive, instead of adding or updating them.

-D   Disable the creation of directory entries in the archive.

-f   Update files in an existing archive if the modification timestamps of the source files are more recent than those in the archive. Doesn't add new files to an existing archive.

-F   Attempt to repair an archive file that has been corrupted or truncated. When doubled (-FF), it performs a more thorough analysis of the archive.

-g   When updating an existing archive, attempt to append to the existing file, rather than creating a new file to replace the old.

-h   Print a usage statement to standard output.

-i *pathname*

Include only the files specified by the additional *pathname* arguments, which usually include wildcards to match filenames of a certain pattern.

-j   Discard the paths of archived files, retaining only the filenames.

-J   Strip data prepended to an archive, such as code to make the archive a self-extracting executable.

-k   Attempt to archive files using DOS-compatible names and attributes.

-l   Translate Unix-style newlines in files to DOS newlines. When doubled (-ll), convert DOS newlines to Unix newlines.

-L   Display the zip license.

-m   Delete the source files after they've been archived.

-n suffixes
   Disable compression for files with names ending in the strings given in *suffixes*. Multiple suffixes are separated by colons or semicolons.

-o   Set the modification timestamp of the ZIP archive to that of the most recently modified item in the archive.

-q   Minimize output.

-r   Perform a recursive traversal of directories specified in the *pathname* arguments, and archive their contents.

-t date
   Archive only files with modification timestamps more recent than *date*. *date* must be in *mmddyyyy* or *yyyy-mm-dd* format.

-tt date
   Ignore files with modification timestamps at or more recent than *date*. *date* must be in *mmddyyyy* or *yyyy-mm-dd* format.

-T   Test the integrity of the ZIP archive created by the command. If the test fails, a preexisting archive file isn't overwritten, and source files aren't deleted (if using -m).

-u   Update files in an existing archive if the modification timestamps of the source files are more recent than those in the archive. Unlike *-f*, new files are also added.

-v   Enable verbose output. If it's the only argument, print version information, compile settings, and environment variable settings to standard output.

-x pathname
   Exclude the files specified by the additional *pathname* arguments, which usually include wildcards to match filenames of a certain pattern.

-X   Disable storage of file metadata in the archive, such as owner, group, and modification date.

-y   Archive symbolic links as symlinks, rather than archiving the targets of symlinks.

-z   Prompt for comments to be stored in the archive file.

-0   Disable compression.

-1   Compress more quickly, at the cost of space efficiency.

-9   Compress better, at the cost of time.

-@   Take the list of source files from standard input.

Examples

Archive the current directory into *source.zip*, including only C source files:

```
$ zip source -i '*.[ch]'
```

Archive the current directory into *source.zip*, excluding the object files:

```
$ zip source -x '*.o'
```

Archive files in the current directory into *source.zip* but don't compress *.tiff* and *.snd* files:

```
$ zip source -z '.tiff:.snd' *
```

Recursively archive the entire directory tree into one archive:

```
$ zip -r /tmp/dist.zip .
```

zipinfo

```
zipinfo [options] file
```
Displays about the specified zip file.

Options

-h Print archive name, size, and number of archived items.

-l As -s, but compressed size is also displayed.

-m As -s, but compression ratio is also displayed.

-M Display output a page at a time.

-s Print information about each item in the archive, in a format similar to the *ls* command's output: permissions, version of *zip* used to create the archive, uncompressed size, file type, compression method, modification timestamp, and name. This is the default behavior if no other options are specified.

-t Print number of archived items, cumulative compressed and uncompressed sizes, and compression ratio.

-T Print timestamps in a sortable format, rather than the default human-readable format.

-v Enable verbose output.

-x Exclude the files specified by the additional *pathname* arguments, which usually include wildcards to match filenames of a certain pattern.

-z Print comments stored in the archive file.

-1 Print only filenames of archived items.

-2 As -1, but -h, -t, and -z flags may be used to print additional information.

zmore

```
zmore [files]
```
Similar to *more*. Uncompresses files and prints them, one screen at a time. Works on files compressed with *compress*, *gzip*, or *pack*, and with uncompressed files.

Commands

Space
> Print next screenful.

i[number]
> Print next screenful, or *number* lines. Set *i* to *number* lines.

d, Ctrl-D
> Print next *i*, or 11 lines.

iz Print next *i* lines or a screenful.

is Skip *i* lines. Print next screenful.

if Skip *i* screens. Print next screenful.

q, Q, :q, :Q
> Go to next file, or, if current file is the last, exit *zmore*.

e, q
> Exit *zmore* when the prompt "--More--(Next file: file)" is displayed.

s   Skip next file and continue.

=   Print line number.

i/expr
> Search forward for *i*th occurrence (in all files) of *expr*, which should be a regular expression. Display occurrence, including the two previous lines of context.

in   Search forward for the *i*th occurrence of the last regular expression searched for.

!command
> Execute *command* in shell. If *command* isn't specified, execute last shell command. To invoke a shell without passing it a command, enter \!.

.   Repeat the previous command.

znew

znew [*options*] [*files*]

Uncompresses .Z files and recompresses them in .*gz* format.

Options

-9   Optimal (and slowest) compression method.

-f   Recompress even if *filename.gz* already exists.

-K   If the original .Z file is smaller than the .*gz* file, keep it.

-P   Pipe data to conversion program. This saves disk space.

-t   Test new .*gz* files before removing .Z files.

-v   Verbose mode.

zprint

zprint [*options*] *name*

Displays information in columnar output about all memory zones. Using command-line switches, you can alter the formatting and amount of information displayed.

Options

-w   Display the space allocated, but not in use, for each memory zone. The output for each zone is displayed in the right-most column.

-s   Produce a sorted output of the memory zones in descending order beginning with the zone that wastes the most memory.

-c   Override the default columnar format with a row-based display that also reduces the information fields shown.

-h   Hide the default columnar headings. This may be useful when sorting output by column.

name is a substring of one or more memory zone names. Only memory zones matching this substring are included in the output.

3

Using the Terminal

The Terminal application (*/Applications/Utilities*) is your gateway between the candy-coated Aqua graphical interface and the no-nonsense command-line interface that Darwin uses. This book (as well as a lot of Apple documentation) tends to use the terms *command line* and *Terminal* interchangeably because, with Mac OS X, to get to the former you must go through the latter.

Using the Terminal

Each window in the Terminal represents a separate *shell* process—a command-line interpreter ready to accept your instructions, as described in "Introduction to the Shell" in Chapter 4.

Terminal Preferences

The Terminal application's user settings control not just the application's look and feel, but the ways you interact with your shells. This section covers important application preferences to know about.

Setting a default shell

There are two ways to set a default shell when using your system, which are suggested by the "When creating a new Terminal window" radio buttons found in Terminal's Preferences window (Terminal → Preferences, or ⌘-,), seen in Figure 3-1.

The lazier way involves activating the "Execute this command" button and typing a shell's path into the neighboring text field. Henceforth, whenever you open a new Terminal window, that shell will launch in place of your default login shell. This is a nice solution if you use only Terminal as a command line and never log in remotely to your machine, or if you're not a member of the machine's admin group and hence can't set your login shell to something else.

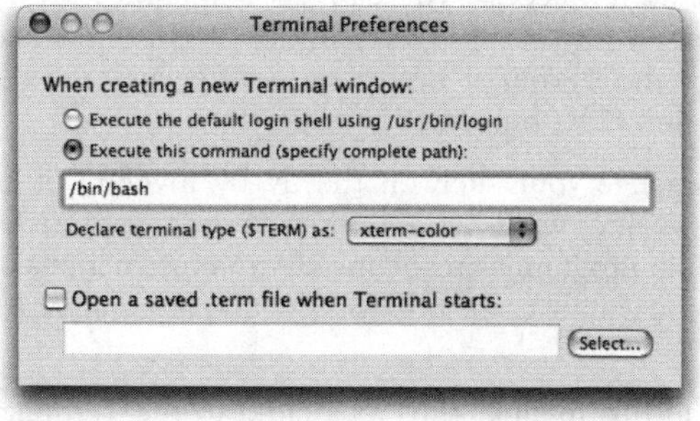

Figure 3-1. The Terminal Preferences dialog

A more permanent, but less obvious, way involves changing your account's default shell. This affects not just the shell Terminal opens by default but the shell that appears when you use a different command-line access application or log in to your machine from some other location via *ssh* (described in "The Secure Shell" in Chapter 11). If you have admin privileges, you can do this through the NetInfo database by adjusting your user account's low-level preferences. Launch NetInfo Manager and navigate to its */users/your-username* directory. (For a complete review of NetInfo, see Chapter 10.) Locate the *shell* property, double-click its value, and type some other shell's path in its place, as shown in Figure 3-2.

Figure 3-2. Changing a user's default shell through NetInfo Manager

If you don't have admin access, you can ask someone who does to take these steps for you. Once your *shell* property under NetInfo has been reset one way or another, select the Terminal preferences' "Execute the default login shell using /usr/bin/login" radio button.

You can always change your shell on the fly by invoking it as a command. If you're running *zsh* and want to temporarily drop into *tcsh* (perhaps you're following some Unix program's arcane installation instructions, which are written only in *tcsh*-ese), you can just type *tcsh* (or the full path, */bin/tcsh*) at the command prompt.

A shell launched in this manner runs as a child to the Terminal window's main shell, so when you exit the second shell you'll pop safely back out to the first shell's command prompt.

 For a *really* lazy way to change your shell, you can make the first line of your default shell's *rc* file a command to switch to your shell of choice! This is a rather slovenly solution and will probably cause you (or others) confusion later. Use one of the other solutions that this section presents, if at all possible.

The Terminal Inspector

If you select File → Show Info (⌘-I) or Terminal → Window Settings, the Terminal Inspector window (shown in Figure 3-3) appears. This window lets you set a variety of visual and shell-interaction options affecting the front-most Terminal window.

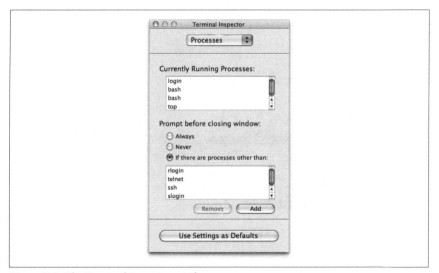

Figure 3-3. The Terminal Inspector window

The pop-up menu at the top of the window lets you navigate between its many panes, summarized in the following list:

Shell

> Lists the shell tied to this Terminal window, and lets you define the application's behavior when you exit a shell (through the *logout* or *exit* commands, or sending an EOF signal to the main shell through Control-D). See the earlier section "Setting a default shell" for information about changing shells.

Processes

> Lists the processes currently running as children of this window's shell. Because closing a Terminal window kills its shell process and any non-backgrounded processes it may contain (see the section "Process Management" later in this chapter), this pane lets you specify the Terminal's behavior if some processes are still running when you close a window. As Figure 3-3 shows, you can have Terminal always prompt you to confirm a window's closure, never prompt you, or prompt you only when processes other than those in the given list exist among the shell's children (use the Remove and Add buttons to modify the list). This can be a lifesaver if you are one of those people who mistakenly hits ⌘-Q frequently (we know who we are). If a program other than the shell is running when you try to exit Terminal, you'll be asked for confirmation.

Emulation

> Terminal is a VT100 emulation program, meaning that it speaks a protocol originally conceived for a certain class of terminals made by (the now-defunct) Digital Equipment Corporation in the late 1970s and early 1980s. Even though the protocol is ancient, it remains the standard. The Terminal's Emulation preferences pane gives you a list of checkboxes that control high-level mapping between your Mac's keyboard and the underlying terminal protocol, as follows:

> *Escape non-ASCII characters*
>
>> If you use either the *bash* or *tcsh* shells, checking this box allows you to enter characters outside those in the standard ASCII set on the command line. Terminal translates the non-ASCII characters into octal ASCII character codes that the shell can interpret properly. (This works as long as character set encoding is set to Unicode in the Display section of the Terminal Inspector.)

> *Option click to position cursor*
>
>> Though it may resemble an Aqua text view in some ways, a Terminal window is normally unresponsive to mouse clicks, making you use keyboard commands to move the cursor around. If you check this box, however, you can option-click a Terminal window to automatically reposition the cursor to that point. This can be a handy function when using Terminal-based text editors, such as Emacs or vi.

> *Paste newlines as carriage returns*
>
>> When this checkbox is active, any newline characters within text that you paste into a Terminal window through the standard Edit → Paste (⌘-V) command are automatically converted to carriage return characters.

Strict VT-100 keypad behavior

When checked, the number keypad functions according to the VT-100 protocol.

Reverse linewrap

In most cases when you move the cursor right to left to the beginning of a wrapped line, it will continue up through the wrap to the end of the previous line. When using some older applications or remote systems, however, you might find that the cursor won't wrap unless this feature is enabled.

Audible bell

Bell characters cause the Mac to sound its system beep.

Visual bell

Bell characters cause the Mac's screen to pulse.

Buffer

Lets you set how many lines of history the Terminal window remembers (and lets you scroll back to via the window's scrollbar), and how it handles line wrapping.

Display

Contains general display options for Terminal's windows, including:

Cursor Style

Sets the cursor's shape and blinking pattern.

Text

Sets the font as well as several font properties, including anti-aliasing and spacing. Also includes a setting that allows you to select and drag text from anywhere in a Terminal window and drop it into the command line or onto the desktop to create a clip file.

Character set encoding

Terminal uses Unicode UTF-8 as its default, but that can be changed here for compatibility with remote systems using other encodings.

Color

Lets you set the window's text, background, cursor and text- selection colors. You can either select from one of the pre-specified combinations or create your own. You can also use an image file instead of a color for window backgrounds. The Transparency slider sets the background's opacity level; setting it to something less than full opacity (by dragging the slider to the right) lets you work with a Terminal window while keeping things behind it visible. This can prove useful when following instructions contained in another window without having to resize either.

Activating the pane's "Disable ANSI color" checkbox prevents your color choices from being overridden by ANSI color-setting instructions the terminal might receive.

Window

Lets you set the window's dimensions in terms of rows and columns of text, and assign it a title based on a number of checkbox-based criteria, as Figure 3-4 shows.

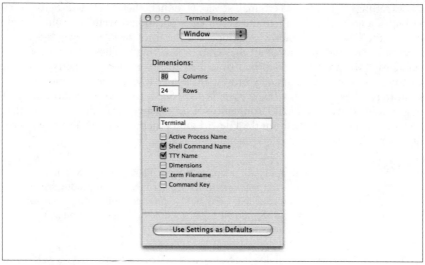

Figure 3-4. The terminal inspector's Window pane

Keyboard

The following options are available for configuring how the Terminal interacts with the keyboard:

Key Mappings

Some Terminal programs, run locally or from a remote machine, allow or even require you to use function keys to issue commands. Key Mappings allows you to add and edit custom key and command pairs using the function, arrow, Home, End and Page keys.

Delete key sends backspace

Some Terminal programs make a distinction between the delete character (which your Delete key normally sends) and a backspace character. Try checking this box if you find the Delete key is not doing what you expect.

Use option key as meta key

Some Terminal programs (such as the Emacs text editor) define a "Meta" key for certain keystrokes. Because your Mac keyboard lacks such a thing, checking this box will have your Option key stand in for it.

Clicking on the "Use Settings as Defaults" button at the bottom of the inspector window saves all the panes' settings as your Terminal application defaults. This means that all future Terminal windows you open, either by launching the Terminal or by selecting File → New Shell (⌘-N) will use the settings you've just configured. See the next section.

Saving and Loading Terminals

After you set up a Terminal window and shell via the Terminal Inspector window (see "The Terminal Inspector" later in this chapter), you have two ways to save these settings for future Terminal sessions: either click the "Use Settings as Defaults" button to make them the Terminal applications' overall default settings, or save the front-most window's settings to a file through File→Save (⌘-S). This creates a *.term* file that stores all the window's settings. (The *.term* file uses the standard XML property list format described in the section "Property Lists" in Chapter 13, so you can manually browse these files if you wish.) It's most convenient to save *.term* files in *~/Library/Application Support/Terminal*, a directory you might need to create initially. You can then access any *.term* files placed in that directory by choosing one from the File → Library menu. You can also open *.term* files using the File → Open (⌘-O) menu command.

 One useful utility for managing *.term* files is Terminal Pal from Freshly Squeezed Software (http://freshsqueeze.com/products/freeware/). When installed, Terminal Pal provides quick access to *.term* files you've saved, allowing you to quickly launch Terminal windows with different settings.

As Figure 3-5 shows, the dialog has an extra set of controls. If you select All Windows (rather than the default Main Window) from the "What to save" pop-up menu, then all the Terminal's open windows, including their onscreen positions, get stored to the resulting *.term* file. This is the option to choose if you like to arrange multiple Terminal windows, perhaps with different properties, in a "just-right" arrangement for a certain task.

Figure 3-5. The Terminal's Save dialog

Activating the "Open this file when Terminal starts up" checkbox will do just what it says. Note that you can set several *.term* files with this function; if you wish to have a single such file as your default and later change your mind about which *.term* file to use, you have to re-save the original window settings with File → Save As (Shift- [⌘-S]) and deactivate that checkbox.

Using the final controls, you can choose to attach to the *.term* file a command that executes each time you open that file. Configure this by selecting the "Execute this command" checkbox and entering the command in the field below it. If you want Terminal to also execute the default shell or login command as specified in the Terminal Preferences dialog, check the "Execute command in a shell" checkbox. With the box unchecked, Terminal will execute only your specified command and close the window once the command is complete.

Connect to Server

Several of Tiger's network daemons advertise their services on the local network using Bonjour's discovery protocol. Terminal's Connect to Server window (File → Connect to Server) allows you to browse and contact these remote *ssh*, *sftp*, *telnet*, and *http* servers without needing to provide a hostname or IP address (Figure 3-6).

Figure 3-6. The Connect to Server dialog box

Clicking on an item in the Service column shows all remote Bonjour-enabled daemons of the selected type in the Server column. When you click on a server name, an appropriate connection command appears in the field at the bottom of the window. Above that field are optional settings specific to the chosen service. You can specify an alternate login name, for example, or choose to use SSH 1 instead of the default SSH 2 protocol for a secure shell connection, and the appropriate change is made to the command.

Clicking the HTTP service lists all user web sites found on each of the supported servers. When you select a site, an appropriate *ping* command appears in the command field (the command is the same for each server, *ping hostname*, regardless of the chosen site).

Each connection command that you use is permanently added to the command field's pop-up list, thereby building a list of connection bookmarks for you.

You can manually add other Bonjour-enabled services (as they become available) to the Services list using the Add button (+) below it. To contact a server without Bonjour-enabled services, you can manually add that server to the Server list using its add button. That way, even without using Bonjour, you can still keep book-marks of commonly used connections.

A Connect to Server command also exists on the pop-up menu for Terminal's icon in the Dock. Selecting it opens the same Connect to Server browse window.

Secure Keyboard Entry

Enabling this feature ensures that all typed characters go directly to the active shell window without risk of another application intercepting them. In high-security environments, Secure Keyboard Entry provides important protection against keystroke recording software attempting to capture passwords and other sensitive data.

If you are using some third-party hot-key or macro-enabling software, however, you might find that it no longer works while Secure Keyboard Entry is enabled.

Focus Follows Mouse

Users of other Unix-like operating systems are often accustomed to making their windows active just by passing the mouse pointer over them, without needing to click in the traditional Macintosh way. This behavior, called focus follows mouse, can be enabled for Terminal windows by executing the following *defaults* command:

```
defaults write com.apple.Terminal FocusFollowsMouse -string YES
```

After issuing that command, you'll need to exit any open Terminal windows for the focus follows mouse behavior to take effect. When you open a new Terminal window, the behavior is activated by the shell; open another window and move the mouse between windows to see the effect. Once activated, any Terminal window beneath the pointer, whether the Terminal is the front-most application or not, will accept text entry. The window won't, however, be raised to the front. To disable the focus follows mouse feature, run the following command and then exit any open Terminal windows:

```
defaults write com.apple.Terminal FocusFollowsMouse -string NO
```

Split-View Scrollback

Split-view windows are nothing new to users of most word-processing software, and Terminal windows provide the same convenience. To split a Terminal window, click the small box just below the right end of the window's titlebar (Figure 3-7). A horizontal dividing bar will appear, which you can drag up and down to resize the height of the two panels. The top panel keeps the scroll bar, allowing you to scroll back up through your entire buffer, while keeping the prompt visible in the other panel. To return to a single pane, click the small box again.

```
⊙ ⊙ ⊙            Terminal — bash (ttyp5)
# neb   NetBSD/FreeBSD
# nec   NEC UX
# nto   QNX Neutrine RTP
# nxt   NEXTSTEP
# nx3   NEXTSTEP 3.x
# osf   OSF/1 (see sos, os4)
# os4   OSF/1 (Digital UNIX) 4
# osx   Mac OS X
# oxp   Mac OS X with Pluggable Authentication Modules (PAM)
# ptx   PTX
# pyr   Pyramid
# qnx   QNX 4
# s40   SUN-OS 4.0 (*not* Solaris)
# sc5   SCO Open Server 5.0.x (see go5)
# sco   Santa Cruz Operation (see sc5, go5)

        $(SH) -c '$(RM) an ua OSTYPE SPECIALS c-client mtest imapd ipopd mailuti ☐
l mlock dmail tmail || true'
        $(CD) tools;$(MAKE) clean


# A monument to a hack of long ago and far away...
love:
        @echo not war?
MyPB:~/Desktop/imap-2004.RC7 chris$ make █
```

Figure 3-7. A split-view Terminal window

Process Management

Each command you invoke or program that you run from a Terminal window becomes a child of that terminal's shell. The Terminal window can juggle many child processes at once, but only one at a time is brought to the foreground, writing its output (through the Unix standard output file handle) to the Terminal, and accepting keyboard input (via Unix standard input) from the user. Any other processes are either placed in the background—running but not displaying any interface or accepting input—or suspended (paused) in the process of execution.

You can control the application in the foreground by sending it Unix signals via the keystrokes listed in Table 3-1. Programs usually respond to them as listed, though individual programs may interpret them differently. (The Emacs text editor, for example, ties a text-searching function to the Control-S keystroke.)

Table 3-1. Foreground process control keystrokes

Keystroke	Description
Control-C	Sends an interrupt signal, which usually causes the program to exit.
Control-D	Sends an end-of-file signal. If a program is accepting multiple lines of input from you, this signals that you're finished providing it.
Control-Z	Suspends the process in the foreground, and returns you to the command line.
Control-S	Suspends the process in the foreground, but keeps it in the foreground.
Control-Q	Resumes a suspended process, and brings it to the foreground.

Control-Q is a good keystroke to try if a Terminal window ceases to update or accept input for no obvious reason, while other Terminal windows continue behaving normally. You may have hit Control-S by mistake.

Terminal aliases Control-C to the File→Send break (Control-C or ⌘.) menu selection. ⌘-- is a legacy Mac keyboard shortcut for interrupting programs; it's often used to quickly invoke the Cancel button in dialog windows.

Table 3-2 lists some Terminal commands that are useful for viewing and controlling backgrounded processes. You can find complete references for them in Chapter 2. See the next section to find out a process's process ID number (PID), which many of these commands require. (You can also use the more convenient %N syntax described by that section when working with processes that are children of the current Terminal window's shell.)

Table 3-2. Process control commands

Command	Description
ps	Lists Terminal-based processes belonging to you.
jobs	Lists processes that are children of this terminal's shell process.
fg pid	Foregrounds (and resumes, if suspended) the process with that *pid*.
bg pid	Backgrounds (and resumes, if suspended) the process with that *pid*.
kill -signal pid	Sends a signal (the terminate signal, by default) to the process with that *pid*.
killall -signal process-name	Sends a signal (the terminate signal, by default) to all processes with that name.

Seeing processes

Typing **ps** by itself displays a simple list of all the shells you are running, as well as all their child processes:

```
andy@honey[~/mosxnut3]$ ps
  PID  TT  STAT     TIME COMMAND
 1692  p1  S     0:00.35 -bash
 3273  p2  S     0:00.02 -bash
 3284  p2  S+    0:00.75 ssh chimpy
 3311  p3  S     0:00.02 -bash
 3313  p3  S+    0:00.05 vim outline.pod
 3883  p4  S     0:00.02 -bash
 3886  p4  S+    0:00.10 make perl
 3950  p4  S+    0:00.01 cc -c -DPERL_CORE -fno-common -DPERL_DARWIN -no-
 3958  p4  S+    0:00.01 powerpc-apple-darwin8-gcc-4.0.0 -c -DPERL_CORE -
 3959  p4  R+    0:00.07 /usr/libexec/gcc/powerpc-apple-darwin8/4.0.0/cc1 -
 3960  p4  S+    0:00.00 as -arch ppc -o op.o
 3961  p4  S+    0:00.00 /usr/libexec/gcc/darwin/ppc/as -arch ppc -o op.o
```

Here you can see that the user andy owns four instances of the *bash* shell. Within these shells, a *vi* session is active, *ssh* has connected to a server called "chimpy", and *make* is building an instance of Perl. *make* itself is calling elements of the GCC compiler suite, such as *cc* and *as*.

The numbers in the first column of the table show the PID number of each process. These are what you can feed to the commands listed in Table 3-2 in order to foreground, background, or send signals to them.

Alternatively, you can use shell-relative PIDs with these commands. Invoking *jobs* lists only those the processes running as children to the current shell:

```
andy@honey[~/mosxnut3]$ jobs
[1]    running    sudo bin/safe_mysqld
[2]  + vi README
andy@honey[~/mosxnut3]$
```

The bracketed numbers leading each row of this output table can be used instead of PIDs when issuing process-control commands. The number can be prefaced with a percentage sign (%) to show that you're using a relative PID. So, to foreground that *vi* process, type *fg %2*. In this particular instance, you can also type *fg* for the same effect; the plus-sign symbol next to the number says it's a child process, and hence the default target for commands like *fg* and *bg*.

 For another view of a Terminal window's child processes, select File→Get Info (⌘-I) and select the Processes choice from the resulting window's pop-up menu. See the section "The Terminal Inspector" earlier in this chapter, for more about this window's views and options.

To see a list of all the processes you're running on this machine, use *ps x*:

```
andy@honey[~/mosxnut3]$ ps x
 PID  TT  STAT      TIME COMMAND
  97  ??  Ss     0:13.66 /System/Library/Frameworks/ApplicationServices
  98  ??  Ss     0:03.03 /System/Library/CoreServices/loginwindow.app/
 212  ??  Ss     0:00.52 /System/Library/CoreServices/pbs
 218  ??  S      0:38.93 /System/Library/CoreServices/Dock.app/Contents/
 220  ??  S      0:13.46 /System/Library/CoreServices/SystemUIServer.app/
 222  ??  S      0:17.76 /System/Library/CoreServices/Finder.app/Contents/
 225  ??  S      0:00.30 /Applications/iTunes.app/Contents/Resources/
 227  ??  S      0:01.10 /Applications/iCal.app/Contents/Resources/
 322  ??  S      0:00.69 /System/Library/Services/AppleSpell.service/
 358  ??  S      0:00.47 /System/Library/CoreServices/RemoteManagement/
 359  ??  S      0:00.04 /System/Library/CoreServices/RemoteManagement/
 388  ??  S      0:34.33 /Applications/Quicksilver.app/Contents/MacOS/
1463  ??  S      0:02.15 /System/Library/CoreServices/Dock.app/Contents/
1469  ??  S      0:01.26 /System/Library/CoreServices/Dock.app/Contents/
1684  ??  S      0:32.87 /Applications/iChat.app/Contents/MacOS/iChat -psn_
1686  ??  S      4:06.34 /Applications/Firefox.app/Contents/MacOS/firefox-
1687  ??  S      1:30.28 /Applications/Utilities/Terminal.app/Contents/
1688  ??  Ss     0:02.53 /System/Library/Frameworks/InstantMessage.framewor
1691  ??  S      0:03.85 /Applications/iCal.app/Contents/MacOS/iCal -psn_0_
1693  ??  S      2:42.60 /Applications/X-Chat Aqua.app/Contents/MacOS/
3180  ??  S      4:53.76 /Applications/Microsoft Office 2004/Microsoft Word
3182  ??  S      0:04.51 /Applications/Microsoft Office 2004/Office/
3261  ??  S      0:00.90 /Applications/Stickies.app/Contents/MacOS/Stickies
3278  ??  S      3:09.86 /Applications/iTunes.app/Contents/MacOS/iTunes
3299  ??  SNs    0:02.06 /System/Library/Frameworks/CoreServices.framework/
```

```
3304  ??  S     0:14.04 /System/Library/CoreServices/Dock.app/Contents/
1692  p1  S     0:00.35 -bash
3273  p2  S     0:00.02 -bash
3284  p2  S+    0:00.76 ssh blitz
3311  p3  S     0:00.02 -bash
3313  p3  S+    0:00.05 vim outline.pod
3883  p4  S     0:00.03 -bash
4405  p4  S+    0:00.09 make perl
4443  p4  S+    0:00.00 /bin/sh -c `sh cflags "optimize='-pg'" toke.o`
4444  p4  S+    0:00.00 /bin/sh -c `sh cflags "optimize='-pg'" toke.o`
4445  p4  R+    0:00.03 sh cflags optimize='-pg' toke.o
```

This lists both the Terminal-controlled programs and the Aqua applications that are running, as well as the frameworks, system services, and plug-ins used by those applications. They are, after all, just Unix programs, all with their own PIDs.

Running *ps* with the *aux* options lists every single process running on the machine, regardless of context or user. This would, at a typical moment in any Mac OS X machine's life, be enough to fill a couple of pages of this book. You can pipe this output through the *grep* command to automatically filter the results: *ps ax | grep bash* shows a table describing all the *bash* processes every user is currently running, for example.

For a friendlier interface to browsing active processes, see the Activity Monitor (*/Applications/Utilities*).

Sending signals with kill and killall

As its name suggests, *kill*'s most common function involves terminating programs, through its default usage: *kill pid*. Actually, *kill* sends a Unix signal of some kind to the program, and the default happens to be the terminate (TERM) signal. You can send different signals through the *kill -signal pid* syntax, where *signal* is a signal name or number.

The even more violent-sounding *killall* is often more convenient than *kill* is. This really just lets you refer to processes by their name, saving you from having to look up their PIDs first. For example, *killall tail* sends the TERM signal to all *tail* processes running under one name.

killall -HUP process is a traditional Unix idiom for having a continually running process (such as a network daemon) reload its configuration information. However, if a Startup Script is available for this service, you should favor running that instead, even if they both ultimately have a similar effect; see the section "StartupItems" in Chapter 11.

Mac OS X's Console Mode

While not quite an alternative to using the Terminal, Mac OS X offers a console login mode that lets you boot into Darwin's command-line interface instead of Aqua.

To enter console mode, you first need to configure Mac OS X's login window so it only displays the name and passwords fields. To do this, launch System Preferences, and go to Accounts → Login Options. In the Login Options pane, turn off automatic login, and set the "Display login window as" option to "Name and password." Next, at the login window, identify yourself as >console and click Log In (or press Return) without providing a password; the login window gets replaced by a standard Unix login prompt. Just type in your username and password as directed, and you're in.

Once you log out (through the *logout* command or by *exit*ing your shell program), the Mac OS X's standard login window appears once more. You need to pull the >console trick again in order to reenter console mode; otherwise, subsequent logins will launch the Finder, as usual.

Using the Terminal

4

Shell Overview

The shell is a program that acts as a buffer between you and the operating system. In its role as a command interpreter, it should (for the most part) act invisibly. It can also be used for simple programming. The shell receives the commands you enter using the Terminal (or a similar program), and decides what to do with it.

This chapter provides a basic overview of the shells included with Mac OS X. Refer to Chapter 5 for specific information about Mac OS X's default user shell, *bash*.

Earlier versions of Mac OS X used the *tcsh* shell as the default user shell. However, all that changed with Panther (Mac OS X v 10.3), when Apple switched the default user shell to *bash*. While many people speculated about the change, the main reason Apple switched to *bash* is for its Unicode support.

Introduction to the Shell

The shell is the user interface to Unix, and by the same token, several shells are available in Unix. Mac OS X provides you with more than one shell to choose from. Each shell has different features, but all of them affect how commands are interpreted and provide tools to create your Unix environment.

Let's suppose that the Unix operating system is a car. When you drive, you issue a variety of "commands": you turn the steering wheel, press the accelerator, or step on the brake. But how does the car translate your commands into the action you want? The car's drive mechanism, which can be thought of as the car's user interface, is responsible. Cars can be equipped with front-wheel drive, rear-wheel drive, four-wheel drive, and sometimes combinations of these.

The shell is simply a program that allows the system to understand your commands. (That's why the shell is often called a *command interpreter*.) For many users, the shell works invisibly behind the scenes and is something they'll never see. Your only concern is that the system does what you tell it to; you don't care about the inner workings. In the car analogy, this is comparable to pressing the brake. Most of us don't care whether the user interface involves disc, drum, or antilock brakes, as long as the car stops when you step on the brake pedal.

There are three main uses for the shell:

Interactive use
> When the shell is used interactively, it waits for you to issue commands, processes them (to interpret special characters such as wildcards), and executes them. Shells also provide a set of commands, known as *built-ins*, to supplement Unix commands.

Customization of your Unix session
> A Unix shell defines *variables*, such as the location of your *Home* directory, to control the behavior of your Unix session. Some variables are preset by the system; you can define others in startup files that are read when you log in or interactively for a single session. Startup files can also contain Unix commands or special shell commands that are executed every time you log in.

Programming
> A series of individual commands, whether shell commands or other Unix commands available on the system, combined into one executable file is called a shell script. Scripts are useful for executing a series of individual commands, but they can also execute commands repeatedly (in a loop) or conditionally (if-else), as in many high-level programming languages.
>
> *bash*, which is Mac OS X Tiger's default user shell, is considered a powerful programming shell, while scripting in *tcsh* (the default user shell for versions of Mac OS X prior to v. 10.3) is rumored to be hazardous to your health.

Shell Flavors

Many different Unix shells are available on Mac OS X Tiger. This book describes the *bash* shell. The Bourne-Again shell (*bash*), which is based on the Bourne shell (*sh*). *bash* is the most commonly used shell for many other Unix variants, including most Linux distributions and FreeBSD.

Most Unix systems have more than one shell, and it's not uncommon to use one shell for writing scripts and another for interactive use. Other popular shells included with Mac OS X Tiger can be found in the */bin* directory and are available to all users on the system.

You can change to another shell by typing the program name at the command line. For example, to change from *bash* to *tcsh*, type:

```
$ tcsh
```

To switch back to *bash*, just exit *tcsh*

```
$ exit   # or ^D
```

Common Features

Table 4-1 is a sampling of features that are common to *bash* and other Unix shells.

Table 4-1. Common shell features

Symbol/command	Meaning/action
>	Redirect output
>>	Append to file
<	Redirect input
<<	Here document (redirect input)
|	Pipe output
&	Run process in background
;	Separate commands on same line
*	Match any character(s) in filename
?	Match single character in filename
!*n*	Repeat command number *n*
[ ]	Match any characters enclosed
( )	Execute in subshell
` `	Substitute output of enclosed command
" "	Partial quote (allows variable and command expansion)
' '	Full quote (no expansion)
\	Quote following character
$var	Use value for variable
$$	Process ID
$0	Command name
$n	*n*th argument ($0<n\leq9$)
$*	All arguments as simple words
#	Begin comment
Tab	Complete current word
bg	Background execution
break	Break from loop statements
cd	Change directory
continue	Resume a program loop
echo	Display output
eval	Evaluate arguments
exec	Execute a new shell
fg	Foreground execution
jobs	Show active jobs
kill	Terminate running jobs
newgrp	Change to a new group
shift	Shift positional parameters
stop	Suspend a background job
suspend	Suspend a foreground job (such as a shell created by *su*)

Table 4-1. Common shell features (continued)

Symbol/command	Meaning/action
time	Time a command
umask	Set default file permissions for new files
unset	Erase variable or function definitions
wait	Wait for a background job to finish

Differing Features

Table 4-2 is a sampling of features that differ between *bash* and *tcsh*, Mac OS X's former default shell.

Table 4-2. Differences between the bash and tcsh shells

Meaning/action	bash	tcsh
Default prompt	$	%
Force redirection	>|	>!
Force append		>>!
Variable assignment	*var=val*	set *var=val*
Set environment variable	export *var=val*	setenv *var val*
Command substitution	$(*command*), `` ` ``	`` ` ``
Number of arguments	$#	$#argv
Execute commands in *file*	. *file*	source *file*
End a loop statement	done	end
End *case* or *switch*	esac	endsw
Loop through variables	for/do	foreach
Sample if statement	if [$i -eq 5]	if ($i==5)
End if statement	fi	endif
Set resource limits	ulimit	limit
Read from terminal	read	$<
Make a variable read-only	readonly	set -r
Show possible completions	Tab	Tab
Ignore interrupts	trap 2	onintr
Begin until loop	until/do	until
Begin while loop	while/do	while

5

bash: The Bourne-Again Shell

bash is the GNU version of the standard Bourne shell—the original Unix shell—and incorporates many popular features from other shells such as *csh*, *tcsh*, and the Korn shell (*ksh*). *tcsh* offers many of the features in this chapter, and is also available on most distributions of Linux. However, *bash* is the default user shell for Mac OS X Tiger.

If executed as part of the user's login, *bash* starts by executing any commands found in */etc/profile*. It executes the commands found in *~/.bash_profile*, *~/.bash_login*, or *~/.profile* (searching for each file only if the previous file is not found).

In addition, every time it starts (as a subshell or a login shell), *bash* looks for a file named *~/.bashrc*. Many system administration utilities create a small *~/.bashrc* automatically, and many users create quite large startup files. Any commands that can be executed from the shell can be included. Here's a small sample file:

```
# Set bash variable to keep 50 commands in history.
HSTSIZE=50
#
# Set prompt to show current working directory and history number of
# command.
PS1='\w: Command \!$ '
#
# Set path to search for commands in my directories, then standard ones.
PATH=~/bin:~/scripts:$PATH
#
# Keep group and others from writing my newly created files.
umask 022
#
# Quick and dirty test of a single-file program.
function gtst ( ) {
    g++ -o $1 $1.C && ./$1
}
#
```

```
# Remove .o files.
alias clean='find ~ -name \*.o -exec rm {  } \;'
```

bash provides the following features:

- Input/output redirection
- Wildcard characters (metacharacters) for filename abbreviation
- Shell variables for customizing your environment
- Powerful programming capabilities
- Command-line editing (using *vi-* or Emacs-style editing commands)
- Access to previous commands (command history)
- Integer arithmetic
- Arithmetic expressions
- Command name abbreviation (aliasing)
- Job control
- Integrated programming features
- Control structures
- Directory stacking (using *pushd* and *popd*)
- Brace/tilde expansion
- Key bindings

Invoking the Shell

The command interpreter for *bash* can be invoked as follows:

bash [*options*] [*arguments*]

bash can execute commands from a terminal (when *-i* is specified), from a file (when the first *argument* is an executable script), or from standard input (if no arguments remain or if *-s* is specified).

Options

Options that appear here with double hyphens also work when entered with single hyphens, but using double hyphens is standard coding procedure.

-, --
  Treat all subsequent strings as arguments, not options.

-D, --dump-strings
  For execution in non-English locales, dump all strings that *bash* translates.

--dump-po-strings
  Same as *--dump-strings*, but uses the GNU *gettext* po (portable object) format suitable for scripting.

-c str
  Read commands from string *str*.

--help
> Print usage information and exit.

-i   Create an interactive shell (prompt for input).

-init-file file
> Substitute *file* for *.bashrc* on startup.

-l, --login
> Behave like a login shell; try to process */etc/profile* on startup. Then process ~/
> *.bash_profile*, ~/*.bash_login*, or ~/*.profile* (searching for each file only if the
> previous file is not found).

--noediting
> Disable line editing with arrow and control keys.

--noprofile
> Don't process */etc/profile*, ~/*.bash_profile*, ~/*.bash_login*, or ~/*.profile* on
> startup.

--norc
> Don't process ~/*.bashrc* on startup.

--posix
> Conform to POSIX standard.

-r, --restricted
> Restrict users to a very secure, limited environment; for instance, they can't
> change out of the startup directory or use the > sign to redirect output.

--rcfile file
> Substitute *file* for *.bashrc* on startup.

-s   Read commands from standard input. Output from built-in commands goes
> to file descriptor 1; all other shell output goes to file descriptor 2.

-v, --verbose
> Print each line as it is executed (useful for tracing scripts).

--version
> Print information about which version of *bash* is installed.

-x   Turn on debugging, as described under the *-x* option to the *set* built-in
> command later in this chapter.

The remaining options to *bash* are listed under the *set* built-in command.

Arguments

Arguments are assigned, in order, to the positional parameters $1, $2, and so
forth. If the first argument is an executable script, it is assigned to $0; then
commands are read from it, and remaining arguments are assigned to $1, $2, and
so on.

Syntax

This subsection describes the many symbols peculiar to *bash*. The topics are arranged as follows:

- Special files
- Filename metacharacters
- Command-line editing
- Quoting
- Command forms
- Redirection forms
- Coprocesses

Special Files

Table 5-1. Special bash configuration files

File	Purpose
/etc/profile	Executed automatically at login.
$HOME/.bash_profile	Executed automatically at login.
$HOME/.bashrc	Executed automatically at shell startup.
$HOME/.bash_logout	Executed automatically at logout.
$HOME/.bash_history	Record of last session's commands.
$HOME/.inputrc	Initialization file for reading input in an interactive shell.
/etc/passwd	Source of home directories for ~name abbreviations.

Filename Metacharacters

Table 5-2. Filename metacharacters

Characters	Meaning
*	Match any string of zero or more characters.
?	Match any single character.
[abc...]	Match any one of the enclosed characters; a hyphen can be used to specify a range (e.g., a–z, A–Z, 0–9).
[!abc...]	Match any character *not* among the enclosed characters.
[^abc...]	Same as [!abc...].
{str1,...}	Brace expansion: match any of the enclosed strings.
~name	Home directory of user *name*. With no *name*, Home directory of current user.
~+	Current working directory (PWD).
~-	Previous working directory from directory stack (OLDPWD; see also the *pushd* built-in command).
~+n	The *n*th entry in the directory stack, counting from the start of the list with the first entry being 0.

Table 5-2. (continued)Filename metacharacters

Characters	Meaning
~-n	The nth entry in the directory stack, counting from the end of the list with the last entry being 0.

Patterns can be a sequence of patterns separated by |. If any subpatterns match, the entire sequence is considered matching. This extended syntax resembles that of *egrep* and *awk*.

Examples

```
$ ls new*        List new and new.1
$ cat ch?        Match ch9 but not ch10
$ vi [D-R]*      Match files that begin with uppercase D through R
```

Command-Line Editing

Command lines can be edited like lines in either Emacs or vi. Emacs is the default. See "Line-Edit Mode" later in this chapter for more information.

vi mode has two submodes, *input mode* and *command mode*. The default is input mode; you can go to command mode by pressing Esc. In command mode, typing a (append) or i (insert) returns you to input mode.

Some users discover that the Del or Backspace key in the Terminal doesn't delete the character before the cursor as it should. Sometimes this problem can be solved by issuing one of the following commands (or placing it in your *.bashrc* file):

```
stty erase ^?
stty erase ^H
```

See the *stty* command in Chapter 2 for more information.

Emacs commands use the Control key and the Meta key—a system-neutral way to describe a function-changing modifier key. On a Mac, this corresponds to the Option key, if you have the Terminal configured correctly. Under the Terminal menu, go to Settings, and select the Keyboard drop down. Check the "use option key as meta key" checkbox, and close the Terminal Inspector.

In this chapter, the notation C- indicates that the Control key is pressed at the same time as the character that follows. Similarly, M- indicates the use of the Meta, or Option key on Mac OS X: either hold Option while typing the next character, *or* press and release the Escape key followed by the next character.

Tables 5-3 through 5-16 show various Emacs and *vi* commands.

Table 5-3. Basic Emacs-mode commands

Command	Description
Ctrl-b	Move backward one character (without deleting).
Ctrl-f	Move forward one character.
Del	Delete one character backward.
Ctrl-d	Delete one character forward.

Table 5-4. Emacs-mode word commands

Command	Description
M-b	Move one word backward.
M-f	Move one word forward.
M-Del	Kill one word backward.
M-d	Kill one word forward.
Ctrl-y	Retrieve (*yank*) last item killed.

Table 5-5. Emacs-mode line commands

Command	Description
Ctrl-a	Move to beginning of line.
Ctrl-e	Move to end of line.
Ctrl-k	Kill forward to end of line.

Table 5-6. Emacs-mode commands for moving through the history file

Command	Description
Ctrl-p	Move to previous command.
Ctrl-n	Move to next command.
Ctrl-r	Search backward.
M-<	Move to first line of history file.
M->	Move to last line of history file.

Table 5-7. Emacs-mode completion commands

Command	Description
Tab	Attempt to perform general completion of the text.
M-?	List the possible completions.
M-/	Attempt filename completion.
Ctrl-x /	List the possible filename completions.
M-~	Attempt username completion.
Ctrl-x ~	List the possible username completions.
M-$	Attempt variable completion.
Ctrl-x $	List the possible variable completions.
M-@	Attempt hostname completion.
Ctrl-x @	List the possible hostname completions.
M-!	Attempt command completion.
Ctrl-x !	List the possible command completions.
M-Tab	Attempt completion from previous commands in the history list.

bash

Table 5-8. Miscellaneous Emacs-mode commands

Command	Description
Ctrl-j	Same as Return.
Ctrl-l	Clear the screen, placing the current line at the top of the screen.
Ctrl-m	Same as Return.
Ctrl-o	Same as Return, then display next line in command history.
Ctrl-t	Transpose character left of and under the cursor.
Ctrl-u	Kill the line from the beginning to point.
Ctrl-v	Insert next keypress literally instead of interpreting it as a command.
Ctrl-[	Same as Esc (most keyboards).
M-c	Capitalize word under or after cursor.
M-u	Change word under or after cursor to all capital letters.
M-l	Change word under or after cursor to all lowercase letters.
M-.	Insert last word in previous command line after point.
M-_	Same as *M-.*.

Table 5-9. Editing commands in vi input mode

Command	Description
Del	Delete previous character.
Ctrl-Shift-W	Erase previous word (i.e., erase until a blank).
Ctrl-Shift-V	Insert next keypress literally instead of interpreting it as a command.
Esc	Enter command mode (see Table 5-8).

Table 5-10. Basic vi command-mode commands

Command	Description
H	Move left one character.
L	Move right one character.
B	Move left one word.
W	Move right one word.
B	Move to beginning of preceding nonblank word.
W	Move to beginning of next nonblank word.
E	Move to end of current word.
E	Move to end of current nonblank word.
0	Move to beginning of line.
^	Move to first nonblank character in line.
$	Move to end of line.

Table 5-11. Commands for entering vi input mode

Command	Description
I	Insert text before current character (insert).

Table 5-11. Commands for entering vi input mode (continued)

Command	Description
A	Insert text after current character (append).
I	Insert text at beginning of line.
A	Insert text at end of line.
R	Replace current character with next keypress.
R	Overwrite existing text.

Table 5-12. Some vi-mode delete commands

Command	Description
Dh	Delete one character backward.
Dl	Delete the current character.
Db	Delete one word backward.
Dw	Delete one word forward.
dB	Delete one nonblank word backward.
dW	Delete one nonblank word forward.
d$	Delete to end-of-line.
d0	Delete to beginning of line.

Table 5-13. Abbreviations for vi-mode delete commands

Command	Description
D	Delete to end of line (equivalent to *d$*).
Dd	Delete entire line (equivalent to *0d$*).
C	Delete to end of line; enter input mode (equivalent to *c$*).
Cc	Delete entire line; enter input mode (equivalent to *0c$*).
X	Delete character backward (equivalent to *dh*).
X	Delete the current character (equivalent to *dl*.)

Table 5-14. vi-mode commands for searching the command history

Command	Description
k or -	Move backward one line.
j or +	Move forward one line.
G	Move to first line in history.
/string	Search backward for *string*.
?string	Search forward for *string*.
N	Repeat search in same direction as previous.
N	Repeat search in opposite direction of previous.

Table 5-15. vi-mode character-finding commands

Command	Description
f*x*	Move right to next occurrence of *x*.
F*x*	Move left to previous occurrence of *x*.
t*x*	Move right to next occurrence of *x*, then back one space.
T*x*	Move left to previous occurrence of *x*, then forward one space.
;	Redo last character-finding command.
,	Redo last character-finding command in opposite direction.

Table 5-16. Miscellaneous vi-mode commands

Command	Description
~	Invert (toggle) case of current character(s).
_	Insert last word of previous command after cursor; enter input mode.
Ctrl-L	Clear the screen and redraw the current line on it; good for when your screen becomes garbled.
#	Prepend # (comment character) to the line and send it to the history file; useful for saving a command to be executed later, without having to retype it.

Quoting

Quoting disables a character's special meaning and allows it to be used literally, as itself. The following characters have special meaning to *bash*:

Table 5-17. Characters with special meaning in bash

Character	Meaning
;	Command separator
&	Background execution
( )	Command grouping (enter a subshell)
{ }	Command block
		Pipe
> < &	Redirection symbols
* ? [ ] ~ !	Filename metacharacters
" ' \	Used in quoting other characters
`	Command substitution
$	Variable substitution (or command substitution)
newline space tab	Word separators
#	Comment

The following characters can be used for quoting:

Table 5-18. Characters used for quoting in bash

Character	Action
" "	Everything between " and " is taken literally, except for the following characters that keep their special meanings:
	$
	Variable substitution will occur.
	`
	Command substitution will occur.
	"
	This marks the end of the double quote.
' '	Everything between 'and' is taken literally, except for another '.
\	The character following \ is taken literally. Use within " " to escape ", $, and '. Often used to escape itself, spaces, or newlines.

Examples

```
$ echo 'Single quotes "protect" double quotes'
Single quotes "protect" double quotes

$ echo "Well, isn't that \"special\"?"
Well, isn't that "special"?

$ echo "You have `ls | wc -l` files in `pwd`"
You have  43 files in /home/andy

$ x=100
$ echo "The value of \$x is $x"
The value of $x is 100
```

Command Forms

Table 5-19. bash command forms

Syntax	Effect
cmd &	Execute cmd in background.
cmd1 ; cmd2	Command sequence; execute multiple cmds on the same line.
(cmd1 ; cmd2)	Subshell; treat cmd1 and cmd2 as a command group.
cmd1 | cmd2	Pipe; use output from cmd1 as input to cmd2.
cmd1 `cmd2`	Command substitution; use cmd2 output as arguments to cmd1.
cmd1 $(cmd2)	Command substitution; nesting is allowed.
cmd1 && cmd2	AND; execute cmd2 only if cmd1 succeeds.
cmd1 || cmd2	OR; execute cmd2 only if cmd1 fails.
{ cmd1 ; cmd2 }	Execute commands in the current shell.

Examples

```
$ cd; ls                          Execute sequentially
$ (date; who; pwd) > logfile      All output is redirected
```

```
$ sort file | pr -3 | lp            Sort file, page output, then print
$ vi `grep -l ifdef *.c`            Edit files found by grep
$ egrep '(yes|no)' `cat list`       Specify a list of files to search
$ egrep '(yes|no)' $(cat list)      Same as previous using bash command
                                    substitution
$ egrep '(yes|no)' $(<list)         Same, but faster
$ grep XX file && lp file           Print file if it contains the pattern
$ grep XX file || echo "XX not found"  Echo an error message if pattern
                                    not found
```

Redirection Forms

Table 5-20. I/O file descriptors

File descriptor	Name	Common abbreviation	Typical default
0	Standard input	stdin	Keyboard
1	Standard output	stdout	Screen
2	Standard error	stderr	Screen

The usual input source or output destination can be changed as shown in Table 5-21.

Table 5-21. I/O redirectors

Redirector	Function
`>file`	Direct standard output to `file`.
`<file`	Take standard input from `file`.
`cmd1	cmd2`	Pipe; take standard output of *cmd1* as standard input to *cmd2*.
`>>file`	Direct standard output to `file`; append to `file` if it already exists.
`>|file`	Force standard output to `file` even if *noclobber* is set.
`n>|file`	Force output from the file descriptor *n* to `file` even if *noclobber* is set.
`<>file`	Use `file` as both standard input and standard output.
`<<text`	Read standard input up to a line identical to `text` (`text` can be stored in a shell variable). Input is usually typed on the screen or in the shell program. Commands that typically use this syntax include *cat, echo, ex,* and *sed.* If `text` is enclosed in quotes, standard input will not undergo variable substitution, command substitution, etc.
`n>file`	Direct file descriptor *n* to `file`.
`n<file`	Set `file` as file descriptor *n*.
`>&n`	Duplicate standard output to file descriptor *n*.
`<&n`	Duplicate standard input from file descriptor *n*.
`&>file`	Direct standard output and standard error to `file`.
`<&-`	Close the standard input.
`>&-`	Close the standard output.
`n>&-`	Close the output from file descriptor *n*.
`n<&-`	Close the input from file descriptor *n*.

Examples

```
$ cat part1 > book
$ cat part2 part3 >> book
$ mail tim < report
$ grep Chapter part* 2> error_file

$ sed 's/^/XX /' << END_ARCHIVE
> This is often how a shell archive is "wrapped",
> bundling text for distribution. You would normally
> run sed from a shell program, not from the command line.
> END_ARCHIVE
XX This is often how a shell archive is "wrapped",
XX bundling text for distribution. You would normally
XX run sed from a shell program, not from the command line.
```

To redirect standard output to standard error:

```
$ echo "Usage error:  see administrator" 1>&2
```

The following command sends output (files found) to *filelist* and sends error messages (inaccessible files) to file *no_access*:

```
$ find / -print > filelist 2>no_access
```

Variables

Preface a variable by a dollar sign ($) to reference its value. You can also optionally enclose it in braces ({ }). You can assign a value to a variable through an equals sign (=) with no whitespace on either side of it:

```
$ TMP=temp.file
```

By default, variables are seen only within the shell itself; to pass variables to other programs invoked within the shell, see the export built-in command.

If followed by an index enclosed by brackets ([ ]), the variable is considered an array variable. For instance:

```
$ DIR_LIST[0]=src
$ DIR_LIST[1]=headers
$ ls ${DIR_LIST[1]}
```

The contents of headers are listed. Many substitutions and commands in this chapter handle arrays by operating on each element separately.

Variable Substitution

In the following substitutions, braces ({ }) are optional, except when needed to separate a variable name from following characters that would otherwise be considered part of the name.

Table 5-22. Substitution variables

Variable	Meaning
${var}	Value of variable var.
$0	Name of the program.
${n}	Individual arguments on command line (positional parameters); 1 n 9.
$#	Number of arguments on command line.
$*	All arguments on command line.
$@	Same as $*, but contents are split into words when the variable is enclosed in double quotes.
$$	Process number of current shell; useful as part of a filename for creating temporary files with unique names.
$?	Exit status of last command (normally 0 for success).
$!	Process number of most recently issued background command.
$-	Current execution options (see the set built-in command). By default, hB for scripts and himBH for interactive shells.
$_	Initially set to name of file invoked for this shell, then set for each command to the last word of the previous command.

Tables 5-23 through Table 5-25 show various types of operators that can be used with *bash* variables.

Table 5-23. Substitution operators

Operator	Substitution
${varname:-word}	If varname exists and isn't null, return its value; otherwise, return word.
	Purpose: Returning a default value if the variable is undefined.
	Example: ${count:-0} evaluates to 0 if count is undefined.
${varname:=word}	If varname exists and isn't null, return its value; otherwise set it to word and then return its value. Positional and special parameters cannot be assigned this way.
	Purpose: Setting a variable to a default value if it is undefined.
	Example: ${count:=0} sets count to 0 if it is undefined.
${varname:?message}	If varname exists and isn't null, return its value; otherwise, print varname: followed by message, and abort the current command or script (noninteractive shells only). Omitting message produces the default message "parameter null or not set."
	Purpose: Catching errors that result from variables being undefined.
	Example: {count:?"undefined"} prints "count: undefined" and exits if count is undefined.
${varname:+word}	If varname exists and isn't null, return word; otherwise, return null.
	Purpose: Testing for the existence of a variable.
	Example: ${count:+1} returns 1 (which could mean true) if count is defined.
${#varname}	Return the number of characters in the value of varname.
	Purpose: Preparing for substitution or extraction of substrings.
	Example: If ${USER} currently expands to root, ${#USER} expands to 4.

Table 5-24. Pattern-matching operators

Operator	Meaning
${*variable#pattern*}	If the pattern matches the beginning of the variable's value, delete the shortest part that matches and return the rest.
${*variable##pattern*}	If the pattern matches the beginning of the variable's value, delete the longest part that matches and return the rest.
${*variable%pattern*}	If the pattern matches the end of the variable's value, delete the shortest part that matches and return the rest.
${*variable%%pattern*}	If the pattern matches the end of the variable's value, delete the longest part that matches and return the rest.
${*var/pat/sub*}	Return *var* with the first occurrence of *pat* replaced by *sub*. Can be applied to $* or $@, in which case each word is treated separately. If *pat* starts with #, it can match only the start of *var*; if *pat* ends with %, it can match only the end of *var*.
${*var//pat/sub*}	Return *var* with every occurrence of *pat* replaced by *sub*.
${*variable:n*}	Truncate the beginning of the variable and return the part starting with character number *n*, where the first character is 0.
${*variable:n:l*}	Starting with character number *n*, where the first character is 0, return a substring of length *l* from the variable.

Table 5-25. Expression evaluation

Operator	Meaning
$((*arithmetic-expression*))	Return the result of the expression. Arithmetic operators are described in the section "Arithmetic Expressions."
	Example: TODAY='date +%-d' ; echo $(($TODAY+7)) stores the number of the current day in $TODAY and then prints that number plus 7 (the number of the same day next week).
[[*$condition*]]	Return 1 if *condition* is true and 0 if it is false. Conditions are described under the *test* built-in command.

Built-in Shell Variables

Built-in variables are set automatically by the shell and are typically used inside shell scripts. Built-in variables can use the variable substitution patterns shown earlier. When setting variables, you don't include dollar signs, but when referencing their values later, the dollar signs are necessary.

Tables 5-26 through Table 5-29 show the commonly used built-in variables in *bash*.

Table 5-26. Behavior-altering variables

Variable	Meaning
auto_resume	Allows a background job to be brought to the foreground simply by entering a substring of the job's command line. Values can be substring (resume if the user's string matches part of the command), exact (string must exactly match command), or another value (string must match at beginning of command).
BASH_ENV	Startup file of commands to execute, if *bash* is invoked to run a script.
CDPATH	Colon-separated list of directories to search for the directory passed in a *cd* command.
EDITOR	Pathname of your preferred text editor.

Table 5-26. Behavior-altering variables (continued)

Variable	Meaning
IFS	Word separator; used by shell to parse commands into their elements. The default separators are space, tab, and newline.
IGNOREEOF	If nonzero, don't allow use of a single Ctrl-D (the end-of-file or EOF character) to log off; use the *exit* command to log off.
PATH	Colon-separated list of directories to search for each command.
PROMPT_COMMAND	Command that *bash* executes before issuing a prompt for a new command.
PS1	Prompt displayed before each new command; see the later section "Variables in Prompt" for ways to introduce into the prompt dynamically changing information such as the current working directory or command history number.
PS2	Prompt displayed before a new line if a command is not finished.
PS3	Prompt displayed by *select* built-in command.
PS4	Prompt displayed by -*x* debugging (see the section "Invoking the Shell") and the *set* built-in command).

Table 5-27. History variables

Variable	Meaning
FCEDIT	Pathname of editor to use with the *fc* command.
HISTCMD	History number of the current command.
HISTCONTROL	If HISTCONTROL is set to the value of ignorespace, lines beginning with a space are not entered into the history list. If set to ignoredups, lines matching the last history line are not entered. Setting it to ignoreboth enables both options.
HISTFILE	Name of history file on which the editing modes operate.
HISTFILESIZE	Maximum number of lines to store in the history file. The default is 500.
HISTSIZE	Maximum number of commands to remember in the command history. The default is 500.

Table 5-28. Mail variables

Variable	Meaning
MAIL	Name of file to check for incoming mail.
MAILCHECK	How often, in seconds, to check for new mail (default is 60 seconds).
MAILPATH	List of filenames, separated by colons (:), to check for incoming mail.

Table 5-29. Status variables

Variable	Meaning
BASH	Pathname of this instance of the shell you are running.
BASH_VERSION	Version number of the shell you are running.
COLUMNS	Number of columns your display has.
DIRSTACK	List of directories manipulated by *pushd* and *popd* commands.
EUID	Effective UID of process running this shell, in the form of the number recognized by the system.
GROUPS	Groups to which user belongs, in the form of the numbers recognized by the system.
HOME	Name of your home (login) directory.

Table 5-29. Status variables (continued)

Variable	Meaning
HOSTNAME	Host the shell is running on.
HOSTTYPE	Short name indicating the type of machine the shell is running on; for instance, *i486*.
LINES	The number of lines your display has.
MACHTYPE	Long string indicating the machine the shell is running on; for instance, *i486-pc-linux-gnu*.
OLDPWD	Previous directory before the last *cd* command.
OSTYPE	Short string indicating the operating system; for instance, *linux-gnu*.
PPID	PID of parent process that invoked this shell.
PWD	Current directory.
SECONDS	Number of seconds since the shell was invoked.
SHELL	Pathname of the shell you are running.
SHLVL	Depth to which running shells are nested.
TERM	The type of terminal that you are using.
UID	Real UID of process running this shell, in the form of the number recognized by the system.

Arithmetic Expressions

The *let* command performs integer arithmetic. *bash* provides a way to substitute integer values (for use as command arguments or in variables); base conversion is also possible.

Table 5-30. Syntax for arithmetic expressions

Expression	Meaning
((*expr*))	Use the value of the enclosed arithmetic expression.

Operators

bash uses arithmetic operators from the C programming language; the following list is in decreasing order of precedence. Use parentheses to override precedence.

Table 5-31. Arithmetic operators

Operator	Meaning
-	Unary minus
! ~	Logical negation; binary inversion (one's complement)
* / %	Multiplication; division; modulus (remainder)
+ -	Addition; subtraction
<< >>	Bitwise left shift; bitwise right shift
<= >=	Less than or equal to; greater than or equal to
< >	Less than; greater than
= = !=	Equality; inequality (both evaluated left to right)
&	Bitwise AND
^	Bitwise exclusive OR

Table 5-31. Arithmetic operators (continued)

Operator	Meaning
|	Bitwise OR
&&	Logical AND
||	Logical OR
=	Assign value
+= -=	Reassign after addition/subtraction
*= /= %=	Reassign after multiplication/division/remainder
&= ^= |=	Reassign after bitwise AND/XOR/OR
<<= >>=	Reassign after bitwise shift left/right

Examples

See the let built-in command for more information and examples.

```
let "count=0" "i = i + 1"        Assign i and count
let "num % 2"; echo $?           Test for an even number
```

Command History

bash lets you display or modify previous commands. Commands in the history list can be modified using:

- Line-edit mode
- The *fc* command

Line-Edit Mode

Line-edit mode lets you emulate many features of the vi and Emacs editors. The history list is treated like a file. When the editor is invoked, you type editing keystrokes to move to the command line you want to execute. In the Terminal, the arrow keys work in both Emacs mode and vi command mode. You can also change the line before executing it. See Table 5-32 for some examples of common line-edit commands. When you're ready to issue the command, press Return. The default line-edit mode is Emacs. To enable *vi* mode, enter:

```
$ set -o vi
```

Note that *vi* starts in input mode; to type a *vi* command, press Esc first.

The mode you use for editing *bash* commands is entirely separate from the editor that is invoked for you automatically within many commands (for instance, the editor invoked by mail readers when you ask them to create a new mail message). To change the default editor, set the VISUALor EDITOR variable to the filename or full pathname of your favorite editor:

```
$ export EDITOR=emacs
```

Table 5-32. Common editing keystrokes

vi	Emacs	Result
K	Ctrl-p	Get previous command.
J	Ctrl-n	Get next command.
/string	Ctrl-r string	Get previous command containing string.
H	Ctrl-b	Move back one character.
L	Ctrl-f	Move forward one character.
b	M-b	Move back one word.
w	M-f	Move forward one word.
X	Del	Delete previous character.
x	Ctrl-d	Delete one character.
dw	M-d	Delete word forward.
db	M-Ctrl-h	Delete word back.
xp	Ctrl-t	Transpose two characters.

The fc Command

Use *fc -l* to list history commands, and *fc -e* to edit them. See the *fc* built-in command for more information.

Examples

$ `history`	*Display the command history list*
$ `fc -l 20 30`	*List commands 20 through 30*
$ `fc -l -5`	*List the last five commands*
$ `fc -l cat`	*List the last command beginning with cat*
$ `fc -ln 5 > doit`	*Save command 5 to file doit*
$ `fc -e vi 5 20`	*Edit commands 5 through 20 using vi*
$ `fc -e emacs`	*Edit previous command using Emacs*
$ `!!`	*Reexecute previous command*
$ `!cat`	*Reexecute last cat command*
$ `!cat foo-file`	*Reexecute last command, adding foo-file to the end of the argument list*

Command Substitution

Table 5-33. Command substitution syntax

Syntax	Meaning
!	Begin a history substitution.
!!	Previous command.
!N	Command number N in history list.
!-N	Nth command back from current command.
!string	Most recent command that starts with string.
!?string?	Most recent command that contains string.
!?string?%	Most recent command argument that contains string.
!$	Last argument of previous command.

Table 5-33. (continued)Command substitution syntax

Syntax	Meaning
!#	The current command up to this point.
!!*string*	Previous command, then append *string*.
!*N string*	Command *N*, then append *string*.
!{*s1*}*s2*	Most recent command starting with string *s1*, then append string *s2*.
^*old*^*new*^	Quick substitution; change string *old* to *new* in previous command, and execute modified command.

Variables in Prompt

Using the following variables, you can display information about the current state of the shell or the system in your *bash* prompt. Set the PS1 variable to a string including the desired variables. For instance, the following command sets PS1 to a string that includes the \w variable to display the current working directory and the \! variable to display the number of the current command. The next line is the prompt displayed by the change.

```
$ PS1='\w: Command \!$ '
~/book/linux: Command 504$
```

Table 5-34. Prompt control sequences

Variable	Meaning
\a	Alarm (bell).
\d	Date in the format "Mon May 8".
\e	Escape character (terminal escape, not backslash).
\h	Hostname.
\j	Number of background jobs (active or stopped).
\l	Current terminal name.
\n	Newline inserted in the prompt.
\r	Carriage return inserted in the prompt.
\s	Current shell.
\t	Time in 24-hour format, where 3:30 p.m. appears as 15:30:00.
\u	User's account name.
\v	Version and release of *bash*.
\w	Current working directory.
\A	Time in 24-hour format, where 3:30 p.m. appears as 15:30.
\D{*format*}	Time in the specified format interpreted by *strftime*; an empty format displays the locale-specific current time.
\H	Like \h.
\T	Time in 12-hour format, where 3:30 p.m. appears as 03:30:00.
\V	Version, release, and patch level of *bash*.
\W	Last element (following last slash) of current working directory.

Table 5-34. Prompt control sequences

Variable	Meaning
\\	Single backslash inserted in the prompt.
\!	Number of current command in the command history.
\#	Number of current command, where numbers start at 1 when the shell starts.
\@	Time in 12-hour format, where 3:30 p.m. appears as 03:30 p.m.
\$	Indicates whether you are *root*: displays # for *root*, $ for other users.
\[	Starts a sequence of nonprinting characters, to be ended by \].
\]	Ends the sequence of nonprinting characters started by \[.
nnn	The character in the ASCII set corresponding to the octal number *nnn* inserted into the prompt.

Job Control

Job control lets you place foreground jobs in the background, bring background jobs to the foreground, or suspend (temporarily stop) running jobs. Job control is enabled by default. Once disabled, it can be reenabled by any of the following commands:

```
bash -m -i
set -m
set -o monitor
```

Many job control commands take *jobID* as an argument. This argument can be specified as follows:

%*n*   Job number *n*

%*s*   Job whose command line starts with string *s*

%?*s* Job whose command line contains string *s*

%%   Current job

%+   Current job (same as preceding)

%-   Previous job

bash provides the following job control commands. For more information on these commands, see the upcoming section "Built-in Commands."

bg   Put a job in the background.

fg   Put a job in the foreground.

jobs
    List active jobs.

kill
    Terminate a job.

stop
    Suspend a background job.

stty tostop
    Stop background jobs if they try to send output to the terminal.

wait

    Wait for background jobs to finish.

Ctrl-Z

    Suspend a foreground job, and use *bg* or *fg* to restart it in the background or foreground. (Your terminal may use something other than *Ctrl-Z* as the suspend character.)

Built-in Commands

Examples to be entered as a command line are shown with the $ prompt. Otherwise, examples should be treated as code fragments that might be included in a shell script. For convenience, some of the reserved words used by multiline commands also are included.

#

#

Ignore all text that follows on the same line. # is used in shell scripts as the comment character and is not really a command.

#!

#!shell

Used as the first line of a script to invoke the named *shell* (with optional arguments) or other program. For example:

```
#!/bin/bash
```

:

:

Null command. Returns an exit status of 0. Sometimes used as the first character in a file to denote a bash script. Shell variables can be placed after the : to expand them to their values.

Example

To check whether someone is logged in:

```
if who | grep -w $1 > /dev/null
    then :    # do nothing
    # if pattern is found
    else echo "User $1 is not logged in"
fi
```

•

. file [*arguments*]

Same as *source*.

alias

alias [*-p*] [*name*[*=cmd*]]

Assign a shorthand *name* as a synonym for *cmd*. If *=cmd* is omitted, print the alias for *name*; if *name* is also omitted or if *-p* is specified, print all aliases. See also *unalias*.

bg

bg [*jobIDs*]

Put current job or *jobIDs* in the background. See the earlier section "Job Control."

bind

bind [*options*]

bind [*options*] *key:function*

Print or set the bindings that allow keys to invoke functions such as cursor movement and line editing. Typical syntax choices for *keys* are "\C-t" for Ctrl-T and "\M-t" or "\et" for Esc-T (quoting is needed to escape the sequences from the shell). Function names can be seen though the *-l* option.

Options

-f *filename*
> Consult *filename* for bindings, which should be in the same format as on the bind command line.

-l Print all Readline functions, which are functions that can be bound to keys.

-m *keymap*
> Specify a keymap for this and further bindings. Possible keymaps are emacs, emacs-standard, emacs-meta, emacs-ctlx, vi, vi-move, vi-command, and vi-insert.

-p Display all functions and the keys that invoke them, in the format by which keys can be set.

-q *function*
> Display the key bindings that invoke *function*.

-r *key*
> Remove the binding attached to *key* so that it no longer works.

-s Display all macros and the keys that invoke them, in the format by which keys can be set.

-u *function*
> Remove all the bindings attached to *function* so that no keys will invoke it.

-v   Display all Readline variables (settings that affect history and line editing) and their current settings, in the format by which variables can be set.

-x *key*:*command*
    Bind key to a shell command.

-P   Display all bound keys and the functions they invoke.

-S   Display all macros and the keys that invoke them.

-V   Display all Readline variables (settings that affect history and line editing) and their current settings.

Example

Bind Ctrl-T to copy-forward-word, the function that copies the part of the word following the cursor so it can be repasted:

```
$ bind "\C-t":copy-forward-word
```

break

break [*n*]

Exit from the innermost (most deeply nested) for, while, or until loop, or from the *n*th innermost level of the loop. Also exits from a select list.

builtin

builtin *command* [*arguments*]

Execute *command*, which must be a shell built-in. Useful for invoking built-ins within scripts of the same name.

case

case *string*

  in

  regex)

  commands

  ;;

  ...

  esac

If *string* matches regular expression *regex*, perform the following *commands*. Proceed down the list of regular expressions until one is found. (To catch all remaining strings, use * as *regex* at the end.)

cd

cd [*options*] [*dir*]

With no arguments, change to user's home directory. Otherwise, change working directory to *dir*. If *dir* is a relative pathname but is not in the current directory, search the CDPATH variable.

Options

-L Force symbolic links to be followed.

-P Don't follow symbolic links, but use the physical directory structure.

command

command [*options*] *command* [*arguments*]

Execute *command*, but don't perform function lookup (i.e., refuse to run any command that is neither in PATH nor a built-in). Set exit status to that returned by *command* unless *command* cannot be found, in which case exit with a status of 127.

Options

-p Search default path, ignoring the PATH variable's value.

-v Print the command or filename that invokes the command.

-V Like *-v*, but also print a description of the command.

-- Treat everything that follows as an argument, not an option.

compgen

compgen [*options*] [*word*]

Generate possible completion matches for *word* for use with bash's programmable completion feature, and write the matches to standard output. If *word* is not specified, display all completions. See complete for the options; any except *-p* and *-r* can be used with *compgen*.

complete

complete [*options*] *names*

Specify completions for arguments to each *name*, for use with *bash*'s programmable completion feature. With no options or with *-p*, print all completion specifications such that they can be reused as input.

Options

-o *comp-option*

> Specify other aspects of the completion specification's behavior besides generating a completion. Possible values of *comp-option* are:

> default

>> Use *readline*'s default filename completion if the completion specification generates no matches.

dirnames

> Use directory name completion if the completion specification generates no matches.

filenames

> Tell *readline* that the completion specification generates filenames so that it can process them accordingly. For use with shell functions.

nospace

> Tell *readline* not to append a space to completions at the end of the line. This is the default.

-p   Print all completion specifications.

-r   Remove completion specification for each *name*, or all specifications if no names are given.

-A *action*

> Specify an action to generate a list of completions. Possible actions are:

alias

> Alias names. May be specified as -*a*.

arrayvar

> Array variable names.

binding

> *readline* key binding names.

builtin

> Shell built-in command names. May be specified as -*b*.

command

> Command names. May be specified as -*c*.

directory

> Directory names. May be specified as -*d*.

disabled

> Disabled shell built-in command names.

enabled

> Enabled shell built-in command names.

export

> Exported shell variable names. May be specified as -*e*.

file

> Filenames. May be specified as -*f*.

function

> Shell function names.

group

> Group names. May be specified as -*g*.

helptopic

> Help topic names accepted by the help built-in command.

hostname

> Hostnames, from the file specified by HOSTFILE.

job

> Job names, if job control is active. May be specified as -*j*.

keyword
>   Shell reserved words. May be specified as *-k*.

running
>   Names of running jobs, if job control is active.

service
>   Service names. May be specified as *-s*.

setopt
>   Valid arguments for the *-o* option to the set built-in command.

shopt
>   Valid shell option names for the *shopt* built-in command.

signal
>   Signal names.

stopped
>   Names of stopped jobs, if job control is active.

user
>   Usernames. May be specified as *-u*.

variable
>   Shell variable names. May be specified as *-v*.

-C *command*
>   Execute the specified command in a subshell and use the output as possible completions.

-F *function*
>   Execute the specified function in the current shell and take the possible completions from the COMPREPLY array variable.

-G *globpat*
>   Expand the specified filename expansion pattern to generate the possible completions.

-P *prefix*
>   Prepend the specified prefix to each possible completion after all other options have been applied.

-S *suffix*
>   Append the specified suffix to each possible completion after all other options have been applied.

-W *list*
>   Split the specified word list and expand each resulting word. The possible completions are the members of the resulting list that match the word being completed.

-X *pattern*
>   Use the specified pattern as a filter and apply it to the list of possible completions generated by all the other options except *-P* and *-S*, removing all matches from the list. A leading ! in the *pattern* negates it so that any completion that doesn't match the pattern is removed.

continue

continue [*n*]

Skip remaining commands in a *for*, *while*, or *until* loop, resuming with the next iteration of the loop (or skipping *n* loops).

declare

declare [*options*] [*name*[*=value*]]

typeset [*options*] [*name*[*=value*]]

Print or set variables. Options prefaced by + instead of - are inverted in meaning.

Options

-a   Treat the following names as array variables.

-f   Treat the following names as functions.

-i   Expect variable to be an integer, and evaluate its assigned value.

-p   Print names and settings of all shell variables and functions; take no other action.

-r   Don't allow variables to be reset later.

-x   Mark variables for subsequent export.

-F   Print names of all shell functions; take no other action.

dirs

dirs [*options*]

Print directories currently remembered for *pushd/popd* operations.

Options

+*entry*
    Print *entry*th entry from start of list (list starts at 0).

-*entry*
    Print *entry*th entry from end of list.

-c   Clear the directory stack.

-l   Long listing.

-p   Print the directory stack, one entry per line.

-v   Like -*p*, but prefix each entry with its position in the stack.

disown

disown [*options*] [*jobIDs*]

Let job run, but disassociate it from the shell. By default, does not even list the job as an active job; commands like *jobs* and *fg* will no longer recognize it. When -*h* is specified, the job is recognized but is kept from being killed when the shell dies.

Options

-a   Act on all jobs.

-h   Do not pass a SIGHUP signal received by the shell on to the job.

---

echo

echo [*options*] [*strings*]

Write each *string* to standard output, separated by spaces and terminated by a newline. If no strings are supplied, echo a newline. (See also *echo* in Chapter 2.)

Options

-e   Enable interpretation of escape characters:

    \a   Audible alert

    \b   Backspace

    \c   Suppress the terminating newline (same as -n)

    \e   Escape character

    \f   Form feed

    \n   Newline

    \r   Carriage return

    \t   Horizontal tab

    \v   Vertical tab

    \\   Backslash

    nnn The character in the ASCII set corresponding to the octal number *nnn*.

    \x*nn* The character in the ASCII set corresponding to the hexadecimal number *nn* (1 or 2 hex digits).

-n   Don't append a newline to the output.

-E   Disable interpretation of escape characters.

---

enable

enable [*options*] [*built-in* ...]

Enable (or when *-n* is specified, disable) built-in shell commands. Without *built-in* argument or with *-p* option, print enabled built-ins. With *-a*, print the status of all built-ins. You can disable shell commands in order to define your own functions with the same names.

Options

-a   Display all built-ins, both enabled and disabled.

-d   Delete a built-in command that was previously loaded with *-f*.

-f *filename*
    On systems that support dynamic loading, load the new built-in command *built-in* from the shared object *filename*.

-n   Disable each specified *built-in*.

-p   Display enabled built-ins.

-s   Restrict display to special built-ins defined by the POSIX standard.

eval

eval [*command args...*]

Perform *command*, passing *args*.

exec

shift [*n*]

Shift positional arguments (e.g., $2 becomes $1). If *n* is given, shift to the left *n* places.

exit

exit [*n*]

Exit a shell script with status *n* (e.g., exit 1). *n* can be zero (success) or nonzero (failure). If *n* is not given, exit status is that of the most recent command. *exit* can be issued at the command line to close a window (log out).

Example

```
if [ $# -eq 0 ]; then
    echo "Usage: $0 [-c] [-d] file(s)"
    exit 1     # Error status
fi
```

export

export [*options*] [*variables*]

export [*options*] [*name*=[*value*]]...

Pass (export) the value of one or more shell *variables*, giving global meaning to the variables (which are local by default). For example, a variable defined in one shell script must be exported if its value will be used in other programs called by the script. When a shell variable has been exported, you can access its value by referencing the equivalent environment variable. If no *variables* are given, export lists the variables exported by the current shell. If *name* and *value* are specified, export assigns *value* to a variable *name* and exports it.

Options

--   Treat all subsequent strings as arguments, not options.

-f   Expect *variables* to be functions.

-n   Unexport variable.

-p   List variables exported by current shell.

fc

fc [*options*] [*first*] [*last*]

fc -s [*oldpattern=newpattern*] [*command*]

Display or edit commands in the history list. (Use only one of *-l* or *-e*.) *fc* provides capabilities similar to the C shell's history and ! syntax. *first* and *last* are numbers or strings specifying the range of commands to display or edit. If *last* is omitted, *fc* applies to a single command (specified by *first*). If both *first* and *last* are omitted, *fc* edits the previous command or lists the last 16. A negative number is treated as an offset from the current command. The second form of *fc* takes a history *command*, replaces *old* string with *new* string, and executes the modified command. If no strings are specified, *command* is reexecuted. If no *command* is given either, the previous command is reexecuted. *command* is a number or string like *first*. See earlier examples under "Command History."

Options

-e [*editor*]
> Invoke editor to edit the specified history commands. The default *editor* is set by the shell variable FCEDIT. If FCEDIT is not set, the value of EDITOR is used, or vi if neither is set.

-l [*first last*]
> List the specified command or range of commands, or list the last 16.

-n   Suppress command numbering from the *-l* listing.

-r   Reverse the order of the *-l* listing.

-s *oldpattern=newpattern*
> Edit command(s), replacing all occurrences of the specified old pattern with the new pattern. Then reexecute.

fg

fg [*jobIDs*]

Bring current job or *jobIDs* to the foreground. See the section "Job Control."

for

for x [*in* list]

> *do*

> commands

> *done*

Assign each word in *list* to x in turn and execute commands. If *list* is omitted, $@ (positional parameters) is assumed.

Examples

Paginate all files in the current directory and save each result:

```
for file in *
do
      pr $file > $file.tmp
done
```

Search chapters for a list of words (like *fgrep -f*):

```
for item in `cat program_list`
do
      echo "Checking chapters for"
      echo "references to program $item..."
      grep -c "$item.[co]" chap*
done
```

function

function command

```
{

   ...

}
```

Define a function. Refer to arguments the same way as positional parameters in a shell script ($1, etc.) and terminate with }.

getopts

getopts string name [args]

Process command-line arguments (or *args*, if specified) and check for legal options. *getopts* is used in shell script loops and is intended to ensure standard syntax for command-line options. *string* contains the option letters to be recognized by *getopts* when running the shell script. Valid options are processed in turn and stored in the shell variable *name*. If an option letter is followed by a colon, the option must be followed by one or more arguments.

hash

hash [options] [commands]

Search for *commands* and remember the directory in which each command resides. Hashing causes the shell to remember the association between a name and the absolute pathname of an executable, so that future executions don't require a search of PATH. With no arguments or only -l, hash lists the current hashed commands. The display shows *hits* (the number of times the command is called by the shell) and *command* (the full pathname).

Options

-d   Forget the remembered location of each specified command.

-l   Display the output in a format that can be reused as input.

-p *filename*
> Assume *filename* is the full path to the command and don't do a path search.

-r Forget the locations of all remembered commands.

-t Print the full pathname for each command. With more than one command, print the command before each full path.

help

help [**-s**] [*string*]

Print help text on all built-in commands or those matching *string*. With *-s*, display only brief syntax; otherwise display summary paragraph also.

history

history [*options*]

history [*lines*]

Print a numbered command history, denoting modified commands with *. Include commands from previous sessions. You may specify how many lines of history to print.

Options
-a *[file]*
> *bash* maintains a file called *.bash_history* in the user's home directory, a record of previous sessions' commands. Ask bash to append the current session's commands to *.bash_history* or to *file*.

-c Clear history list: remove all previously entered commands from the list remembered by the shell.

-d *offset*
> Delete the history entry at the specified offset from the beginning of the history list.

-n [*file*]
> Append to the history list those lines in *.bash_history* or in *file* that haven't yet been included.

-p *args*
> Perform history substitution on the specified arguments, and display the result on standard output. The results aren't stored in the history list. Each argument must be quoted to disable normal history expansion.

-r [*file*]
> Use *.bash_history* or *file* as the history list, instead of the working history list.

-s *args*
> Remove the last command in the history list, and then add the specified arguments to the list as a single entry (but don't execute the entry).

-w [*file*]
> Overwrite *.bash_history* or *file* with the working history list.

if

if *test-cmds*

Begin a conditional statement. The possible formats, shown here side by side, are:

```
if test-cmds      if test-cmds      if test-cmds
   then              then              then
      cmds1             cmds1             cmds1
fi                   else            elif test-cmds
                        cmds2            then
                     fi                    cmds2
                                        ...
                                     else
                                        cmdsn
                                  fi
```

Usually, the initial *if* and any *elif* lines execute one *test* or [ ] command (although any series of commands is permitted). When *if* succeeds (that is, the last of its *test-cmds* returns 0), *cmds1* are performed; otherwise, each succeeding *elif* or *else* line is tried.

jobs

jobs [*options*] [*jobIDs*]

List all running or stopped jobs, or those specified by *jobIDs*. For example, you can check whether a long compilation or text format is still running. This can also useful before logging out. See also the earlier section "Job Control."

Options

-l   List job IDs and process GIDs.

-n   List only jobs whose status has changed since last notification.

-p   List process GIDs only.

-r   List active, running jobs only.

-s   List stopped jobs only.

-x *command* [*arguments*]
    Execute *command*. If *jobIDs* are specified, replace them with *command*.

kill

kill [*options*] *IDs*

Terminate each specified PID or job ID. You must own the process or be a privileged user (either with *su* or *sudo*). See also the earlier section "Job Control" and the *killall* command in Chapter 2.

Options

-*signal*

    The *signal* number (from *ps -f*) or name (from *kill -l*). The default is TERM (signal number 15). With a signal number of 9, the *kill* is unconditional. If nothing else works to kill a process, *kill -9* almost always kills it, but it doesn't allow the process any time to clean up.

--   Consider all subsequent strings to be arguments, not options.

-l [*arg*]

    With no argument, list the signal names. (Used by itself.) The argument can be a signal name or a number representing either the signal number or the exit status of a process terminated by a signal. If it is a name, the corresponding number is returned; otherwise, the corresponding name is returned.

-n *signum*

    Specify the signal number to send.

-s *signal*

    Specify *signal*. May be a signal name or number.

---

let

let *expressions*

Perform arithmetic as specified by one or more integer *expressions*. *expressions* consist of numbers, operators, and shell variables (which don't need a preceding $), and must be quoted if they contain spaces or other special characters. For more information and examples, see the earlier section "Arithmetic Expressions," and "expr" in Chapter 2.

Examples

Both of the following examples add 1 to variable i:

```
let i=i+1
let "i = i + 1"
```

---

local

local [*options*] [*variable*[=*value*]] [*variable2*[=*value*]] ...

Without arguments, print all local variables. Otherwise, create (and set, if specified) one or more local variables. See the *declare* built-in command for options. Must be used within a function.

---

logout

logout [*status*]

Exit the shell, returning *status* as exit status to invoking program if specified. Can be used only in a login shell. Otherwise, use *exit*.

popd

popd [*options*]

Manipulate the directory stack. By default, remove the top directory, and *cd* to it. If successful, run *dirs* to show the new directory stack.

Options

+*n*   Remove the *n*th directory in the stack, counting from 0.

-*n*   Remove the *n*th entry from the bottom of the stack, counting from 0.

-n   Don't do a *cd* when removing directories from the stack.

printf

printf *string* [*arguments*]

Format the *arguments* according to *string*. Works like the C library *printf* function. Standard *printf* percent-sign formats are recognized in *string*, such as %i for integer. Escape sequences such as \n can be included in *string* and are automatically recognized; if you want to include them in *arguments*, specify a *string* of %b. You can escape characters in *arguments* to output a string suitable for input to other commands by specifying a *string* of %q.

Examples

```
$ printf "Previous command: %i\n" "$(($HISTCMD-1))"
Previous command: 534
$ echo $PAGER
less -E
$ printf "%q\n" "\t$PAGER"
\\tless\ -E
```

The last command would probably be used to record a setting in a file where it could be read and assigned by another shell script.

pushd

pushd [*directory*]

pushd [*options*]

By default, switch top two directories on stack. If specified, add a new directory to the top of the stack instead, and *cd* to it.

Options

+*n*   Rotate the stack to place the *n*th (counting from 0) directory at the top.

-*n*   Rotate the stack to place the *n*th directory from the bottom of the stack at the top.

-n   Don't do a *cd* when adding directories to the stack.

pwd

pwd [*option*]

Display the current working directory's absolute pathname. By default, any symbolic directories used when reaching the current directory are displayed, but with *-P*, or if the *-o* option to the set built-in is set, the real names are displayed instead.

Options

-L   Include any symbolic links in the pathname.

-P   Don't include symbolic links in the pathname.

---

read

read [*options*] [*variable1 variable2 ...*]

Read one line of standard input and assign each word (as defined by IFS) to the corresponding *variable*, with all leftover words assigned to the last variable. If only one variable is specified, the entire line is assigned to that variable. The return status is 0 unless EOF is reached, a distinction that is useful for running loops over input files. If no variable names are provided, read the entire string into the environment variable REPLY.

Options

-a *var*
> Read each word into an element of *var*, which is treated as an array variable.

-d *char*
> Stop reading the line at *char* instead of at the newline.

-e   Line editing and command history are enabled during input.

-n *num*
> Read only *num* characters from the line.

-p *string*
> Display the prompt *string* to the user before reading each line, if input is interactive.

-r   Raw mode; ignore \ as a line continuation character.

-s   Don't echo the characters entered by the user (useful for reading a password).

-t *seconds*
> Time out and return without setting any variables if input is interactive and no input has been entered for *seconds* seconds.

-u *fd*
> Read input from specified file descriptor *fd* instead of standard input.

Examples

```
$ read first last address
Sarah Caldwell 123 Main Street
$ echo "$last, $first\n$address"
Caldwell, Sarah
123 Main Street
```

The following commands, which read a password into the variable $user_pw and then display its value, use recently added options that are not in all versions of *bash* in current use:

```
$ read -sp "Enter password (will not appear on screen)" user_pw
Enter password (will not appear on screen)
$ echo $user_pw
You weren't supposed to know!
```

The following script reads input from the system's password file, which uses colons to delimit fields (making it a popular subject for examples of input parsing):

```
IFS=:
cat /etc/passwd |
while
read account pw user group gecos home shell
do
echo "Account name $account has user info: $gecos"
done
```

readonly

readonly [*options*] [*variable1 variable2...*]

Prevent the specified shell variables from being assigned new values. Variables can be accessed (read) but not overwritten.

Options

-a   Treat the following names as array variables.

-f   Treat the following names as functions and set them read-only so that they can't be changed.

-p   Display all read-only variables (default).

return

return [*n*]

Normally used inside a function to exit the function with status *n* or with the exit status of the previously executed command. Can be used outside a function during execution of a script by the . command to cause the shell to stop execution of the script. The return status is *n* or the script's exit status.

select

select name [*in* wordlist *;*]

  do

  commands

  done

Choose a value for *name* by displaying the words in *wordlist* to the user and prompting for a choice. Store user input in the variable REPLY and the chosen word in *name*. Then execute *commands* repeatedly until they execute a break or return. The default prompt can be changed by setting the PS3 shell variable.

---

set

set [*options*] [*arg1 arg2 ...*]

With no arguments, set prints the values of all variables known to the current shell. Options can be enabled (*-option*) or disabled (*+option*). Options can also be set when the shell is invoked, via *bash*. Arguments are assigned in order to $1, $2, and so on.

Options

-    Turn off *-v* and *-x*, and turn off option processing.

--   Used as the last option; turn off option processing so that arguments beginning with - are not misinterpreted as options. (For example, you can set $1 to -1.) If no arguments are given after --, unset the positional parameters.

-a   From now on, automatically mark variables for export after defining or changing them.

-b   Report background job status at termination instead of waiting for next shell prompt.

-e   Exit if a command yields a nonzero exit status.

-f   Don't expand filename metacharacters (e.g., * ? [ ]). Wildcard expansion is sometimes called *globbing*.

-h   Locate and remember commands as they are defined.

-k   Assignment of environment variables (*var=value*) take effect regardless of where they appear on the command line. Normally, assignments must precede the command name.

-m   Monitor mode. Enable job control; background jobs execute in a separate process group. *-m* usually is set automatically.

-n   Read commands, but don't execute. Useful for checking errors, particularly for shell scripts.

-o [*m*]
     List shell modes, or turn on mode *m*. Many modes can be set by other options. The modes can be turned off through the *+o* option. Modes are:

allexport
     Same as *-a*.

braceexpand
     Same as *-B*.

emacs
     Enter Emacs editing mode (on by default).

errexit
     Same as *-e*.

hashall
     Same as *-h*.

histexpand
     Same as *-H*.

history
> Default. Preserve command history.

ignoreeof
> Don't allow use of a single Control-D (the end-of-file or EOF character) to log off; use the exit command to log off. This has the same effect as setting the shell variable IGNOREEOF=1.

interactive-comments
> Allow comments to appear in interactive commands.

keyword
> Same as -*k*.

monitor
> Same as -*m*.

noclobber
> Same as -*C*.

noexec
> Same as -*n*.

noglob
> Same as -*f*.

notify
> Same as -*b*.

nounset
> Same as -*u*.

onecmd
> Same as -*t*.

physical
> Same as -*P*.

posix
> Match POSIX standard.

privileged
> Same as -*p*.

verbose
> Same as -*v*.

vi
> Enable vi-style command-line editing.

xtrace
> Same as -*x*.

+o [*m*]
> Display the set commands that recreate the current mode settings or turn off mode *m*. See the -*o* option for a list of modes.

-p   Start up as a privileged user; don't process $HOME/.profile.

-t   Exit after one command is executed.

-u   Indicate an error when user tries to use a variable that is undefined.

-v   Show each shell command line when read.

-x   Show commands and arguments when executed, preceded by a + or the prompt defined by the PS4 shell variable. This provides step-by-step debugging of shell scripts. (Same as -o xtrace.)

-B   Default. Enable brace expansion.

-C   Don't allow output redirection (>) to overwrite an existing file.

-H   Default. Enable ! and !! commands.

-P   Print absolute pathnames in response to *pwd*. By default, *bash* includes symbolic links in its response to *pwd*.

Examples

`set -- "$num" -20 -30`	*Set $1 to $num, $2 to -20, $3 to -30*
`set -vx`	*Read each command line; show it; execute it;*
	show it again (with arguments)
`set +x`	*Stop command tracing*
`set -o noclobber`	*Prevent file overwriting*
`set +o noclobber`	*Allow file overwriting again*

shift

shift [*n*]

Shift positional arguments (e.g., $2 becomes $1). If *n* is given, shift to the left *n* places.

shopt

shopt [*options*] [*optnames*]

Set or unset variables that control optional shell behavior. With no options or with -p, display the settable *optnames*.

Options

-o   Allow only options defined for the set -o built-in to be set or unset.

-p   Display output in a form that can be reused as input.

-q   Quiet mode. Suppress normal output.

-s   Set (enable) each specified option. With no *optname*, list all set options.

-u   Unset (disable) each specified option. With no *optname*, list all unset options.

Settable shell options

Unless otherwise noted, options are disabled by default.

cdable_vars
    If an argument to the cd built-in is not a directory, assume that it's a variable containing the name of the directory to change to.

cdspell
    For interactive shells, check for minor errors in the name of a directory component (transposed characters, a missing character, or an extra character). Print the corrected name and proceed.

checkhash

Check that a command found in the hash table actually exists before trying to execute it; if it is not found, do a path search.

checkwinsize

Check the window size after each command, and update LINES and COLUMNS as necessary.

cmdhist

Attempt to save all lines of a multiline command in one history entry to facilitate re-editing.

dotglob

Include filenames beginning with . in the results of pathname expansion.

execfail

For a noninteractive shell, don't exit if the file specified as an argument to exec cannot be executed. For an interactive shell, don't exit from the shell if exec fails.

expand_aliases

Expand aliases. Enabled by default for interactive shells.

extglob

Enable the shell's extended pattern-matching features for pathname expansion.

histappend

Append the history list to the file specified by HISTFILE when the shell exits, instead of overwriting the file.

histreedit

Give the user a chance to re-edit a failed history substitution.

histverify

Load a history substitution into the readline editing buffer so it can be further edited, instead of immediately passing it to the shell parser.

hostcomplete

Try to provide hostname completion when a word containing @ is being completed. Set by default.

huponexit

Send SIGHUP to all jobs when an interactive login shell exits.

interactive_comments

In an interactive shell, treat any word beginning with a #, and any subsequent characters, as a comment. Set by default.

lithist

If cmdhist is also enabled, save multiline commands to the history file separated by embedded newlines rather than semicolons (;) when possible.

login_shell

Set by the shell if it is started as a login shell. Can't be changed by the user.

mailwarn

Warn if a mail file has been accessed since the last time bash checked it.

no_empty_cmd_completion

Don't attempt to search the PATH for possible completions when completion is attempted on an empty line.

nocaseglob

Use case-insensitive filename matching during pathname expansion.

---

nullglob
> Allow patterns that don't match any files to expand to a null string.

progcomp
> Enable the programmable completion facilities. Set by default.

promptvars
> Perform variable and parameter expansion on prompt strings after performing normal expansion. Set by default.

restricted_shell
> Set by the shell if started in restricted mode. This option can't be changed by the user and is not reset when the startup files are executed.

shift_verbose
> Cause the shift built-in to print an error message when the shift count is greater than the number of positional parameters.

sourcepath
> Cause the source built-in (.) to search the PATH to find the directory containing a file supplied as an argument. Set by default.

xpg_echo
> Cause the echo built-in to expand backslash-escape sequences by default.

---

source

source *file* [*arguments*]

Read and execute lines in *file*. *file* doesn't have to be executable but must reside in a directory searched by PATH. Any *arguments* are passed as positional parameters to the file when it is executed.

---

suspend

suspend [*-f*]

Same as Ctrl-Z.

Option

-f   Force suspend, even if shell is a login shell.

---

test

test *condition*

[condition]

Evaluate a *condition* and, if its value is true, return a zero exit status; otherwise, return a nonzero exit status. An alternate form of the command uses [ ] rather than the word *test*. *condition* is constructed using the following expressions. Conditions are true if the description holds true.

File conditions

-a *file*
> *file* exists.

-b *file*
> *file* is a block special file.

-c *file*
> *file* is a character special file.

-d *file*
> *file* is a directory.

-e *file*
> *file* exists.

-f *file*
> *file* is a regular file.

-g *file*
> *file* has the set-group-ID bit set.

-h *file*
> *file* is a symbolic link.

-k *file*
> *file* has its sticky bit (no longer used) set.

-p *file*
> *file* is a named pipe (FIFO).

-r *file*
> *file* is readable.

-s *file*
> *file* has a size greater than 0.

-t [*n*]
> The open file descriptor *n* is associated with a terminal device (default *n* is 1).

-u *file*
> *file* has its set-user-ID bit set.

-w *file*
> *file* is writable.

-x *file*
> *file* is executable.

-G *file*
> *file*'s group is the process's effective GID.

-L *file*
> *file* is a symbolic link.

-N *file*
> *file* has been modified since its last time of access.

-O *file*
> *file*'s owner is the process's effective UID.

-S *file*
> *file* is a socket.

f1 -ef *f2*
> Files *f1* and *f2* are linked (refer to the same file through a hard link).

---

f1 -nt *f2*
> File *f1* is newer than *f2*.

f1 -ot *f2*
> File *f1* is older than *f2*.

String conditions

-n *s1*
> String *s1* has nonzero length.

-o *s1*
> Shell option *s1* is set. Shell options are described under the set built-in command.

-z *s1*
> String *s1* has 0 length.

s1 = *s2*
> Strings *s1* and *s2* are identical.

s1 = = *s2*
> Strings *s1* and *s2* are identical.

s1 != *s2*
> Strings *s1* and *s2* aren't identical.

s1 < *s2*
> String *s1* is lower in the alphabet (or other sort in use) than *s2*. By default, the check is performed character-by-character against the ASCII character set.

s1 > *s2*
> String *s1* is higher in the alphabet (or other sort in use) than *s2*.

string
> *string* is not null.

Integer comparisons

n1 -eq *n2*
> *n1* equals *n2*.

n1 -ge *n2*
> *n1* is greater than or equal to *n2*.

n1 -gt *n2*
> *n1* is greater than *n2*.

n1 -le *n2*
> *n1* is less than or equal to *n2*.

n1 -lt *n2*
> *n1* is less than *n2*.

n1 -ne *n2*
> *n1* does not equal *n2*.

Combined forms

! *condition*
> True if *condition* is false.

condition1 -a *condition2*
> True if both conditions are true.

condition1 -o condition2
> True if either condition is true.

Examples

Each of the following examples shows the first line of various statements that might use a test condition:

while test $# -gt 0	*While there are arguments ...*
while [-n "$1"]	*While the first argument is nonempty ...*
if [$count -lt 10]	*If $count is less than 10 ...*
if [-d RCS]	*If the RCS directory exists ...*
if ["$answer" != "y"]	*If the answer is not y ...*
if [! -r "$1" -o ! -f "$1"]	*If the first argument is not a readable file or a regular file ...*

times

times

Print accumulated process times for user and system.

trap

trap [*option*] [*commands*] [*signals*]

Execute *commands* if any of *signals* is received. Each *signal* can be a signal name or number. Common signals include 0, 1, 2, and 15. Multiple commands should be quoted as a group and separated by semicolons internally. If *commands* is the null string (e.g., *trap "" signals*), then *signals* is ignored by the shell. If *commands* is omitted entirely, reset processing of specified signals to the default action. If both *commands* and *signals* are omitted, list current trap assignments. See the examples at the end of this entry and under exec.

Options

-l   List signal names and numbers.

-p   Used with no *commands* to print the trap commands associated with each *signal*, or all signals if none is specified.

Signals

Signals are listed along with what triggers them.

0   Exit from shell (usually when shell script finishes).

1   Hang up (usually logout).

2   Interrupt (usually through Ctrl-C).

3   Quit.

4   Illegal instruction.

5   Trace trap.

6   Abort.

7   Unused.

8   Floating-point exception.

9   Termination.

10   User-defined.

11   Reference to invalid memory.

12   User-defined.

13   Write to a pipe without a process to read it.

14   Alarm timeout.

15   Software termination (usually via *kill*).

16   Unused.

17   Termination of child process.

18   Continue (if stopped).

19   Stop process.

20   Process suspended (usually through Control-Z).

21   Background process has *tty* input.

22   Background process has *tty* output.

23-28
    Unused.

29   I/O possible on a channel.

Examples

> **trap** **""** **2**   *Ignore signal 2 (interrupts)*
> **trap** **2**   *Obey interrupts again*

Remove a *$tmp* file when the shell program exits or if the user logs out, presses Control-C, or does a *kill*:

> **trap** **"rm -f $tmp; exit"** **0 1 2 15**

---

type

type [*options*] *commands*

Report absolute pathname of programs invoked for *commands* and whether or not they are hashed.

Options

--   Consider all subsequent strings to be arguments, not options.

-a, -all
    Print all occurrences of *command*, not just that which would be invoked.

-f   Suppress shell function lookup.

-p, -path
    Print the hashed value of *command*, which may differ from the first appearance of *command* in the PATH.

-t, -type
    Determine and state if *command* is an alias, keyword, function, built-in, or file.

-P   Force a PATH search for each name, even if -t would not return a value of "file" for the name.

Example
```
$ type mv read
mv is /bin/mv
read is a shell built-in
```

typeset

typeset

Obsolete. See *declare.*

ulimit

ulimit [*options*] [*n*]

Print the value of one or more resource limits or, if *n* is specified, set a resource limit to *n*. Resource limits can be either hard (*-H*) or soft (*-S*). By default, *ulimit* sets both limits or prints the soft limit. The options determine which resource is acted on. Values are in 1024-byte increments unless otherwise indicated.

Options
--   Consider all subsequent strings to be arguments, not options.

-a   Print all current limits.

-H   Hard resource limit.

-S   Soft resource limit.

Specific limits
These options limit specific resource sizes.

-c   Core files.

-d   Size of processes' data segments.

-f   Size of shell-created files.

-l   Size of memory that the process can lock.

-m   Resident set size.

-n   Number of file descriptors. On many systems, this can't be set.

-p   Pipe size, measured in blocks of 512 bytes.

-s   Stack size.

-t   Amount of CPU time, counted in seconds.

-u   Number of processes per user.

-v   Virtual memory used by shell.

umask

umask [*options*] [*nnn*]

Display file creation mask or set file creation mask to octal value *nnn*. The file creation mask determines which permission bits are turned off (e.g., *umask 002* produces rw-rw-r--).

Options

-p   Display mask within a *umask* command so that a caller can read and execute it.

-S   Display *umask* symbolically rather than in octal.

unalias

unalias [*-a*] *names*

Remove *names* from the alias list. See also *alias*.

Option

-a   Remove all aliases.

unset

unset [*options*] *names*

Erase definitions of functions or variables listed in *names*.

Options

-f   Expect *name* to refer to a function.

-v   Expect *name* to refer to a variable (default).

until

until *test-commands*

   do

   commands

   done

Execute *test-commands* (usually a *test* or [ ] command); if the exit status is nonzero (that is, the test fails), perform *commands*. Repeat.

wait

wait [*ID*]

Pause in execution until all background jobs complete (exit status 0 is returned), or until the specified background PID or job ID completes (exit status of *ID* is returned).

Note that the shell variable $! contains the PID of the most recent background process. If job control is not in effect, *ID* can only be a PID number. See the earlier section "Job Control."

Example

wait $!   *Wait for last background process to finish*

while

while

    test-commands

   do

    commands

  done

Execute *test-commands* (usually a *test* or [ ] command); if the exit status is 0, perform *commands*. Repeat.

Text Editing and Processing

Part II summarizes the command set for the text editors and related utilities in Unix. Chapter 6 reviews pattern matching, an important aspect of text editing.

Chapters in this part of the book include:

- Chapter 6, Pattern Matching
- Chapter 7, The vi Editor
- Chapter 8, The Emacs Editor

6

Pattern Matching

A number of Unix text-processing utilities let you search for, and in some cases change, text patterns rather than fixed strings. These utilities include the editing programs *ed*, *ex*, *vi*, Emacs, and *sed*, the *gawk* scripting language, and the commands *grep* and *egrep*. Text patterns (also called *regular expressions*) contain normal characters mixed with special characters (called *metacharacters*).

Perl's regular expression support is so rich that it does not fit into this book; you can find a description in the O'Reilly books *Mastering Regular Expressions*, *Perl in a Nutshell*, *Perl 5 Pocket Reference*, or *Programming Perl*. The Emacs editor also provides regular expressions similar to those shown in this chapter.

ed and *ex* are hardly ever used as standalone, interactive editors nowadays. But *ed* can be found as a batch processor invoked from shell scripts, and *ex* commands are often invoked within *vi* through the colon (:) command. We use *vi* in this chapter to refer to the regular expression features supported by both *vi* and the *ex* editor on which it is based. *sed* and *gawk* are widely used in shell scripts and elsewhere as filters to alter text.

Filenames Versus Patterns

When you issue a command on the command line, special characters are seen first by the shell, and then by the program; therefore, unquoted metacharacters are interpreted by the shell for filename expansion. The command:

```
$ grep [A-Z]* chap[12]
```

can, for example, be transformed by the shell into:

```
$ grep Array.c Bug.c Comp.c chap1 chap2
```

and can then try to find the pattern Array.c in files Bug.c, Comp.c, chap1, and chap2. To bypass the shell and pass the special characters to *grep*, use quotes:

```
$ grep "[A-Z]*" chap[12]
```

Double quotes suffice in most cases, but single quotes are the safest bet.

Note also that in pattern matching, ? matches zero or one instance of a regular expression; in filename expansion, ? matches a single character.

Metacharacters, Listed by Unix Program

Some metacharacters are valid for one program but not for another. Those that are available to a Unix program are marked by a checkmark (×) in Table 6-1. Items marked with a P are specified by POSIX; double-check your system's version. Full descriptions are provided after the table.

Table 6-1. Unix metacharacters

Symbol	ed	ex	vi	sed	awk	grep	egrep	Action
.	✓	✓	✓	✓	✓	✓	✓	Match any character.
*	✓	✓	✓	✓	✓	✓	✓	Match zero or more preceding.
^	✓	✓	✓	✓	✓	✓	✓	Match beginning of line/string.
$	✓	✓	✓	✓	✓	✓	✓	Match end of line/string.
\	✓	✓	✓	✓	✓	✓	✓	Escape following character.
[ ]	✓	✓	✓	✓	✓	✓	✓	Match one from a set.
(\)	✓	✓	✓	✓		✓		Store pattern for later replay.[a]
\n	✓	✓	✓	✓		✓		Replay subpattern in match.
{ }					✓P		✓P	Match a range of instances.
\{ \}	✓			✓		✓		Match a range of instances.
\< \>	✓	✓	✓					Match word's beginning or end.
+					✓		✓	Match one or more preceding.
?					✓		✓	Match zero or one preceding.
|					✓		✓	Separate choices to match.
( )					✓]		✓	Group expressions to match.

[a] Stored subpatterns can be replayed during matching. See Table 6-2.

Note that in *ed*, *ex*, *vi*, and *sed*, you specify both a search pattern (on the left) and a replacement pattern (on the right). The metacharacters in Table 6-1 are meaningful only in a search pattern.

In *ed*, *ex*, *vi*, and *sed*, the metacharacters in Table 6-2 are valid only in a replacement pattern.

Table 6-2. Metacharacters in replacement patterns

Symbol	ex	vi	sed	ed	Action
\	✓	✓	✓	✓]	Escape following character.
\n	✓	✓	✓]	✓	Text matching pattern stored in \(\).
&	✓	✓	✓	✓	Text matching search pattern.
~	✓	✓			Reuse previous replacement pattern.
%				✓	Reuse previous replacement pattern.
\u \U	✓	✓			Change character(s) to uppercase.
\l \L	✓	✓			Change character(s) to lowercase.
\E	✓	✓			Turn off previous \U or \L.
\e	✓				Turn off previous \u or \l.

Metacharacters

The characters in Table 6-3 have special meaning only in search patterns.

Table 6-3. Metacharacters used in search patterns

Character	Pattern
.	Match any single character except newline. Can match newline in *awk*.
*	Match any number (or none) of the single character that immediately precedes it. The preceding character can also be a regular expression; e.g., since . (dot) means any character, .* means match any number of any character.
^	Match the following regular expression at the beginning of the line or string.
$	Match the preceding regular expression at the end of the line or string.
[ ]	Match any one of the enclosed characters. A hyphen (-) indicates a range of consecutive characters. A circumflex (^) as the first character in the brackets reverses the sense of the character set, so that it matches any one character not in the list. A hyphen or close bracket (]) as the first character is treated as a member of the list. All other metacharacters are treated as members of the list (i.e., literally).
{n,m}	Match a range of occurrences of the single character that immediately precedes it. The preceding character can also be a metacharacter. {n} matches exactly n occurrences, {n,} matches at least n occurrences, and {n,m} matches any number of occurrences between n and m. n and m must be between 0 and 255, inclusive.
\{n,m\}	Just like {n,m}, above, but with backslashes in front of the braces.
	Turn off the special meaning of the character that follows.
\(\)	Save the pattern enclosed between \(and \) into a special holding space. Up to nine patterns can be saved on a single line. The text matched by the subpatterns can be replayed in substitutions by the escape sequences \1 to \9.
\n	Replay the nth subpattern enclosed in \(and \) into the pattern at this point. n is a number from 1 to 9, with 1 starting on the left. See "Examples of Searching" later in this chapter.
\< \>	Match characters at beginning (\<) or end (\>) of a word.
+	Match one or more instances of preceding regular expression.
?	Match zero or one instances of preceding regular expression.
		Match the regular expression specified before or after.
( )	Apply a match to the enclosed group of regular expressions.

Many Unix systems allow the use of POSIX character classes within the square brackets that enclose a group of characters. These classes, listed in Table 6-4, are typed enclosed in [: and :]. For example, [[:alnum:]] matches a single alphanumeric character.

Table 6-4. Character classes

Class	Characters matched
alnum	Alphanumeric characters
alpha	Alphabetic characters
blank	Space or tab
cntrl	Control characters
digit	Decimal digits
graph	Nonspace characters
lower	Lowercase characters
print	Printable characters
space	Whitespace characters
upper	Uppercase characters
Xdigit	Hexadecimal digits

The characters in Table 6-5 have special meaning only in replacement patterns.

Table 6-5. Metacharacters used in replacement patterns

Character	Pattern
\	Turn off the special meaning of the character that follows.
\n	Restore the text matched by the nth pattern previously saved by \(and \). n is a number from 1 to 9, with 1 starting on the left.
&	Reuse the text matched by the search pattern as part of the replacement pattern.
~	Reuse the previous replacement pattern in the current replacement pattern. Must be the only character in the replacement pattern. (*ex* and *vi*)
%	Reuse the previous replacement pattern in the current replacement pattern. Must be the only character in the replacement pattern. (*ed*)
\u	Convert first character of replacement pattern to uppercase.
\U	Convert entire replacement pattern to uppercase.
\l	Convert first character of replacement pattern to lowercase.
\L	Convert entire replacement pattern to lowercase.
\e, \E	Turn off previous \u, \U, \l, and \L.

Examples of Searching

When used with *grep* or *egrep*, regular expressions should be surrounded by quotes. (If the pattern contains a $, you must use single quotes; e.g., `'pattern'`.) When used with *ed*, *ex*, *sed*, and *awk*, regular expressions are usually surrounded by /, although (except for *awk*) any delimiter works. Tables 6-6 through Table 6-9 show some example patterns.

Table 6-6. General search patterns

Pattern	What does it match?
bag	The string bag anywhere in the line
^bag	bag at the beginning of the line.
bag$	bag at the end of the line.
^bag$	bag as the only word on the line.
[Bb]ag	Bag or bag anywhere in the line.
b[aeiou]g	b, a vowel, and g.
b[^aeiou]g	b, a consonant (or uppercase or symbol), and g.
b.g	b, any character, and g.
^...$	Any line containing exactly three characters.
^\.	Any line that begins with a dot.
^\.[a-z][a-z]	Same, followed by two lowercase letters (e.g., *troff* requests).
^\.[a-z]\{2\}	Same as previous; *ed*, *grep*, and *sed* only.
^\[^.]	Any line that doesn't begin with a dot.
bugs*	bug, bugs, bugss, etc, anywhere on the line
"word"	A word in quotes.
"*word"*	A word, with or without quotes.
[A-Z][A-Z]*	One or more uppercase letters.
[A-Z]+	Same; *egrep* or *awk* only.
[[:upper:]]+	Same; POSIX *egrep* or *awk*.
[A-Z].*	An uppercase letter, followed by zero or more characters.
[A-Z]*	Zero or more uppercase letters.
[a-zA-Z]	Any letter.
[^0-9A-Za-z]	Any symbol or space (not a letter or a number).
[^[:alnum:]]	Same, using POSIX character class.

Table 6-7. egrep and awk search patterns

egrep or awk pattern	What does it match?
[567]	One of the digits 5, 6, or 7.
five|six|seven	One of the words five, six, or seven.
80[2-4]?86	8086, 80286, 80386, or 80486.
80[2-4]?86|(Pentium(-II)?)	8086, 80286, 80386, 80486, Pentium, or Pentium-II.
compan(y|ies)	company or companies.

Table 6-8. ex and vi search patterns

ex or vi pattern	What does it match?
\<the	Words like theater or the.
the\>	Words like breathe or the.
\<the\>	The word the.

Table 6-9. ed, sed and grep search patterns

ed, sed or grep pattern	What does it match?
0\{5,\}	Five or more zeros in a row.
[0-9]\{3\}-[0-9]\{2\}-[0-9]{4\ }	U.S. Social Security number (*nnn-nn-nnnn*).
\(why\).*\1	A line with two occurrences of why.
\([[:alpha:]_][[:alnum:]_.]*\) = \1;	C/C++ simple assignment statements.

Examples of Searching and Replacing

The examples in Table 6-10 show the metacharacters available to *sed* and *vi*. We have shown *vi* commands with an initial colon because that is how they are invoked with *vi*. A space is marked by a ■; a tab is marked by *tab*.

Table 6-10. Searching and replacing

Command	Result
s/.*/(&)/	Redo the entire line, but add parentheses.
s/.*/mv & &.old/	Change a word list (one word per line) into *mv* commands.
/^$/d	Delete blank lines.
:g/^$/d	Same as previous, in *vi* editor.
/^[■*tab*]*$/d	Delete blank lines, plus lines containing only spaces or tabs.
:g/^[■*tab*]*$/d	Same as previous, in *vi* editor.
s/■*/■/g	Turn one or more spaces into one space.
:%s/■*/■/g	Same as previous, in *ex* editor.
:s/[0-9]/Item &:/	Turn a number into an item label (on the current line).
:s	Repeat the substitution on the first occurrence.
:&	Same as previous.
:sg	Same, but for all occurrences on the line.
:&g	Same as previous.
:%&g	Repeat the substitution globally (i.e., on all lines).
:.,$s/Fortran/\U&/g	On current line to last line, change word to uppercase.
:%s/.*/\L&/	Lowercase entire file.
:s/\<./\u&/g	Uppercase first letter of each word on current line (useful for titles).
:%s/yes/No/g	Globally change a word to *No*.
:%s/Yes/~/g	Globally change a different word to *No* (previous replacement).

Finally, here are some *sed* examples for transposing words. A simple transposition of two words might look like this:

    s/die or do/do or die/   *Transpose words*

The real trick is to use hold buffers to transpose variable patterns. For example:

    s/\([Dd]ie\) or \([Dd]o\)/\2 or \1/   *Transpose, using hold buffers*

7

The vi Editor

vi is the classic screen-editing program for Unix. A number of enhanced versions exist, including *nvi*, *vim*, *vile*, and *elvis*. On Mac OS X Tiger, the *vi* command is linked to *vim*. The Emacs editor, covered in Chapter 8, has several *vi* modes that allow you to use the same commands covered in this chapter.

The *vi* editor operates in two modes, *command mode* and *insert mode*. The dual mode makes *vi* an attractive editor for users who separate text entry from editing. For users who edit as they type, Emacs modeless editing can be more comfortable.

vi is based on an older line editor called *ex*. A user can invoke powerful editing capabilities within *vi* by typing a colon (:), entering an *ex* command, and pressing the Return key. Furthermore, you can place *ex* commands in a startup file called *~/.exrc*, which *vi* reads at the beginning of your editing session. Because *ex* commands are still an important part of *vi*, they are also described in this chapter.

One of the most common versions of *vi* is Bram Moolenaar's Vi IMproved, or *vim*. On Mac OS X Tiger, *vim* is the default version of *vi* and runs when you invoke *vi*. *vim* changes some of the basic features of *vi*, most notoriously changing the undo key to support multiple levels of undo. While seasoned users of *vi* find *vim*'s changes disturbing, those new to *vi* find *vim*'s extensive features attractive.

Wherever a command or option applies to *vim* only, those items are flagged in this chapter with (**vim**) after their description.

Fully documenting *vim* is beyond the scope of this chapter, but we do cover some of its most commonly used options and features. Beyond what we cover here, *vim* offers enhanced support to programmers through an integrated build and debugging process, syntax highlighting, extended *ctags* support, and support for Perl and Python, as well as GUI fonts and menus, function key mapping, independent mapping for each mode, and more. Fortunately, *vim* comes with a powerful help program you can use to learn more about the things we just couldn't fit into this chapter.

For more information, including details on *vim*'s extensions, see the O'Reilly book *Learning the vi Editor*.

Review of vi Operations

This section provides a review of the following:

- Command-line options
- *vi* modes
- Syntax of *vi* commands
- Status-line commands

Command Mode

Once the file is opened, you are in command mode. From command mode, you can:

- Invoke insert mode.
- Issue editing commands.
- Move the cursor to a different position in the file.
- Invoke *ex* commands.
- Invoke a Linux shell.
- Save or exit the current version of the file.

Insert Mode

In *insert mode*, you can enter new text in the file. Press the Esc or Ctrl-[keys to exit insert mode and return to command mode. The following commands invoke insert mode:

a Append after cursor.

A Append at end of line.

c Begin change operation (must be followed by a movement command).

C Change to end of line.

i Insert before cursor.

I Insert at beginning of line.

o Open a line below current line.

O Open a line above current line.

r Replace character under cursor.

R Begin overwriting text.

s Substitute a character.

S Substitute entire line.

Syntax of vi Commands

In *vi*, commands have the following general form:

    [n] operator [m] object

Here are the basic editing operators:

c   Begin a change.

d   Begin a deletion.

y   Begin a yank (or copy).

If the current line is the object of the operation, the operator is the same as the object: cc, dd, yy. Otherwise, the editing operators act on objects specified by cursor-movement commands or pattern-matching commands. *n* and *m* are the number of times the operation is performed or the number of objects the operation is performed on. If both *n* and *m* are specified, the effect is *n m*.

An object can represent any of the following text blocks:

Word
> Includes characters up to a space or punctuation mark. A capitalized object is a variant form that recognizes only blank spaces.

Sentence
> Extends to ., !, or ? followed by two spaces.

Paragraph
> Extends to next blank line or *nroff/troff* paragraph macro (defined by *para= option*).

Section
> Extends to next *nroff/troff* section heading (defined by *sect=option*).

Examples

2cw
> Change the next two words

d}   Delete up to next paragraph

*d^*   Delete back to beginning of line

5yy
> Copy the next five lines into temporary buffer (for future pasting)

y]]
> Copy up to the next section into temporary buffer (for future pasting)

Status-Line Commands

Most commands aren't echoed on the screen as you input them. However, the status line at the bottom of the screen is used to echo input for the following commands:

/   Search forward for a pattern

?   Search backward for a pattern

:   Invoke an ex command

!   Pipe the text indicated by a subsequent movement command through the following shell command, and replace the text with the output of the shell command

Commands that are input on the status line must be entered by pressing the Return key. In addition, error messages and output from the Ctrl-G command are displayed on the status line.

vi Command-Line Options

Here are the three most common ways to start a *vi* session:

```
vi file
vi +n file
vi +/pattern file
```

You can open a *file* for editing, optionally at line *n* or at the first line matching *pattern*. If no file is specified, *vi* opens with an empty buffer. The command-line options that can be used with *vi* are as follows (*vim*-only options are labeled):

+*[num]*
> Start editing at line number *num*, or the last line of the file if num is omitted.

+/*pattern*
> Start editing at the first line matching *pattern*. (Fails if nowrapscan is set in your .exrc startup file.)

-*b*   Edit the file in binary mode. (vim)

-*c command*
> Run the given *vi command* upon startup. Only one -*c* option is permitted. *ex* commands can be invoked by prefixing them with a colon. An older form of this option, +*command*, is still supported.

--*cmd command*
> Like -*c*, but execute the command before any resource files are read. (vim)

-*d*   Run in *diff* mode. Works like *vimdiff*. (vim)

-*e*   Run as *ex* (line editing rather than full-screen mode).

-*h*   Print help message, then exit.

-*i file*
> Use the specified *file* instead of the default *.viminfo* to save or restore *vim*'s state. (vim)

-*l*   Enter LISP mode for running LISP programs (not supported in all versions).

-*m* Start the editor with the write option turned off so the user can't write to files. (vim)

-*n*   Don't use a swap file; record changes in memory only. (vim)

--*noplugin*
> Don't load any plug-ins. (vim)

-o[n]

Start *vim* with *n* open horizontal windows. The default is to open one window for each file. (vim)

-r [file]

Recovery mode; recover and resume editing on *file* after an aborted editor session or system crash. Without file, list files available for recovery.

-s, -s scriptfile

When running in *ex* mode (*-e*), suppress prompts or informative messages sent to the console. Otherwise, read and execute commands given in *scriptfile* as if they were typed in from the keyboard. (vim)

-t tag

Edit the *file* containing *tag* and position the cursor at its definition.

-u file

Read configuration information from *file* instead of default *.vimrc* resource files. If the file argument is NONE, *vim* won't read resource files, load plug-ins, or run in compatible mode. If the argument is NORC, it doesn't read resource files, but it will load plug-ins. (vim)

-v   Run in full-screen mode (default).

--version

Print version information, then exit.

-w rows

Set the window size so *rows* lines at a time are displayed; useful when editing over a slow dial-up line.

-x   Prompt for a key that will be used to try to encrypt or decrypt a file using crypt (not supported in all versions).

-y   Modeless *vi*; run *vim* in insert mode only, without a command mode. This is the same as invoking *vim* as *evim*. (vim)

-C   Same as *-x*, but assume the file is encrypted already (not supported in all versions). For *vim*, this option starts the editor in *vi*-compatible mode.

-D   Debugging mode for use with scripts. (vim)

-L   List files that were saved due to an aborted editor session or system crash (not supported in all versions). For *vim* this option is the same as *-r*.

-M   Don't allow text in files to be modified. (vim)

-N   Run *vim* in a non-*vi*-compatible mode. (vim)

-O[n]

Start *vim* with *n* open windows arranged vertically on the screen. (vim)

-R   Edit files read-only.

-S commandfile

Source commands given in *commandfile* after loading any files for editing specified on the command line. Shorthand for the option *-c* source. (vim)

-T type
> Set the terminal *type*. This value overrides the $TERM environment variable. (vim)

-V[n]
> Verbose mode; print messages about what options are being set and what files are being read or written. You can set a level of verbosity to increase or decrease the number of messages received. The default value is 10 for high verbosity. (vim)

-W scriptfile
> Write all typed commands from the current session to the specified *scriptfile*. The file created can be used with the *-s* command. (vim)

-Z Start *vim* in restricted mode. Don't allow shell commands or suspension of the editor. (vim)

ex Command-Line Options

While most people know *ex* commands only by their use within *vi*, the editor also exists as a separate program and can be invoked from the shell (for instance, to edit files as part of a script). Within *ex*, you can enter the *vi* or visual command to start *vi*. Similarly, within *vi*, you can enter Q to quit the *vi* editor and enter *ex*.

If you invoke ex as a standalone editor, you can include the following options:

+[num]
> Start editing at line number *num*, or the last line of the file if *num* is omitted.

+/pattern
> Start editing at the first line matching *pattern*. (Fails if nowrapscan is set in your *.exrc* startup file.)

-c command
> Run the given ex *command* at startup. Only one *-c* option is permitted. An older form of this option, *+command*, is still supported.

-e Run as a line editor rather than full-screen *vi* mode (default).

-l Enter LISP mode for running LISP programs (not supported in all versions).

-r [file]
> Recover and resume editing on *file* after an aborted editor session or system crash. Without file, list files available for recovery.

-s Silent; don't display prompts. Useful when running a script. This behavior also can be set through the older - option.

-t tag
> Edit the file containing *tag* and position the cursor at its definition.

-v Run in full-screen mode (same as invoking *vi*).

-w rows
> Set the window size so *rows* lines at a time are displayed; useful when editing by a slow dial-up line.

-x Prompt for a key that tries to encrypt or decrypt a file using *crypt* (not supported in all versions).

-C Same as *-x*, but assume the file is encrypted already (not supported in all versions).

-L List files that were saved due to an editor or system crash (not supported in all versions).

-R Edit files read-only; don't allow changes to be saved.

You can exit *ex* in several ways:

:x Exit (save changes and quit).

:q! Quit without saving changes.

:vi Enter the *vi* editor.

Movement Commands

Some versions of *vi* don't recognize extended keyboard keys (e.g., arrow keys, Page Up, Page Down, Home, Insert, and Delete); some do. All, however, recognize the keys in this section. Many users of *vi* prefer to use these keys, because it helps them keep their fingers on the home row of the keyboard. A number preceding a command repeats the movement. Movement commands are also objects for change, delete, and yank operations.

Character

Command	Action
h, j, k, l	Left, down, up, right (←, ↑, ↓, →,)
Spacebar	Right
Backspace	Left
Ctrl-H	Left

Text

Command	Action
w, b	Forward, backward by word (treating punctuation marks as words).
W, B	Forward, backward by word (recognizing only whitespace, not punctuation, as separators).
e	End of word (treating a punctuation mark as the end of a word).
E	End of word (recognizing only whitespace as the end of a word).
ge	End of previous word (treating a punctuation mark as the end of a word). (vim)
gE	End of previous word (recognizing only whitespace as the end of a word). (vim)
), (	Beginning of next, current sentence.
}, {	Beginning of next, current paragraph.
]], [[	Beginning of next, current section.
][, []	End of next, current section. (vim)

Lines

Long lines in a file may show up on the screen as multiple lines. While most commands work on the lines as defined in the file, a few commands work on lines as they appear on the screen.

Command	Action
0, $	First, last position of current line.
^, _	First nonblank character of current line.
+, -	First character of next, previous line.
Return	First nonblank character of next line.
n|	Column n of current line.
g0, g$	First, last position of screen line. (vim)
g^	First nonblank character of screen line. (vim)
gm	Middle of screen line. (vim)
gk, gj	Move up, down one screen line. (vim)
H	Top line of screen.
M	Middle line of screen.
L	Last line of screen.
nH	n lines after top line of screen.
nL	n lines before last line of screen.

Screens

Command	Action
Ctrl-F, Ctrl-B	Scroll forward, backward one screen.
Ctrl-D, Ctrl-U	Scroll down, up one-half screen.
Ctrl-E, Ctrl-Y	Show one more line at bottom, top of window.
z Return	Reposition line with cursor to top of screen.
z.	Reposition line with cursor to middle of screen.
z-	Reposition line with cursor to bottom of screen.
Ctrl-L	Redraw screen (without scrolling).

Searches

Command	Action
/pattern	Search forward for pattern.
/	Repeat previous search forward.
/pattern/+n	Go to line n after pattern.
?pattern	Search backward for pattern.
?	Repeat previous search backward.
?pattern?-n	Go to line n before pattern.
n	Repeat previous search.

Command	Action
N	Repeat previous search in opposite direction.
%	Find match of current parenthesis, brace, or bracket.
*	Search forward for word under cursor. Matches only exact words. (vim)
#	Search backward for word under cursor. Matches only exact words. (vim)
g*	Search backward for word under cursor. Matches the characters of this word when embedded in a longer word. (vim)
g#	Search backward for word under cursor. Matches the characters of this word when embedded in a longer word. (vim)
fx	Move forward to x on current line.
Fx	Move backward to x on current line.
tx	Move forward to just before x in current line.
Tx	Move backward to just after x in current line.
,	Reverse search direction of last f, F, t, or T.
;	Repeat last character search (f, F, t, or T).
:noh	Suspend search highlighting until next search. (vim).

Line numbering

Command	Action
Ctrl-G	Display current filename and line number.
gg	Move to first line in file. (vim)
nG	Move to line number n.
G	Move to last line in file.
:n	Move to line number n.

Marking position

Command	Action
mx	Mark current position with character x.
`x	(backquote) Move cursor to mark x.
'x	(apostrophe) Move to start of line containing x.
``	(backquotes) Return to previous mark (or location prior to search).
''	(apostrophes) Like preceding, but return to start of line.
`"	(apostrophe quote) Move to position when last editing the file. (vim)
`[`]	(backquote bracket) Move to beginning/end of previous text operation. (vim)
'[']	(apostrophe bracket) Like preceding, but return to start of line where operation occurred. (vim)
`.	(backquote period) Move to last change in file. (vim)
`.	(apostrophe period) Like the previous item, but return to start of line. (vim)
:marks	List active marks. (vim)

Edit Commands

Recall that c, d, and y are the basic editing operators.

Inserting New Text

Command	Action
a	Append after cursor.
A	Append to end of line.
i	Insert before cursor.
I	Insert at first nonblank character of line.
gI	Insert at beginning of line. (vim)
o	Open a line below cursor.
O	Open a line above cursor.
Esc	Terminate insert mode.

The following commands work in insert mode.

Command	Action
Tab	Insert a tab.
Backspace	Delete previous character.
Ctrl-E	Insert character found just below cursor. (vim)
Ctrl-Y	Insert character found just above cursor. (vim)
Ctrl-H	Delete previous character (same as Backspace).
Delete	Delete current character.
Ctrl-W	Delete previous word. (vim)
Ctrl-A	Repeat last insertion. (vim)
Ctrl-I	Insert a tab.
Ctrl-N	Insert next completion of the pattern to the left of the cursor. (vim)
Ctrl-P	Insert previous completion of the pattern to the left of the cursor. (vim)
Ctrl-T	Shift line right to next shift width. (vim)
Ctrl-D	Shift line left to previous shift width. (vim)
Ctrl-U	Delete current line.
Ctrl-V	Insert next character verbatim.
Ctrl-[	Terminate insert mode.

Some of the control characters listed in the previous table are set by *stty*. Your terminal settings may differ.

Changing and Deleting Text

The following table isn't exhaustive but illustrates the most common operations.

Command	Action
cw	Change through end of current word.
cc	Change line.
c$	Change text from current position to end of line.
C	Same as c$.

Command	Action
dd	Delete current line.
d$	Delete remainder of line.
D	Same as d$.
*n*dd	Delete *n* lines.
dw	Delete a word.
d}	Delete up to next paragraph.
d^	Delete back to beginning of line.
d/*pattern*	Delete up to first occurrence of *pattern*.
dn	Delete up to next occurrence of pattern.
dfa	Delete up to and including a on current line.
dta	Delete up to (not including) a on current line.
dL	Delete up to last line on screen.
dG	Delete to end of file.
gqap	Reformat current paragraph to textwidth. (vim)
g~w	Switch case of word. (vim)
guw	Change word to lowercase. (vim)
gUw	Change word to uppercase. (vim)
p	Insert last deleted or yanked text after cursor.
gp	Same as p, but leave cursor at end of inserted text. (vim)
]p	Same as p, but match current indention. (vim)
[p	Same as P, but match current indention. (vim)
P	Insert last deleted or yanked text before cursor.
gP	Same as P, but leave cursor at end of inserted text. (vim)
r*x*	Replace character with *x*.
Rtext	Replace text beginning at cursor.
s	Substitute character.
*n*s	Substitute *n* characters.
S	Substitute entire line.
u	Undo last change.
Ctrl-R	Redo last change. (vim)
U	Restore current line.
x	Delete current character.
X	Delete back one character.
*n*X	Delete previous *n* characters.
.	Repeat last change.
~	Reverse case.
&	Repeat last substitution.
Y	Copy (yank) current line to temporary buffer.
yy	Same as Y.
"*x*yy	Copy current line to buffer *x*.
ye	Copy text to end of word into temporary buffer.
yw	Same as ye.

Command	Action
y$	Copy rest of line into temporary buffer.
"xdd	Delete current line into buffer x.
"Xdd	Delete current line and append to buffer x.
"xp	Put contents of buffer x.
J	Join previous line to current line.
gJ	Same as J, but without inserting a space. (vim)
:j!	Same as J.
Ctrl-A	Increment number under cursor. (vim)
Ctrl-X	Decrement number under cursor. (vim)

Saving and Exiting

Writing a file means saving the edits and updating the file's modification time.

Command	Action
ZZ	Quit vi, writing the file only if changes were made.
:x	Same as ZZ.
:wq	Write and quit file.
:w	Write file.
:w *file*	Save copy to *file*.
:n1,n2w *file*	Write lines *n1* to *n2* to new *file*.
:n1,n2w >> *file*	Append lines *n1* to *n2* to existing *file*.
:w!	Write file (overriding protection).
:w! *file*	Overwrite file with current buffer.
:w %.new	Write current buffer named *file* as *file.new*.
:q	Quit file.
:q!	Quit file (discarding edits).
Q	Quit *vi* and invoke *ex*.
:vi	Return to *vi* after Q command.
%	Current filename.
#	Alternate filename.

Accessing Multiple Files

Command	Action
:e *file*	Edit *file*; current file becomes the alternate file.
:e!	Restore last saved version of current file.
:e+ *file*	Begin editing at end of new *file*.
:e+ *n file*	Open new *file* at line *n*.
:e#	Open to previous position in alternate (previously edited) file.
:ta *tag*	Edit file containing *tag* at the location of the tag.

Command	Action
:n	Edit next file.
:n!	Force next file into buffer (don't save changes to current file).
:n *files*	Specify new list of *files*.
:args	Display multiple files to be edited.
:rew	Rewind list of multiple files to top.

Window Commands

The following table lists common commands for controlling windows in vim. See also the *split*, *vsplit*, and *resize* commands in Chapter 2. For brevity, control characters are marked in the following list by ^.

Command	Action
:new	Open a new window.
:new *file*	Open *file* in a new window.
:sp *file*	Split the current window.
:sv *file*	Same as :sp, but make new window read-only.
:sn *file*	Edit next *file* in new window.
:clo	Close current window.
:hid	Hide current window, unless it is the only visible window.
:on	Make current window the only visible one.
:res *n*	Resize window to *n* lines.
:wa	Write all changed buffers to file.
:qa	Close all buffers and exit.
^W s	Same as :sp.
^W n	Same as :new.
^W ^	Open new window with alternate (previously edited) file.
^W c	Same as :clo.
^W o	Same as :only.
^W j, ^W k	Move cursor to next/previous window.
^W p	Move cursor to previous window.
^W h, ^W l	Move cursor to window on left/right.
^W t, ^W b	Move cursor to window on top/bottom of screen.
^W K, ^W B	Move current window to top/bottom of screen.
^W H, ^W L	Move current window to far left/right of screen.
^W r, ^W R	Rotate windows down/up.
^W +, ^W -	Increase/decrease current window size.
^W =	Make all windows same height.

Interacting with the Shell

Command	Action
:r *file*	Read in contents of file after cursor.
:r !*command*	Read in output from *command* after current line.
:nr !*command*	Like preceding, but place after line *n* (0 for top of file).
:!*command*	Run *command*, then return.
!*object command*	Send object, indicated by a movement command, as input to shell command *command*; replace object with *command*'s output.
:n1,n2! *command*	Send lines *n1* through *n2* to *command*; replace with output.
n!!*command*	Send *n* lines to *command*; replace with output.
!!	Repeat last system command.
!!*command*	Replace current line with output of *command*.
:sh	Create subshell; return to file with EOF.
Ctrl-Z	Suspend editor; resume with *fg*.
:so *file*	Read and execute *ex* commands from *file*.

Macros

Command	Action
:ab *in out*	Use *in* as abbreviation for *out*.
:unab *in*	Remove abbreviation for *in*.
:ab	List abbreviations.
:map *c* sequence	Map character *c* as sequence of commands.
:unmap *c*	Disable map for character *c*.
:map	List characters that are mapped.
:map! *c* sequence	Map character *c* to input mode *sequence*.
:unmap! *c*	Disable input mode map (you may need to quote the character with Ctrl-V).
:map!	List characters that are mapped to input mode.
q*x*	Record typed characters into register specified by letter *x*. If letter is uppercase, append to register. (vim)
q	Stop recording. (vim)
@x	Execute the register specified by letter x. (vim)

In *vi*, the following characters are unused in command mode and can be mapped as user-defined commands:

Letters
    g K q V v

Control keys
    ^K ^O ^T ^W ^X

Symbols
    _ * \ =

The = is used by *vi* if LISP mode is set. *vim* uses all of these characters, but you can create macros for function keys and multiple character commands. See `:help :map` for details. Other versions of *vi* may use some of these characters as well, so test them before using them.

Miscellaneous Commands

Command	Action
<	Shift line left to position indicated by following movement command.
>	Shift line right to position indicated by following movement command.
<<	Shift line left one shift width (default is eight spaces).
>>	Shift line right one shift width (default is eight spaces).
>}	Shift right to end of paragraph.
<%	Shift left until matching parenthesis, brace, bracket, etc. (Cursor must be on the matching symbol.)
=	Indent line in C-style, or using program specified in equalprg option. (vim)
K	Look up word under cursor in manpages (or program defined in keywordprg). (vim)
^[	Abort command or end input mode.
^]	Perform a tag lookup on the text under the cursor.
^\	Enter *ex* line-editing mode.
^^	(Caret key with Ctrl key pressed) Return to previously edited file.

Alphabetical List of Keys in Command Mode

For brevity, control characters are marked by ^.

Command	Action
a	Append text after cursor.
A	Append text at end-of-line.
^A	Search for next occurrence of word under cursor. Increment number in *vim* when cursor is on a number.
b	Back up to beginning of word in current line.
B	Back up one word, treating punctuation marks as words.
^B	Scroll backward one window.
c	Change text up to target of next movement command.
C	Change to end of current line.
^C	End insert mode; interrupts a long operation.
d	Delete up to target of next movement command.
D	Delete to end of current line.
^D	Scroll down half-window; in insert mode, unindent to shiftwidth if autoindent is set (or when using *vim*).
e	Move to end of word.
E	Move to end of word, treating punctuation as part of word.

Command	Action
^E	Show one more line at bottom of window.
f	Find next character typed forward on current line.
F	Find next character typed backward on current line.
^F	Scroll forward one window.
g	Unused in *vi*. Begins many multiple-character commands in *vim*.
G	Go to specified line or end of file.
^G	Print information about file on status line.
h	Left arrow cursor key.
H	Move cursor to home position.
^H	Left arrow cursor key; backspace key in insert mode.
i	Insert text before cursor.
I	Insert text before first nonblank character on line.
^I	Unused in command mode; in insert mode, same as Tab key.
j	Down arrow cursor key.
J	Join previous line to current line.
^J	Down arrow cursor key; in insert mode, move down a line.
k	Up arrow cursor key.
K	Unused in *vi*. Look up word using keywordprg in *vim*.
^K	Unused in *vi*. Insert multiple-keystroke character in *vim*.
l	Right arrow cursor key.
L	Move cursor to last position in window.
^L	Redraw screen.
m	Mark the current cursor position in register (a–z).
M	Move cursor to middle position in window.
^M	Move to beginning of next line.
n	Repeat the last search command.
N	Repeat the last search command in reverse direction.
^N	Down arrow cursor key.
o	Open line below current line.
O	Open line above current line.
^O	Unused in *vi*. Return to previous jump position in *vim*.
p	Put yanked or deleted text after or below cursor.
P	Put yanked or deleted text before or above cursor.
^P	Up arrow cursor key.
q	Unused in *vi*. Record keystrokes in *vim*.
Q	Quit *vi* and enter *ex* line-editing mode.
^Q	Unused in *vi*. Same as ^V in *vim* (On some terminals, resume data flow.)
r	Replace character at cursor with the next character you type.
R	Replace characters.
^R	Redraw the screen.
s	Change the character under the cursor to typed characters.
S	Change entire line.

Command	Action
^S	Unused. (On some terminals, stop data flow.)
t	Find next character typed forward on current line and position cursor before it.
T	Find next character typed backward on current line and position cursor after it.
^T	Unused in command mode for *vi*. Pop tag from tagstack in *vim*. In insert mode, move to next tab setting.
u	Undo the last change made. In *vi*, a second undo redoes an undone command. *vim* supports multiple levels of undo. To redo, use Ctrl-R.
U	Restore current line, discarding changes.
^U	Scroll the screen upward a half-window.
v	Unused in *vi*. Enter visual mode in *vim*.
V	Unused in *vi*. Enter linewise visual mode in *vim*.
^V	Unused in command mode for *vi*. Enter blockwise visual mode in *vim*. In insert mode, insert next character verbatim.
w	Move to beginning of next word.
W	Move to beginning of next word, treating punctuation marks as words.
^W	Unused in command mode in *vi*. Begins window commands in *vim*. In insert mode, back up to beginning of word.
x	Delete character under cursor.
X	Delete character before cursor.
^X	Unused in *vi*. Decrement number in vim when cursor is on a number. In insert mode in *vim*, begins several commands.
y	Yank or copy text up to target of following movement command into temporary buffer.
Y	Make copy of current line.
^Y	Show one more line at top of window.
z	Reposition line containing cursor. z must be followed by Return (reposition line to top of screen), . (reposition line to middle of screen), or - (reposition line to bottom of screen).
ZZ	Exit the editor, saving changes.

Syntax of ex Commands

To enter an ex command from vi, type:

    :[address] command [options]

An initial : indicates an *ex command*. As you type the *command*, it is echoed on the status line. Enter the *command* by pressing Return. *address* is the line number or range of lines that are the object of *command*. *options* and *addresses* are described in the following sections. ex commands are described in "Syntax of ex commands."

Options

! Indicates a variant command form, overriding the normal behavior.

count
The number of times the *command* is to be repeated. Unlike *vi* commands, the count comes after the *command*, not before it. Numbers preceding an *ex* command are considered to be part of the *address*. For example, 3d deletes line 3, while d3 deletes three lines beginning with the current line.

file

> The name of a *file* that is affected by the command. % stands for current file; # stands for previous file.

Addresses

If no *address* is given, the current line is the object of the *command*. If the *address* specifies a range of lines, the format is:

> x,y

where *x* and *y* are the first and last addressed lines (*x* must precede *y* in the buffer). *x* and *y* may be line numbers or symbols. Using ; instead of , sets the current line to *x* before interpreting *y*.

Address Symbols

Symbol	Meaning
1,$	All lines in the file
%	All lines; same as 1,$
x,y	Lines x through y
x;y	Lines x through y, with current line reset to x
0	Top of file
.	Current line
n	Absolute line number n
$	Last line
x-n	n lines before x
x+n	n lines after x
-[n]	One or n lines previous
+[n]	One or n lines ahead
'x	Line marked with x
"	Previous mark
/pattern/	Forward to line matching *pattern*
?pattern?	Backward to line matching *pattern*

Alphabetical Summary of ex Commands

ex commands can be entered by specifying any unique abbreviation. In this listing, the full name appears in the margin, and the shortest possible abbreviation is used in the syntax line. Examples are assumed to be typed from *vi*, so they include the : prompt.

abbrev

ab [string text]

Define string when typed to be translated into text. If string and text aren't specified, list all current abbreviations.

Examples

Note: ^M appears when you type Ctrl-V followed by Return.

```
:ab ora O'Reilly Media, Inc.
:ab id Name:^MRank:^MPhone:
```

append

[address] a[!]

Append new text at specified *address*, or at present address if none is specified. Add a ! to switch the autoindent setting that will be used during input (e.g., if autoindent is enabled, ! disables it). Enter new text after entering the command. Terminate input of new text by entering a line consisting of just a period.

Example

```
:a      Begin appending to current line
        Append this line
        and this line too.
.       Terminate input of text to append
```

args

ar

Print filename arguments (the list of files to edit). The current argument is shown in brackets ([ ]).

cd

cd *dir*

chdir *dir*

Change current directory within the editor to *dir*.

bdelete

[*n*] bd[!] [*n*]

Unload buffer *n* and remove it from the buffer list. Add a ! to force removal of an unsaved buffer. The buffer may also be specified by filename. If no buffer is specified, remove the current buffer. (vim)

buffer

[*n*] b[!] [*n*]

Begin editing buffer *n* in the buffer list. Add a ! to force a switch from an unsaved buffer. The buffer may also be specified by filename. If no buffer is specified, continue editing the current buffer. (vim)

buffers

buffers[!]

Print the listed members of the buffer list. Some buffers (e.g., deleted buffers) won't be listed. Add ! to show unlisted buffers. *ls* is another abbreviation for this command. (vim)

center

[*address*] ce [*width*]

Center line within the specified *width*. If *width* is not specified, use textwidth. (vim)

change

[address] c[!] text

Replace the specified lines with text. Add a ! to switch the autoindent setting during input of text. Terminate input by entering a line consisting of just a period.

close

clo[!]

Close current window unless it is the last window. If buffer in window is not open in another window, unload it from memory. This command won't close a buffer with unsaved changes, but you can add ! to hide it instead. (**vim**)

copy

[address] co destination

Copy the lines included in *address* to the specified destination address. The command t is the same as copy.

Example

:1,10 co 50   *Copy first 10 lines to just after line 50*

delete

```
[address] d [buffer]
```
Delete the lines included in *address*. If *buffer* is specified, save or append the text to it.

Examples

`:/Part I/,/Part II/-1d`	*Delete to line above "Part II"*
`:/main/+d`	*Delete line below "main"*
`:.,$d`	*Delete from this line to last line*

edit

```
e[!] [+n] [file]
```
Begin editing *file*. Add a ! to discard any changes to the current file. If no file is given, edit another copy of the current file. With the *+n* argument, begin editing on line *n*.

Examples

`:e file`	
`:e#`	*Return to editing the previous file*
`:e!`	*Discard edits since last save*

exusage

```
exu [command]
```
Print a brief usage message describing command or a list of available commands if command is omitted. (In vim, use the help command instead.)

file

```
f [filename]
```
Change the filename for the current buffer to *filename*. The next time the buffer is written, it is written to file *filename*. When the name is changed, the buffer's notedited flag is set, to indicate you aren't editing an existing file. If the new filename is the same as a file that already exists on the disk, you need to use :w! to overwrite the existing file. When specifying a *filename*, the % character indicates the current filename. If no *filename* is specified, print the current name and status of the buffer.

Example

```
:f %.new
```

fold

```
address fo
```
Fold the lines specified by address. A fold collapses several lines on the screen into one line, which can later be unfolded. It doesn't affect the text of the file. (**vim**)

The vi Editor

foldclose

[address] foldc[!]

Close folds in specified address or at present address if none is specified. Add a ! to close more than one level of folds. (vim)

foldopen

[address] foldo[!]

Open folds in specified address, or at present address if none is specified. Add a ! to open more than one level of folds. (vim)

global

[*address*] g[!]/*pattern*/[*commands*]

Execute commands on all lines that contain *pattern* or, if *address* is specified, on all lines within that range. If commands aren't specified, print all such lines. If ! is used, execute *commands* on all lines that don't contain pattern. See *v*.

Examples

```
:g/Unix/p              Print all lines containing "Unix"
:g/Name:/s/tom/Tom/    Change "tom" to "Tom" on all lines  containing "Name:"
```

help

h

Print a brief help message. Information on particular commands can be obtained through the *exusage* and *viusage* commands. (In *vim* this command provides extensive information for all commands, and neither *exusage* nor *viusage* is used.)

hide

hid

Close current window unless it is the last window, but don't remove the buffer from memory. This is a safe command to use on an unsaved buffer. (vim)

insert

address i[!]

Insert new text at line before the specified address, or at present address if none is specified. Add a ! to switch the autoindent setting during input of text. Enter new text after entering the command. Terminate input of new text by entering a line consisting of just a period.

join

[*address*] j[!] [*count*]

Place the text in the specified *address* on one line, with whitespace adjusted to provide two blank characters after a period, no blank characters after a), and one blank character otherwise. Add a ! to prevent whitespace adjustment.

Example

:1,5j!   *Join first five lines, preserving whitespace*

jumps

ju

Print jump list used with Control-I and Control-O commands. The jump list is a record of most movement commands that skip over multiple lines. It records the position of the cursor before each jump. (vim)

k

[address] k char

Mark the given address with *char*. Return later to the line with '*char*.

list

[address] l [count]

Print the specified lines so that tabs display as ^I, and the ends of lines display as $. The l command is a temporary version of :set list.

left

[*address*] le [*count*]

Left-align lines specified by *address*, or current line if no address is specified. Indent lines by count spaces. (vim)

map

map[!] [*char commands*]

Define a keyboard macro named *char* as the specified sequence of *commands*. *char* is usually a single character, or the sequence #n, representing a function key on the keyboard. Use a ! to create a macro for input mode. With no arguments, list the currently defined macros.

Examples

:map K dwwP   *Transpose two words*

map | 357

```
:map q :w^M:n^M        Write current file; go to next
:map! + ^[bi(^[ea      Enclose previous word in parentheses
```

mark

[*address*] ma *char*

Mark the specified line with *char*, a single lowercase letter. Return later to the line with '*char*. *vim* also uses uppercase and numeric characters for marks. Lowercase letters work the same as in *vi*. Uppercase letters are associated with filenames and can be used between multiple files. Numbered marks, however, are maintained in a special *viminfo* file and can't be set using this command. Same as *k*.

marks

marks [*chars*]

Print list of marks specified by *chars* or all current marks if no chars specified. (**vim**)

Example

:marks abc   Print marks a, b and c.

mkexrc

mk[!] *file*

Create an *.exrc* file containing a set command for every *ex* option, set to defaults.

move

[*address*] m *destination*

Move the lines specified by *address* to the destination address.

Example

:.,/Note/m /END/   Move text block after line containing "END"

new

[*count*]new

Create a new window *count* lines high with an empty buffer. (**vim**)

next

n[!] [[+*command*] *filelist*]

Edit the next file from the command-line argument list. Use args to list these files. If *filelist* is provided, replace the current argument list with *filelist* and begin editing on the first file; if *command* is given (containing no spaces), execute *command* after editing the first such file. Add a ! to discard any changes to the current file.

Example

> :n chap*   *Start editing all "chapter" files*

nohlsearch

noh

Temporarily stop highlighting all matches to a search when using the *hlsearch* option. Highlighting is resumed with the next search. (**vim**)

number

> [*address*] nu [*count*]

Print each line specified by *address*, preceded by its buffer line number. Use # as an alternate abbreviation for number. *count* specifies the number of lines to show, starting with *address*.

open

> [*address*] o [/*pattern*/]

Enter *vi*'s open mode at the lines specified by *address* or at the lines matching *pattern*. Enter and exit open mode with Q. Open mode lets you use the regular *vi* commands, but only one line at a time. May be useful on slow connections.

preserve

pre

Save the current editor buffer as though the system had crashed.

previous

prev[!]

Edit the previous file from the command-line argument list.

print

> [*address*] p [*count*]

> [*address*] P [*count*]

Print the lines specified by *address*. *count* specifies the number of lines to print, starting with *address*. Add a ! to discard any changes to the current file.

Example

:100;+5p   *Show line 100 and the next 5 lines*

put

[*address*] pu [*char*]

Restore the lines that were previously deleted or yanked from named buffer *char*, and put them after the line specified by *address*. If *char* is not specified, restore the last deleted or yanked text.

qall

qa[!]

Close all windows and terminate current editing session. Use ! to discard changes made since the last save. (vim)

quit

q[!]

Terminate current editing session. Use ! to discard changes made since the last save. If the editing session includes additional files in the argument list that were never accessed, quit by typing q! or by typing q twice. (In *vim*, if multiple windows are open, this command only closes the current window; use qall to quit multiple windows.)

read

[*address*] r *file*

Copy in the text from file on the line below the specified *address*. If *file* is not specified, the current filename is used.

Example

:0r $HOME/data   *Read file in at top of current file*

read

[*address*] r !*command*

Read the output of shell *command* into the text after the line specified by *address*.

Example

:$r !cal   *Place a calendar at end of file*

recover

rec [*file*]

Recover *file* from system save area.

redo

red

Restore last undone change. Same as Control-R. (vim)

resize

res [[+|-]*n*]

Resize current window to be *n* lines high. If + or - is specified, increase or decrease the current window height by *n* lines. (vim)

rewind

rew[!]

Rewind argument list and begin editing the first file in the list. The ! flag rewinds, discarding any changes to the current file that haven't been saved.

right

[*address*] le [*width*]

Right-align lines specified by *address*, or current line if no *address* is specified, to column *width*. Use textwidth option if no width is specified. (vim)

sbuffer

[*n*] sb [*n*]

Split the current window and begin editing buffer *n* from the buffer list in the new window. The buffer to be edited may also be specified by filename. If no buffer is specified, open the current buffer in the new window. (**vim**)

sbnext

[*count*] sbn [*count*]

Split the current window and begin editing the *count* next buffer from the buffer list. If no count is specified, edit the next buffer in the buffer list. (**vim**)

snext

[*count*] sn [[+*n*] *filelist*]

Split the current window and begin editing the next file from the command-line argument list. If *count* is provided, edit the *count* next file. If *filelist* is provided, replace the current argument list with *filelist* and begin editing the first file. With the +*n* argument, begin editing on line *n*. Alternately, *n* may be a pattern of the form /pattern. (vim)

split

[*count*] sp [+*n*] [*filename*]

Split the current window and load *filename* in the new window, or the same buffer in both windows if no file is specified. Make the new window *count* lines high, or if count is not specified, split the window into equal parts. With the +*n* argument, begin editing on line *n*. *n* may also be a pattern of the form /pattern. (vim)

sprevious

[*count*] spr [+*n*]

Split the current window and begin editing the previous file from the command-line argument list in the new window. If *count* is specified, edit the *count* previous file. With the +*n* argument, begin editing on line *n*. *n* may also be a pattern of the form /pattern. (vim)

script

sc[!] [*file*]

Create a new shell in a buffer that can be saved, optionally specifying *file* where the buffer can be saved. Can be used only in *vi*.

set

se *parameter1 parameter2* ...

Set a value to an option with each parameter, or if no parameter is supplied, print all options that have been changed from their defaults. For Boolean-valued options, each parameter can be phrased as option or nooption; other options can be assigned with the syntax *option=value*. Specify all to list current settings.

Examples

```
:set nows wm=10
:set all
```

shell

`sh`

Create a new shell. Resume editing when the shell is terminated.

source

`so file`

Read and execute *ex* commands from *file*.

Example

`:so $HOME/.exrc`

stop

`st`

Suspend the editing session. Same as Control-Z. Use *fg* to resume session.

substitute

`[address] s [/pattern/replacement/] [options] [count]`

Replace each instance of *pattern* on the specified lines with *replacement*. If pattern and replacement are omitted, repeat last substitution. *count* specifies the number of lines on which to substitute, starting with *address*. When preceded by the global (g) or v command, this command can be specified with a blank pattern, in which case the pattern from the g or v command is used.

Options

c

Prompt for confirmation before each change.

g

Substitute all instances of pattern on each line.

p

Print the last line on which a substitution was made.

Examples

`:1,10s/yes/no/g`	*Substitute on first 10 lines*
`:%s/[Hh]ello/Hi/gc`	*Confirm global substitutions*
`:s/Fortran/\U&/ 3`	*Uppercase first instance of "Fortran" on next three lines*
`:g/^[0-9][0-9]*/s//Line &:/`	*For every line beginning with one or more digits, add the "Line" and a colon*

suspend

su

Suspend the editing session. Same as Control-Z. Use *fg* to resume session.

sview

[*count*] sv [*+n*] [*filename*]

Same as the *split* command, but set the readonly option for the new buffer. (vim)

t

[*address*] t *destination*

Copy the lines included in *address* to the specified *destination*. *t* is an alias for copy.

Example

:%t$ *Copy the file and add it to the end*

tag

[*address*] ta[!] *tag*

Switch the editing session to the file containing *tag*.

Example

Run *ctags*, then switch to the file containing *myfunction*:

```
:!ctags *.c
:tag myfunction
```

tags

tags

Print list of tags in the tag stack. (vim)

unabbreviate

una *word*

Remove *word* from the list of abbreviations.

undo

u

Reverse the changes made by the last editing command. In *vi* the *undo* command will undo itself, redoing what you undid. *vim* supports multiple levels of undo. Use *redo* to redo an undone change in *vim*.

unhide

[*count*] unh

Split screen to show one window for each active buffer in the buffer list. If specified, limit the number of windows to *count*. (**vim**)

unmap

unm[!] *char*

Remove *char* from the list of keyboard macros. Use ! to remove a macro for input mode.

v

[*address*] v/*pattern*/[*commands*]

Execute *commands* on all lines not containing *pattern*. If *commands* aren't specified, print all such lines. v is equivalent to g!. See *global*.

Example

    :v/#include/d   *Delete all lines except "#include" lines*

version

ve

Print the editor's current version number.

vi

vi [+n] file

Begin editing file, optionally at line *n*. Can be used only in *vi*.

view

vie[[+n] *filename*]

Same as edit, but set file to readonly. When executed in *ex* mode, return to normal or visual mode. (**vim**)

visual

[*address*] vi [*type*] [*count*]

Enter visual mode (*vi*) at the line specified by address. Exit with Q. *type* can be either -, ^, or . . (See the *z* command.) *count* specifies an initial window size.

viusage

viu [*key*]

Print a brief usage message describing the operation of *key*, or a list of defined keys if *key* is omitted. (In *vim* use the help command instead.)

vsplit

[*count*] vs [*+n*] [*filename*]

Same as the *split* command but split the screen vertically. The *count* argument can specify a width for the new window. (**vim**)

wall

wa[!]

Write all changed buffers with filenames. Add ! to force writing of any buffers marked readonly. (**vim**)

wnext

[*count*] wn[!] [[*+n*] *filename*]

Write current buffer and open next file in argument list, or the *count* next file if specified. If *filename* is specified, edit it next. With the +*n* argument, begin editing on line *n*. *n* may also be a pattern of the form /*pattern*. (vim)

wq

wq[!]

Write and quit the file in one command. The ! flag forces the editor to write over any current contents of file.

wqall

wqa[!]

Write all changed buffers and quit the editor. Add ! to force writing of any buffers marked readonly. *xall* is another alias for this command. (**vim**)

write

[*address*] w[!] [[>>] *file*]

Write lines specified by address to *file*, or write full contents of buffer if address is not specified. If file is also omitted, save the contents of the buffer to the current filename. If >>*file* is used, write contents to the end of an existing file. The ! flag forces the editor to write over any current contents of file.

write

[address] w !command

Write lines specified by address to *command*.

Examples

```
:1,10w name_list       Copy first 10 lines to name_list
:50w >> name_list      Now append line 50
```

X

X

Prompt for an encryption key. This can be preferable to :set key as typing the key is not echoed to the console. To remove an encryption key, just reset the key option to an empty value. (*vim*)

xit

x

Write the file if it was changed since the last write, then quit.

yank

[*address*] ya [*char*] [*count*]

Place lines specified by address in named buffer *char*. If no *char* is given, place lines in general buffer. *count* specifies the number of lines to yank, starting with *address*.

Example

```
:101,200 ya a
```

z

[*address*] z [*type*] [*count*]

Print a window of text, with the line specified by *address* at the top. *count* specifies the number of lines to be displayed.

Type

+   Place specified line at top of window (the default).

-    Place specified line at bottom of window.

.   Place specified line in center of window.

^   Move up one window.

=   Place specified line in center of window, and leave as the current line.

!

[*address*] !*command*

Execute external *command* in a shell. If address is specified, apply the lines contained in *address* as standard input to *command*, and replace the lines with the output.

Examples

```
:!ls              List files in the current directory
:11,20!sort -f    Sort lines 11-20 of current file
```

=

[*address*] =

Print the line number of the next line matching *address*. If no address is given, print the number of the last line.

< >

[*address*]<[*count*]

[*address*]>[*count*]

Shift lines specified by *address* either left (<) or right (>). Only blanks and tabs are removed in a left shift. *count* specifies the number of lines to shift, starting with *address*.

---

address

address

Print the line specified in *address*.

Return

Return

Print the next line in the file.

@

[*address*] @ [*char*]

Execute contents of register specified by *char*. If *address* is given, move cursor to the specified address first. Both star and * are aliases for this command. (**vim**)

@@

[*address*] @

Repeat the last @ command. If *address* is given, move cursor to the specified address first. (vim)

&

& [*options*] [*count*]

Repeat the previous substitution (s) command. *count* specifies the number of lines on which to substitute, starting with *address*.

Examples

:s/Overdue/Paid/	*Substitute once on current line*
:g/Status/&	*Redo substitution on all "Status" lines*

~

[*address*] ~ [*count*]

Replace the previous regular expression with the previous replacement pattern from a *substitute* (s) command.

vi Configuration

This section describes the following:

- The *:set* command
- Options available with *:set*
- Sample *~/.exrc* file

The :set Command

The *:set* command lets you specify options that change characteristics of your editing environment. Options may be put in the *~/.exrc* file or set during a *vi* session.

The colon shouldn't be typed if the command is put in *~/.exrc*.

Command	Action
:set *x*	Enable option *x*.
:set no*x*	Disable option *x*.
:set *x=val*	Give *value* to option *x*.
:set	Show changed options.
:set all	Show all options.
:set *x?*	Show value of option *x*.

Options Used by :set

The following table describes the options to *:set*. The first column includes the optional abbreviation, if there is one, and uses an equals sign to show that the option takes a value. The second column gives the default, and the third column describes the behavior of the enabled option.

Option	Default	Description
autoindent (ai)	noai	In insert mode, indent each line to the same level as the line above or below.
autoprint (ap)	ap	Display changes after each editor command. (For global replacement, display last replacement.)
autowrite (aw)	noaw	Automatically write (save) file if changed, before opening another file with :*n* or before giving an external command with : !.
background (bg)		Describe the background so the editor can choose appropriate highlighting colors. Default value of dark or light depends on the environment in which the editor is invoked. (**vim**)
backup (bk)	nobackup	Create a backup file when overwriting an existing file. (**vim**)
backupdir= (bdir)	.,~/tmp/,~/	Name directories in which to store backup files if possible. The list of directories is comma-separated and in order of preference. (**vim**)
backupext= (bex)	~	String to append to filenames for backup files. (**vim**)
beautify (bf)	nobf	Ignore all control characters during input (except tab, newline, or formfeed).
cindent (cin)	nocindent	Insert indents in appropriate C format. (**vim**)
compatible (cp)	cp	Make *vim* behave more like *vi*. Default is nocp when a ~/.vimrc file is found. (**vim**)
directory= (dir)	/tmp	Name the directory in which *ex* stores buffer files. (Directory must be writable.)
edcompatible	noed-compatible	Use *ed*-like features on substitute commands.
equalprg= (ep)		Use the specified program for the = command. When the option is blank (the default), the key invokes the internal C indention function or the value of the *indentexpr* option. (**vim**)
errorbells (eb)	errorbells	Sound bell when an error occurs.
exrc (ex)	noexrc	Allow the execution of ~/.exrc files that reside outside the user's home directory.

Option	Default	Description
formatprg= (fp)		The *gq* command will invoke the named external program to format text. It will call internal formatting functions when this option is blank (the default). (**vim**)
gdefault (gd)	nogdefault	Set the *g* flag on for substitutions by default. (**vim**)
hardtabs= (ht)	8	Define boundaries for terminal hardware tabs.
hidden (hid)	nohidden	Hide buffers rather than unload them when they are abandoned. (**vim**)
hlsearch (hls)	hlsearch	Highlight all matches of most recent search.
history= (hi)	20	Number of *ex* commands to store in the history table. (**vim**)
ignorecase (ic)	noic	Disregard case during a search.
incsearch (is)	noincsearch	Highlight matches to a search pattern as it is typed. (**vim**)
lisp	nolisp	Insert indents in appropriate LISP format. ( ), { }, [[, and]] are modified to have meaning for LISP.
list	nolist	Print tabs as ^I; mark ends of lines with $. (Use *list* to tell if tabs or spaces are at the end of a line.)
magic	magic	Wildcard characters . (dot), * (asterisk), and [ ] (brackets) have special meaning in patterns.
mesg	mesg	Permit system messages to display on terminal while editing in *vi*.
mousehide (mh)	mousehide	When characters are typed, hide the mouse pointer. (**vim**)
number (nu)	nonu	Display line numbers on left of screen during editing session.
paste	nopaste	Change the defaults of various options to make pasting text into a terminal window work better. All options are returned to their original value when the *paste* option is reset. (**vim**)
redraw (re)	noredraw	Terminal redraws screen whenever edits are made (in other words, insert mode pushes over existing characters, and deleted lines immediately close up). Default depends on line speed and terminal type. *noredraw* is useful at slow speeds on a dumb terminal: deleted lines show up as @, and inserted text appears to overwrite existing text until you press Esc.
remap	remap	Allow nested map sequences.
report=	5	Display a message on the prompt line whenever you make an edit that affects at least a certain number of lines. For example, 6dd reports the message "6 lines deleted."
ruler (ru)	ruler	Show line and column numbers for the current cursor position. (**vim**)
scroll=	<1/2 window>	Amount of screen to scroll.
sections= (sect)	SHNHH HUnhsh	Define section delimiters for [[ ]] movement. The pairs of characters in the value are the names of *nroff/troff* macros that begin sections.
shell= (sh)	/bin/sh	Pathname of shell used for shell escape (:*!*) and shell command (:*sh*). Default value is derived from SHELL variable.

Option	Default	Description
shiftwidth= (sw)	8	Define number of spaces used by the indent commands (^T, ^D, >>, and <<).
showmatch (sm)	nosm	In *vi*, when) or } is entered, cursor moves briefly to matching (or {. (If the match is not on the screen, rings the error message bell.) Very useful for programming.
showmode	noshowmode	In insert mode, displays a message on the prompt line indicating the type of insert you are making, such as "Open Mode" or "Append Mode."
slowopen (slow)		Hold off display during insert. Default depends on line speed and terminal type.
smartcase (scs)	nosmartcase	Override the *ignorecase* option when a search pattern contains uppercase characters. (**vim**)
tabstop= (ts)	8	Define number of spaces that a tab indents during editing session. (Printer still uses system tab of 8.)
taglength= (tl)		Define number of characters that are significant for tags. Default (0) means that all characters are significant.
tags=	tags /usr/lib/tags	Define pathname of files containing tags. By default, the system looks for files *tags* (in the current directory) and */usr/lib/tags*.
term=		Set terminal type.
terse	noterse	Display shorter error messages.
timeout (to)	timeout	Keyboard maps timeout after 1 second.
ttytype=		Set terminal type. Default is inherited from TERM environment variable.
undolevels= (ul)	1000	Number of changes that can be undone. (**vim**)
warn	warn	Display the message "No write since last change."
window= (w)		Show a certain number of lines of the file on the screen. Default depends on line speed and terminal type.
wrapmargin= (wm)		Define right margin. If greater than 0, automatically insert carriage returns to break lines.
wrapscan (ws)	ws	Searches wrap around either end of file.
writeany (wa)	nowa	Allow saving to any file.
writebackup (wb)	wb	Back up files before attempting to overwrite them. Remove the backup when the file has been successfully written.

Sample ~/.exrc File

The following lines of code are an example of a customized *.exrc* file:

```
set nowrapscan wrapmargin=7
set sections=SeAhBhChDh nomesg
map q :w^M:n^M
map v dwElp
ab ORA O'Reilly Media, Inc.
```

8

The Emacs Editor

The Emacs editor is found on many Unix systems, including Mac OS X Tiger, because it is a popular alternative to *vi*. Many versions are available. This book documents GNU Emacs. For more information, see the O'Reilly book *Learning GNU Emacs*.

Emacs is much more than "just an editor"; in fact, it provides a fully integrated user environment. From within Emacs you can issue individual shell commands, or open a window where you can work in the shell, read and send mail, read news, access the Internet, write and test programs, and maintain a calendar. To fully describe Emacs would require more space than we have available. In this chapter, therefore, we focus on the editing capabilities of Emacs.

To start an Emacs editing session, type:

> *emacs*

You can also specify one or more files for Emacs to open when it starts:

> *emacs files*

Emacs Concepts

This section describes some Emacs terminology that may be unfamiliar if you haven't used Emacs before.

Modes

One of the features that makes Emacs popular is its editing modes. The modes set up an environment designed for the type of editing you are doing, with features such as having appropriate key bindings available and automatically indenting according to standard conventions for that type of document. There are two types of modes—major and minor. The major modes include modes for various programming languages such as C or Perl, for text processing (e.g., SGML or even straight text), and many more. One particularly useful major mode is Dired (Directory Editor), which has commands that let you manage directories. Minor modes set or unset features that are independent of the major mode, such as auto-fill (which controls word wrapping), insert versus overwrite, and auto-save. For a full discussion of modes, see *Learning GNU Emacs* or the Emacs Info documentation system (C-h i).

Buffer and Window

When you open a file in Emacs, the file is put into a buffer so you can edit it. If you open another file, that file goes into another buffer. The view of the buffer contents that you have at any point in time is called a *window*. For a small file, the window might show the entire file; for a large file, it shows only a portion of a file. Emacs allows multiple windows to be open at the same time to display the contents of different buffers or different portions of a single buffer.

Point and Mark

When you are editing in Emacs, the position of the cursor is known as *point*. You can set a *mark* at another place in the text to operate on the region between point and mark. This is useful for deleting or moving an area of text.

Kill and Yank

Emacs uses the terms *kill* and *yank* for the concepts more commonly known today as cut and paste. You cut text in Emacs by killing it, and paste it by yanking it back. If you do multiple kills in a row, you can yank them back all at once.

Typical Problems

A common problem with Emacs is that the Del or Backspace key doesn't delete the character before the cursor, as it should, but instead invokes a help prompt. This is caused by an incompatible terminal setup file. A fairly robust fix is to create a file named *.emacs* in your home directory (or edit one that's already there) and add the following lines:

```
(keyboard-translate ?\C-h ?\C-?)
(keyboard-translate ?\C-\\ ?\C-h)
```

Now the Del or Backspace kill should work, and you can invoke help by pressing C-\ (an arbitrarily chosen key sequence).

Another potential problem is that on some systems, C-s causes the terminal to hang. This is due to an old-fashioned handshake protocol between the terminal and the system. You can restart the terminal by pressing C-q, but that doesn't help you enter commands that contain the sequence C-s. The solution (aside from using a more modern dial-in protocol) is to create new key bindings that replace C-s or to enter those commands as M-x *command-name*. This isn't specifically an Emacs problem, but it can cause problems when you run Emacs in a terminal window because C-s and C-q are commonly used Emacs key sequences.

Notes on the Tables

Emacs commands use the Control key and the Meta key—a system-neutral way to describe a function-changing modifier key. On a Mac, this corresponds to the Option key, if you have the Terminal configured correctly. Under the Terminal menu, go to Settings, and select the Keyboard drop down. Check the "use option key as meta key" checkbox, and close the Terminal Inspector.

In this chapter, the notation C- indicates that the Control key is pressed at the same time as the character that follows. Similarly, M- indicates the use of the Meta, or Option key on Mac OS X: either hold Option while typing the next character, *or* press and release the Escape key followed by the next character.

Absolutely Essential Commands

If you're just getting started with Emacs, Table 8-1 lists some of the most important commands to know.

Binding	Action
C-h	Enter the online help system.
C-x C-s	Save the file.
C-x C-c	Exit Emacs.
C-x u	Undo last edit (can be repeated).
C-g	Get out of current command operation.
C-p	Up by one line.
C-n	Down by one line.
C-f	Forward by one character.
C-b	Back by one character.
C-v	Forward by one screen.
M-v	Backward by one screen.
C-s	Search forward for characters.
C-r	Search backward for characters.
C-d	Delete current character.
Del	Delete previous character.
Backspace	Delete previous character.

Summary of Commands by Group

Tables list keystrokes, command name, and description. C- indicates the Ctrl key; M- indicates the Meta key.

File Handling Commands

Binding	Command	Action
C-x C-f	find-file	Find file and read it.
C-x C-v	find-alternate-file	Read another file; replace the one read currently in the buffer.
C-x i	insert-file	Insert file at cursor position.
C-x C-s	save-buffer	Save file. (If terminal hangs, C-q restarts.)
C-x C-w	write-file	Write buffer contents to file.
C-x C-c	save-buffers-kill-emacs	Exit Emacs.
C-z	suspend-emacs	Suspend Emacs (use *exit* or *fg* to restart).

Cursor Movement Commands

In addition to the key bindings shown in this table, you can use the arrow keys to move around in Emacs. When you run Emacs in a graphical display environment (e.g., in the X Window System), you can also use the mouse for operations such as moving the cursor or selecting text.

Binding	Command	Action
C-f	forward-char	Move forward one character (right).
C-b	backward-char	Move backward one character (left).
C-p	previous-line	Move to previous line (up).
C-n	next-line	Move to next line (down).
M-f	forward-word	Move one word forward.
M-b	backward-word	Move one word backward.
C-a	beginning-of-line	Move to beginning of line.
C-e	end-of-line	Move to end-of-line.
M-a	backward-sentence	Move backward one sentence.
M-e	forward-sentence	Move forward one sentence.
M-{	backward-paragraph	Move backward one paragraph.
M-}	forward-paragraph	Move forward one paragraph.
C-v	scroll-up	Move forward one screen.
M-v	scroll-down	Move backward one screen.
C-x [	backward-page	Move backward one page.
C-x]	forward-page	Move forward one page.
M->	end-of-buffer	Move to end-of-file.
M-<	beginning-of-buffer	Move to beginning of file.

Binding	Command	Action
(none)	goto-line	Go to specific line of file.
(none)	goto-char	Go to specific character of file.
C-l	recenter	Redraw screen with current line in the center.
M-*n*	digit-argument	Repeat the next command *n* times.
C-u *n*	universal-argument	Repeat the next command *n* times.

Deletion Commands

Binding	Command	Action
Del	backward-delete-char	Delete previous character.
C-d	delete-char	Delete character under cursor.
M-Del	backward-kill-word	Delete previous word.
M-d	kill-word	Delete the word the cursor is on.
C-k	kill-line	Delete from cursor to end-of-line.
M-k	kill-sentence	Delete sentence the cursor is on.
C-x Del	backward-kill-sentence	Delete previous sentence.
C-y	yank	Restore what you've deleted.
C-w	kill-region	Delete a marked region (see next section "Paragraphs and Regions").
(none)	backward-kill-paragraph	Delete previous paragraph.
(none)	kill-paragraph	Delete from the cursor to the end of the paragraph.

Paragraphs and Regions

Binding	Command	Action
C-@	set-mark-command	Mark the beginning (or end) of a region.
C-Space	(Same as preceding)	(Same as preceding)
C-x C-p	mark-page	Mark page.
C-x C-x	exchange-point-and-mark	Exchange location of cursor and mark.
C-x h	mark-whole-buffer	Mark buffer.
M-q	fill-paragraph	Reformat paragraph.
(none)	fill-region	Reformat individual paragraphs within a region.
M-h	mark-paragraph	Mark paragraph.
M-{	backward-paragraph	Move backward one paragraph.
M-}	forward-paragraph	Move forward one paragraph.
(none)	backward-kill-paragraph	Delete previous paragraph.
(none)	kill-paragraph	Delete from the cursor to the end of the paragraph.

Stopping and Undoing Commands

Binding	Command	Action
C-g	keyboard-quit	Abort current command.
C-x u	advertised-undo	Undo last edit (can be done repeatedly).
(none)	revert-buffer	Restore buffer to the state it was in when the file was last saved (or auto-saved).

Transposition Commands

Binding	Command	Action
C-t	transpose-chars	Transpose two letters.
M-t	transpose-words	Transpose two words.
C-x C-t	transpose-lines	Transpose two lines.
(none)	transpose-sentences	Transpose two sentences.
(none)	transpose-paragraphs	Transpose two paragraphs.

Capitalization Commands

Binding	Command	Action
M-c	capitalize-word	Capitalize first letter of word.
M-u	upcase-word	Uppercase word.
M-l	downcase-word	Lowercase word.
M- - M-c	negative-argument; capitalize-word	Capitalize previous word.
M- - M-u	negative-argument; upcase-word	Uppercase previous word.
M- - M-l	negative-argument; downcase-word	Lowercase previous word.
(none)	capitalize-region	Capitalize initial letters in region.
C-x C-u	upcase-region	Uppercase region.
C-x C-l	downcase-region	Lowercase region.

Incremental Search Commands

Binding	Command	Action
C-s	isearch-forward	Start or repeat incremental search forward.
C-r	isearch-backward	Start or repeat incremental search backward.
Return	(none)	Exit a successful search.
C-g	keyboard-quit	Cancel incremental search; return to starting point.
Del	(none)	Delete incorrect character of search string.
M-C-r	isearch-backward-regexp	Incremental search backward for regular expression.
M-C-s	isearch-forward-regexp	Incremental search forward for regular expression.

Word Abbreviation Commands

Binding	Command	Action
(none)	abbrev-mode	Enter (or exit) word abbreviation mode.
C-x a -	inverse-add-global-abbrev	Define previous word as global (mode-independent) abbreviation.
C-x a i l	inverse-add-mode-abbrev	Define previous word as mode-specific abbreviation.
(none)	unexpand-abbrev	Undo the last word abbreviation.
(none)	write-abbrev-file	Write the word abbreviation file.
(none)	edit-abbrevs	Edit the word abbreviations.
(none)	list-abbrevs	View the word abbreviations.
(none)	kill-all-abbrevs	Kill abbreviations for this session.

Buffer Manipulation Commands

Binding	Command	Action
C-x b	switch-to-buffer	Move to specified buffer.
C-x C-b	list-buffers	Display buffer list.
C-x k	kill-buffer	Delete specified buffer.
(none)	kill-some-buffers	Ask about deleting each buffer.
(none)	rename-buffer	Change buffer name to specified name.
C-x s	save-some-buffers	Ask whether to save each modified buffer.

Window Commands

Binding	Command	Action
C-x 2	split-window-vertically	Divide the current window in two vertically, resulting in one window on top of the other.
C-x 3	split-window-horizontally	Divide the current window in two horizontally, resulting in two side-by-side windows.
C-x >	scroll-right	Scroll the window right.
C-x <	scroll-left	Scroll the window left.
C-x o	other-window	Move to the other window.
C-x 0	delete-window	Delete current window.
C-x 1	delete-other-windows	Delete all windows but this one.
(none)	delete-windows-on	Delete all windows on a given buffer.
C-x ^	enlarge-window	Make window taller.
(none)	shrink-window	Make window shorter.
C-x }	enlarge-window-horizon-tally	Make window wider.
C-x {	shrink-window-horizon-tally	Make window narrower.
M-C-v	scroll-other-window	Scroll other window.
C-x 4 f	find-file-other-window	Find a file in the other window.

Binding	Command	Action
C-x 4 b	switch-to-buffer-other-window	Select a buffer in the other window.
C-x 5 f	find-file-other-frame	Find a file in a new frame.
C-x 5 b	switch-to-buffer-other-frame	Select a buffer in another frame.
(none)	compare-windows	Compare two buffers; show first difference.

Special Shell Mode Characters

The following table shows commands that can be used in Shell mode. To enter Shell mode, run the command M-x shell.

Binding	Command	Action
C-c C-c	interrupt-shell-subjob	Terminate the current job.
C-c C-d	shell-send-eof	End-of-file character.
C-c C-u	kill-shell-input	Erase current line.
C-c C-w	backward-kill-word	Erase the previous word.
C-c C-z	stop-shell-subjob	Suspend the current job.

Indentation Commands

Binding	Command	Action
C-x .	set-fill-prefix	Prepend each line in paragraph with characters from beginning of line up to cursor column; cancel prefix by typing this command in column 1.
(none)	indented-text-mode	Major mode: each tab defines a new indent for subsequent lines.
(none)	text-mode	Exit indented text mode; return to text mode.
M-C-\	indent-region	Indent a region to match first line in region.
M-m	back-to-indentation	Move cursor to first character on line.
M-^	delete-indentation	Join this line to the previous line.
M-C-o	split-line	Split line at cursor; indent to column of cursor.
(none)	fill-individual- paragraphs	Reformat indented paragraphs, keeping indentation.

Centering Commands

Binding	Command	Action
(none)	center-line	Center line that cursor is on.
(none)	center-paragraph	Center paragraph that cursor is on.
(none)	center-region	Center currently defined region.

Macro Commands

Binding	Command	Action
C-x (	start-kbd-macro	Start macro definition.
C-x)	end-kbd-macro	End macro definition.
C-x e	call-last-kbd-macro	Execute last macro defined.
M-n C-x e	digit-argument and call-last-kbd-macro	Execute last macro defined n times.
C-u C-x (	start-kbd-macro	Execute last macro defined, then add keystrokes.
(none)	name-last-kbd-macro	Name last macro you created (before saving it).
(none)	insert-last-keyboard- macro	Insert the macro you named into a file.
(none)	load-file	Load macro files you've saved.
(none)	*macroname*	Execute a keyboard macro you've saved.
C-x q	kbd-macro-query	Insert a query in a macro definition.
C-u C-x q	(none)	Insert a recursive edit in a macro definition.
M-C-c	exit-recursive-edit	Exit a recursive edit.

Detail Information Help Commands

Binding	Command	Action
C-h a	command-apropos	What commands involve this concept?
(none)	apropos	What commands, functions, and variables involve this concept?
C-h c	describe-key-briefly	What command does this keystroke sequence run?
C-h b	describe-bindings	What are all the key bindings for this buffer?
C-h k	describe-key	What command does this keystroke sequence run, and what does it do?
C-h l	view-lossage	What are the last 100 characters I typed?
C-h w	where-is	What is the key binding for this command?
C-h f	describe-function	What does this function do?
C-h v	describe-variable	What does this variable mean, and what is its value?
C-h m	describe-mode	Tell me about the mode the current buffer is in.
C-h s	describe-syntax	What is the syntax table for this buffer?

Help Commands

Binding	Command	Action
C-h t	help-with-tutorial	Run the Emacs tutorial.
C-h i	info	Start the Info documentation reader.
C-h n	view-emacs-news	View news about updates to Emacs.
C-h C-c	describe-copying	View the Emacs General Public License.
C-h C-d	describe-distribution	View information on ordering Emacs from the FSF.
C-h C-w	describe-no-warranty	View the (non)warranty for Emacs.

Summary of Commands by Key

Emacs commands are presented next in two alphabetical lists. Tables list keystrokes, command name, and description. C- indicates the Ctrl key; M- indicates the Meta key.

Control-Key Sequences

Binding	Command	Action
C-@	set-mark-command	Mark the beginning (or end) of a region.
C-Space	(Same as preceding)	(Same as preceding)
C-]	abort-recursive-edit	Exit recursive edit and exit query-replace.
C-a	beginning-of-line	Move to beginning of line.
C-b	backward-char	Move backward one character (left).
C-c C-c	interrupt-shell-subjob	Terminate the current job.
C-c C-d	shell-send-eof	End-of-file character.
C-c C-u	kill-shell-input	Erase current line.
C-c C-w	backward-kill-word	Erase previous word.
C-c C-z	stop-shell-subjob	Suspend current job.
C-d	delete-char	Delete character under cursor.
C-e	end-of-line	Move to end-of-line.
C-f	forward-char	Move forward one character (right).
C-g	keyboard-quit	Abort current command.
C-h	help-command	Enter the online help system.
C-h a	command-apropos	What commands involve this concept?
C-h b	describe-bindings	What are all the key bindings for this buffer?
C-h c	describe-key-briefly	What command does this keystroke sequence run?
C-h C-c	describe-copying	View the Emacs General Public License.
C-h C-d	describe-distribution	View information on ordering Emacs from the FSF.
C-h C-w	describe-no-warranty	View the (non)warranty for Emacs.
C-h f	describe-function	What does this function do?
C-h i	info	Start the Info documentation reader.
C-h k	describe-key	What command does this keystroke sequence run, and what does it do?
C-h l	view-lossage	What are the last 100 characters I typed?
C-h m	describe-mode	Tell me about the mode the current buffer is in.
C-h n	view-emacs-news	View news about updates to Emacs.
C-h s	describe-syntax	What is the syntax table for this buffer?
C-h t	help-with-tutorial	Run the Emacs tutorial.
C-h v	describe-variable	What does this variable mean, and what is its value?
C-h w	where-is	What is the key binding for this command?
C-k	kill-line	Delete from cursor to end-of-line.
C-l	recenter	Redraw screen with current line in the center.
C-n	next-line	Move to next line (down).

Binding	Command	Action
C-p	previous-line	Move to previous line (up).
C-q	quoted-insert	Insert next character typed. Useful for inserting a control character.
C-r	isearch-backward	Start or repeat nonincremental search backward.
C-r	(none)	Enter recursive edit (during query replace).
C-s	isearch-forward	Start or repeat nonincremental search forward.
C-t	transpose-chars	Transpose two letters.
C-u n	universal-argument	Repeat the next command n times.
C-u C-x (	start-kbd-macro	Execute last macro defined, then add keystrokes.
C-u C-x q	(none)	Insert recursive edit in a macro definition.
C-v	scroll-up	Move forward one screen.
C-w	kill-region	Delete a marked region.
C-x (	start-kbd-macro	Start macro definition.
C-x)	end-kbd-macro	End macro definition.
C-x [	backward-page	Move backward one page.
C-x]	forward-page	Move forward one page.
C-x ^	enlarge-window	Make window taller.
C-x {	shrink-window-horizontally	Make window narrower.
C-x }	enlarge-window-horizontally	Make window wider.
C-x <	scroll-left	Scroll the window left.
C-x >	scroll-right	Scroll the window right.
C-x .	set-fill-prefix	Prepend each line in paragraph with characters from beginning of line up to cursor column; cancel prefix by typing this command in column 1.
C-x 0	delete-window	Delete current window.
C-x 1	delete-other-windows	Delete all windows but this one.
C-x 2	split-window-vertically	Divide current window in two vertically, resulting in one window on top of the other.
C-x 3	split-window-horizontally	Divide current window in two horizontally, resulting in two side-by-side windows.
C-x 4 b	switch-to-buffer-other-window	Select a buffer in the other window.
C-x 4 f	find-file-other-window	Find a file in the other window.
C-x 5 b	switch-to-buffer-other-frame	Select a buffer in another frame.
C-x 5 f	find-file-other-frame	Find a file in another frame.
C-x a -	inverse-add-global-abbrev	Define previous word as global (mode-independent) abbreviation.
C-x a i l	inverse-add-mode-abbrev	Define previous word as mode-specific abbreviation.
C-x b	switch-to-buffer	Move to the buffer specified.
C-x C-b	list-buffers	Display the buffer list.
C-x C-c	save-buffers-kill-emacs	Exit Emacs.
C-x C-f	find-file	Find file and read it.
C-x C-l	downcase-region	Lowercase region.
C-x C-p	mark-page	Place cursor and mark around whole page.
C-x C-q	(none)	Toggle read-only status of buffer.

Binding	Command	Action
C-x C-s	save-buffer	Save file. (If terminal hangs, C-q restarts.)
C-x C-t	transpose-lines	Transpose two lines.
C-x C-u	upcase-region	Uppercase region.
C-x C-v	find-alternate-file	Read an alternate file, replacing the one currently in the buffer.
C-x C-w	write-file	Write buffer contents to file.
C-x C-x	exchange-point-and-mark	Exchange location of cursor and mark.
C-x Del	backward-kill- sentence	Delete previous sentence.
C-x e	call-last-kbd-macro	Execute last macro defined.
C-x h	mark-whole-buffer	Place cursor and mark around whole buffer.
C-x i	insert-file	Insert file at cursor position.
C-x k	kill-buffer	Delete the buffer specified.
C-x o	other-window	Move to the other window.
C-x q	kbd-macro-query	Insert a query in a macro definition.
C-x s	save-some-buffers	Ask whether to save each modified buffer.
C-x u	advertised-undo	Undo last edit (can be done repeatedly).
C-y	yank	Restore killed text.
C-z	suspend-emacs	Suspend Emacs (use *exit* or *fg* to restart).

Meta-Key Sequences

Binding	Command	Action
M— M-c	negative-argument; capitalize-word	Capitalize previous word.
M— M-l	negative-argument; downcase-word	Lowercase previous word.
M— M-u	negative-argument; upcase-word	Uppercase previous word.
M-$	spell-word	Check spelling of word after cursor.
M-%	query-replace	Search for and replace a string.
M-!	shell-command	Prompt for a shell command and run it.
M-<	beginning-of-buffer	Move to beginning of file.
M->	end-of-buffer	Move to end-of-file.
M-{	backward-paragraph	Move backward one paragraph.
M-}	forward-paragraph	Move forward one paragraph.
M-^	delete-indentation	Join this line to the previous one.
M-n	digit-argument	Repeat the next command n times.
M-n C-x e	digit-argument; call-last-kbd-macro	Execute the last defined macro n times.
M-a	backward-sentence	Move backward one sentence.
M-b	backward-word	Move one word backward.
M-c	capitalize-word	Capitalize first letter of word.
M-C-\	indent-region	Indent a region to match first line in region.
M-C-c	exit-recursive-edit	Exit a recursive edit.
M-C-o	split-line	Split line at cursor; indent to column of cursor.

Binding	Command	Action
M-C-r	isearch-backward-regexp	Incremental search backward for regular expression.
M-C-s	isearch-forward-regexp	Incremental search forward for regular expression.
M-C-v	scroll-other-window	Scroll other window.
M-d	kill-word	Delete word that cursor is on.
M-Del	backward-kill-word	Delete previous word.
M-e	forward-sentence	Move forward one sentence.
M-f	forward-word	Move one word forward.
(none)	fill-region	Reformat individual paragraphs within a region.
M-h	mark-paragraph	Place cursor and mark around whole paragraph.
M-k	kill-sentence	Delete sentence that cursor is on.
M-l	downcase-word	Lowercase word.
M-m	back-to-indentation	Move cursor to first nonblank character on line.
M-q	fill-paragraph	Reformat paragraph.
M-t	transpose-words	Transpose two words.
M-u	upcase-word	Uppercase word.
M-v	scroll-down	Move backward one screen.
M-x	(none)	Execute a command by typing its name.

Summary of Commands by Name

The following Emacs commands are presented alphabetically by command name. Use M-x to access the command name. Tables list command name, keystroke, and description. C- indicates the Ctrl key; M- indicates the Meta key.

Command	Binding	Action
macroname	(none)	Execute a keyboard macro you've saved.
abbrev-mode	(none)	Enter (or exit) word abbreviation mode.
abort-recursive-edit	C-]	Exit recursive edit and query replace.
advertised-undo	C-x u	Undo last edit (can be done repeatedly).
apropos	(none)	What functions and variables involve this concept?
back-to-indentation	M-m	Move cursor to first nonblank character on line.
backward-char	C-b	Move backward one character (left).
backward-delete-char	Del	Delete previous character.
backward-kill-paragraph	(none)	Delete previous paragraph.
backward-kill-sentence	C-x Del	Delete previous sentence.
backward-kill-word	C-c C-w	Delete previous word.
backward-kill-word	M-Del	Delete previous word.
backward-page	C-x [	Move backward one page.
backward-paragraph	M-{	Move backward one paragraph.

Command	Binding	Action
backward-sentence	M-a	Move backward one sentence.
backward-word	M-b	Move backward one word.
beginning-of-buffer	M-<	Move to beginning of file.
beginning-of-line	C-a	Move to beginning of line.
call-last-kbd-macro	C-x e	Execute last macro defined.
capitalize-region	(none)	Capitalize region.
capitalize-word	M-c	Capitalize first letter of word.
center-line	(none)	Center line that cursor is on.
center-paragraph	(none)	Center paragraph that cursor is on.
center-region	(none)	Center currently defined region.
command-apropos	C-h a	What commands involve this concept?
compare-windows	(none)	Compare two buffers; show first difference.
delete-char	C-d	Delete character under cursor.
delete-indentation	M-^	Join this line to previous one.
delete-other-windows	C-x 1	Delete all windows but this one.
delete-window	C-x 0	Delete current window.
delete-windows-on	(none)	Delete all windows on a given buffer.
describe-bindings	C-h b	What are all the key bindings for in this buffer?
describe-copying	C-h C-c	View the Emacs General Public License.
describe-distribution	C-h C-d	View information on ordering Emacs from the FSF.
describe-function	C-h f	What does this function do?
describe-key	C-h k	What command does this keystroke sequence run, and what does it do?
describe-key-briefly	C-h c	What command does this keystroke sequence run?
describe-mode	C-h m	Tell me about the mode the current buffer is in.
describe-no-warranty	C-h C-w	View the (non)warranty for Emacs.
describe-syntax	C-h s	What is the syntax table for this buffer?
describe-variable	C-h v	What does this variable mean, and what is its value?
digit-argument	M-n	Repeat next command n times.
downcase-region	C-x C-l	Lowercase region.
downcase-word	M-l	Lowercase word.
edit-abbrevs	(none)	Edit word abbreviations.
end-kbd-macro	C-x)	End macro definition.
end-of-buffer	M->	Move to end-of-file.
end-of-line	C-e	Move to end-of-line.
enlarge-window	C-x ^	Make window taller.
enlarge-window-horizontally	C-x }	Make window wider.
exchange-point-and-mark	C-x C-x	Exchange location of cursor and mark.
exit-recursive-edit	M-C-c	Exit a recursive edit.
fill-individual-paragraphs	(none)	Reformat indented paragraphs, keeping indentation.
fill-paragraph	M-q	Reformat paragraph.
fill-region	(none)	Reformat individual paragraphs within a region.

Command	Binding	Action
find-alternate-file	C-x C-v	Read an alternate file, replacing the one currently in the buffer.
find-file	C-x C-f	Find file and read it.
find-file-other-frame	C-x 5 f	Find a file in another frame.
find-file-other-window	C-x 4 f	Find a file in another window.
forward-char	C-f	Move forward one character (right).
forward-page	C-x]	Move forward one page.
forward-paragraph	M-}	Move forward one paragraph.
forward-sentence	M-e	Move forward one sentence.
forward-word	M-f	Move forward one word.
goto-char	(none)	Go to numbered character of file.
goto-line	(none)	Go to numbered line of file.
help-command	C-h	Enter the online help system.
help-with-tutorial	C-h t	Run the Emacs tutorial.
indent-region	M-C-\	Indent a region to match first line in region.
indented-text-mode	(none)	Major mode: each tab defines a new indent for subsequent lines.
info	C-h i	Start the Info documentation reader.
insert-file	C-x i	Insert file at cursor position.
insert-last-keyboard-macro	(none)	Insert the macro you named into a file.
interrupt-shell-subjob	C-c C-c	Terminate the current job (shell mode).
inverse-add-global-abbrev	C-x a -	Define previous word as global (mode-independent) abbreviation.
inverse-add-mode-abbrev	C-x a i l	Define previous word as mode-specific abbreviation.
isearch-backward	C-r	Start incremental search backward.
isearch-backward-regexp	M-C-r	Same, but search for regular expression.
isearch-forward	C-s	Start incremental search forward.
isearch-forward-regexp	M-C-s	Same, but search for regular expression.
kbd-macro-query	C-x q	Insert a query in a macro definition.
keyboard-quit	C-g	Abort current command.
kill-all-abbrevs	(none)	Kill abbreviations for this session.
kill-buffer	C-x k	Delete the buffer specified.
kill-line	C-k	Delete from cursor to end-of-line.
kill-paragraph	(none)	Delete from cursor to end of paragraph.
kill-region	C-w	Delete a marked region.
kill-sentence	M-k	Delete sentence the cursor is on.
kill-shell-input	C-c C-u	Delete current line.
kill-some-buffers	(none)	Ask about deleting each buffer.
kill-word	M-d	Delete word the cursor is on.
list-abbrevs	(none)	View word abbreviations.
list-buffers	C-x C-b	Display buffer list.
load-file	(none)	Load macro files you've saved.
mark-page	C-x C-p	Place cursor and mark around whole page.

Command	Binding	Action
mark-paragraph	M-h	Place cursor and mark around whole paragraph.
mark-whole-buffer	C-x h	Place cursor and mark around whole buffer.
name-last-kbd-macro	(none)	Name last macro you created (before saving it).
negative-argument; capitalize-word	M-- M-c	Capitalize previous word.
negative-argument; downcase-word	M-- M-l	Lowercase previous word.
negative-argument; upcase-word	M-- M-u	Uppercase previous word.
next-line	C-n	Move to next line (down).
other-window	C-x o	Move to the other window.
previous-line	C-p	Move to previous line (up).
query-replace	M-%	Search for and replace a string.
query-replace-regexp	(none)	Query-replace a regular expression.
quoted-insert	C-q	Insert next character typed. Useful for inserting a control character.
recenter	C-l	Redraw screen, with current line in center.
rename-buffer	(none)	Change buffer name to specified name.
replace-regexp	(none)	Replace a regular expression unconditionally.
re-search-backward	(none)	Simple regular-expression search backward.
re-search-forward	(none)	Simple regular-expression search forward.
revert-buffer	(none)	Restore buffer to the state it was in when the file was last saved (or auto-saved).
save-buffer	C-x C-s	Save file. (If terminal hangs, C-q restarts.)
save-buffers-kill-emacs	C-x C-c	Exit Emacs.
save-some-buffers	C-x s	Ask whether to save each modified buffer.
scroll-down	M-v	Move backward one screen.
scroll-left	C-x <	Scroll the window left.
scroll-other-window	M-C-v	Scroll other window.
scroll-right	C-x >	Scroll the window right.
scroll-up	C-v	Move forward one screen.
set-fill-prefix	C-x .	Prepend each line in paragraph with characters from beginning of line up to cursor column; cancel prefix by typing this command in column 1.
set-mark-command	C-@ or C-Space	Mark the beginning (or end) of a region.
shell-command	M-!	Prompt for a shell command and run it.
shell-send-eof	C-c C-d	End-of-file character (shell mode).
shrink-window	(none)	Make window shorter.
shrink-window-horizontally	C-x {	Make window narrower.
spell-buffer	(none)	Check spelling of current buffer.
spell-region	(none)	Check spelling of current region.
spell-string	(none)	Check spelling of string typed in minibuffer.
spell-word	M-$	Check spelling of word after cursor.
split-line	M-C-o	Split line at cursor; indent to column of cursor.

Command	Binding	Action
split-window-horizontally	C-x 3	Divide current window horizontally into two.
split-window-vertically	C-x 2	Divide current window vertically into two.
start-kbd-macro	C-x (	Start macro definition.
stop-shell-subjob	C-c C-z	Suspend current job.
suspend-emacs	C-z	Suspend Emacs (use *fg* to restart).
switch-to-buffer	C-x b	Move to the buffer specified.
switch-to-buffer-other-frame	C-x 5 b	Select a buffer in another frame.
switch-to-buffer-other-window	C-x 4 b	Select a buffer in another window.
text-mode	(none)	Enter text mode.
transpose-chars	C-t	Transpose two characters.
transpose-lines	C-x C-t	Transpose two lines.
transpose-paragraphs	(none)	Transpose two paragraphs.
transpose-sentences	(none)	Transpose two sentences.
transpose-words	M-t	Transpose two words.
unexpand-abbrev	(none)	Undo the last word abbreviation.
universal-argument	C-u *n*	Repeat the next command *n* times.
upcase-region	C-x C-u	Uppercase region.
upcase-word	M-u	Uppercase word.
view-emacs-news	C-h n	View news about updates to Emacs.
view-lossage	C-h l	What are the last 100 characters I typed?
where-is	C-h w	What is the key binding for this command?
write-abbrev-file	(none)	Write the word abbreviation file.
write-file	C-x C-w	Write buffer contents to file.
yank	C-y	Restore what you've deleted.

Extending Emacs

Emacs' many modes come courtesy of *elisp* files, programs written in Emacs' own LISP-based language and stored in *.el* and *.elc* files (the latter for compiled files). Getting into the Elisp language is outside the topic of this book,[*] but be aware that all the modes you're working with are written in *elisp*.

Darwin's directory for Emacs extensions is */usr/share/emacs/emacs-version-number/lisp*. Generally speaking, installing Emacs extensions that you download is as simple as moving them into this folder or into the neighboring *site-lisp* directory. Some *.el* files need to be compiled in order to work; this involves using the *M-x byte-compile-file* command from within Emacs. Packages that contain many interdependent files, such as the PSGML extension for editing SGML and XML files (*http://www.lysator.liu.se/projects/about_psgml.html*), may make this process easier by including standard Unix *configure* and *Makefile* files, which often just run Emacs in batch mode to compile the files in the right order.

---

[*] However, there are books on this topic alone, such as *Writing GNU Emacs Extensions* (O'Reilly).

Many modes require you to activate various Emacs variables and settings before they'll work. This usually involves editing your *.emacs* file (see the next section) in some way and is usually described in the extension's *README* file, or perhaps in the comment section of the *elisp* file itself.

Many Emacs modes and main functions are centered around programming. The *elisp* files that ship with Mac OS X include full-featured (which is to say, many-variabled) major modes for C, Java, Perl, and many other languages. Through Meta-X commands such as *compile*, *debug*, and the *compilation-mode* major mode, you can even use Emacs as a complete build-and-debug environment.

That said, there's not much reason to use Emacs as your IDE, unless you're working with a very obscure language that lacks editor support outside of Emacs modes (such as *elisp*) or with a rapid-development language with a console-based interface that doesn't really need an IDE, such as Perl or shell scripting. For all other Mac OS X programming, investigate what Project Builder can do.

The .emacs File

You can configure Emacs' default behavior by creating and editing a special *elisp* file called *.emacs* in your Home folder. (As with all dotfiles, the Finder hides *.emacs* from sight; see "Hidden files" in Chapter 10.) Emacs executes all the commands in this file whenever you launch the program, so it's a great place to set variables, activate and customize major mode options, and so on.

Even if you don't know *elisp*, it's good to know about *.emacs* because Emacs extensions often require it. If you use Emacs a lot, you may find your *.emacs* file growing over time. A well-organized *elisp* file maintains scalability through grouping similar commands together into well-commented blocks, so that you know what everything does each time you return to add to (or debug) the file.

As an example, here's part of the *.emacs* file on a Mac OS X system:

```
; First, adjust my loadpath so I can see me own .el files
(setq load-path (cons (expand-file-name "/Users/jmac/emacs-lisp/") load-
path)
)
; Activate and configure PSGML mode

(autoload 'sgml-mode "psgml" "Major mode to edit SGML files." t )
(custom-set-variables)
(custom-set-faces
 '(font-lock-comment-face (((((class color) (background dark)) (:foreground
"orchid1")))))
;; required for Emacs 21
(setq after-change-function nil)


;; Activate XSL-editing mode
(autoload 'xsl-mode "xslide" "Major mode for XSL stylesheets." t)
```

```
;; Turn on font lock when in XSL mode
(add-hook 'xsl-mode-hook
          'turn-on-font-lock)

(setq auto-mode-alist
      (append
       (list
        '("\\.xsl" . xsl-mode))
       auto-mode-alist))

;; Activate the 'time-clock' minor mode, which adds time-tracking
functionality.

    (require 'timeclock)

;; Define some keystrokes to trigger timeclock functions quickly.
    (define-key ctl-x-map "ti" 'timeclock-in)
    (define-key ctl-x-map "to" 'timeclock-out)
    (define-key ctl-x-map "tc" 'timeclock-change)
    (define-key ctl-x-map "tr" 'timeclock-reread-log)
    (define-key ctl-x-map "tu" 'timeclock-update-modeline)
    (define-key ctl-x-map "tw" 'timeclock-when-to-leave-string)

;; The M-x-erase-buffer command will warn you about your rash deed unless
;; you have the following variable set:
(put 'erase-buffer 'disabled nil)
```

You can find plenty of other *.emacs* examples online, including a whole repository just for them at *http://www.dotfiles.com.*

Note the path-extending command, *(setq load-path ...)*, at the top of the previous example. If you're not a member of the machine's *admin* group, and thus lack the *sudo* powers necessary to write to the */usr/share/emacs/21.2/* directory, you can define your own space to place *elisp* files, just as we have here with the directory */Users/jmac/emacs-lisp*. This tells Emacs to add that directory to the paths it scans when it seeks extension files.

GUI Emacs

The Emacs that comes with Mac OS X Tiger is a console application that runs in the Terminal. There's no interaction with the GUI, and so many features such as menus, mouse and scroll wheel support, and syntax coloring are not supported. However, there are currently at least two distributions of Emacs that take advantage of Mac OS X and the Carbon and Aqua frameworks.

Emacs for Mac OS X
   http://www.mindlube.com/products/emacs/

Aquamacs
   http://aquamacs.org/

Finally, if you're running X Windows on your Macintosh, you can compile Emacs and run it with X support.

## PART III

Managing Mac OS X

This part of the book offers chapters on managing your Mac OS X Tiger system. Chapters in this part of the book include:

- Chapter 9, Filesystem Overview
- Chapter 10, Directory Services
- Chapter 11, Running Network Services
- Chapter 12, The X Window System
- Chapter 13, The Defaults System

Filesystem Overview

This chapter examines how Mac OS X works with files, both in the lower level of its filesystems, and more generally in the specific directory layouts it uses to organize its most important files and keep track of installed applications.

Mac OS X Filesystems

Like earlier versions of Mac OS, Mac OS X filesystems favor the Mac OS Extended Format, better known as HFS+ (Hierarchical File System),* but they also work well with the Universal File System (UFS) that most other Unix-based operating systems use as their primary filesystem.

Most Mac OS X volumes use HFS+ as their format for two reasons. First, until Mac OS X 10.3, HFS+ has performed much better than UFS (though UFS performance in Tiger has improved greatly, close to matching that of HFS+). The other reason is that HFS+ natively supports multiple file forks (see the later section "File Forks".) Still, through strong UFS support, a Mac OS X machine can work seamlessly with other Unix volumes, such as network-mounted ones that may be accessible over NFS.

Differences Between HFS+ and UFS

Here are the most noticeable differences between the HFS+ and UFS file formats:

- UFS is case-sensitive in its file path interpretation, while standard HFS+ is not. The paths */tmp/foo*, */tmp/Foo*, and */TMP/FOO* all point to the same location on an HFS+ system but to three different ones on a UFS filesystem. However, using Mac OS X Server 10.3 and higher, you can format case-

---

* Mac OS 8.1 and later used HFS+, while versions prior to 8.1 used the older Mac OS Standard Format, known as just HFS (without the plus).

sensitive HFS+ volumes, and these volumes will maintain case-sensitivity when mounted on a Mac OS X client system.

 Some software from the UFS world might assert case-sensitivity despite HFS+'s permissiveness. The Tab-completion feature of the *bash* or *zsh* shell command lines, for example, is case-sensitive, even if the filesystem they're working with is not.

- UFS uses slashes (/) as its path separator, while HFS+ uses colons (:). However, various Mac OS X applications accept slash-using path notation no matter the underlying filesystem format. The Finder's Go → Go To Folder (Shift-⌘-G) command lets you type a path to travel to that point on the computer's filesystem. On the other hand, the Finder's Get Info window displays the real, colon-based path of the selected Finder object if it's on an HFS+ system.

  The two filesystems have a different concept of "root," or what the path / or : means, respectively. A UFS system's root directory is the top level of some designated disk volume, while the root to an HFS+ filesystem contains no data but has a list of available volumes. This is why absolute filenames expressed in HFS+ terms always lead in with a volume name, such as *Volume:tmp:foo*. (It's also philosophically similar to the filesystem *root* as the Finder displays it, through its Go → Computer (Shift-⌘-C) command.)

 Mac OS X often expects absolute paths to act as they would look on a UFS system. In the Terminal, *cd /* takes you to the top level of the boot volume, not to the HFS+ *root*. (Other volumes are accessible from */Volumes*.)

- HFS+ stores two time-related pieces of metadata with each file: its creation date and its modification date. UFS stores only modification dates.

File Forks

HFS+ is perhaps most distinctive among filesystems concerning how it allows files to store information in multiple *forks*. A typical non-Carbonized application for Mac OS 9 stores its executable binary code in a *data fork*, and supplemental information—such as icons, dialogs, and sounds—is stored in a *resource fork*. Each fork is a separate subsection of the file. Documents can also have both data and resources forks, which applications can read from and write to as they see fit.

However, Mac OS X is based on Unix, which was built to work with single-forked files, holding nothing except their own data. Modern Mac OS applications eschew all use of resource forks, instead taking one of two paths. They either store all their resources in a separate file with an *.rsrc* extension, kept inside the application package, or they simply store their resources as separate files inside the package. Carbon applications usually take the former, single-file route for their resources, and Cocoa applications favor the latter.

To accommodate traditional Macintosh applications and files, Mac OS X provides native support for multiple forks on HFS+ volumes, and native-like support on

UFS volumes. Copying and moving such files with the Finder works as expected, whether the files reside on an HFS+ or a UFS volume.

Under the hood, however, you'll find that this task required some special engineering on Apple's part. Mac OS X stores any resource fork that happens to reside on a UFS volume as a separate *file*, whose original name is prefixed with ._. For example, when a copy of the SimpleText application resides on a UFS volume, it's comprised of a data file named *SimpleText*, and a resource file named ._*SimpleText*. The Finder shows only the data file but does the work of splitting, moving, and recombining both files as they move between UFS and HFS+ volumes.

Similarly, because the Unix subsystem can't directly recognize multiple file forks residing on HFS+ volumes, the OS handles them differently. When viewed from the Unix command line, resource forks appear as separate files of the same name, but with */rsrc* appended. These special files will not show up in a directory listing, but will when explicitly listed (for example, "ls Simpletext/rsrc").

For both of these reasons, then, special care is required when handling dual-fork files from the command line. Traditional Unix file-transfer tools such as *cp*, *mv*, *tar*, *cpio*, and *rsync*, have not recognized resource forks and would leave them behind when moving the data fork, rendering application files useless. Mac OS X provides the *CpMac*, *MvMac*, and *ditto* utilities that do handle resource forks properly, and these are detailed in Chapter 2. As of Mac OS X Tiger, *cp* and *mv* also preserve resource forks, but *CpMac* and *MvMac* are included for compatibility with older scripts.

Attribute forks

HFS+ files can store metainformation in a third fork, called an *attribute fork*. Most commonly, this fork, if used, holds the file's application and creator codes.

As with resource forks, Mac OS X supports this fork and its codes but considers them deprecated. Modern Mac applications link files to themselves through filename extensions, not creator codes. As a user, you can also modify these application-document links as you wish, through the "Open with application" page of the Finder's Get Info window.

Journaling

The Disk Utility application enables *journaling* on HFS+ volumes. Disk journaling is a feature that both increases filesystem stability and decreases recovery time in the event filesystem directory damage occurs.

With journaling enabled, the OS keeps a record, or *journal*, of all write operations to the disk. If the system ever stops unexpectedly due to a crash or power failure, the OS automatically "replays" the journal upon restart, ensuring that the disk and its directory are again consistent with each other, a processes that takes only a few seconds.

Without journaling enabled, the OS must perform a check of the entire filesystem following a crash to restore consistency. This can take up to several hours, depending on the size of the disk.

Journaling does slightly decrease disk-write performance, but this should only be an issue when working with high-end multimedia, for example, when disks need to perform as fast as possible.

Other Supported Filesystem Formats

Mac OS X can recognize and work with several local filesystem formats beyond UFS and HFS+, as listed in Table 9-1.

Table 9-1. Mac OS X's supported filesystem formats

Filesystem type	Description
HFS+	Mac OS Extended Format. The standard filesystem format for Mac OS Versions 8.1 and later (including Mac OS X).
HFS	Mac OS Standard Format. Used by Mac OS versions prior to 8.1.
UFS	Universal File System, used by most Unix-based systems.
UDF	Universal disk format, used by DVDs.
ISO 9660	Used by CD-ROMs.
FAT	Used primarily by DOS and older versions of Windows, sometimes other media (such as some digital cameras).
FAT32	Used by newer versions of Windows.
NFS	The Network File System (see Chapter 10).

This list doesn't include the remote filesystems that Mac OS X can mount as network-shared volumes.

Filesystem Organization

Mac OS X defines several folders across the filesystem as holding special significance to the system. Individual applications, as well as the system software itself, consult these directories when scanning for certain types of software or resources installed on the machine. For example, a program that wants a list of fonts available to the whole system can look in */Library/Fonts* and */System/Library/Fonts*. Font files can certainly exist elsewhere in the filesystem, but relevant applications aren't likely to find them unless they're in a predictable place.

Domains

You might also have a */Library/Fonts* folder inside your home folder and perhaps yet another inside */Network/Library/Fonts*. Each *Fonts* folder exists inside a separate *domain*—Mac OS X's term for the scope that a folder resides in (in terms of both function and permission from the current user's point of view). The system defines four domains:

The term "domain" is a contender for the most overloaded word used to describe Mac OS X. While reading this section, try not to confuse the concept of filesystem domains with that of Internet domain names (such as *oreilly.com*) or NetInfo domains (as covered in Chapter 10). None of these have anything to do with each other.

User

Contains folders that are under complete control of the current user. Generally speaking, this includes the user's Home folder and everything inside it.

Local

Holds folders and files usable by all users of this machine, which may be modified by system administrators (users in the admin group) but are not crucial to the operating system. Folders directly under the *root* directory (/) that don't belong to other domains fall into the Local domain. On most systems, these include the */Library* and */Applications* folders.

Network

Works like the Local domain, except that its folders are hosted on the network, accessible to users of that network and modifiable by network administrators. Usually, this domain extends to cover all folders (but not the servers) found within the */Network* directory.

System

Contains folders and files that exist to support the computer's operating system and are not intended for direct human use. Nobody except the root account has permission to modify anything in the */System* domain.

The */System* folder contains a typical Mac OS X machine's System domain.

 Not every folder on the system lies in a domain. Other users' Home folders, for example, are always out of reach, even for administrative users, and the system has no special use for them. From the current user's point of view, they have no relevance; hence, they have no domain.

When an application needs to scan a system-defined folder for information, it usually seeks that folder in each of these four domains and scans its content, if it exists. The search order it uses is usually as follows:

1. User
2. Local
3. Network
4. System

An individual application can use a different order if it wishes, but this order suffices for most. It starts at the User domain (the scope where the current user has the most control), continues through the Local and Network domains (where system administrators might have put files for users' shared use), and ends at the System domain (where files critical to the operating system live and whose presence is usually a decision of Apple's).

Filesystem
Overview

For example, a program that wishes to find a particular font knows that it can find that font's file in a */Library/Font* folder. This folder can exist in any of the four domains, so it scans the directories in the following order:

1. */Users/username/Library/Fonts/*
2. */Library/Fonts/*
3. */Network/Library/Fonts/*
4. */System/Library/Fonts/*

If it finds the font, it stops its search. If that same application wishes to build a list of all fonts available to the user, it scans all the previous folders in their entirety. In the case of duplicates—for example, Courier is defined in both the User and System domains—the earlier domain in the search order (User, in this case) takes precedence.

Special Folders

There are two interpretations of the *root* directory on Mac OS X: one that's displayed for Finder views, and a Unix one that is mainly accessible from the Terminal. For more information on accessing the Unix *root* directory from the Finder, see "Exploring root" later in this chapter.

When you click on the icon of the boot hard drive in the Sidebar, you will see the folders listed in Table 9-2. These folders contain essential system files, applications, and the directories for all the system's users.

Table 9-2. Special folders in the root directory

Directory	Domain	Description
Applications	Local, System[a]	Holds applications available to all users of this machine.
Library	Local	Contains resources available to all users of this machine, such as fonts, plug-ins, and documentation.
System	System	This is the system folder for Mac OS X.
Users	User	Contains user home directories
System Folder	System	This is the system folder for Mac OS 9. Present only if Mac OS 9 is also installed on this volume.
Documents	-	Miscellaneous files from a Mac OS 9 installation.
Applications (Mac OS 9)	-	Applications from a Mac OS 9 installation.

[a] This folder exists in both the local and system domains. Most of its content belongs to the admin group, but some applications, such as Printer Setup Utility, can't be modified by even admin-group users.

User directories

Once created, each user is provided with a series of subdirectories in the home directory (*/Users/username*). These directories, listed here, can be used for storing anything, although some have specific purposes:

Desktop
  This directory contains the items found on your Desktop, including any files, folders, or application aliases placed there.

Documents

While it isn't mandatory, the */Documents* directory can be used as a repository for any files or folders you create.

Library

This directory is similar to the */System/Preferences* directory found in earlier versions of the Mac OS; it contains resources used by applications but not the applications themselves.

Movies

This is a place to store movies you create with iMovie or can use to hold QuickTime movies you create or download from the Internet.

Music

This directory can store music and sound files, including *.aiff*, *.mp3*, and so on. This directory also stores the iTunes Library.

Pictures

This directory can store photos and other images. iPhoto also uses the *~/Pictures* directory to house its iPhoto Library directory, which contains the photo albums you create.

Public

If you enable file or web sharing (System Preferences → Sharing → Services), this is where you can place items you wish to share with other users. Users who access the */Public* directory can see and copy items from this directory. Also in the */Public* directory is the Drop Box (*/Public/Drop Box*), a place in which other users can put files for you. If you have file sharing enabled, guest users anywhere on the network can also view and copy from */Public* and add items to the Drop Box.

Sites

If you enable Personal Web Sharing (System Preferences → Sharing → Services), this is the directory that houses the web site for your user account.

The Shared user directory

Because users are allowed to add or modify files only within their own home directories, the */Users/Shared* directory exists as a place to drop items to be shared with other users on the system. Guest network users can't access this directory.

The Library folder

Every domain contains a Library folder. Applications searching for additional resources and software available to it scan through the Library folders in the order noted in the earlier section "Domains."

Library folders hold system-specific application resources. Unlike the application-specific icons, sounds, and other resource files found within an application's package, Library resources are either shared among many applications (as fonts are) or are specific to both individual applications and the current system (as user preference files are).

A running application has access to the resources in all the Library folders within the domains the current user can see. Thus, if the user *chris* is running an application, the application combs through */Users/chris/Library*, */Library*, */Network/Library*, and */System/Library* for resource files. If searching for a particular resource, such as a font or a configuration file, it looks through the folders in the usual User → Local → Network → System domain search order, unless the application specifies a different order.

Anything a user places in her own User domain's Library folder, either directly or through an application, is available to that user alone. For example, all applications on the system are stored in */Applications*; however, a user's preferences for an application are stored in */Users/username/Library/Preferences*, usually as *plist* files. This separation allows multiple users on the system to use the same applications and yet have a different set of preferences to suit their needs. A system administrator can place resources in the Local domain's Library folder to allow all users of that computer access to them, and a network administrator can place files in the Network domain's Library so that all users of all computers across a network can use them. Nobody should ever need to modify the System domain's Library folder; leave that up to Apple's own system software installer and updater applications.

Mac OS X's Library folders are somewhat analogous to the *lib* directories found in key places around a typical Unix system, such as */usr/lib* and */usr/local/lib*. Unix *lib* directories usually hold code libraries and modules, and Mac OS X Library folders hold frameworks (the dynamic code libraries that Cocoa applications can link to in their Frameworks subfolders). As this section illustrates, though, Library folders also hold all manner of other application resources.

It's worth noting that a typical Mac OS X system does, in fact, have a number of more traditional Unix *lib* directories in the usual places, which the underlying Darwin OS uses when compiling software.

The following list briefly describes the folders often found in Library folders. Unless otherwise noted, they might be found in any domain.

Application Support
> This folder acts as a "scratch pad" for various applications. By convention, each application creates its own subfolder in this one, within which it can write whatever files it wishes.
>
> Some applications do, however, place their own folders directly underneath the Library folder, rather than in */Library/Application Support*. (For example, Apple's iTunes application does this.)

Assistants
> Programs that assist with the configuration of other applications or services (also known as *wizards*).

Audio
> Audio-related resources, including system alerts and audio plug-ins for various applications' use.

ColorPickers

Programs for choosing a color according to various models. The available color pickers appear as choices when an application displays a color well panel (Figure 9-1). Mac OS X's default pickers, including the color wheel, slider, and image-based pickers, live in */System/Library/ColorPickers*.

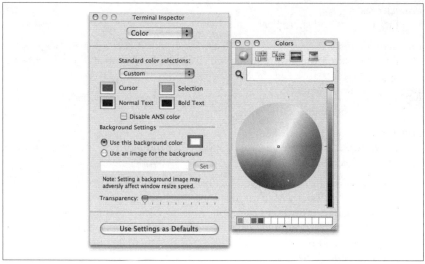

Figure 9-1. A color well panel

ColorSync

ColorSync profiles and scripts.

Components

Miscellaneous components and extensions. This folder tends to exist solely in the System domain.

Documentation

Documentation files. Can be in Apple Help format, plaintext files, collections of HTML, or just about anything else.

As with */Library/Application Support*, applications usually place their files within their own, eponymous subfolders.

Extensions

Device drivers and kernel extensions. Appropriate only in the system domain.

 Don't confuse the */System/Library/Extension* folder with Mac OS 9's */System Folder/Extensions* folder. The two are somewhat analogous in that both contain device drivers and low-level system extensions, but Mac OS 9's */Extensions* folder often contains all the sorts of things that Mac OS X's Library folders now hold, in one big, unsorted directory.

Favorites

Found only in the User domain, this folder contains aliases to files, folders, and disks.

Fonts

Font files, for both printing and display.

Frameworks

Frameworks and shared code libraries.

Internet Plug-ins

Plug-ins, libraries, and filters used by web browsers and other Internet applications.

Keyboards

Keyboard mapping definitions.

Preferences

Preference files for various applications. Depending upon the domain, these can be for an individual user, or system- or network-wide.

Applications can use whatever file format they wish for storing their preferences. Many modern Mac applications use XML property list files, with a .*plist* extension; this allows its application to access it through the standard user-defaults programming APIs and allows other applications to see how that application is configured. (Unix's permission system prevents users from spying on one another's config files!)

 The files in */Library/Preferences* usually apply to system-wide things, such as login window preferences. However, a system administrator can place an individual application's preferences file here to override individual users' preferences for that application.

See Chapter 13 for more information about Mac OS X's preferences system known as the defaults database.

Printers

Printer drivers and PPD plug-ins, organized by printer vendor.

QuickTime

QuickTime components and extensions.

Scripting Additions

AppleScript extensions.

Scripts

Scripts to display under the Script menu extra. The menu extra's content is an aggregation of all the filesystem domains' */Library/Scripts* folders. Subfolders show up as submenus.

WebServer

/Library/WebServer is the default document *root* of the Apache web server that ships with Mac OS X. See Chapter 12 for more on running Apache.

Hidden Files

By default, the Finder hides many files and folders from view, including the entirety of Darwin's directory layout, under the philosophy that most Mac OS X users will never need to access the system's Unix underpinnings. Savvier users, on the other hand, have a number of ways to see and work with all the filesystem's files.

Seeing Hidden Files

There are two ways to see files that don't appear in the Finder. The most direct way involves simply viewing a folder's contents by running the *ls* command on it in the Terminal. The Terminal sees the world simply as a tree of directories and files, and nothing more; files that have special, Mac-specific system roles appear like any other file. (However, you'll have to run *ls* with the *-a* flag.)

The other way involves changing the Finder preference that keeps these files hidden from sight. (Apple gets points for making this a user-adjustable preference, albeit not a very obvious one.) You'll need to add a value to the Finder preferences' file. You can accomplish this by operating the *defaults* command-line program on your *com.apple.finder* user defaults domain (described in Chapter 13), or by directly editing your */Users/username/Library/Preferences/com.apple.finder.plist* file with the Property List Editor application, as shown in Figure 9-2.

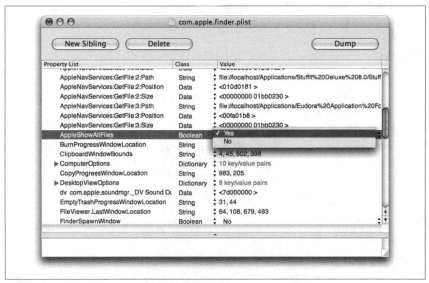

Figure 9-2. The Finder's preferences, as seen in Property List Editor

To add a value to the *com.apple.finder.plist* file, follow these steps:

1. Launch the Property List Editor (*/Developer/Applications/Utilities*).

2. Open the *com.apple.finder.plist* file located in */Users/username/Library/ Preferences*.

3. Click on the disclosure triangle next to Root to reveal the values and keys for the Finder's preferences.

4. Select Root by clicking on it once.

5. Click on the New Child button.

6. In the first column, enter AppleShowAllFiles.

7. Change its class to Boolean.

8. Change its value to Yes.

9. Save the changes to the *plist* file (File → Save, or ⌘-S).

10. Quit the Property List Editor (⌘-Q).

Your work's almost over. To make the changes take effect, you need to relaunch the Finder, as follows:

1. Go to → Force Quit (or Option-⌘-Esc).

2. Select the Finder.

3. Click the Relaunch button.

There will be a short pause while the process for the Finder quits and restarts, after which the changes you made will take effect.

 If you already know about a Finder-hidden folder's existence, you can view its contents in the Finder by choosing Go to Folder (Shift-⌘-G) and then typing the path to that folder. Typing */bin*, for example, reveals the contents of that directory.

Dotfiles

Following the traditional Unix model, the Finder hides all *dotfiles*, which are simply files (or folders) whose names begin with a period (dot) character. Applications can access dotfiles like any other file.

Your Mac's filesystem will likely accrue many dotfiles over time, particularly in users' Home folders, since this is the typical location for legacy Unix applications to store preference and configuration files. (Mac OS X-specific applications prefer to store this sort of information in Library folders, as described in the earlier section "The Library folder".) The following list covers some of particular interest:

.bash_history
> Found in the user's Home directory, this file is used by the *bash* shell to record previously entered commands.

.FBCIndex, .FBCLockFolder
> The Finder creates these dotfiles in each directory that it indexes by content. The binary file, *FBCIndex*, acts as an index to the content of all the folder's files. When performing a by-content search via the Finder's Find command, the Finder quickly reads from these index files, rather than picking through all the individual files again.

.ssh

When you access another computer via the Secure Shell (SSH), an encrypted RSA key is stored in the *known_hosts* file within this directory.

.Trash

Found in users' Home folders, this directory contains all the files and folders that a user has sent to the Trash (through either the Dock's Trash icon or the Finder's Move to Trash (⌘-Delete) command) but not yet deleted. When a user clicks once on the Dock's Trash icon, this folder's contents appear in a special Finder window labeled Trash.

This knowledge is useful for accessing users' Trash folders from the Terminal, or doing it programmatically through Perl or a shell script.

 Mac OS 9, if present, also keeps its system-wide Trash as a hidden folder, separate from the Trash folder in each Mac OS X user's Home folder. See "Hidden Mac OS 9 files", later in this chapter.

Exploring root

The *root* directory of a Mac OS X boot disk has the most to hide, from the Finder's point of view; it may play *root* to as many as three separate operating systems' filesystems, all at once! Beyond holding the lowest-level directories of the Mac OS X filesystem, such as the */System* and */Library* folders, the *root* directory also contains the basic directories that Darwin—the pure Unix system running at Mac OS X's core—needs. These include the directories that any Unix user would recognize, such as */etc* and */tmp*. Compare Figure 9-3 with Figure 9-4.

Furthermore, if Mac OS 9 is installed on the boot disk, its System Folder appears under the *root* directory, as do several Mac OS 9 configuration files. Other arbitrary files and folders created by the Mac OS 9 application might also exist at *root* because that operating system lacks Mac OS X's permission system and doesn't view the *root* directory as "sacred ground." For example, many Mac OS 9 software installers create new folders directly under *root*; Mac OS X installers place their software in locations such as */Applications/Library*.

Mac OS X's Finder, when displaying the boot disk's *root* folder, will show most of the low-level Mac OS X and Mac OS 9 filesystems' folders, but keep several special files hidden from sight, and it won't show any of Darwin's directories.

Hidden Mac OS 9 files

This isn't a book about Mac OS 9, so we won't go into detail about these files' functions. However, it's worthwhile to point out their presence on disks on which Mac OS 9 and Mac OS X are both installed because their mysterious existence might otherwise prove confusing.

All of these exist under the boot volume's *root* directory (/). Mac OS 9 is a single-user system, so it finds no fault in writing files directly to /, even though that's considered sacred ground to any Unix system, including Mac OS X.

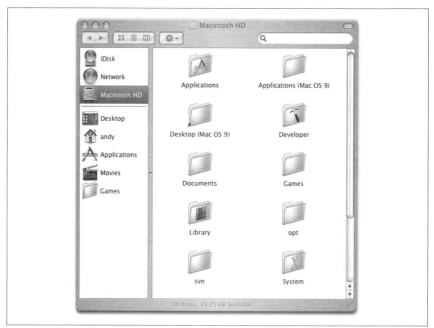

Figure 9-3. A typical Finder view of the boot disk's root

Figure 9-4. The same view, with hidden files revealed

Here are a few of the more common Mac OS 9 hidden files:

- Cleanup At Startup
- Desktop DB

- Desktop DF
- Temporary Items
- TheFindByContentFolder
- TheVolumeSettingsFolder
- Trash

As a rule of thumb, if you see mysterious, hidden files lurking directly under the *root* directory, they're probably the doing of Mac OS 9.

Hidden Darwin files

This book frequently mentions "traditional Unix systems" when comparing Mac OS X to other Unix-based operating systems. The truth is that Darwin (already noted) *is* a rather traditional Unix system, when considered all by itself. It has its own directory structure that subtly shares disk space with the more visible Mac OS X structure covered in the earlier section "Filesystem Organization."

All these files and directories exist under the *root* directory (/). (This may make them sound like the hidden Mac OS 9 files described in the previous section, but they're quite different. They serve as the core of the Darwin system, and hence of Mac OS X itself, in a way.)

mach

mach.sym

mach_kernel
> These files make up the Mach kernel, the heart of Darwin and Mac OS X.

etc

private/etc
> */etc* is actually a symbolic link to */private/etc*, a directory that holds Darwin's system configuration files. While many of these files, such as *hosts* and *passwd*, have roles superceded by Mac OS X's Directory Service technologies, others, such as *hostconfig*, are central to the whole operating system's configuration, especially during the startup process.

tmp

private/tmp
> Again, */tmp* is a symbolic link to */private/tmp*. The usual Unix *tmp* directory is readable and writeable by all users and processes, despite the fact that it's hidden in the invisible */private* directory. Lots of command-line programs and utilities use this directory as a scratch pad to write temporary files to disk. (Modern Mac OS X applications are more likely to use users' *Library* folders.)

var

private/var
> */var* is a symbolic link to the */private/var* directory, which holds logs, spools, PID files, and other file-based resources used by active processes. Most importantly, */private/var/db* holds vital configuration data including the NetInfo databases.

bin

Core Terminal commands, such as *cp* and *mkdir*. (As with all Unix command-line functions, all these commands, even the seemingly simple ones such as *ls*, are executable program files.)

sbin

Command-line utilities to perform basic filesystem and other administrative operations, such as mounting, unmounting, configuring, and diagnosing disks. Because these commands affect the whole system, they must usually be run as *root*.

automount

The system uses this directory as a mount point when statically mounting networked volumes.

dev

Device files, each a pointer to some kind of Unix device the system supports, are both real (such as disks and their partitions) and virtual (such as */dev/ null*).

Volumes

This is the default mount point Mac OS X uses for the filesystems of disks and partitions other than the boot volume. One subdirectory appears here for every disk (except for the boot disk and Network icon) that the Finder displays in the top-half of the Sidebar.

The File Permissions System

Mac OS X uses the Unix file permission system to control who has access to the filesystem's files, folders, and disks, and what they can do with them.

Ownership and permissions are central to security. It's important to get them right, even when you're the only user, because odd things can happen if you don't. For most users' interaction with Mac OS X, the system will do the right thing, without their having to think much about it. (Things get a little trickier when viewing the system as an administrator, though.)

Permissions refer to the ways in which someone can use a file. There are three such permissions under Unix:

Read

Allows you to look at a file's contents.

Write

Allows you to change or delete a file.

Execute

Allows you to run a file as a program. (This isn't so important when using Mac OS X's GUI, though; see the sidebar "What About the Execute Bit?" later in this section.)

When each file is created, the system assigns some default permissions that work most of the time. For instance, it gives you both read and write permission, but most of the world has only read permission. If you have a reason to be concerned, you can set things up so that other people have no permissions at all.

There are times when defaults don't work, though. For instance, if you create a shell script or Perl program in the Terminal, you have to assign executable permission so that you can run it. We'll show how to do that later in this section, after we get through the basic concepts.

Permissions have different meanings for a directory:

Read
> Allows you to list the contents of that directory.

Write
> Allows you to add or remove files in that directory.

Execute
> Allows you to make that directory your working directory and list information about its contents.

If you allow people to add files to a directory, you are also letting them remove files. The two privileges go together when you assign write permission. However, there is a way you can let users share a directory and keep them from deleting each other's files: you can set that directory's *sticky bit*. (See the entry for *chmod* in Chapter 2.)

The differences between the Read and Execute bits allow you to set up special kinds of directories such as drop boxes and pickup boxes. A Drop Box is a directory with only write and execute access allowed. Users are therefore able to place items inside the directory but not see what's inside. A Pickup Box has only execute access allowed, forcing users to specify a full pathname to access any items inside and preventing them from adding anything to the directory.

There are more files on Unix systems than the plain files and directories we've talked about so far. These are special files (devices), sockets, symbolic links, and so forth; each type observes its own rules regarding permissions. However you don't need to know the details on each type.

Owners and Groups

Now, who gets these permissions? To allow people to work together, Unix has three levels of permission: *owner*, *group*, and *other*. The *other* covers everybody who has access to the system and who isn't the *owner* or a member of the *group*.

The idea behind having groups is to give a set of users, such as a team of programmers, access to a file or set of applications. For instance, a programmer creating source code may reserve write permission to himself, but allow members of his group to have read access through a *group* permission. As for *other*, it might have no permission at all.

Each file has an *owner* and a *group*. The *owner* is generally the user who created the file. Each user also belongs to a default *group* that has the same name as the user account, if that account was created in Tiger (older versions of Mac OS X assigned the group *staff* to new accounts). Therefore, by default, each user is the only member or their group. That *group*, then, is assigned to every file the user creates. You can create other groups, though, and assign each user to multiple groups. By changing the *group* assigned to a file, you can give this level of access to any collection of people you want.

Mac OS 9 had something similar to this system with its Users & Groups Control panel, but this was relevant mainly to configuring who could mount your machine's hard drive over a network. Mac OS X's permission system also applies itself to this use but is far more pervasive, affecting every user's interaction with every part of the filesystem whether they are logged in locally or over a network.

Viewing and Modifying File Permissions

The permissions system is another part of Mac OS X with two distinct interfaces: you can either use the traditional Unix command-line tools through the Terminal to view and change a file's permissions, or you can use the Finder's Get Info window for a graphical interface to the same task.

Figure 9-5 shows the Finder's interface to the permission system, a section of the Finder's Info window .

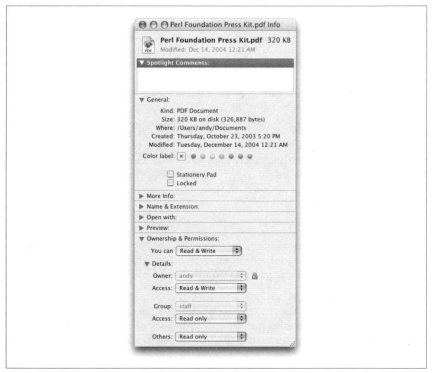

Figure 9-5. The Get Info window's Ownership & Permissions view

The pop-up menus display the object's current owner and group, as well as the owner, group, and other access permissions.

If you are the file's owner, you can modify the three permission menus, setting them to Read & Write, Read Only, or No Access for that type of user. If you have administrative privileges, you can also modify the object's owner and group.

What About the Execute Bit?

Unix veterans will note that the Finder offers no interface to any of a file's "execute" bits, which determine whether someone is allowed to try launching a file as a program. Simply put, this type of distinction doesn't exist in Mac OS X's Aqua layer, in which the Finder recognizes only certain kinds of files or directories as launchable, including *.app* application bundles and *.jar* Java archive files.

Furthermore, directories created in the Finder—through File→New Folder (Shift-⌘-N)—always have their execute bits set, and there's no way to unset them in the Finder. Again, you have to use *chmod* for that.

If you run the *ls* command with the *-l* option, it lists the requested files in a tabular format, with columns specifying the group, owner, and permissions of each file. Here is the Terminal's view of the same file depicted in Figure 9-5:

```
honey:~/Documents andy$ ls -l Perl\ Foundation\ Press\ Kit.pdf
-rw-r--r--  1 andy staff 326887 Dec 14  2004 Perl Foundation Press Kit.pdf
```

The code of letters and dashes in the first column lists the permissions. The first hyphen means it's a plain file (as opposed to a directory, which would be designated with a *d*). The next three characters list the read, write, and execute bits for the file's owner; rw- means that the read and write permissions are active, but the execute permission is not. (If it were, you'd see rwx instead.) Then there are three characters showing the group permissions (read-only, in this case) and three more for "other" permission (read-only, again).

After this, we see the file's owner (andy) and group (andy), followed by the file's size in bytes, a timestamp, and finally, the file's name.

To change permissions, you must use the *chmod* command, while the *chown* and *chgrp* commands change a file or directory's owner and group, respectively. Consult Chapter 2 or your Mac's manpages for more information on these commands. You may also wish to consult the *ls* command's documentation to see other ways you can list files in the Terminal.

10

Directory Services

A *directory service* manages information about users and resources such as printers and servers. It can manage this information for anything from a single machine to an entire corporate network. The Directory Service architecture in Mac OS X is called *Open Directory*. Open Directory encompasses flat files (such as */etc/hosts*), NetInfo (the legacy directory service brought over from earlier versions of Mac OS X and NeXTSTEP), LDAPv3, and other services through third-party plug-ins.

This chapter describes how to perform common configuration tasks, such as adding a user or host on Mac OS X with the default configuration. If your system administrator has configured your Macintosh to consult an external directory server, some of these instructions may not work. If that's the case, you should ask your system administrator to make these kinds of changes anyhow.

Understanding Directory Services

In Mac OS X 10.1.*x* and earlier, the system was configured to consult the NetInfo database for all directory information. If you needed to do something simple, such as adding a host, you couldn't just add it to */etc/hosts* and be done with it. Instead, you had to use the NetInfo Manager (or NetInfo's command-line utilities) to add the host to the system.

However, as of Mac OS X 10.2 (Jaguar), NetInfo functions started to become more of a legacy protocol and were reduced to handling the local directory database for machines that did not participate in a network-wide directory, such as Active Directory or OpenLDAP. NetInfo is still present in Mac OS X 10.3 and 10.4, but you can perform many configuration tasks by editing the standard Unix flat files. By default, Mac OS X is now configured to consult the local directory (also known as the NetInfo database) for authentication, which corresponds to */etc/passwd* and */etc/group* on other Unix systems. You can override this setting with the Directory Access application. For more information, see "Configuring Directory Services," later in this chapter.

For users whose network configuration consists of an IP address, a default gateway, and some DNS addresses, this default configuration should be fine. You'll need to tap into Open Directory's features for more advanced configurations, such as determining how a user can log into a workstation and find his home directory, even when that directory is hosted on a shared server.

In order to work with Mac OS X's Directory Services, you must first understand the overall architecture, which is known as Open Directory. Directory Services is the part of Mac OS X (and the open source Darwin operating system) that implements this architecture. Figure 10-1 shows the relationship of Directory Services to the rest of the operating system. On the top, server processes, as well as the user's desktop and applications, act as clients to Directory Services, which delegates requests to a directory service plug-in (see "Configuring Directory Services," later in this chapter, for a description of each plug-in).

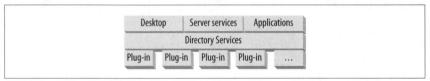

Figure 10-1. The Directory Services architecture

Programming with Directory Services

As a programmer, you frequently need to deal with directory information, whether you realize it or not. Your application uses Directory Services each time it looks up a host entry or authenticates a password. The Open Directory architecture unifies what used to be a random collection of flat files in /etc. The good news is that the flat files still work. The other good news is that there is a brave new world just beyond those flat files. So, while all your old Unix code should work with the Open Directory architecture, you should look for new ways to accomplish old tasks, especially if you can continue writing portable code.

To get at directory information, Unix applications typically go through the C library using such functions as gethostent( ). The C library connects to *lookupd,* a thin shim that is the doorway to the *DirectoryService* daemon. The *DirectoryService* daemon consults the available plug-ins until it finds the one that can answer the directory query.

Working with Passwords

One traditional route to user and password information was through the getpw* family of functions. However, those functions are not ideal for working with systems that support multiple directories (flat files, NetInfo, LDAP, etc.). Also, in the interest of thwarting dictionary attacks against password files, many operating systems have stopped returning encrypted passwords through those APIs. Many Unix and Linux systems simply return an "x" when you invoke a function like getpwnam( ). However, those systems can return an encrypted password through functions like getspnam( ), which consult shadow password entries and can generally be invoked by the root user only. Example 10-1 shows the typical usage of such an API, where the user enters her plaintext password, and the program encrypts it and then compares it against the encrypted password stored in the system.

Example 10-1. Using getpwnam( ) to retrieve an encrypted password

```
/*
 * getpw* no longer returns a crypted password.
 *
 * Compile with gcc checkpass.c -o checkpass
 * Run with: ./checkpass
 */

#include <pwd.h>
#include <stdio.h>
#include <stdlib.h>

int main(int argc, char *argv[])
{
  const char *user = NULL;
  struct passwd *pwd;

  /* Set the user name if it was supplied on the command
   * line.  Bail out if we don't end up with a user name.
   */
  if (argc == 2)
    user = argv[1];
  if(!user)
  {
    fprintf(stderr, "Usage: checkpass <username>\n");
    exit(1);
  }

  /* Fetch the password entry. */
  if (pwd = getpwnam(user))
  {
    char *password = (char *) getpass("Enter your password: ");

    /* Encrypt the password using the encrypted password as salt.
     * See crypt(3) for complete details.
     */
    char *crypted  = (char *) crypt(password, pwd->pw_passwd);

    /* Are the two encrypted passwords identical? */
    if (strcmp(pwd->pw_passwd, crypted) == 0)
      printf("Success.\n");
    else
    {
      printf("Bad password: %s != %s\n", pwd->pw_passwd, crypted);
      return 1;
```

```
    }
  }
  else
  {
    fprintf(stderr, "Could not find password for %s.\n", user);
    return 1;
  }
  return 0;

}
```

As of Mac OS X Panther (v 10.3), your code no longer has a chance to look at an encrypted password. There are no functions such as getspnam( ), and if you invoke a function like getpwnam( ), you'll get one or more asterisks as the result. For example:

```
$ gcc checkpass.c -o checkpass
$ ./checkpass bjepson
Enter your password:
Bad password: ******** != **yRnqib5QSRI
```

> There are some circumstances where you can obtain an encrypted password, but this is not the default behavior of Mac OS X. See the *getpwent(3)* manpage for complete details.

Instead of retrieving and comparing encrypted passwords, you should go through the Linux-PAM APIs. Since Linux-PAM is included with (or available for) many flavors of Unix, you can use it to write portable code. Example 10-2 shows a simple program that uses Linux-PAM to prompt a user for his password.

Example 10-2. Using Linux-PAM to authenticate a user

```
/*
 * Use Linux-PAM to check passwords.
 *
 * Compile with gcc pam_example.c -o pam_example -lpam
 * Run with: ./pam_example <username>
 */
#include <stdio.h>
#include <pam/pam_appl.h>
#include <pam/pam_misc.h>

int main(int argc, char *argv[])
{

  int retval;
  static struct pam_conv pam_conv;
  pam_conv.conv = misc_conv;
  pam_handle_t *pamh = NULL;
  const char *user = NULL;

  /* Set the username if it was supplied on the command
```

Example 10-2. Using Linux-PAM to authenticate a user (continued)

```
 * line. Bail out if we don't end up with a username.
 */
if (argc == 2)
  user = argv[1];
if(!user)
{
  fprintf(stderr, "Usage: pam_example <username>\n");
  exit(1);
}

/* Initialize Linux-PAM. */
retval = pam_start("pam_example", user, &pam_conv, &pamh);
if (retval != PAM_SUCCESS)
{
  fprintf(stderr, "Could not start pam: %s\n",
      pam_strerror(pamh, retval));
  exit(1);
}

/* Try to authenticate the user. This could cause Linux-PAM
 * to prompt the user for a password.
 */
retval = pam_authenticate(pamh, 0);
if (retval == PAM_SUCCESS)
  printf("Success.\n");
else
  fprintf(stderr, "Failure: %s\n", pam_strerror(pamh, retval));

/* Shutdown Linux-PAM. Return with an error if
 * something goes wrong.
 */
return pam_end(pamh, retval) == PAM_SUCCESS ? 0 : 1;
}
```

In order for this to work, you must create a file called *pam_example* in */etc/pam.d* with the following contents (the filename must match the first argument to pam_ start( ), which is shown in bold in Example 10-2):

```
auth       required    pam_securityserver.so
account    required    pam_permit.so
password   required    pam_deny.so
```

Be careful when making any changes in the */etc/pam.d* directory. If you change one of the files that is consulted for system login, you may lock yourself out of the system. For more information on Linux-PAM, see the *pam(8)* manpage.

Once you've compiled this program and created the *pam_example* file in */etc/pam.d*, you can test it out:

```
$ gcc pam_example.c -o pam_example -lpam
$ ./pam_example bjepson
Password: ********
Success.
```

Configuring Directory Services

In order to configure Directory Services, use the Directory Access application (*/Applications/Utilities*), shown in Figure 10-2.

You can enable or disable various directory service plug-ins, or change their configuration.

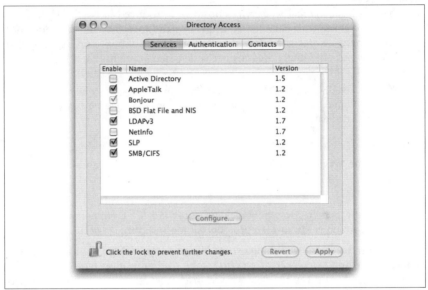

Figure 10-2. The Directory Access application shows the available plug-ins

Directory Access supports the following plug-ins:

Active Directory
> This plug-in lets Mac OS X consult an Active Directory domain on a server running Windows 2000 or Windows 2003.

AppleTalk
> This is the ultimate Mac OS legacy protocol. AppleTalk was the original networking protocol supported by Mac OS versions prior to Mac OS X. Linux and the server editions of Windows also support AppleTalk.

Bonjour
> Formerly known as Rendezvous, Bonjour is Apple's zero-configuration protocol for discovering file sharing, printers, and other network services. It uses a peer-to-peer approach to announce and discover services automatically as devices join a network.

BSD Flat File and NIS
> This includes the Network Information Service (NIS) and the flat files located in the */etc* directory, such as *hosts*, *exports*, and *services*. By default, this option is switched off. After you enable it, click Apply, switch to the Authentication tab, choose Custom Path from the search menu, click the Add button, choose */BSD/Local*, and click Apply again.

LDAPv3

This is the same version of LDAP used by Microsoft's Active Directory and Novell's NDS. In addition to the client components, Mac OS X includes *slapd*, a standalone LDAP daemon. Mac OS X's LDAP support comes through OpenLDAP (*http://www.openldap.org*), an open source LDAPv3 implementation.

NetInfo

This is a legacy Directory Services protocol introduced in NeXTSTEP. If the checkbox is off (the default), NetInfo uses the local domain but does not consult network-based NetInfo domains. If the checkbox is on, NetInfo also looks for and potentially uses any network-based domains that it finds.

 NetInfo and LDAP both use the same data store, which is contained in */var/db/netinfo/*. The data store is a collection of embedded database files.

SLP

This is the Service Location Protocol, which supports file and print services over IP.

SMB/CIFS

This is the Server Message Block protocol (a.k.a., Common Internet File System), which is Microsoft's protocol for file and print services.

Under the Services tab, everything except NetInfo and BSD Configuration Files is enabled by default. However, if you go to the Authentication tab (Figure 10-3), you'll see that NetInfo is the sole service in charge of authentication (which is handled by */etc/passwd* and */etc/group* on other Unix systems).

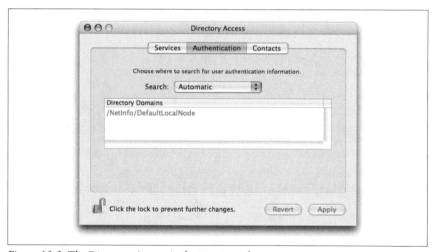

Figure 10-3. The Directory Access Authentication tab

By default, the Authentication tab is set to Automatic. You can set the Search popup to any of the following:

Automatic
> This is the default, which searches (in order) the local NetInfo directory, a shared NetInfo domain, and a shared LDAPv3 domain.

Local directory
> This searches only the local NetInfo directory.

Custom path
> This allows you to use BSD flat files (*/etc/passwd* and */etc/group*). After you select Custom path from the pop up, click Add and select */BSD/local*.

After you have changed the Search setting, click Apply. The Contact tab is set up identically to the Authentication tab and is used by programs that search Directory Services for contact information (office locations, phone numbers, full names, etc.).

Enabling BSD flat files does not copy or change the information in the local directory (the NetInfo database). If you want to rely only on flat files, you would need to find all the user entries from the local directory (you could use the command *nidump passwd .* to list them all) and add them to the password flat files (*/etc/passwd* and */etc/master.passwd*) by running the *vipw* utility with no arguments (do not edit either file directly). When you are done editing the password file, *vipw* invokes *pwd_mkdb* to rebuild the databases (*/etc/spwd.db* and */etc/pwd.db*) used for looking up usernames and passwords, and also updates */etc/passwd*. Switching over to flat files would allow you to access encrypted passwords through getpwnam( ) and friends, but would also mean you could no longer use the GUI tools to manage user accounts.

> If you change any settings in the Directory Access applications, you may find that some invalid credentials are temporarily cached by Directory Services. To clear out the cache immediately, run the following command as *root*:
>
> ```
> $ lookupd -flushcache
> ```

NetInfo Manager

The local directory is organized hierarchically, starting from the *root*, which, like a filesystem's *root*, is called /. However, this is not meant to suggest that there is a corresponding directory or file for each entry. Instead, the data is stored in a collection of files under */var/db/netinfo*.

You can browse or modify the local directory using NetInfo Manager, which is located in */Applications/Utilities*. Figure 10-4 shows NetInfo Manager displaying the properties of the *mysql* user.

Figure 10-4. Browsing the local directory

Directory Services Utilities

This chapter demonstrates four Directory Services utilities: *dscl*, *nireport*, *nidump*, and *niload*. Table 10-1 describes these and other NetInfo utilities.

Table 10-1. NetInfo tools

Tool	Description
dscl	Provides a command-line interface to Directory Services.
nicl	Provides a command-line interface to NetInfo.
nidump	Extracts flat file format data (such as */etc/passwd*) from NetInfo.
nifind	Finds a NetInfo directory.
nigrep	Performs a regular expression search on NetInfo.
niload	Loads flat file format data (such as */etc/passwd*) into NetInfo.
nireport	Prints tables from NetInfo.
niutil	NetInfo utility for manipulating the database.

The *nidump* and *nireport* utilities display the contents of the local directory. *niload* loads the contents of flat files (such as */etc/passwd* or */etc/hosts*) into Directory Services. *niutil* directly manipulates the Directory Services database; it's the command-line equivalent of NetInfo Manager. To make changes, use *sudo* with these commands or first log in as the *root* user. The commands that can be performed as a normal user are shown without the *sudo* command in the examples that follow.

Unlike other *ni** utilities, *nicl* acts directly on the database files. Consequently, you can use *nicl* to modify the local directory even when Directory Services is not running (such as when you boot into single-user mode).

 When you use any of these utilities you are making potentially dangerous changes to your system. But even if you trash the local directory with reckless usage of these commands, you can restore the NetInfo database from your last backup. For more details, see "Restoring the Directory Services Database," later in this chapter. To back up the local NetInfo database, use the command:

```
$ nidump -r / -t localhost/local > backup.nidump
```

Managing Groups

Directory Services stores information about groups in its */groups* directory. This is different from the */etc/group* file, which is consulted only in single-user mode.

To list all of the group IDs (GIDs) and group names for the local domain, invoke *nireport* with the NetInfo domain (., the local domain), the directory (*/groups*), and the properties you want to inspect—in this case, *gid* and *name*:

```
$ nireport . /groups gid name
-2       nobody
-1       nogroup
0        wheel
1        daemon
2        kmem
3        sys
4        tty
5        operator
6        mail
7        bin
20       staff
26       lp
27       postfix
28       postdrop
29       certusers
45       utmp
66       uucp
68       dialer
69       network
70       www
74       mysql
[... and so on ...]
```

Although the flat file format is called *group* (after the */etc/group* file), the group directory is */groups*. If you forget that last *s*, *nireport* looks for the wrong directory. However, if you want to dump the groups directory in the */etc/group* file format, use the command *nidump group* . without that last *s*.

Creating a Group with niload

The *niload* utility can be used to read the flat file format used by */etc/group* (name:password:gid:members). To add a new group, you can create a file that adheres to that format, and load it with *niload*. For ad hoc work, you can use a here document (an expression that functions as a quoted string, but spans multiple lines) rather than a separate file:

```
$ sudo niload group . <<EOF
> writers:*:1001:
> EOF
```

Creating a Group with dscl

To create a group with *dscl*, you'll need to create a directory under */groups* and set the *gid* and *passwd* properties. An asterisk (*) specifies no password; be sure to quote it so that the shell does not attempt to expand it. The following creates a group named *writers* as GID 5005 with no password and no members:

```
$ sudo dscl . create /groups/writers gid 5005
$ sudo dscl . create /groups/writers passwd '*'
```

Adding Users to a Group

You can add users to the group by appending values to the *users* property with *dscl*'s *merge* command at the command line (or by using the *merge* command interactively; start *dscl* in interactive mode with *sudo dscl .*). If the *users* property does not exist, *dscl* creates it. If the users are already part of the group, they are not added to the list (contrast this with the *-append* command, which can result in the same user being added more than once if the command is invoked multiple times):

```
$ sudo dscl . merge /groups/writers users bjepson rothman
```

Listing Groups with nidump

Use *nidump* to confirm that the new group was created correctly. To list groups with *nidump*, pass in the format (in this case, the *group* file) and the domain (., the local domain):

```
$ nidump group . | grep writers
writers:*:5005:bjepson,rothman
```

Because you can use *nireport* to dump any directory, you could also use it to see this information:

```
$ nireport . /groups name passwd gid users | grep writers
writers *       5005    bjepson,rothman
```

Deleting a Group

To delete a group, use *dscl*'s *delete* command. Be careful with this command, since it deletes everything in and below the specified NetInfo directory:

```
$ sudo dscl . delete /groups/writers
```

Managing Users and Passwords

The Directory Services equivalent of the *passwd* file resides under the */users* portion of the directory. Although Mac OS X includes */etc/passwd* and */etc/master. passwd* files, they are consulted only while the system is in single-user mode, or if the system has been reconfigured to use BSD Flat Files (see "Configuring Directory Services," earlier in this chapter).

To add a normal user to your system, you should use System Preferences → Accounts. However, if you want to bulk-load NetInfo with many users or create a user while logged in over *ssh*, you can use *dscl* or *niload*.

You can list all users with the *nireport* utility. Supply the NetInfo domain (., the local domain), the directory (*/users*), and the properties you want to inspect (*uid*, *name*, *home*, *realname*, and *shell*):

```
$ nireport . /users uid name home realname shell
-2      nobody  /var/empty      Unprivileged User       /usr/bin/false
0       root    /var/root       System Administrator    /bin/sh
1       daemon  /var/root       System Services /usr/bin/false
99      unknown /var/empty      Unknown User    /usr/bin/false
26      lp      /var/spool/cups Printing Services       /usr/bin/false
27      postfix /var/spool/postfix      Postfix User    /usr/bin/false
70      www     /Library/WebServer      World Wide Web Server    /usr/bin/
71      eppc    /var/empty      Apple Events User        /usr/bin/false
74      mysql   /var/empty      MySQL Server    /usr/bin/false
75      sshd    /var/empty      sshd Privilege separation       /usr/bin/
false
76      qtss    /var/empty      QuickTime Streaming Server      /usr/bin/
false
77      cyrusimap       /var/imap       Cyrus IMAP User /usr/bin/false
78      mailman /var/empty      Mailman user    /usr/bin/false
79      appserver       /var/empty      Application Server      /usr/bin/
[... and so on ...]
```

Creating a User with niload

The *niload* utility understands the flat file format used by */etc/passwd* (which is name:password:uid:gid:class:change:expire:gecos:home_dir:shell). See the *passwd(5)* manpage for a description of each field. To add a new user, create a file that adheres to that format and load it with *niload*. You can use a here document rather than a separate file. This example creates a user for Ernest Rothman with a UID of 701 and membership in the group numbered 701, which you'll create next:

```
$ sudo niload passwd . <<EOF
> rothman:*:701:701::0:0:Ernest Rothman:/Users/rothman:/bin/bash
> EOF
```

Next, create a group with the same name as the new user and a GID that matches his UID (as of Mac OS X 10.3, users are given their own groups):

```
$ sudo niload group . <<EOF
> rothman:*:701:
> EOF
```

As you can see from the example, we set the user's password field to *, which disables logins for that account. To set the password, we'll use the *passwd* command:

```
$ sudo passwd rothman
Changing password for rothman.
New password: ********
Retype new password: ********
```

If you *niload* a user that already exists, that user's entry will be updated with the new information. Before the user can log in, you must create his home directory (see "Creating a User's Home Directory," later in this chapter).

Creating a User with dscl

To create a user with *dscl*, you'll need to create a directory under */users*, and set the *uid*, *gid*, *shell*, *realname*, and *home* properties.

The following commands will create the same user shown in the previous section:

```
$ sudo dscl . create /users/rothman uid 701
$ sudo dscl . create /users/rothman gid 701
$ sudo dscl . create /users/rothman shell /bin/bash
$ sudo dscl . create /users/rothman home /Users/rothman
$ sudo dscl . create /users/rothman realname "Ernest Rothman"
$ sudo dscl . create /users/rothman passwd \*
$ sudo dscl . create /groups/rothman gid 701
$ sudo dscl . create /groups/rothman passwd \*
```

Be sure to quote or escape the asterisk (*) in the passwd entries. After you create the user, you should set the password as shown in the previous section.

Creating a User's Home Directory

One thing that NetInfo can't do for you is create the user's home directory. Mac OS X keeps a skeleton directory under the */System/Library/User Template* directory. If you look in this directory, you'll see localized versions of a user's home directory. To copy the localized English version of the home directory, use the *ditto* command with the *--rsrc* flag to preserve any resource forks that may exist:

```
$ sudo ditto --rsrc \
    /System/Library/User\ Template/English.lproj /Users/rothman
```

Then, use *chown* to recursively set the ownership of the home directory and all its contents (make sure you set the group to a group of which the user is a member):

```
$ sudo chown -R rothman:rothman /Users/rothman
```

This change makes the new user the owner of his home directory and all its contents.

Granting Administrative Privileges

To give someone administrative privileges, add that user to the *admin* group (*/groups/ admin*). This gives him or her the ability to use *sudo* and run applications (such as software installers) that require such privileges:

```
$ sudo dscl . merge /groups/admin users rothman
```

If you want this setting to take place immediately, you can run the command *sudo lookupd -flushcache* to flush any cached credentials.

Modifying a User

You can change a user's properties by using the *create* command, even if that property already exists. For example, to change *rothman*'s shell to *zsh*, use:

```
$ sudo dscl . -create /users/rothman shell /bin/zsh
```

 You can also modify most user settings with System Preferences → Accounts. If you want to do things the traditional Unix way, Mac OS X includes *chsh*, *chfn*, and *chpass* in Version 10.3 and beyond.

Listing Users with nidump

Use *nidump* to confirm that *rothman* was added successfully. To list users with *nidump*, pass in the format (in this case, the *passwd* file) and the domain (use . for the local domain):

```
$ nidump passwd . | grep rothman
rothman:********:701:701::0:0:Ernest Rothman:/Users/rothman:/bin/zsh
```

Deleting a User

To delete a user, use *dscl*'s *delete* command. Since *delete* recursively deletes everything under the specified directory, use this command with caution:

```
$ sudo dscl . delete /users/rothman
```

If you want to also delete that user's home directory, you'll have to do it manually.

 Be sure to delete the group you created for this user as well ("rothman" in this example), as shown in "Deleting a Group," earlier in this chapter.

Managing Hostnames and IP Addresses

Mac OS X consults both the */etc/hosts* file and the */machines* portion of the local directory. For example, the following entry in */etc/hosts* would map the hostname *xyzzy* to 192.168.0.1:

```
192.168.0.1   xyzzy
```

Creating a Host with niload

The *niload* utility understands the flat file format used by */etc/hosts* (*ip_address name*). See the *hosts(5)* manpage for a description of each field. To add a new host, create a file using that format and load it with *niload*. This example ads the host *xyzzy*:

```
$ sudo niload hosts . <<EOF
> 192.168.0.1 xyzzy
> EOF
```

If you add an entry that already exists, it will be overwritten.

The */etc/hosts* file takes precedence over the local directory, so if you enter the same hostname with different IP addresses in both places, Mac OS X uses the one in */etc/hosts*.

Exporting Directories with NFS

You can use the */etc/exports* file to store folders that you want to export over NFS. For example, the following line exports the */Users* directory to two hosts (192. 168.0.134 and 192.168.0.106):

```
/Users  -ro 192.168.0.134 192.168.0.106
```

The NFS server will start automatically at boot time if there are any exports in that file. After you've set up your exports, you can reboot, and NFS should start automatically. NFS options supported by Mac OS X include the following (see the *exports(5)* manpage for complete details):

-maproot=user
> Specifies that the remote *root* user should be mapped to the specified user. You may specify either a username or numeric user ID.

-maproot=user:[group[:group...]]
> Specifies that the remote *root* user should be mapped to the specified user with the specified group credentials. If you include the colon with no groups, as in -maproot=*username*:, it means the remote user should have no group credentials. You may specify a username or numeric user ID for *user* and a group name or numeric group ID for *group*.

-mapall=user
> Specifies that all remote users should be mapped to the specified user.

-mapall=user:[group[:group...]]
> Specifies that all remote users should be mapped to the specified user with the specified group credentials. If you include the colon with no groups, as in mapall=*username*:, it specifies that a remote user shouldn have no group credentials.

-kerb
> Uses a Kerberos authentication server to authenticate and map client credentials.

-ro
> Exports the filesystem as read-only. The synonym -o is also supported.

Flat Files and Their Directory Services Counterparts

As mentioned earlier, Directory Services manages information for several flat files in earlier releases of Mac OS X, including */etc/printcap*, */etc/mail/aliases*, */etc/protocols*, and */etc/services*. For a complete list of known flat file formats, see the *nidump* and *niload* manpages.

Although you can edit these flat files directly as you would on any other Unix system, you can also use Directory Services to manage this information. You can use *niload* with a supported flat file format to add entries, or you can use *dscl* or NetInfo Manager to directly manipulate the entries. Table 10-2 lists each flat file, the corresponding portion of the directory, and important properties associated with each entry. See the *netinfo(5)* manpage for complete details. Properties marked with (list) can take multiple values using the *dscl merge* command (for an example, see "Adding Users to a Group," earlier in this chapter.)

The "Flat files or local database?" column in Table 10-2 indicates whether Directory Services consults the flat file, the local database, or both. You can use Directory Access to modify the way information is looked up on your Macintosh.

Table 10-2. Flat files and their NetInfo counterparts

Flat file	NetInfo directory	Important properties	Flat files or local database?
/etc/exports	*/exports*	name, clients (list), opts (list)	Flat files
/etc/fstab	*/mounts*	name, dir, type, opts (list), passno, freq	Local database
/etc/group	*/groups*	name, passwd, gid, users (list)	Local database
/etc/hosts	*/machines*	ip_address, name (list)	Both; entries in */etc/hosts* take precedence
/etc/mail/aliases	*/aliases*	name, members (list)	Flat files
/etc/networks	*/networks*	name (list), address	Flat files
/etc/passwd, /etc/master.passwd	*/users*	name, passwd, uid, gid, realname, home, shell	Local database
/etc/printcap	*/printers*	*name*, and various *printcap* properties (see the *printcap(5)* manpage)	Flat files
/etc/protocols	*/protocols*	name (list), number	Flat files
/etc/rpc	*/rpcs*	name (list), number	Flat files
/etc/services	*/services*	*name* (list), *port, protocol* (list)	Flat files

Restoring the Directory Services Database

If the local directory database is damaged, boot into single-user mode by holding down ⌘-S as the system starts up. Next, check to see if you have a backup of the NetInfo database. The *daily periodic* job backs up the database each time it is run. You can find the backup in */var/backups/local.nidump*. If you don't have a backup, you won't be able to restore. The *local.nidump* file is overwritten each time the *cron* job runs, so make sure you back it up regularly (preferably to some form of removable media).

If your computer is generally not turned on at 3:15 a.m. (the default time for the *daily periodic* job), you'll never get a backup of your local directory. You can solve this problem by editing *com.apple. periodic-daily.plist* to run this job at a different time, or to run the job periodically with the command *sudo periodic daily*.

If you totally mess up and find that you forgot to backup your Net-Info database, you can stop at step 5 and issue the command *rm /var/db/.AppleSetupDone*. This makes Mac OS X think that it's being booted for the first time when you restart, forcing it to run the Setup Assistant so you can create the initial user for the system, thus bringing your system to a usable state for further repairs.

After the system boots in single-user mode, you should:

1. Wait for the root# prompt to come up.
2. Fix any filesystem errors:

   # **/sbin/fsck -fy**

3. Mount the *root* filesystem as read/write:

   # **/sbin/mount -uw /**

4. Change directories and go to the NetInfo database directory:

   # **cd /var/db/netinfo/**

5. Move the database out of the way and give it a different name:

   # **mv local.nidb/ local.nidb.broken**

6. Start enough of the system to use NetInfo. The */etc/rc* script also creates a blank NetInfo database when it sees that it no longer exists:

   # **sh /etc/rc**

7. Wait for a while for the system to become ready—just before it's ready, you should see the screen go blue as though it's going to show you the login window. However, it will return to the verbose boot screen with the black background, and you can press Control-L or Return to get your shell prompt back. Next, load the backup into NetInfo:

   # **/usr/bin/niload   -d -r / . < /var/backups/local.nidump**

8. When it saw that the NetInfo database needed to be recreated, */etc/rc* deleted the *.AppleSetupDone* file, so you need to recreate it:

   # **touch /var/db/.AppleSetupDone**

After you have completed these steps, reboot the system with the *reboot* command.

11

Running Network Services

A *network service* is a program running on a local machine that other machines can connect to and use over a network. Common examples include web, email, and file-transfer servers.

This chapter describes how network services work in general, and how several of the more popular services work on Mac OS X.

Network Services Overview

Generally, a network service operates through a *daemon* program that listens for incoming connections on a certain port; web servers usually listen on port 80, for example, and *ssh* connections typically happen on port 22. (The precise way it accomplishes this is implementation-specific; it might choose to handle the whole connection itself or fork off another process to handle it so the daemon can get back to listening.)

Running Services in Mac OS X

Like so many other administrative tasks in Mac OS X, you have two ways to run the network services. The classic Unix way involves invoking the daemon on the command line, either manually through the Terminal or with a script. The Sharing preference pane, though, provides a very simple on/off switch for many network services.

Running Services Through the Sharing Pane

The Sharing pane contains three tabbed panes shown in Figure 11-1 .

Services
   Lists several service daemons you can control.

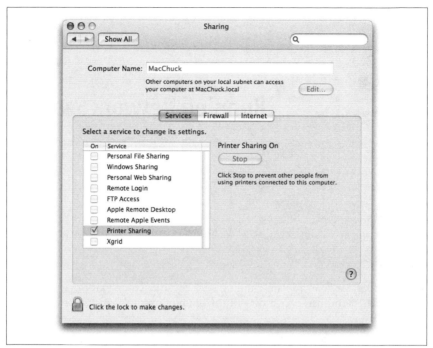

Figure 11-1. The Sharing preference panel's Services pane

Firewall
Contains controls for the system's built-in firewall.

Internet
Lets you enable/disable Internet sharing.

Every item in the Services list is visually paired with an On checkbox and is (behind the scenes) associated with a daemon program. Generally, when you check a checkbox, the related daemon launches; unchecking the checkbox kills the daemon, making the service unavailable. In some cases, the system service remains running in either state, but toggling the checkbox causes the system to rewrite its configuration file and then restart it.

Personal File Sharing
When active, other computers can mount disks and folders on your file-system via AFP. See the later section "File Sharing Services."

Windows Sharing
The same as Personal file sharing but uses the SMB protocol to share disks and folders, making access easier for users of Microsoft Windows machines—though other operating systems, including Mac OS X, can also mount SMB shares easily. See the later section "File Sharing Services."

Personal Web Sharing
Checking this launches the computer's Apache web server. See the later section "Web Services."

Remote Login
> Launches the Mac's SSH server. See the later section "The Secure Shell."

FTP Access
> Runs the FTP server, as described later in "File Transfer Protocol (FTP)."

Apple Remote Desktop
> Runs the Apple Remote Desktop (ADR) client daemons, which allow a remote machine running the ADR administrations software (available separately) to manage the client machine. A teacher running ADR, for example, can remotely view a student's display, install software, or generate system information reports on any computer running the client. When you click to enable the client, an Access Privileges button on the pane is enabled as well, allowing the client to specify how much access a remote ADR user can have.

Remote Apple Events
> When activated, every active application that responds to Apple Events (i.e., is controllable by AppleScript) also becomes a web service that responds to the SOAP protocol, accessible from anywhere on the Internet.

Printer Sharing
> Activates printer sharing.

Xgrid
> Allows your Mac to be controlled by an Xgrid server to distribute tasks for your computer to perform. For additional information about Xgrid, see *http:// www.apple.com/macosx/features/xgrid*.

Mail Services

Email-related daemons can be put into two categories: *mail transport agents* (MTAs), which send new email messages to their destination machines, and *mail delivery agents* (MDAs), which send mail that's landed in a user's mailbox to that user's personal computer.

Mail Transport Agents (Postfix)

A mail transport agent sends email to other computers, most often via the SMTP protocol. Mac OS X ships with Postfix, an improved alternative to the more common *sendmail* program that shipped with versions of Mac OS X before Panther.

 Run Postfix only if you need to provide mail-sending services to yourself or your network. You don't need to run this service to simply send email as long as there is an SMTP server that will accept connections from your machine; most ISPs provide mail services on their own servers, for example. Try sending through *mail. yourispname.com* and see.

Using Postfix

You can configure Postfix to work in two ways on your machine. The first, as a local mailer, allows you to send and receive local messages, as well as send messages to external Internet addresses. This mode is useful for receiving the regular *cron* reports that get sent to *root*, for allowing scripts to send mail, and for sending quick messages from the command line using the *mail* command.

Postfix can also run as a standalone mail server, able to exchange mail with other servers on the Internet. Even if you don't need to run your own full-fledged mail server, this mode lets you use your regular GUI email client and send mail directly from your Mac to any Internet address, eliminating the need for you to first relay your mail through an external SMTP server. This option can be very helpful when, for whatever reasons, your ISP's server becomes unreachable.

Configuring a local mailer

By default, Mac OS X runs a program called *master* that monitors the outgoing mail queue and runs Postfix on the queue as needed. This daemon is controlled by the *launchd* script */System/Library/LaunchDaemons/org.postfix.master.plist*. Without any configuration, Tiger lets you send local mail. To confirm, try sending a message to yourself:

```
MacChuck:~ chuck$ mail chuck
Subject: Test
Testing...1, 2, 3
.
EOT
MacChuck:~ chuck$
```

Check local mail using the *mail* command by itself:

```
MacChuck:~ chuck$ mail
Mail version 8.1 6/6/93.  Type ? for help.
"/var/mail/chuck": 1 message 1 new
>N  1 chuck@dhcp-172-24-31  Tue Aug  2 10:21  14/566   "Test"
& [RETURN]
Message 1:
From chuck@dhcp-172-24-31-10.west.ora.com  Tue Aug  2 10:21:48 2005
X-Original-To: chuck
Delivered-To: chuck@dhcp-172-24-31-10.west.ora.com
To: chuck@dhcp-172-24-31-10.west.ora.com
Subject: Test
Date: Tue,  2 Aug 2005 10:21:47 -0700 (PDT)
From: chuck@dhcp-172-24-31-10.west.ora.com (Chuck Toporek)

Testing...1, 2, 3

& q
Saved 1 message in mbox
dhcp-172-24-31-10:~ chuck$
```

However, even with local mail working, you might still have a problem passing mail to other mail servers because most require that any incoming messages be from a valid domain (one whose name resolves to an IP number). If a valid domain isn't part of your machine's hostname, you need to specify one (your ISP's, for example) in the Postfix configuration file, */etc/postfix/main.cf*. Depending on your situation, you'll need to define up to three parameters. Find each in *main.cf*, and uncomment their lines (remove the #s) before replacing the values with your own:

#myhostname = host.domain.tld

> This parameter identifies your machine to other servers. The full hostname doesn't have to be resolvable, but its domain does (e.g., *domain.tld*). You'll need to define at least this parameter.

#mydomain = domain.tld

> This parameter identifies the domain you're sending from, which must be resolvable. You need to define this parameter only if you're defining *myorigin* as well.

#myorigin = *$mydomain*

> This parameter serves two purposes. It's used in the *from* header of outgoing messages as the domain part of the sender's address, and it also gets appended to any recipient address that has no domain specified. For the second reason, then, any mail locally addressed to a simple username, such as root, is sent to root@*myorigin* and not the local root account.

> If you use Postfix as more than just a local mailer, and this is the desired behavior, specify a resolvable domain name for *myorigin*. (In most cases, this value is the same used for *mydomain*, so you can instead use *$mydomain* as the value for *myorigin*.)

> If, on the other hand, you want locally addressed mail to stay local, don't define this parameter, and Postfix will use the value set for *myhostname* in the outgoing *from* headers. In that case, you should use only a domain name, and not a full hostname, for *myhostname*'s value.

If you've made your changes while Postfix is running, execute the command postfix reload as root, and the changes will take effect without interrupting mail services.

Chapter 2 contains a list of Postfix's command-line arguments. If you need to customize your Mac's Postfix setup, you should read a good reference book on the topic, such as *Postfix: The Definitive Guide* (O'Reilly) or the online materials found at *http://www.postfix.com*.

 During installation of Tiger, a script is supposed to run that creates the user accounts required by several system daemons, including Postfix. If you've performed an upgrade to Tiger, however, it's possible that this didn't happen, so starting Postfix will fail with an unknown user error. You can easily fix this by running the script manually as root. You'll find the script at */Library/Receipts/Essentials.pkg/Contents/Resources/CreateSystemUsers*.

Configuring a mail server

Once you have Postfix running as a local mailer, you can then configure it to operate as a standalone mail server, which requires the services of the SMTP daemon, *smtpd*. As a security precaution, Postfix is configured by default with *smtpd* disabled so it won't accept incoming mail. However, it's not difficult to enable *smtpd* so Postfix can at least relay messages from a local email client.

To do this, first modify the file */etc/hostconfig* so the line `MAILSERVER=-AUTOMATIC-` instead reads `MAILSERVER=-YES-`. This ensures that Postfix is running at all times to accept mail. Next, uncomment this line from */etc/postfix/master.cf*:

```
#smtpinetn -  n  -  -smtpd
```

You can then start Postfix by running `/System/Library/StartupItems/Postfix/ Postfix start` as *root* (or using `restart` if Postfix is already running).

Finally, configure your email client (including Apple's Mail application, Microsoft's Entourage, and Qualcomm's Eudora) to use either `localhost` or `127. 0.0.1` as its SMTP server. Once you do, Postfix will deliver outgoing mail from your Mac directly to your recipients' servers.

By default, Postfix is configured to accept only local connections, so you still won't be able to receive mail from the network. Allowing this involves changing the `inet_ interfaces` and `mynetworks_style` parameters in *main.cf*. There are several ways to do this, and security considerations are involved as well, so you should have a strong understanding of the issues before putting a mail server on the network. The Postfix references mentioned previously are a good place to start.

Mail Delivery Agents

Most email users don't read mail directly from their mailhosts; instead, they download their mail from the host to their personal computers. A daemon running on the mailhost called a Mail Delivery Agent (MDA) facilitates this by supporting a mail-delivery protocol, and individual mail clients (Apple's Mail, for example) connect to this service to check for and download new messages.

The two most common MDA protocols are the Post Office Protocol (POP) and the Internet Message Access Protocol (IMAP). POP, the older and more commonly supported of the two, comprises a very simple command set, allowing users to do little besides download their mail and delete it from the server. IMAP represents a newer and more sophisticated protocol that lets users store and organize all their mail on the server-side. This offers much greater convenience to users, but at the cost of more server resources; consider using the *quota* command (see Chapter 2) to set users' storage capacities if you support IMAP.

Unfortunately, Mac OS X ships with neither *popd* nor *imapd*, the daemons that give you POP and IMAP services, respectively. You can cover both these bases by installing the UW IMAP server, available as a source code tarball (*http://www. washington.edu/imap/*).

If you would like to forgo compiling UW IMAP altogether, a shareware utility exists that provides a simple GUI interface allowing you to easily enable Postfix as well as the UW IMAP and POP services. Postfix Enabler is available from *http:// www.cutedgesystems.com/software/PostfixEnabler/*.

Web Services

Mac OS X comes with Apache, an open source web server responsible for more than half of all the Internet's web sites.[*] At its most basic level, Apache runs as a daemon named *httpd* that supports the Hypertext Transfer Protocol (HTTP); it listens to web surfers' requests (on port 80, by default) and replies with response codes and web pages.

Apache Configuration

Apache's configuration information lies in the */etc/httpd* directory, mainly in the file */etc/httpd/httpd.conf*. This file sets up options through lists of directives and values, often mapped to filesystem directories and other criteria. Many of its options are highly specific to Mac OS X, so that Apache works "out of the box"; turning on web services with a single click in the Sharing pane (see the earlier section "Running Services Through the Sharing Pane") launches a full-featured web server on a fresh Mac OS X installation. Here are some highlights (and variances from the defaults that are in a platform-independent Apache installation):

- The DirectoryRoot directive defines the location of the server's default location for HTML files and other web-servable documents—in other words, what you'd see if you pointed your web browser to *http://localhost/*. Mac OS X sets this directive to */Library/WebServer/Documents/*.

- Following the usual Unix tradition, Mac OS X Apache lets a host's individual users build personal web sites in their own home folders, accessible by pointing a web browser to *http://network_address/~username*. To find your network address, go to the Sharing preferences panel, as shown in Figure 11-1. Most Unix systems define users' personal document roots at *~username/public_ html*; Mac OS X Apache sets it to *~username/Sites*.

- An Include directive at the bottom of the file reads in several additional Apache configuration files located in */etc/httpd/users/*. One *username.conf* file exists for every user created through the Accounts pane. Each one defines Apache options and directives for serving that user's */Sites* folder over the Web, thus allowing an administrator to set different options on different users' personal web sites.

- Apache keeps two log files, *access_log* and *error_log*, in the */var/log/httpd/* directory. The *access_log* file keeps a record of the files served (graphics, web pages, etc.) and to whom the files were served by displaying the IP address of the machine that accessed the server. The *error_log* file reports any errors, such as from people who have attempted to access a file on the web server that doesn't exist. If anything is ever wrong with your web pages or web serving, this file is the first place to check for problems.

---

[*] Netcraft tracks the changing popularity levels of Apache and other web servers on its web site at *http://www.netcraft.com/survey/*.

Apache Modules

Apache modules are code libraries that extend Apache's abilities beyond funda-mental HTTP serving. Apache lets you install modules two ways: *static* modules are "baked in" to the *httpd* program at compile time, while *dynamic* modules are separate files that *httpd* can load and include into its functionality without any recompiling needed.

Mac OS X's Apache setup uses the latter of these strategies. To enable an existing but inactive module, simply locate the LoadModule and AddModule directives within */etc/httpd/httpd.conf* and remove the # characters from the start of both lines, turning the lines from comments into actual directives. To disable an active module, just insert a # at the start of both lines, commenting them out; then restart the web server.

To install new modules, place their *.so* files (compiling them first, if necessary) into the */usr/libexec/httpd/* directory, and then add new LoadModule and AddModule lines to */etc/httpd/httpd.conf*.

File Transfer Protocol (FTP)

FTP services run courtesy of the *ftpd* daemon. It allows the machine's users to remotely access the filesystem, so that they can browse directory listings and transfer files to and from the machine. Normally, it obeys the filesystem permis-sions just as a login shell does. However, if you would like to restrict FTP users' access to their respective home directories, simply add the users' names, one per line, to a file named *ftpchroot* and, as root, save it in */etc*.

Enabling Anonymous FTP

First, as described in Chapter 10, use NetInfo Manager to create a group named *ftp*, making sure to give it an unused GID. Next, use NetInfo Manager again to create a nonhuman user also named *ftp*, under which all-anonymous FTP activity will occur. For consistency, use the same number you specified for the *ftp* group's GID as this new account's UID, again making sure that it's not already being used by another account.

Create a home directory for *ftp*. (Be sure that *ftp*'s NetInfo directory correctly refers to this directory as its home.) Whether or not an */etc/ftpchroot* file exists, the FTP server always forbids an anonymous user from accessing anywhere in the filesystem outside the *ftp* user's Home directory.

You can now populate this directory with whatever you wish to permit anony-mous users to browse and download. To make a typical FTP site, add a *pub/* folder containing all the downloadables, as well as an introductory blurb in an *ftpwelcome* file in */etc*; upon connection, the FTP server provides the contents of that file to the FTP client to display or record in the session transcript.

For security's sake, consider changing the ownership of all these files and folders to root using the *chown* command and using *chmod* to make them read-only for all users. This will prevent anonymous FTP users from uploading (and perhaps overwriting) files as well as keep the directory safe from tampering by local users. (A */pub/incoming* directory, writeable by the FTP user, is the typical spot for anonymous file uploads, if you'd like to allow that to a limited degree.)

Remote Login Services

There may come a time when you need to log into your Mac from another machine or log into another Mac (or Unix system) from your machine. For this, Mac OS X offers remote login services such as the Secure Shell, Telnet, and the remote shell.

The Secure Shell

The Secure Shell (SSH) is a protocol for using key-based encryption to allow secure communication between machines. As its name suggests, it is most commonly used for interactive sessions with shells on remote machines, so that you can use the *ssh* command.

Mac OS X ships with the OpenSSH (*http://www.openssh.com*) client and server software. This includes the *ssh* command, which you use to open SSH connections to other machines, and the *sshd* daemon program, which you run to allow other machines to SSH into your Mac.

As with FTP (see the earlier section "File Transfer Protocol (FTP)"), running an SSH service (the *sshd* daemon) on Mac OS X is easy: just activate the Remote Login checkbox in the Sharing pane.

Telnet

Mac OS X versions prior to 10.1.0 shipped with *telnetd*, a daemon that runs the Telnet protocol, as its default remote login server. Telnet is a decades-old method for getting a virtual terminal on a remote machine through a network. However, it's inherently insecure, because all its transmissions are *cleartext*, lacking any sort of encryption, and hence easily readable by malevolent entities monitoring the traffic that enters and leaves your network. Use of Telnet has, in recent years, fallen out of favor for Internet-based remote logins now that such tools as SSH are freely available.

If you must, you can run *telnetd* on your Mac OS X machine. You'll find it in */usr/libexec/telnetd* but won't be able to launch it directly from there. *telnetd* is one of several network services, including *ftpd* and *sshd*, controlled by the super-server process *xinetd*, which listens on the network for service requests and launches the proper daemon on-demand. The easiest way to have *xinetd* begin passing Telnet requests to *telnetd* is to run the *service* command (a script, actually) as root:

```
sudo service telnet start
```

This command modifies the proper *xinet.d* file (*/etc/xinet.d/telnet*) to enable Telnet services and then force *xinetd* to re-read its configuration files. Once the command is performed, any incoming Telnet requests will cause *telnetd* to launch and receive that connection. To turn this off, simply run the similar command:

```
sudo service telnet stop
```

If you do enable *telnetd*, consider carefully configuring your firewall to allow Telnet connections only from other machines on the local subnetwork. Incoming Telnet traffic from the global Internet can be snooped by outside eavesdroppers, even if connections are limited to trusted machines. Logging into a machine through Telnet is tantamount to shouting your password across a crowded roomful of strangers so that your friend down the hall can hear it. Whenever possible, use *ssh* instead of *telnet*.

The Remote Shell

The *remote shell*, or RSH, is used to issue commands on another system. The *rsh* command allows you to quickly log in and execute a command on a remote host; however, like Telnet, *rsh* is insecure and has been disabled under Mac OS X. You should use SSH instead for remote access to other machines.

File Sharing Services

Mac OS X's native file-sharing method is the Apple Filing Protocol (AFP). As with related technologies such as SMB and NFS, it lets users of other computers (often, but not necessarily, other Macs) mount volumes of your local filesystem onto their own.

Both the command-line and GUI interfaces for administering AFP are very simple. To turn on AFP, activate the Personal File Sharing checkbox in the Sharing preference pane's Services tab. This simply launches the *AppleFileServer* daemon (which resides in */usr/sbin*). *AppleFileServer* takes no arguments; it makes all your machine's volumes and User folders available for mounting on other computers. The program stores its configuration information (including the location of log files, whether it allows Guest access, and so on) in the */Library/Preferences/com. apple.AppleFileServer.plist* file.

Toggling this checkbox in the Sharing pane also modifies the AFPSERVER line in */etc/hostconfig*, read by the startup script */System/Library /StartupItems/ AppleShare/AppleShare* (see the next section).

The AFP server handles user authentication through Directory Services, in most cases referring to NetInfo for the list of volumes it's allowed to provide to the requesting user. This list, of course, varies depending on the type of account that user has on the server.

Users with no accounts can log in as Guest and are allowed only to mount the Public directories (as defined by the sharedDir property of each user's NetInfo record) within each home directory on the server. Once the volume is mounted, its permission system applies just as if that same user were logged into the machine and accessing the filesystem directly. Therefore, guest users can copy items from Public and add items to */Public/Drop Box*, as those items' Unix permissions dictate.

Users with Standard accounts on the server can also access the Public folders of the other user accounts, and additionally have access to their own entire home directories. Users with Admin accounts can choose to mount not only their own entire home directory but also any physical partition or mounted volume on the server.

You can specify additional share points by adding a SharePoints subdirectory to the */config* directory in NetInfo and for each share point creating a subdirectory to it with these properties:

Name
> Label for the NetInfo subdirectory.

afp_name
> Label to identify the share point on the network.

directory_path
> Absolute path to the local directory to be shared.

afp_shared
> Use a value of 1 to turn on sharing for the share point or 0 to turn it off.

afp_use_parent_owner
> Switches whether items added to the shared directory should inherit their owner and group properties from the parent directory (use a value of 1) or maintain the default behavior of inheriting ownership from the user (use a value of 0).

afp_use_parent_privs
> Switches whether items added to the shared directory should inherit their permissions from the parent directory (use a value of 1), or maintain the default behavior of giving read/write permissions to the owner and read-only permissions to everyone else (use a value of 0).

You can allow or disallow guest access to the share point by adjusting those permissions locally on the shared directory. Stop and restart Personal File Sharing once you've configured the share point to make it available. Note that Admin users will not see these share points listed when connecting since they already can access all directories on the server.

If you prefer the convenience of an all-in-one GUI application, the donation-ware utility SharePoints (*http://www.hornware.com/sharepoints*) makes adding share points quick and easy.

Daemon Management

Panther relies on the services of a large number of system daemons for its operation, and every network service you enable adds to the count of potential background processes. While it would be easiest to simply have all the daemons launch at startup, it's much more efficient to do this for just the handful that require it and launch the other daemons only as needed. To coordinate this complex task, Tiger uses three mechanisms: *bootstrap daemons*, *StartupItems*, and *launchd*.

Bootstrap Daemons

Introduced with Panther, the *register_mach_bootstrap_servers* tool, provides a way to have system daemons launch on demand (that is, not until they receive their first service request). In fact, this method will eventually take the place of the *StartupItems* (see the following section) as Mac OS X evolves in future releases.

This tool assembles a list of daemons by reading each file in */etc/mach_init.d/* (for system daemons to be run as root) and */etc/mach_init_per_user.d/* (for user daemons to be run under normal user accounts). It then registers each daemon in the list and the service it provides with the *mach_init* daemon, itself launched by the Mach kernel early in the startup.

Once a daemon is registered, *mach_init* waits for requests from other processes for the services the daemon provides, launching (or relaunching) the daemon only when it detects a request. Such daemons, available to the system so early in the startup process, are known as *bootstrap daemons*. For now, only about a dozen system daemons are handled this way, none of which are network services.

StartupItems

The second mechanism, though now legacy, is still responsible for starting many system and network daemons. During system startup, the *SystemStarter* application scans and runs special scripts kept in */Library/StartupItems/*. If you've installed a daemon yourself and wish to have it launch at startup and be owned by the root user (so that it is running when the first user logs in, and continues to run until the machine is shut down or it's explicitly killed), add another item to this collection of startup items or copy or modify an existing one, if applicable. (More startup scripts are in */System/Library/StartupItems/*, but, like everything else in the */System/* folder, are not meant to be messed with.)

Each object under *StartupItems* is a folder named after its function. Inside it are two important files: a parameter list of options in *StartupParameters.plist* and the script itself, which must have the same name as the folder.

Example 11-1 shows a simplified version of the contents of the Apache startup item (*/System/Library/StartupItems/Apache /Apache*).

Example 11-1. The Apache startup item, simplified

```
[1] #!/bin/sh

    ##
    # Apache HTTP Server
    ##

[2] /etc/rc.common

[4] StartService ()
    {
        if [ "${WEBSERVER:=-NO-}" = "-YES-" ]; then
            echo "Starting Apache web server"
            if [ ! -e /etc/httpd/httpd.conf ] ; then
                cp -p /etc/httpd/httpd.conf.default /etc/httpd/httpd.conf
```

Example 11-1. The Apache startup item, simplified (continued)

```
            fi
            apachectl start
        fi
    }

[5] StopService ( )
    {
        echo "Stopping Apache web server"
        apachectl stop
    }

[6] RestartService ( )
    {
        if [ "${WEBSERVER:=-NO-}" = "-YES-" ]; then
            echo "Restarting Apache web server"
            apachectl restart
        else
            StopService
        fi
    }

[3] RunService "$1"
```

Here's what it does, in order:

1. The "shebang" line (#!/bin/sh) marks this file as a shell script.

2. It uses the shell's dot command (.) to execute the shell script at */etc/rc.common*. This script sets up many environment variables useful to startup scripts.

3. The script's next command actually comes with this last line, which calls one of the three functions* found in the preceding lines. The RunService command calls a function (defined by *rc.common*) that tells the script which of its own three functions to call next, based on the argument provided with this script's execution command. Possible arguments are start, stop, or restart.

4. If the argument is start, the script then knows to execute its StartService( ) function, which determines what to do next based on what's in the WEBSERVER environment variable (set by *rc.common*, after it reads the */etc/hostconfig* file). If its value is -YES-, it dumps a status message to the console (which passes it along to the startup screen) and executes the *apachectl start* command.

5. If the argument is stop, the script executes its StopService ( ) function, which dumps a status message and stops Apache.

6. If the argument is restart, the script executes its RestartService ( ) function. If WEBSERVER's value is -YES-, a status message displays, and Postfix is told to re-read its configuration. Otherwise, the StopService function is executed.

---

* A function is a chunk of code, defined here within curly braces, that works like a script-within-a-script. Functions are read and stored in memory as the script is executed, but aren't themselves executed unless called by name elsewhere in the same script or from within a different script.

Manually running StartupItems

Much like their counterparts, the */etc/rc.init* scripts found on Linux and BSD systems, *StartupItems* can also be run on the command line. When available, it's generally a better idea to use a daemon's *StartupItems* rather than invoke it directly (i.e., by using */System/Library/StartupItems/Apache/Apache* instead of directly calling */usr/sbin/apachectl*) because the script is "safer"; it ensures that the machine's software and network environment is set up correctly for the daemon's use.

Typically, you must run *StartupItems* as *root* (or under the auspices of the *sudo* command), and, as with the Postfix *StartupItem*, provide one of three standard arguments:

start
> Launch the service this *StartupItem* represents. It usually fails if it's already running.

stop
> Kill this service.

restart
> Equivalent to stop-ing and then start-ing the service; often it actually sends a HUP (hang-up) signal to the service's process. This causes it to reread its configuration files and act appropriately, allowing it to reconfigure itself without suffering any downtime.

The /etc/hostconfig file

Many *StartupItems* (like the one for Apache) must make a choice about whether they're supposed to perform their stated function. If you don't want your machine to run as a web server, for example, then you won't want the Apache startup script to launch the *httpd* daemon. You could modify or remove the */System/Library/StartupItems/Apache* folder, but that's a messy solution that would probably lead to confusion if you (or, worse, another administrator on the machine) want to activate Apache later on.

A better solution, and the one that Mac OS X intends you to use, involves modifying the */etc/hostconfig* file. This file, which is nothing more than a newline-separated list of key/value pairs (as well as a few comments), is loaded by */etc/rc. common*, a shell script which itself is run as an initial step by most startup scripts. This means that all the variables it sets become accessible to scripts that load *rc. common*, such as the Apache startup item. Thus, if you simply set *hostconfig*'s WEBSERVER key to -NO-, the Apache startup script deduces that you don't want web services activated on startup and quietly exits rather than launch the *httpd* daemon. (This is, in fact, exactly what happens when you deactivate the Sharing preference pane's Personal Web Sharing checkbox. Many other System Preferences controls can also modify lines in */etc/hostconfig*.

StartupParameters.plist

The *StartupParameters.plist* file (an example of a property list XML file, detailed in Chapter 13) can contain the following keys:

Description
> A brief description of this startup item's function, such as "Apache web server."

Provides
> A list of keywords that name the services this startup item provides, when run.

Requires
> A list of keywords that name the services that must already be running before this startup item can be launched.

Uses
> A list of keywords that names the services this startup item could use, but doesn't absolutely require.

Messages
> A dictionary of status messages that get sent to the console (and the startup screen, if it's visible) when the startup item starts or stops.

OrderPreference
> For cases in which the Requires and Uses keys specify the same startup order for multiple items, this key specifies in a relative way when the startup item should launch. Possible values are First, Early, None, Late, and Last.

The *SystemStarter* program determines the order in which to run all the system's startup items by scanning their *StartupParameters.plist* files and comparing the values of their Provides, Requires, Uses, and OrderPreference keys. It then determines which items will provide other items' Required service; those run first, so that later items' prerequisites will be met.

launchd

Mac OS X Tiger introduces the latest and greatest startup scheme, *launchd*. It has launch-on-demand capabilities and also supports on-demand launching via Mach ports (as does the *mach_init.d* scheme). *launchd* also offers the ability to launch on demand based on file system and Unix domain socket events. The property list (*.plist*) files for system-installed daemons are in */System/Library/LaunchDaemons*. Locally-installed daemons can be installed into */Library/LaunchDaemons*. Table 11-1 lists and describes the system-installed daemons, most of which have counterparts in Linux and Unix systems.

You can control launch daemons with the *launchctl* utility. For example, to enable and load a daemon that's disabled (there will be a Disabled key in its property list file), use launchctl load -w followed by the path to the property list. For example, the following command would be enabled and start the telnet server:

```
# launchctl load -w /System/Library/LaunchDaemons/telnet.plist
```

You can stop and disable this daemon with unload -w:

```
# launchctl unload -w /System/Library/LaunchDaemons/telnet.plist
```

For more information, see *launchctl* in Chapter 2, or the *launchctl* manpage.

Table 11-1. Default Mac OS X launch daemons

Property List File	Description	Enabled by default?
bootps.plist	Starts the DHCP/BOOTP daemon.	No
com.apple.atrun.plist	Launches the *atrun* daemon.	Yes
com.apple.KernelEventAgent.plist	Runs the kernel event agent, which responds to low-level kernel events (such as disk and network events).	Yes
com.apple.mDNSResponder.plist	Starts the Multicast DNS responder, needed by Bonjour.	Yes
com.apple.nibindd.plist	Launches the NetInfo binder daemon.	Yes
com.apple.periodic-daily.plist	Runs the daily *periodic* job.	Yes
com.apple.periodic-monthly.plist	Runs the monthly *periodic* job.	Yes
com.apple.periodic-weekly.plist	Runs the weekly *periodic* job.	Yes
com.apple.portmap.plist	Starts the portmapper.	Yes
com.apple.syslogd.plist	Launches the system log daemon.	Yes
com.apple.xgridagentd.plist	Runs the Xgrid agent.	No
com.apple.xgridcontrollerd.plist	Runs the Xgrid controller.	No
com.vix.cron.plist	Starts the *cron* daemon.	Yes
eppc.plist	Runs the Apple Events server.	No
exec.plist	Starts *rexecd*, the remote execution server.	No
finger.plist	Launches the finger daemon.	No
ftp.plist	Starts the FTP server.	No
login.plist	Starts the remote login (*rlogin*) daemon.	No
nmbd.plist	Launches Samba's *nmbd* daemon.	No
ntalk.plist	Starts the *ntalk* daemon.	No
org.isc.named.plist	Runs *named*.	No
org.postfix.master.plist	Launches the postfix master process.	Yes
org.xinetd.xinetd.plist	Starts the Internet superserver (*xinetd*) (see xinetd below).	Yes
printer.plist	Starts the CUPS *lpd* server.	No
shell.plist	Starts the remote shell daemon (*rshd*).	No
smbd.plist	Launches Samba's *smbd* daemon.	No
ssh.plist	Starts the SSH server.	No
swat.plist	Runs the Samba Web Administration Tool.	No
telnet.plist	Launches the telnet server.	No
tftp.plist	Starts the Trivial FTP server daemon.	No

xinetd

xinetd, the extended Internet services daemon, is responsible for launching several of Mac OS X's Internet and other IP-based daemons, including *sshd* (for secure shell services), *ftpd* (for FTP services), and *smbd* (for Windows filesharing and printing services). As you can see by looking at the *IPServices* startup script, *xinetd* itself is actually one of the daemons launched by *SystemStarter*.

Also called a *super-server*, *xinetd* launches daemons on-demand, much like *mach_init*. Super-servers—including *xinetd* or its simpler predecessor, *inetd*—are found on most other Unix-like platforms. *xinetd* determines which daemons it's responsible for by reading the files, each named for a service, in */etc/xinetd.d/*. Each file defines a service and series of attributes, including `disable`, which defines whether the service is disabled or not, and `server`, which specifies the daemon to launch when that service is enabled and requested.

Enabling a *xinetd* service typically means setting that service's `disable` attribute to `no` and sending *xinetd* a *kill -HUP* signal so it will reload its configuration files. This can of course be done manually with a text editor, but two easier methods exist that make that rarely necessary. First, for the following items the Sharing preference pane does all you need: Windows Sharing, Remote Login, FTP Access, and Remote Apple Events, since they are all controlled by *xinetd*.

For any other items in */etc/xinetd.d/*, you can use the *service* command, as shown previously in the *telnet* section. To stop or start a service, the command must be run as *root* and takes two arguments: the service name and an action, either `start` or `stop`. To list all *xinetd*-controlled items, run `service --list` as any user.

12

The X Window System

Although the X in "Mac OS X" is not the same X as in "The X Window System," you can get them to play nice together.

Most Unix systems use the X Window System as their default GUI. (We'll refer to the X Window System as X11 instead of X, to avoid confusion with Mac OS X.) X11 includes development tools and libraries for creating graphical applications for Unix-based systems. Mac OS X does not use X11 as its GUI, relying instead on Quartz (and, on compatible hardware, Quartz Extreme), a completely different graphics system. However, Apple's own implementation of X11 for Mac OS X, based on the open source XFree86 Project's X11 (*http://www.xfree86.org*), was initially released as a beta for Jaguar and is bundled with Mac OS X Tiger as an optional installation. Apple also provides an X11 software development kit (the X11 SDK) as an optional installation with Xcode, which is located in the Xcode Tools folder on the Mac OS X Tiger Installation DVD.

This chapter highlights some of the key features of Apple's X11 distribution and explains how to install Apple's X11 and the X11 SDK. It also explains how to use X11 in both rootless and full-screen modes (using the GNOME and KDE desktops). You'll also learn how to connect to other X Window systems using Virtual Network Computing (VNC), as well as how to remotely control the Mac OS X Aqua desktop from other X11 systems.

From Aqua to X11, there's no shortage of graphical environments for Mac OS X. The operating system's solid Unix underpinnings and powerful graphics subsystem make it possible for developers to support alternative graphical environments. For this reason, a humble iBook can make a fine cockpit for a network of heterogeneous machines!

About Apple's X11

As noted earlier, Apple's X11 distribution is based on the open source XFree86 Project's XFree86, Version 4.4. The X11 package has been optimized for Mac OS X and has the following features:

- X11R6.6 window server.
- Support for the RandR (Resize and Rotate) extension.
- Strong integration with Mac OS X environment.
- A Quartz window manager that provides Aqua window decorations, ability to minimize windows to the Dock, and pasteboard integration.
- Can use other window managers.
- Compatible with Exposé.
- Supports rootless and full-screen modes.
- A customizable Application menu, which allows you to add applications for easy launching and to map keyboard shortcuts.
- A customizable Dock menu, which allows you to add applications for easy launching, to map keyboard shortcuts, and to list all open windows.
- Finder integration, which supports auto-detection of X11 binaries and double-clicking to launch X11 binaries, starting the X server if it is not already running.
- Preference settings for system color map, key equivalents, system alerts, keyboard mapping, and multi-button mouse emulation.
- Hardware acceleration support for OpenGL (GLX) and Direct CG (AIPI).

Installing X11

Apple's X11 for Mac OS X is available as an optional installation bundled with Mac OS X. To install it when you first install Mac OS X Tiger (or upgrade an existing installation), you must customize the installation (in the Selection Type phase) and select the X11 checkbox. If you don't install X11 during the Mac OS X installation, you can install it later by inserting the Install Mac OS X DVD, then double-clicking the *System* folder, followed by the *Installation* folder, and then the *Packages* folder. Here you'll find the *X11User.pkg* package, which you must also double-click to start the installation process.

The installation places the double-clickable X11 application in the */Applications/ Utilities* folder. If you're going to build X11-based applications, you'll need to install the Xcode Tools, which installs X11SDK by default. To install Xcode Tools along with X11SDK, insert the Mac OS X Install DVD, and double-click the Xcode Tools folder to find XcodeTools.mpkg, which you must double-click to begin the installation process.

If you don't install X11SDK when you install Xcode Tools, you can install it later by once again inserting the Mac OS X Install DVD, double-clicking the Xcode Tools folder, followed by the Packages folder, where you will find the X11SDK.

pkg installer. Double-click the *X11SDK.pkg* installer to begin the installation of X11SDK. This chapter simply focuses on using X11.

The *X11User.pkg* can be downloaded from *http://www.apple.com/ macosx/features/x11/download*, while Xcode Tools can be downloaded from the Apple Developer Connection located at *http:// developer.apple.com*.

Running X11

X11 can be run in two modes, *full screen* or *rootless* (the default). Both of these modes run side-by-side with Aqua, although full-screen mode hides the Finder and Mac OS X's desktop. (To hide X11 and return to the Finder, press Option-⌘-A.)

To launch the X server, double-click the X11 application (in */Applications/ Utilities*). An *xterm* window (which looks similar to a Mac OS X Terminal window) opens, sporting Aqua-like buttons for closing, minimizing, and maximizing the window. Also, X11 windows minimize to the Dock, just like other Aqua windows. Figure 12-1 shows a Terminal window and an *xterm* window side-by-side.

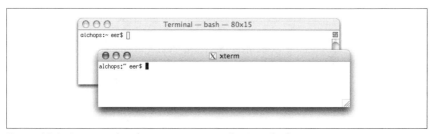

Figure 12-1. A Terminal and an xterm sporting the Aqua look

If you're using the default configuration, you'll also notice three obvious differences from a Terminal window. In particular:

- The *xterm* window has a titlebar that reads "xterm"
- The *xterm* window does not have vertical and/or horizontal scrollbars
- The *xterm* window does not have a split window option

A less obvious difference between a Terminal window and an X11 *xterm* window is that Control-clicking (or right-clicking) in an *xterm* window does not invoke the same contextual menu that it does in a Terminal window. Control-clicking, Control-Option-clicking, and Control-⌘-clicking in an *xterm* invokes *xterm*-specific contextual menus, as shown in Figures 12-2, 12-3, and 12-4. If you have a three-button mouse, Control-clicking with the right mouse button does the same thing as Control-⌘-clicking; Control-clicking with the middle button does the same thing as Control-Option-clicking.

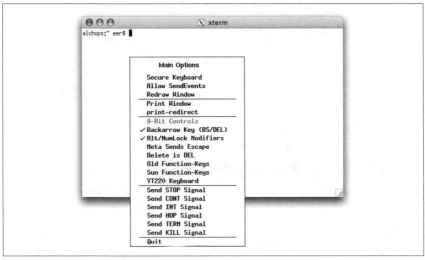

Figure 12-2. Control-click (or Control-left-click) in an xterm window

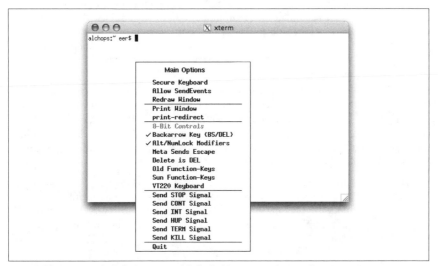

Figure 12-3. Control-click (or Control-left-click) in an xterm window

 You can use Fink to install an *xterm* replacement such as *rxvt* or *eterm*. For more information about Fink, see *http://fink.sourceforge.net*.

The X Window System

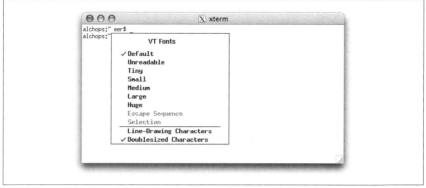

Figure 12-4. Control-⌘-click (or Control-right-click) in an xterm window

Mac OS X emulates right-mouse clicks with Control-click. In X11, you can configure key combinations that simulate two- and three-button mice.

By default, Option-click simulates the middle mouse button, and ⌘-click simulates the right mouse button. You can use X11 → Preferences to enable or disable this, but you cannot change which key combinations are used (although you can use *xmodmap* as you would under any other X11 system to remap pointer buttons).

In rootless mode, X11 applications take up their own window on your Mac OS X desktop. In full-screen mode, X11 takes over the entire screen and is suitable for running an X11 desktop environment (DTE) like GNOME, KDE, or Xfce. If you want to run X11 in full-screen mode, you'll have to enable this mode in the X11's preferences by clicking the Output tab and selecting the full-screen mode checkbox.

You can still access your Mac OS X desktop while in full-screen mode by pressing Option-⌘-A. To go back to the X11 desktop, click on the X11 icon in the Dock or use ⌘-Tab and then press Option-⌘-A.

Customizing X11

There are a number of things you can customize in X11. For example, you can customize your *xterm* window, set X11 application preferences, customize the X11 application and Dock menus, and specify which window manager to use.

Dot-files, Desktops, and Window Managers

To customize X11, you can create an *.xinitrc* script in your Home directory. A sample *.xinitrc* script is provided in */etc/X11/xinit/xinitrc*.

Using the script as a starting point, you can specify which X11-based applications to start when X11 is launched, including which window manager you'd like to use as your default. The default window manager for X11 is the Quartz window manager (or *quartz-wm*). The tab window manager (or *twm*) is also bundled with X11, but many other window managers are available. You can visit the following web sites to get instructions and binaries for a wide variety of window managers and DTEs:

Fink
> *http://fink.sourceforge.net*

DarwinPorts
> *http://darwinports.opendarwin.org*

GNU-Darwin
> *http://gnu-darwin.sourceforge.net*

OroborOSX
> *http://oroborosx.sourceforge.net*

If you're going to use your own *.xinitrc* file and want to use the Quartz window manager, make sure you start the Quartz window manager with the command:

```
exec /usr/X11R6/bin/quartz-wm
```

Once you've installed X11, you'll probably want to install additional X11 applications, window managers, and perhaps other DTEs. (Even if you are using Apple's window manager, you can still run most binaries from other DTEs, such as GNOME and KDE, without using that DTE as your desktop.) One of the easiest ways to install additional window managers is to use Fink. Table 12-1 lists some of the window managers and desktops offered by Fink.

Table 12-1. Window managers available for Fink

Window manager/desktop	Fink package name
Blackbox	Blackbox
Enlightenment	enlightenment
FVWM	fvwm, fvwm2
GNOME	bundle-gnome
IceWM	Icewm
KDE	bundle-kde
mwm	Lesstif
Oroborus	Oroborus, oroborus2
PWM	Pwm
Sawfish	Sawfish
Window Maker	windowmaker
XFce	Xfce

Fink has entire sections (*http://fink.sourceforge.net/pdb/sections.php*) devoted to GNOME and KDE, where you will find an extensive set of libraries, utilities, and plug-ins. Also included in the GNOME section are GTK+, *glib*, and Glade.

Installing GNOME and KDE may be especially useful if you want to develop software for these desktops.

Fink installs everything in its */sw* directory. So, for example, if you've installed *lesstif* and want to use the *mwm* window manager, you must include */sw/bin* in your path, or include /sw/bin/mwm & in your .xinitrc file to start the Motif window manager. However, if you've installed Fink according to its instructions, */sw/bin* is automatically added to your command path.

You can customize the *xterm* window in Apple's X11 in the same way you would customize *xterm* on any other system running X11. You can, for example, set resources in an *.Xdefaults* file in your home directory or use escape sequences to set the title bar.

X11 Preferences, Application Menu, and Dock Menu

You can also customize your X11 environment by setting X11's preferences via the X11 → Preferences window (⌘-,) and adding programs to its Application menu. X11's preferences are organized into two categories: Input and Output. The X11 preferences have the following options:

Input

The following options are used for controlling how X11 interacts with input devices:

Emulate three-button mouse
> Determines whether Option-click and ⌘-click mimic the middle and right buttons.

Use the system keyboard layout
> Allows input menu changes to overwrite the current X11 keymap.

Enable keyboard shortcuts under X11
> Enabled menu bar key equivalents, which may interfere with X11 applications that use the Meta modifier.

By default, all three of these options are enabled.

Output

The following options are used for configuring X11's look and feel:

Colors
> This pop-up menu offers the following options:
>
> • From Display
> • 256 Colors
> • Thousands
> • Millions
>
> By default, the Color pop-up is set to "From Display"; if you change this setting to something else, you will need to relaunch X11 for the change to take effect.

Enable the Enter Full Screen Menu
> This option is unchecked by default. When unchecked, X11 runs in rootless mode, which means that X11 windows can reside side-by-side with Aqua windows. In full-screen mode, use Option-⌘-A to toggle full-screen X11 and Aqua.

Use system alert sounds
> Determines whether X11's beeps use the system alert sound, as specified in the Sound Effects preference pane (System Preferences → Sound → Sound Effects). If left unchecked, X11 windows use the standard Unix system beep to sound an alert.

Customizing X11's Applications menu

X11's Applications menu can be used to quickly launch X11 applications, so you don't have to enter their command path. You can add other X11 applications to this menu and assign keyboard shortcuts by selecting Applications → Customize to bring up the X11 Application Menu dialog window, shown in Figure 12-5.

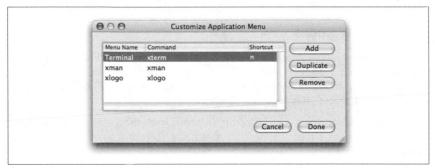

Figure 12-5. X11 Application Menu customization window

The same X11 Application Menu customization window can be opened by Control-clicking on X11's Dock icon and selecting Applications → Customize from the contextual menu. When you Control-click on X11's Dock icon, you'll see that the applications shown in Figure 12-5 are listed there as well. X11's contextual menu allows you to quickly launch other X11 applications and to switch between windows of currently running X11 applications.

X11-based Applications and Libraries

You can use Fink or DarwinPorts to install many X11-based applications, such as the GNU Image Manipulation Program (GIMP), *xfig/transfig*, ImageMagick, *nedit*, and many others. Since Fink understands dependencies, installing some of these applications will cause Fink to first install several other packages. For example, since the text editor *nedit* depends on Motif libraries, Fink will first install *lesstif*. (This also gives you the Motif window manager, *mwm*.) Similarly, when you install the GIMP via Fink, you will also install the packages for GNOME, GTK+, and *glib* since Fink handles any package dependencies you might encounter. DarwinPorts can be used in a similar manner.

You can also use Fink or DarwinPorts to install libraries directly. For example, the following command can be used to install the X11-based Qt libraries with Fink:

```
$ sudo fink install qt
```

There is an Aqua version of Qt for Mac OS X (available from Trolltech, *http://www.trolltech.com*); however, Qt applications won't automatically use the library. Instead, you'll need to recompile and link the application against the Aqua version of Qt, which may not always be a trivial task. If you want the Aqua version of qt, you can alternatively use DarwinPorts to install it with the following command:

```
$ sudo port install qt3-mac
```

Another interesting development is the port of KDE to Mac OS X. As of this writing, Konqueror had been ported and a port of Koffice was underway. To keep abreast of developments pertaining to KDE on Mac OS X, see *http://ranger.befunk.com/blog/*.

Aqua-X11 Interactions

Since X11-based applications rely on different graphics systems, even when running XDarwin in rootless mode, you would not necessarily expect to see GUI interactions run smoothly between these two graphics systems. But actually, there are several such interactions that run very well.

First, it is possible to open X11-based applications from the Terminal application. To launch an X11-based application from the Terminal, use the *open-x11* command as follows:

```
$ open-x11 /sw/bin/gimp
```

You can also copy and paste between X11 and Mac OS X applications. For example, to copy from an *xterm* window, select some text with your mouse and use the standard Macintosh keyboard shortcut to copy, ⌘-C. This places the selected text into the clipboard. To paste the contents of the clipboard into a Mac OS X application (such as the Terminal), simply press ⌘-V to paste the text.

To copy from a Mac OS X application, highlight some text and press ⌘-C. The copied text can be pasted into an *xterm* window by pressing the middle button of a three-button mouse or by Option-clicking in the X11 application.

TKAqua

Although TKAqua has been available for pre-Tiger releases of Mac OS X (from *http://tcltkaqua.sourceforge.net/*), Tiger is the first release of Mac OS X that ships with this Aqua-fied version of the Tcl scripting language and its Tk toolkit. The double-clickable Wish Shell is installed in */Developer/Applications/Utilities* when you install Xcode. An X11-based version of Tcl/Tk can be installed with Fink or DarwinPorts.

Connecting to Other X Window Systems

You can connect from Mac OS X to other X Window systems using *ssh* with X11 forwarding. If you use OpenSSH (which is included with Mac OS X), you must use the *-X* option to request X11 forwarding. When used with the *ssh* command, the *-2* option specifies the SSH Version 2 protocol, as opposed to the older Version 1 protocol. For example:

```
$ ssh -2 -X remotemachine -l username
```

As long as X11 is running, this can be entered in either an *xterm* window or in the Terminal. To have the X11 forwarding enabled in Terminal, you must have the DISPLAY variable set prior to making the connection. Under the *bash* shell (and other Bourne-compatible shells) use:

```
DISPLAY=:0.0; export DISPLAY
```

Under *csh* and *tcsh*, use:

```
setenv DISPLAY :0.0
```

It is also possible to create a double-clickable application that connects to a remote machine via SSH 2, with X11 forwarding enabled. For example, you can use the following script for this purpose:

```
#!/bin/sh
DISPLAY=:0.0; export DISPLAY
/usr/X11R6/bin/xterm -e ssh -2 -X remotemachine -l username
```

If you've installed the commercial version of SSH from *http://www.ssh.com*, the equivalent of the preceding script is as follows:

```
#!/bin/sh
DISPLAY=:0.0; export DISPLAY
/usr/X11R6/bin/xterm -e ssh2 remotemachine -l username
```

 The X11 forwarding flag is *+x* with the commercial SSH, but it is enabled by default, so you need not include it in the command.

Using Apple's X11, you can add an Application menu item to accomplish the same task. To do this, start by saving the above script to whatever you'd like to call this application. For example, suppose we want to connect to a remote machine named *mrchops* with a username of *eer*. We'll name the application *sshmrchops* and save it as *~/bin/sshmrchops.sh*. In X11, select Applications → Customize, and then click the Add button, as shown in Figure 12-6.

That's it! Now you'll be ready to launch the connection to the remote machine via the menu bar and the Dock. Once you've connected to a machine running X11, you can start X11-based applications on the remote machine and display them on your Mac OS X machine.

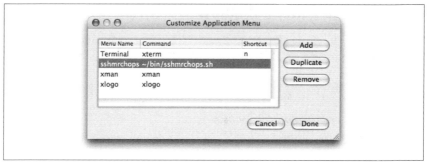

Figure 12-6. Adding an item to the X11 application menu

You can also do the reverse (SSH to your Mac and run X11 applications on the Mac, but display them on the local machine), but be sure to edit */etc/sshd_config* and change this line:

```
#X11Forwarding no
```

to this:

```
X11Forwarding yes
```

> You also need to stop and restart Remote Login using System Preferences → Sharing for this change to take effect.

OSX2X

These days, it's fairly common to find a Mac sitting next to a Linux or Unix system running an X11-based desktop. You may also have more than one Mac on your desk. In such situations, it would be convenient to use only one keyboard and mouse to control all of your Mac OS X and X11-based desktops, saving valuable desktop space. Enter Michael Dales' free BSD-licensed application *osx2x* (*http://opendarwin.org/projects/osx2x/*).

To use this handy little application, log into your Linux/Unix box running an X11 server, and enter the command:

```
xhost + mymachost
```

Then, double-click the *osx2x* application, and once the main window appears, click New Connection to open a drop-down window. In the drop-down window's Hostname field, supply the hostname or IP address of the Unix box running the X11 desktop, followed by either :0 or :0.0 (without any spaces), as in *myhost*:0.0. Next, select the Edge detection (East, West, North, or South), and the connection type X11. If, on the other hand, you are connecting your Mac to a machine running a VNC (Virtual Network Computer, described in the next section) server (for example, another Mac), select VNC as the Connection type rather than X11, and enter the VNC server password. You can switch back and forth between the Mac and the remote machine with Control-T, or you can enable edge detection and choose the position of your X11 system relative to your Mac. For example, if your Mac is to the right of your destination X11 machine, select West as illustrated in Figure 12-7.

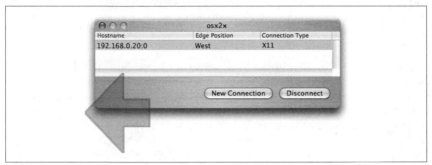

Figure 12-7. Controlling a neighboring X11 desktop with osx2x

In addition to using one keyboard and mouse to control up to four systems, you can use *osx2x* to copy text from an X11 clipboard using ⌘-C and paste on the Mac OS X side using ⌘-V.

Virtual Network Computing

One of the attractive features of Mac OS X is the ease with which you can integrate a Mac OS X system into a Unix environment consisting of multiple Unix workstations that typically rely on X11 for their GUI. In the previous section, for example, we explained how to log in to a remote Unix machine, launch an X11 application, and display the application on your Mac. The reverse process is also possible. You can log into a remote Mac OS X machine from another computer, launch an application on the remote Mac OS X machine, and have the application display on your local machine. The local machine, meanwhile, can be running the X Window System, Microsoft Windows, or any another platform supported by Virtual Network Computing (VNC).

VNC consists of two components:

- A VNC server, which must be installed on the remote machine
- A VNC viewer, which is used on the local machine to view and control applications running on the remote machine

The VNC connection is made through a TCP/IP connection.

The VNC server and viewer may not only be on different machines, but they can also be installed on different operating systems. This allows you to, for example, connect from Solaris to Mac OS X. Using VNC, you can launch and run both X11 and Aqua applications on Mac OS X, but view and control them from your Solaris box.

VNC can be installed on Mac OS X with the Fink package manager (look for the *vnc* package), but that version (the standard Unix version of the VNC server) only supports X11 programs, not Aqua applications. This standard Unix version of VNC translates X11 calls into the VNC protocol. All you need on the client machine is a VNC viewer. Two attractive Mac-friendly alternatives to the strictly X11-based VNC server are *OSXvnc* (*http://www.redstonesoftware.com/vnc.html*), and Apple's powerful desktop management software, Apple Remote Desktop 2.x. (ARD2) *OSXvnc* is freeware, and although Apple Remote Desktop is commercial software, the client portion of it ships with Tiger and includes a full VNC server, named *AppleVNCServer*.

The standard Unix version of the VNC server is quite robust. Rather than interacting with your display, it intercepts and translates the X11 network protocol. (In fact, the Unix version of the server is based on the XFree86 source code.) Applications that run under the Unix server are not displayed on the server's screen (unless you set the DISPLAY environment variable to :0.0, in which case it would be displayed only on the remote server, but not on your VNC client). Instead, they are displayed on an invisible X server that relays its virtual display to the VNC viewer on the client machine. *OSXvnc* and *AppleVNCServer* work in a similar manner except they support the Mac OS X Aqua desktop instead of X11. With either *OSXvnc* or *AppleVNCServer* running on your Mac OS X system, you can use a VNC client on another system—for example, a Unix system—to display and control your Mac OS X Aqua desktop. You can even tunnel these VNC connections (both X11 and Aqua) through SSH.

Launching VNC

If you installed VNC on your Mac OS X system via Fink (or on any Unix system for that matter), you can start the VNC server by issuing the following command:

```
vncserver
```

If you don't have physical access to the system on which you want to run the VNC server, you can login into it remotely and enter the command before logging out:

```
nohup vncserver
```

This starts the VNC server, and nohup makes sure that it continues to run after you log out. In either case, the first time you start vncserver, you need to supply a password, which you need anyway when connecting from a remote machine. (This password can be changed using the command *vncpasswd*.) You can run several servers; each server is identified by its hostname with a *:number* appended. For example, suppose you start the VNC server twice on a machine named *abbott*; the first server is identified as *abbott:1* and the second as *abbott:2*. You need to supply this identifier when you connect from a client machine.

By default, the VNC server runs *twm*. So, when you connect, you will see an X11 desktop instead of Mac OS X's desktop. You can specify a different window manager in *~/.vnc/xstartup*. To terminate the VNC server, use the following command syntax:

```
vncserver -kill :display
```

For example, to terminate *abbott:1*, you would issue the following command while logged into *abbott* as the user who started the VNC server:

```
vncserver -kill :1
```

VNC and SSH

VNC passwords and network traffic are sent over the wire as plaintext. However, you can use SSH with VNC to encrypt this traffic.

There is a derivative of VNC, called TightVNC (*http://www.tightvnc.com*), which is optimized for bandwidth conservations. (If you are using Fink, you can install it with the command *fink install tightvnc*). TightVNC also offers automatic SSH tunneling on Unix and backward compatibility with the standard VNC.

If you want to tunnel your VNC connection through SSH, you can do it even without TightVNC. To illustrate this process, let's consider an example using a SUN workstation running Solaris named *mrchops* and a PowerBook G4 named *mug* running Mac OS X Tiger. In the following example, the VNC server is running on the Solaris machine and a VNC client on the Mac OS X machine. To display and control the remote Solaris GNOME desktop on your local Mac OS X system, do the following:

1. Log into the Solaris machine, *mrchops*, via SSH if you need to login remotely.

2. On *mrchops*, enter the following command to start the VNC server on *display :1*:

   ```
   nohup vncserver :1
   ```

3. In your *~/.vnc* directory, edit the *xstartup* file so *gnome* starts when you connect to the VNC server with a VNC client. In particular, your *xstartup* file should look like this:

   ```
   #!/bin/sh
   xrdb $HOME/.Xresources
   xterm  -geometry 80x24+10+10 -ls -title "$VNCDESKTOP Desktop" &

   exec /usr/bin/gnome-session
   ```

4. Logout from the Solaris box, *mrchops*.

5. From a Terminal window (or *xterm*) on your Mac OS X machine, log into *mrchops* via *ssh*:

   ```
   ssh -L 5902:127.0.0.1:5901 mrchops
   ```

   Any references to *display :2* on your Mac will connect to the Solaris machine's *display :1* through an SSH tunnel (*display :1* uses port 5901, *display :2* uses 5902). You may need to add the *–l* option to this command if your username on the Solaris machine is different from the one you're using on your Mac OS X machine. For example, say your username on *mrchops* is *brian,* but on *mug* it's *ernie*. The following command would be issued instead of the one above:

   ```
   ssh -L 5902:127.0.0.1:5901 mrchops -l brian
   ```

   Additionally, you may need to open ports through any firewalls you may have running. Open ports 5900-5902 for VNC, and 22 for *ssh*.

6. On your Mac, you can either start X11 or run *vncviewer* from the command line:

   ```
   vncviewer localhost:2
   ```

   You can also run an Aqua VNC client like *VNCDimension* (*http://www. mdimension.com/*) or *Chicken of the VNC* (*http://sourceforge.net/projects/*

cotvnc/). Figure 12-8 shows a Chicken of the VNC connection to a Solaris GNOME desktop.

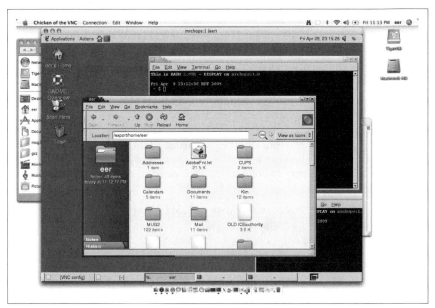

Figure 12-8. Chicken of the VNC displaying a remote GNOME desktop

Connecting to the Mac OS X VNC Server

To connect to a Mac OS X machine that is running a VNC server, you need to install a VNC viewer. We mentioned two Mac OS X viewers (*VNCDimension* and *Chicken of the VNC*) earlier, and additional Mac OS X viewers can be found on Version Tracker or MacUpdate (*http://www.versiontracker.com/macosx/* or *http://www.macupdate.com*) by searching for "VNC". VNC or TightVNC provide viewers for Unix systems. These viewers can be used to display and control the Mac OS X client machines.

To connect, start your viewer and specify the hostname and display number, such as *chops:1* or *chops:2*. If all goes well, you'll be asked for your password and then be connected to the remote Mac OS X desktop. VNC connections to Mac OS X Aqua desktops can be established through SSH tunnels.

To illustrate this process, let's do the reverse of what we did in our last example; let's make an SSH-secured connection from a Solaris machine to the Mac OS X machine running the VNC server. Again, let's assume that the name of the Solaris machine is *mrchops* and the Mac OS X machine has a hostname of *alchops*.

1. On *alchops*, double-click the *OSXvnc* application. Select a display number (we've selected 1 in this example). The port number will be filled in automatically once you've selected the display number. Next, enter a password that will be used to connect to the VNC server and click the Start Server button. This step is illustrated in Figure 12-9.

You can also *ssh* to *alchops* and start *OSXvnc* from the command line. For a list of command-line options enter:

```
/Applications/OSXvnc.app/OSXvnc-server -help
```

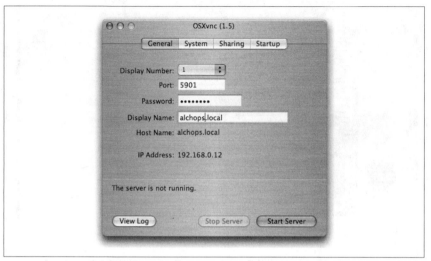

Figure 12-9. Starting the OSXvnc server

2. On the Solaris machine, *mrchops*, enter:

```
ssh -L 5902:localhost:5901 alchops
```

3. In another *xterm* window on *mrchops,* enter:

```
vncviewer -depth 24 -truecolor localhost:2
```

4. The resulting VNC connection is shown in shown in Figure 12-10.

 If you're running *OSXvnc* on your Mac, you can control the Mac OS X desktop from the SUN Solaris machine, but the image quality of the Mac OS X desktop will be poor unless you invoke the *vncviewer* with the options *-depth 24 truecolor*. In our testing, these options are needed to connect the Solaris *vncviewer* to the *AppleVNCServer*.

OSXvnc has several configuration options. If you click the System button when you open *OSXvnc*, you can select Swap Mouse Buttons 2 and 3, and two energy savings: Allow Display Dimming and Allow machine to Sleep. You can choose from several sharing options under *OSXvnc*'s Sharing button, as shown in Figure 12-11.

If you want *OSXvnc-server* to run whenever the Mac OS X system is running, *OSXvnc* provides a way to install and configure a system-wide VNC server that starts when you boot your Mac. To take advantage of this feature, click the Startup button in *OSXvnc*, click the Configure Startup Item, and authenticate as an administrative user, as shown in Figure 12-12.

Figure 12-10. Mac OS X desktop displayed and controlled on a Solaris GNOME desktop

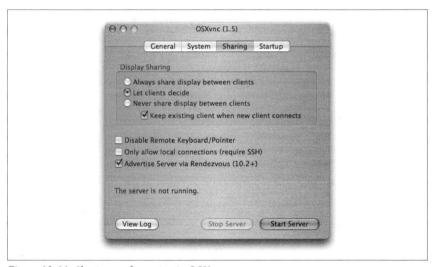

Figure 12-11. Sharing configuration in OSXvnc

Configuring *OSXvnc* as a startup item places *OSXvnc* in */Library/StartupItems*. Subsequently, the OSXvnc-server application starts automatically when you boot up your Mac. In this case, the *OSXvnc* GUI doesn't run, and you won't have access to the pasteboard between machines.

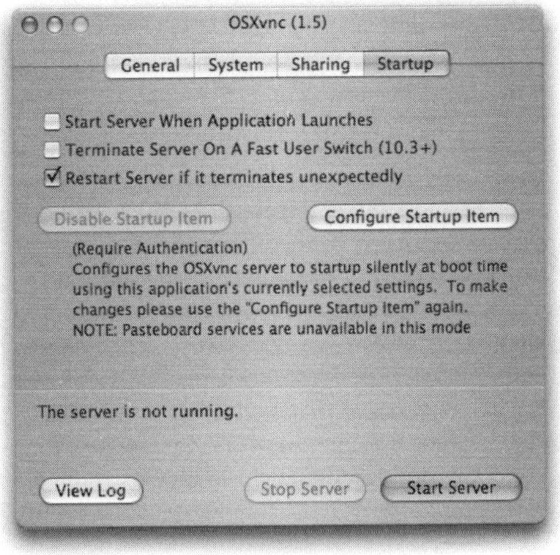

Figure 12-12. Installing OSXvnc as a Startup Item

To enable *AppleVNCServer* check Apple Remote Desktop in the Sharing System Preference, click the Access Privileges button, check "VNC viewers may control screen with password," select a password, and click OK, as shown in Figure 12-13.

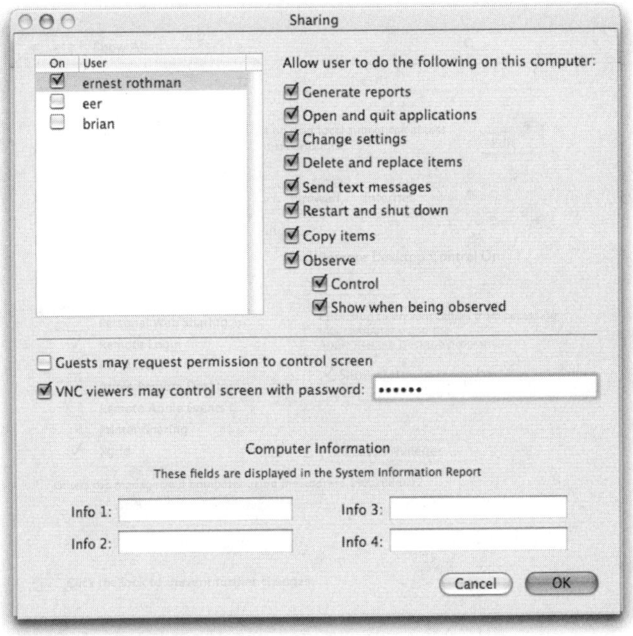

Figure 12-13. Enabling AppleVNCServer

At the time of this writing *OSXvnc* does not support multiple monitors, while *AppleVNCServer* does. Though, according to the *OSXvnc* web site, support for multiple monitors is planned for a future release. You can run both *OSXvnc* and *AppleVNCServer* on the same system, but since *AppleVNCServer* listens for clients on port 5900, you'll need to avoid using this port for *OSXvnc*.

 VNC clients and servers are available for Windows machines, so Windows clients can connect to Mac OS X and other UNIX VNC servers. Mac OS X clients can also connect to and control Windows VNC servers. (See *http://www.realvnc.com/.*) As an alternative to VNC, you can use Microsoft's free Remote Desktop Client (RDC, available at *http://www.microsoft.com/mac/otherproducts/ otherproducts.aspx?pid=remotedesktopclient*) to remotely control a Windows desktop from a Mac OS X machine. An open source X11-based remote desktop client for Windows, named rdesktop (*http:// www.rdesktop.org*), is also available and can be installed with DarwinPorts or Fink).

13

The Defaults System

Native Mac OS X applications store their preferences in the *defaults database*. This is made up of each application's property list (*plist*) file, which is an XML file consisting of key/value pairs that define the preferences for an application or service of the operating system.

If an application has a *plist* file, every time you change its preferences, the changes are saved back to the *plist* file. Also included in the defaults database system are the changes you make to your system via the panels found in System Preferences (*/Applications*).

As an administrator, you may need to access your or another user's preferences. This is done from the Terminal using the *defaults* command. This chapter covers Mac OS X's preferences system, including the format and location of application and system preference files, how they work, and how to view and adjust their settings using the Property List Editor (*/Developer/Applications/Utilities*) and the Terminal.

Property Lists

User-defined property lists are stored in *~/Library/Preferences*, and the appropriate *plist* is called up when an application launches. Property lists can contain literal preferences set through the application's ApplicationPreferences dialog, or subtler things such as window coordinates or the state of an option (such as whether to display the battery menu extra in the menu bar, as shown in Example 13-1).

Example 13-1. The com.apple.menuextra.battery.plist file in XML format

```
<?xml version="1.0" encoding="UTF-8"?>
<!DOCTYPE plist PUBLIC "-//Apple Computer//DTD PLIST 1.0//EN" "http://www.apple.
com/DTDs/PropertyList-1.0.dtd">
<plist version="1.0">
```

```
<dict>
        <key>ShowPercent</key>
        <string>YES</string>
        <key>ShowTime</key>
        <string>NO</string>
</dict>
</plist>
```

Each property list is named after its *domain*, the unique namespace that an application uses when working with its preference files. Domains can look like any string, but the Apple-recommended format is similar to a URL, just in reverse. The naming convention is based on the developer's company or organization's name, using the application's name as the domain. All of the *plist* files for the System Preferences and other iApps use the syntax *com.apple.domain.plist*, where *domain* is the name of the service or application. For example, the *plist* file for the Dock's preferences is *com.apple.dock.plist*, while the preferences file for Omni-Graffle (if you have it installed) is *com.omnigroup.OmniGraffle.plist*.

> Not all application preference files are part of the preferences system. Some applications may write their user preference files in a proprietary format to *~/Library/Preferences*. These are typically Carbon applications not packaged into bundles, and hence lacking the *Info.plist* files they need to claim a preferences domain. As such, these preference files can't be read or altered by the *defaults* command (described later), even though they are stored in *~/Library/ Preferences*.
>
> Classic applications, on the other hand, are even more antisocial, always writing their preference files in opaque formats in Mac OS 9's *System Folder/Preferences* folder.

To get a list of the *com.apple*.domain *plist* files in the *~/Library/Preferences* directory, issue the following commands:

```
$ cd ~/Library/Preferences
$ ls com.apple.* > ~/Desktop/plists.txt
```

The first command places you in the *~/Library/Preferences* directory; the second gives a wildcard search for all files that begin with *com.apple*, and then redirects that listing to a file named *plists.txt* and saves that file on your Desktop. Because each application, including the menu extras, creates its own *plist* file, this listing can be long.

Note that *plists* can be in one of two formats: Binary and XML. By default, Mac OS X will use binary *plist* files, which is more efficient for space, but makes it impossible for human readers to read. Here's what a binary format file looks like if you try to display it like a text file:

```
$ cd ~/Library/Preferences
$ cat com.apple.windowclock.plist
bplist00<D1>^A^B_^P^TNSWindow Frame Clock_^P^^1081 788 128 128 0 0 1280 938
```

The output may include strange garbage characters. To look at it in a friendly format, you'll need to convert it to XML using the *plutil* command to convert to *xml1* (that's "ex-em-el-one" format):

```
$ plutil -convert xml1 com.apple.windowclock.plist
$ cat com.apple.windowclock.plist
<?xml version="1.0" encoding="UTF-8"?>
<!DOCTYPE plist PUBLIC "-//Apple Computer//DTD PLIST 1.0//EN" "http://www.
apple.com/DTDs/PropertyList-1.0.dtd">
<plist version="1.0">
<dict>
        <key>NSWindow Frame Clock</key>
        <string>1081 788 128 128 0 0 1280 938 </string>
</dict>
</plist>
```

There's no need to convert back to binary format, since Mac OS X will handle them identically, but if you really want to:

```
$ plutil -convert binary1 com.apple.windowclock.plist
```

Looking at Example 13-1, you can see the basic structure of a *plist* file. At the most basic level, a *plist* file can be broken down into three parts: dictionaries, keys, and values for the keys. The dictionary sections, denoted with <dict/>, set the structure; keys (<key/>) define an available preference, and the values for the keys in this example are strings (<string/>).

The values for a key are defined within either a <data/>, <date/>, <boolean/>, <string/>, or <integer/> tag. Keys can also contain nested dictionary sections or arrays (<array/>) sections for holding encoded values or a series of strings. Nested dictionaries are referred to as children of the parent dictionary. For example, *com.apple.dock.plist* has a *persistent-apps* key, which contains an array for all of the applications in the Dock (to the left of the divider bar). Within the array, you'll see a number of nested dictionaries that define the parameters for the application's icon in the Dock. Example 13-2 shows the array item for *Mail.app*'s Dock icon.

Example 13-2. Mail.app's array in com.apple.dock.plist in XML format

```
<key>persistent-apps</key>
<array>
....
```

Example 13-2. Mail.app's array in com.apple.dock.plist in XML format (continued)

```
<dict>
    <key>GUID</key>
    <integer>1871630911</integer>
    <key>tile-data</key>
    <dict>
        <key>file-data</key>
        <dict>
            <key>_CFURLAliasData</key>
            <data>
            AAAAAACQAAMAAQAAu77rNQAASCsAAAAAAAAD
            KgAARrIAALthjLAAAAAACSD//gAAAAAAAAA
            /////wABAAQAAAMqAA4AEgAIAEOAYQBpAGwA
            LgBhAHAAcAAPABAABwBQAGEAbgBOAGgAZQBy
            ABIAFUFwcGxpY2F0aW9ucy9NYWlsLmFwcAAA
            EwABLwD//wAA
            </data>
            <key>_CFURLString</key>
            <string>/Applications/Mail.app</string>
            <key>_CFURLStringType</key>
            <integer>0</integer>
        </dict>
        <key>file-label</key>
        <string>Mail</string>
        <key>file-mod-date</key>
        <integer>-1136549615</integer>
        <key>file-type</key>
        <integer>9</integer>
        <key>parent-mod-date</key>
        <integer>-1134631645</integer>
    </dict>
    <key>tile-type</key>
    <string>file-tile</string>
</dict>
...
</array>
```

Because a *plist* file is nothing more than text, you can use any text editor (such as TextEdit, BBEdit, *vi*, or Emacs) to view and edit its contents; however, the preferred method is to use the Property List Editor (*/Developer/Applications/ Utilities*), described later. The Property List Editor application is installed when you install the Xcode Tools.

Viewing and Editing Property Lists

There are two ways you can view and edit the contents of an application's preferences file:

- With the Property List Editor (*/Developer/Applications/Utilities*)
- From the command line, using the *defaults* command

The Property List Editor is available on your system only after installing the Xcode Tools; however, the *defaults* command is available with the base installation of Mac OS X, and doesn't require you to install any additional software.

Viewing is one thing, but knowing what you can enter into a *plist* file requires a bit of investigative work. An application asserts its domain through the *CFBundleIdentifier* key in its internal *Info.plist* file, which is stored in an application's */Contents* directory. For example, the *Info.plist* file for the Dock can be found in */System/Library/CoreServices/Dock.app/Contents*.

The preferences available to an application are defined via the *CFBundleExecutable* key in the *Info.plist* file. Typically, the string for *CFBundleExecutable* is the short name for the application (e.g., Dock). This executable can be found in an application's */Contents/MacOS* directory; e.g., the Dock executable is located in */System/Library/CoreServices/Dock.app/Contents/MacOS*.

To see a listing of available keys and strings for an application, use the *strings* command in the Terminal, followed by the path to the application's short name as defined by *CFBundleExecutable*:

```
$ strings /System/Library/CoreServices/Dock.app/Contents/MacOS/Dock
```

Unfortunately, the output from *strings* doesn't have a discernible structure. You'll need to sift through the output to find hints about the preferences you can set and alter using the Property List Editor or the *defaults* command, defined in the following sections.

Using the Property List Editor

The Property List Editor, shown in Figure 13-1, is a GUI tool that lets you view and edit property list files.

At their base, every *plist* has a Root item, which contains all the dictionaries, arrays, keys, and values that define the preferences for an application. When you initially open a *plist* file, all its elements are hidden inside the Root item. If you click on the disclosure triangle next to Root (this is similar to the List View of the Finder), the keys of the *plist* are revealed in the first column.

If you select a Dictionary or Array item in the Property List column that has a disclosure triangle next to it, you can use ⌘-right (or left) arrow to respectively open or close a disclosure triangle. Likewise, Option-⌘-right (or left) Arrow respectively opens or closes all of the disclosure triangles in the Property List Editor. For example, if you select Root and hit Option-⌘-right arrow, all of the contents of that *plist* file are shown in the upper display; Option-⌘-left arrow closes them again.

As shown in Figure 13-1, there are three columns in the Property List Editor's display:

Property List
> The Property List column lists the items seen in the <key/> tags of a *plist*'s XML file.

Figure 13-1. The Property List Editor

Class

The Class column lists the classes available for each key definition. Clicking on the set of up/down arrows next to a class reveals a pop-up menu, from which you can select from one of seven possible classes including:

String

A string can contain alphanumeric text, such as an application path (e.g., */Applications/Mail.app/*), a single-word response that defines the action of a key, or the default position of the application's window (e.g., {{125, 0}, {205, 413}}).

Dictionary

Dictionary items are grayed out in the Property List Editor's display and give you details on the number of key/value pairs listed in that dictionary item. Dictionaries are tagged as <dict/> in the XML file.

Array

Like dictionaries, the Value column is grayed out for an Array, showing you the number of ordered objects available in that array. Within each array, you will find another Dictionary item listing its key/value pairs. Arrays are tagged as <array/> in the XML file.

Boolean

Contains YES or NO responses as its value, and are tagged as <true/> or <false/>, respectively, as the value in the XML file.

Number

Contains a floating-point value for the key, such as a percentage value for the opaqueness of the Terminal application (e.g., 0.750000 for 75 percent) or the version number for an application. Values in the Number class are tagged in the *plist* file using <integer/>.

Date

Contains the date in MM/DD/YY format. The Date Value can also include a time, in HH:MM:SS format.

Data

Data information is stored as a string of encoded alphanumeric data, inside a set of opening and closing angle brackets. If you look closely at the Value, you'll see that the numbers are in blocks of eight characters (digits or letters from A to F), which reveal its form as binary data. Example 13-3 shows the Data Value for *Mail.app*'s icon alias in the Dock.

Example 13-3. The Data Value for _CFURLAliasData as binary data

```
<00000000 00900003 00010000 bbbeeb35 0000482b 00000000 0000032a
000046b2 0000bb61 8cb00000 00000920 fffe0000 00000000 0000ffff
ffff0001 00040000 032a000e 00120008 004d0061 0069006c 002e0061
00700070 000f0010 00070050 0061006e 00740068 00650072 00120015
4170706c 69636174 696f6e73 2f4d6169 6c2e6170 70000013 00012f00
ffff0000 >
```

Value

Contains the value for the Class.

To view the XML source for the *plist* file, click on the Dump button in the upper-right corner of the Property List Editor's window. You can't edit the XML source in the Property List Editor; edits to the *plist* file are made in the upper portion of the window.

> You should avoid changing a *plist* file used by an application that's currently in use, because it can crash the application or cause it and your system to behave strangely.

To edit an item, double-click on the item you want to edit to select it, type in the new value, and then hit Return to accept the new value. If you want to see the change in the XML source, hit the Dump button again. After the changes have been entered, save the file before closing (File → Save, or ⌘-S).

The defaults Command

Another way to view and change the contents of a *plist* file is with the *defaults* command from the Terminal. The *defaults* command gives you an abstract way to read from and write to the preferences system. It lets you quickly modify any or all of an application's saved-state settings, which can prove quite handy when debugging your own applications. As with any command-line program, you can write shell scripts to run several invocations of *defaults* with a single command, letting you set the application's stage however you like in an instant.

If the preferences domain is bound to a specific host, you must specify a host with the *-host* option or refer to the current machine with the *-currentHost* option.

The following section contains a complete reference for the *defaults* command.

defaults

defaults [*host*] *subcommand domain* [*option*] [*key*]

        defaults [-currentHost | -host *hostname*] read [*domain* [*key*]]
        defaults [-currentHost | -host *hostname*] read-type *domain key*
        defaults [-currentHost | -host *hostname*] write *domain* { 'plist' | *domain*
        key ' *value* ' }
        defaults [-currentHost | -host *hostname*] rename *domain old_key new_key*
        defaults [-currentHost | -host *hostname*] delete [*domain* [*key*]]
        defaults [-currentHost | -host *hostname*] { *domains* | find *word* | help }

Used to access Mac OS X's user defaults database to read, write (set or change), and delete system and application preferences.

The *defaults* command allows users and administrators to read, write, and delete Mac OS X user defaults from a command-line shell. An application's defaults belong to a *domain*, which typically correspond to individual applications; however, they can apply to system settings made via the System Preferences panels. Each domain has a dictionary of keys and values representing its defaults. Keys are always strings, but values can be complex data structures comprising arrays, dictionaries, strings, and binary data. These data structures are stored as XML property lists.

Though all applications, system services, and other programs have their own domains, they also share a domain named NSGlobalDomain. If a default isn't specified in the application's domain but is specified in NSGlobalDomain, the application uses the value in that domain.

Host

-currentHost

Restricts the actions of the *defaults* command to the domains listed in ~/*Library/ Preferences/ByHost*.

-host hostname

Used to specify the *hostname*, based on the Ethernet MAC address of the system the user is logged in to.

Subcommands

read

Prints all the user's defaults, for every domain, to standard output.

read domain

Prints all the user's defaults for *domain* to standard output.

read-type domain key

Prints the type of *key* for the given *domain*.

read domain key

Prints the value for the default of *domain* identified by *key*.

write domain key 'value'

Writes value as the value for *key* in *domain*. The *value* must be a property list and must be enclosed in single quotes. For example:

```
defaults write com.companyname.appname "Default Color" '(255, 0, 0)'
```

sets the application's *value* for the *key* (Default Color) to an array, which contains the string 255, 0, 0 (for the RGB values). Note that the *key* is enclosed in quotation marks because it contains a space.

write domain plist

Overwrites the defaults information in a domain with that given as *plist*. *plist* must be a property list representation of a dictionary and must be enclosed in single quotes. For example:

```
defaults write com.companyname.appname '{ "Default Color" = (255, 0, 0);
"Default Font" = Helvetica; }';
```

erases any previous defaults for *com.companyname.appname* and writes the values for the two names into the defaults system.

delete domain

Removes all default information for *domain*.

delete domain key

Removes the default named *key* from *domain*.

domains

Prints the names of all defaults *domains* on the user's system.

find word

Searches for *word* in the domain names, keys, and values of the user's defaults, and prints the results to standard output.

help

Prints a list of possible command formats.

-h

Prints an abbreviated list of possible command formats.

Options

-g
Used as a synonym for the domain NSGlobalDomain. You can also use "*Apple Global Domain*" (including the quotation marks) as a synonym for the domain NSGlobalDomain. For example:

```
$ defaults read "Apple Global Domain"
```

displays the same thing as:

```
$ defaults read -g
```

or:

```
$ defaults read NSGlobalDomain
```

or:

```
$ defaults read -globalDomain
```

The following list specifies values for preference keys:

-app
Specifies an application found in the */Applications* directory, rather than using its domain. For example:

```
$ defaults read -app Mail
```

outputs the defaults data for the Mail application.

-array

> Allows the user to specify an array as the value for the given preference key:
>
> ```
> defaults write somedomain preferenceKey -array element1 element2
> element3
> ```
>
> The specified array overwrites the value of the *key* if the *key* is present at the time of the write. If the *key* isn't present, it's created with the new value.

-array-add

> Allows the user to add new elements to the end of an array for a *key*, which has an array as its value. Usage is the same as *-array*. If the *key* isn't present at the time of the write, it's created with the specified array as its value.

-dict

> Allows the user to add a dictionary to the defaults database for a domain. Keys and values are specified in order:
>
> ```
> defaults write somedomain preferenceKey -dict key1 value1 key2 value2
> ```
>
> The specified dictionary overwrites the *value* of the *key* if the *key* is present at the time of the write. If the *key* isn't present, it's created with the new *value*.

-dict-add

> Allows the user to add new key/value pairs to a dictionary for a *key* that has a dictionary as its value. Usage is the same as *-dict*. If the *key* isn't present at the time of the write, it is created with the specified dictionary as its value.

Host-Specific Preferences

A folder called *ByHost* can exist within *~/Library/Preferences*. *ByHost* contains property list files defining preferences specific to an application on a certain host. These files have filenames following the format of *com.apple.address.plist*, in which *address* is the Ethernet MAC address associated with the *-currentHost*.

To read the *plist* files located in the *ByHost* directory, you need to specify the *-currentHost* option, as follows:

```
$ defaults -currentHost read com.apple.screensaver
```

Notice that you don't need to specify the Ethernet address that's part of the filename. The *-currentHost* option tells the *defaults* command to read the specified domain from the *ByHost* directory.

Index

We'd like to hear your suggestions for improving our indexes. Send email to *index@oreilly.com*.

M

Mac OS 9
  hidden files, 407, 408
  /System Folder/Extensions
     folder, 403
Mac OS Extended Format, 395
Mac OS X
  built-in console login mode, 272
  default launch daemons, 446
  Directory Services architecture, 415
  emulation of right-mouse clicks, 452
machine command, 134
/machines file, 427
mail
  notification, 26
  retrieving from mail servers, 76
  services, 433
mail delivery agents (MDAs), 436
mail, monitoring outgoing queue, 434
mail transport agents (MTAs), 433
  Postfix, 433
mailemail command, 76
mailq command, 134
mailstat command, 135
mailx command, 5
make command, 6
makekey command, 135
man command, 8, 135
manpages, flat file formats and, 429
map command (ex), 357
mark command (ex), 358
marks command (ex), 358
master program, 434
md5 command, 136
MDAs (mail delivery agents), 436
mdcheckschema command, 138
mdfind command, 138
mdimport command, 140
mdls command, 141
mDNS, 137
mDNSResponder, 137
mdutil command, 141
merge command, 141
  dscl, 424
metacharacters
  listed by Unix program, 330
  replacement patterns, 332
  search patterns, 331
Meta-key (Emacs) commands, 384
Microsoft Remote Desktop Client
    (RDC), 466

middle mouse button, simulation with
    Option-click, 452
mkbom command, 142
mkdir command, 5, 142
mkexrc command (ex), 358
more command, 5, 143
  commands, 144
  examples, 144
  options, 143
Motif window manager (mwm), 455
mount command, 145
mount_afp command, 146
mount_autofs command, 146
mount_cd9660 command, 147
mount_cddafs command, 147
mount_devfs command, 147
mount_fdesc command, 148
mount_ftp command, 148
mount_hfs command, 148
mounting disks and diskarbitrationd
    command, 61
mount_msdos command, 149
mount_nfs command, 150
mount_ntfs command, 150
mount_smbfs command, 151
  options, 152
mount_synthfs command, 153
mount_udf command, 153
mount_volfs command, 153
mount_webdav command, 154
mouse buttons
  emulation of three-button mouse in
    X11, 454
  xterm vs. Terminal windows, 450
move command (ex), 358
Move to Trash option (File menu), 407
/Movies directory (user directory), 401
MS-DOS, 398
MTAs (mail transport agents), 433
multiuser systems, 401
/Music directory (user directory), 401
mv command, 5, 154
MvMac, 155
mwm (Motif window manager), 455

N

nedit text editor, 455
NetInfo, 420
  backing up database, 423
  in Directory Services
    architecture, 414

Z

About the Authors

Andy Lester has been a professional programmer for 18 years and a Perl evangelist for a decade. By day, he manages programmers for Follett Library Resources in McHenry, Illinois. By night, he spreads the gospel of automated testing and maintains over a dozen CPAN modules. Lester also writes for *The Perl Journal*, and three of his hacks have been published in *Spidering Hacks* by O'Reilly.

Chris Stone (*cjstone@mac.com*) is a senior systems administrator (the Mac guy) at O'Reilly. He's written several Mac OS X-related articles for the O'Reilly MacDevCenter (*http://www.macdevcenter.com*) and has contributed to *Mac OS X: The Missing Manual, Panther Edition*, published by Pogue Press/O'Reilly. Chris grew up on the San Francisco peninsula, went to Humboldt State University, and spent 10 years hidden away in the Japanese countryside before returning to California and settling in the North Bay area, where he now lives with his wife Miho and two sons Andrew and Jonathan.

Chuck Toporek (*chuckdude@mac.com*) is a MacHead, through and through. He has used Macs since 1988, when he first cut his teeth on a Mac II system. Chuck is a senior editor for O'Reilly, mainly working on Macintosh-related books, and is also a member of the Program Committee for O'Reilly's Mac OS X Conference. He is a coauthor of *Hydrocephalus: A Guide for Patients, Families and Friends*, and author of two other Mac books from O'Reilly: the *Mac OS X Tiger Pocket Guide* (now in its fourth edition) and *Inside .Mac*.

Jason McIntosh (*jmac@jmac.org*) lives in Somerville, Massachusetts, and works as a senior web programmer with the Institute for Chemistry and Cellular Biology at Harvard Medical School in Boston. His previous technical publications include *Perl and XML* (coauthored with Erik T. Ray and published by O'Reilly), and an occasional series of columns and weblog entries on XML or Mac OS X for the O'Reilly Network, particularly *http://www.macdevcenter.com*. His primary hobby is playing and designing obscure board and card games. All these things, as well as other inventions and reflections, may be found at his online home at *http://www.jmac.org*. Jason has worked with Macintosh computers (selling them, administrating them, programming them, and writing about them) since 1991. He agrees that, yes, that is pretty funny about his name, now that you mention it.

Colophon

Our look is the result of reader comments, our own experimentation, and feedback from distribution channels. Distinctive covers complement our distinctive approach to technical topics, breathing personality and life into potentially dry subjects.

The animal on the cover of *Mac OS X Tiger in a Nutshell* is a Siberian tiger. The Siberian tiger is the largest member of the cat family, including lions. A male averages 7 to 9 feet in length, and it usually weighs about 500 pounds. A female weighs slightly less, averaging about 300 pounds. This animal is native to Siberia and parts of China. Its fur color ranges from yellow to orange, with black stripes, although a few white tigers with black stripes have been spotted. The fur is long and thick, to help the animal survive its native cold climates. An interesting fact about tiger stripes is that the pattern of each tiger's stripes is unique to that tiger. Therefore, stripes are a useful tool for identifying different tigers.

The Siberian tiger is endangered. Although there are about 1,000 living in captivity, only about 200 to 300 live in the wild. This is partly due to industrial encroachment on its natural habitat, limiting the tiger's hunting resources. Poaching is also a serious problem; in some areas of the world, tiger parts are thought to have great medicinal value, so these parts bring great financial gain to sellers.

Philip Dangler was the production editor, and Linley Dolby was the copyeditor for *Mac OS X Tiger in a Nutshell*. Philip Dangler proofread the book. Darren Kelly and Claire Cloutier provided quality control. Julie Hawks wrote the index.

Emma Colby designed the cover of this book, based on a series design by Edie Freedman. The cover image is an original illustration created by Susan Hart. Karen Montgomery produced the cover layout with Adobe InDesign CS using Adobe's ITC Garamond font.

David Futato designed the interior layout. This book was converted by Keith Fahlgren to FrameMaker 5.5.6 with a format conversion tool created by Erik Ray, Jason McIntosh, Neil Walls, and Mike Sierra that uses Perl and XML technologies. The text font is Linotype Birka; the heading font is Adobe Myriad Condensed; and the code font is LucasFont's TheSans Mono Condensed. The illustrations that appear in the book were produced by Robert Romano, Jessamyn Read, and Lesley Borash using Macromedia FreeHand MX and Adobe Photoshop CS. The tip and warning icons were drawn by Christopher Bing. This colophon was written by Mary Brady.

Better than e-books

Buy *Mac OS X Tiger in a Nutshell* and access
the digital edition FREE on Safari for 45 days.

Go to www.oreilly.com/go/safarienabled
and type in coupon code IDDF-HI4D-9S96-RFEX-CU85

Search
thousands of
top tech books

Download
whole chapters

Cut and Paste
code examples

Find
answers fast

Search Safari! The premier electronic reference
library for programmers and IT professionals.

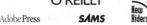

Related Titles from O'Reilly

Macintosh

AppleScript: The Definitive Guide

AppleScript: The Missing Manual

Appleworks 6: The Missing Manual

The Best of the Joy of Tech

FileMaker Pro: The Missing Manual

GarageBand: The Missing Manual

iBook Fan Book

iLife '04: The Missing Manual

iMovie HD & iDVD 5: The Missing Manual

iPhoto 5: The Missing Manual

iPod Playlists '05

iPod Shuffle Fan Book

iPod & iTunes: The Missing Manual, *3rd Edition*

iWork '05: The Missing Manual

Mac Annoyances

Mac OS X Panther in a Nutshell

Mac OS X Tiger Pocket Guide

Mac OS X Panther Power User

Mac OS X: The Missing Manual, *Tiger Edition*

Mac OS X Unwired

Modding Mac OS X

Office 2004 for the Macintosh: The Missing Manual

Revolution in The Valley: The Insanely Great Story of How the Mac was Made

Switching to the Mac, *Tiger Edition*

Mac Developers

Building Cocoa Applications: A Step-By-Step Guide

Cocoa in a Nutshell

Essential Mac OS X Panther Server Administration

Learning Carbon

Learning Cocoa with Objective-C, *2nd Edition*

Learning Unix for Mac OS X Tiger

Mac OS X for Java Geeks

Mac OS X Panther Hacks

Mac OS X Tiger in a Nutshell

Mac OS X Tiger for Unix Geeks

Objective-C Pocket Reference

RealBasic: The Definitive Guide, *2nd Edition*

Running Mac OS X Tiger

Keep in touch with O'Reilly

Download examples from our books

To find example files from a book, go to: *www.oreilly.com/catalog* select the book, and follow the "Examples" link.

Register your O'Reilly books

Register your book at *register.oreilly.com* Why register your books? Once you've registered your O'Reilly books you can:

- Win O'Reilly books, T-shirts or discount coupons in our monthly drawing.
- Get special offers available only to registered O'Reilly customers.
- Get catalogs announcing new books (US and UK only).
- Get email notification of new editions of the O'Reilly books you own.

Join our email lists

Sign up to get topic-specific email announcements of new books and conferences, special offers, and O'Reilly Network technology newsletters at:

elists.oreilly.com

It's easy to customize your free elists subscription so you'll get exactly the O'Reilly news you want.

Get the latest news, tips, and tools

www.oreilly.com

- "Top 100 Sites on the Web"—PC Magazine
- CIO Magazine's Web Business 50 Awards

Our web site contains a library of comprehensive product information (including book excerpts and tables of contents), downloadable software, background articles, interviews with technology leaders, links to relevant sites, book cover art, and more.

Work for O'Reilly

Check out our web site for current employment opportunities:

jobs.oreilly.com

Contact us

O'Reilly Media, Inc.
1005 Gravenstein Hwy North
Sebastopol, CA 95472 USA
Tel: 707-827-7000 or 800-998-9938
   (6am to 5pm PST)
Fax: 707-829-0104

Contact us by email

For answers to problems regarding your order or our products:
order@oreilly.com

To request a copy of our latest catalog:
catalog@oreilly.com

For book content technical questions or corrections: **booktech@oreilly.com**

For educational, library, government, and corporate sales: **corporate@oreilly.com**

To submit new book proposals to our editors and product managers:
proposals@oreilly.com

For information about our international distributors or translation queries:
international@oreilly.com

For information about academic use of O'Reilly books:
adoption@oreilly.com
or visit:
academic.oreilly.com

For a list of our distributors outside of North America check out:
international.oreilly.com/distributors.html

Order a book online

www.oreilly.com/order_new